HOMILIES ON ROMANS

ST. JOHN CHRYSOSTOM

Homilies on Romans

Volume 1

Second Edition

Translated by
Panayiotis Papageorgiou

HOLY CROSS
ORTHODOX PRESS
Brookline, Massachusetts

Second Edition 2024
© 2012 Panayiotis Papageorgiou

Published by Holy Cross Orthodox Press
50 Goddard Avenue
Brookline, Massachusetts 02445

ISBN 978-1-960613-09-7

All rights reserved. No part of this publication may be reproduced, stored in a retrieval system, or transmitted in any form or by any means—electronic, mechanical, photocopy, recording, or any other—without the prior written permission of the author. The only exception is brief quotations in printed reviews.
On the cover: Icon of Saints Paul the Apostle and John Chrysostom by Marina Papageorgiou, Iconographer

Publisher's Cataloging in Publication
(Provided by Cassidy Cataloging Services, Inc.)
Names: John Chrysostom, Saint, -407, author. | Papageōrgiou, Panagiōtēs, translator.
Title: Homilies on Romans / St. John Chrysostom ; translated by Panayiotis Papageorgiou.
Other titles: Homilies on Romans. English
Description: Second edition. | Brookline, Massachusetts : Holy Cross Orthodox Press, [2024-] | Revision of the 2013 edition. | Includes bibliographical references and index.
Identifiers: ISBN: 978-1-960613-09-7 (v. 1)
Subjects: LCSH: John Chrysostom, Saint, -407—Sermons. | Bible. Romans—Sermons. | Orthodox Eastern Church—Sermons.
Classification: LCC: BS2665.54 .J64 2024 | DDC: 227/.106—dc23

Contents

Abbreviations	vi
Preface to the Second Edition	vii
Preface to the First Edition	ix
Introduction	xi
Prologue	1
Homily 1	9
Homily 2	22
Homily 3	43
Homily 4	56
Homily 5	67
Homily 6	90
Homily 7	108
Homily 8	134
Homily 9	160
Homily 10	174
Homily 11	192
Homily 12	213
Homily 13	240
Homily 14	273
Homily 15	305
Bibliography	323
Index	327

ABBREVIATIONS

DB	*Dictionary of the Bible*, ed. John L. McKenzie
ΕΠΕ	Ἕλληνες Πατέρες τῆς Ἐκκλησίας
FOTC	The Fathers of the Church: A New Translation
JB	Jerusalem Bible
JBC	*Jerome Biblical Commentary*, ed. Raymond E. Brown, Joseph A. Fitzmyer, and Roland E. Murphy
LXX	Septuagint, ed. Alfred Rahlfs
NAB	New American Bible
NCE	New Catholic Encyclopedia
NPNF	The Nicene and Post-Nicene Fathers, ed. Philip Schaff and Henry Wace
OT	Old Testament
PG	Patrologia Graeca (Patrologia Cursus Completus, Series Graeca), ed. Jacques-Paul Migne
RNT	New Testament of the New American Bible

PREFACE TO THE SECOND EDITION

It is with great joy that we bring back this first volume of the Homilies of St. John Chrysostom on Romans after several years of being out of print.

Experience has shown over the last few years that the demand for these homilies transcends the scholarly world, for which they were originally intended. Having used this text in numerous Bible Studies and received a very positive response from lay people and priests alike, I realized how important it is to make this book available again. In the meantime, I am also encouraged to proceed to complete the second volume containing Homilies 16-32.

Many thanks go to His Grace bishop Anthony Vrame whose patient and diligent efforts have made it possible to improve this edition and make it easier and more pleasant to use.

Many thanks go also to many of my friends and parishioners who have encouraged me over the years to provide this volume again.

Finally, I would like to give Glory to God who has given me the opportunity, privilege and blessing to study St. John Chrysostom's works over the years and bring these particular homilies to modern English readers at a time when the patristic interpretation of the Holy Scriptures need be heard louder than any other time.

Fr. Panayiotis Papageorgiou, Ph.D.
Marietta, GA
December 4, 2024

PREFACE TO THE FIRST EDITION

It is proper that tribute be paid for this translation to a man of blessed memory, Prof. Paul W. Harkins, whom I met during my years as a graduate student at the North American Patristics Society conference at Loyola University in 1989. Prof. Harkins was glad to let me use the unfinished manuscript of his translation of Chrysostom's Homilies on Romans for the purposes of my dissertation.[1] At the time he was hoping to complete and publish it before the end of his life, but he requested that I pick it up and finish it if he was not able. It was not until after the completion of my doctoral work and after his death that I proceeded to finish this modern translation of the homilies. I reached out to Dr. Patrick Harkins, the son of Prof. Paul Harkins, who was glad to hear of my desire to complete and publish the work and encouraged me to proceed. Besides completing the translation of the unfinished homilies and correcting the finished ones against the Greek text, my main contribution to this publication is the enriching of the text with references and clarifications that draw from my dissertation research.

I must apologize for not making this valuable text available earlier. My main excuse is my immersion in parish work and my family, both during my tenure with the Church of Cyprus (1993–2001) and subsequently with the Church in the United States. I am glad to be able finally to re-embark on this noble task.

Although I walked in Prof. Harkins' footsteps with regard to this labor of love, I must take full responsibility for the weaknesses of the final product without claiming credit for all its strengths. The experience of Paul Harkins as a veteran translator pervades this work, although my intervention seeks to bring it up to date and

---

[1] Fr. Panayiotis Papageorgiou, "A Theological Analysis of Selected Themes in the Homilies of St. John Chrysostom on the Epistle of St. Paul to the Romans," PhD dissertation, The Catholic University of America, Washington D.C., 1995.

give it a theological touch born from my personal studies and doctoral research.

I hope that this text, which enriched my own theological knowledge and facilitated my maturity in the Christian life, will be a positive contribution to the life of Christians who seek a deeper understanding of the Scriptures as interpreted by this great father of the early Church. I also hope that my notes and comments will be useful to the scholar who seeks to understand the mind and theology of St. John Chrysostom.

The current first volume of this translation is comprised of the prologue and St. John's first fifteen homilies covering the first eight chapters of St. Paul's Epistle to the Romans. The remaining seventeen homilies covering the remaining chapters of the Epistle will be published in the second volume in the near future.

I would like to thank Peter Schadler for his insightful comments and recommendations that helped me to bring this work up to date. My very special thanks also to Gabriela Jessica Fulton for her patient and careful reading and valuable suggestions and corrections that helped improve the text of the homilies.

>Fr. Panayiotis Papageorgiou
>Marietta, GA
>September 8, 2012

INTRODUCTION

Prehistory

Although St. Paul's writings were considered to be "Scripture" and were used by both orthodox and heretical writers very early in the Christian period,[2] it was not until the third century that we encounter the first serious Pauline commentators: the great Alexandrian scholars, Clement and Origen.[3] Of the two, Origen is the one who can be justly credited with beginning what

---

[2] Paul's writings were used as authoritative Christian writings as early as the first half of the second century by Polycarp of Smyrna (a representative of the mainstream Christian life and thought of this time) in his epistle to the Philippians, chap. 12, written at about AD 135, where he quotes Eph 4:26 along with a quotation from the Old Testament as "Scripture." The Gnostic Vasilides (from the same time) is reported by Hippolytus, in his Elenchos 7.26.3, as having quoted 1 Cor 2:13 as ἡ γραφή. Later writers do likewise. See Maurice F. Wiles, The Divine Apostle: The Interpretation of St. Paul's Epistles in the Early Church (Cambridge: Cambridge University Press, 1967), 4–5. See also William Sanday and Arthur C. Headlam, A Critical and Exegetical Commentary on the Epistle to the Romans (Edinburg:...Clark, 1902), lxxiv–lxxxii, for lists of parallel passages between Romans and 1 Peter, Hebrews, James, Jude, 1 Clement, and the Epistle of Polycarp. Paul was a favorite of the Gnostics because of his apparent attacks on the Jews, and his idea that we have now moved from the precepts of the Old to the New Testament. The Gnostics read in Paul's writings, and especially in the Epistle to the Romans, their strong dichotomy between the creator God of the OT (who was responsible for the promulgation of sin and death in the human race) and Christ, the God of redeeming love. See Peter Gorday, Principles of Patristic Exegesis: Romans 9–11 in Origen, John Chrysostom and Augustine, Studies in the Bible and Early Christianity, vol. 4 (New York and Toronto: Edwin Mellen Press, 1983), 44–45.

[3] Origen's objective was to set himself squarely in opposition to the Gnostic interpretation of Paul's message in Romans (see P. Gorday, Principles of Patristic Exegesis, 44).

we know as real exegetical commentary.[4] Origen's tremendous productivity left behind a large number of commentaries on the Pauline Epistles, of which unfortunately very little survives today, and that only in fragments.[5] The only one of his works that survives in a substantial form seems to be the first commentary on Romans; it was preserved for us in Latin by Rufinus, whose translation has been vindicated by some recent findings of Greek fragments of the work among the Tura papyri discovered in 1941.[6] It was not until a century and a half after Origen, and in a different setting, that the next Romans commentaries were to appear.[7] These were produced by the two Antiochenes, Chrysostom and Theodore of Mopsuestia, who began their careers as friends and classmates at the feet of Diodore of Tarsus in Antioch. Although Chrysostom's commentary on Romans has been preserved intact, that of Theodore survived only in fragments after his condemnation by the Council of Constantinople in AD 553, unlike some of his other works, which have been preserved in Latin.[8]

---

[4] For the history of the "commentary" form and the influences on Origen, see Peter Gorday, Principles of Patristic Exegesis, 46.

[5] Wiles, Divine Apostle, 6.

[6] See H. Chadwick, "Rufinus and the Tura Papyrus of Origen's Commentary on Romans," *Journal of Theological Studies*, n.s. 10 (1959): 10–42.

[7] One reason for the absence of extant commentaries from this period between Origen and Chrysostom is the practice of the creation of catenae of extracts from previous writers in an effort to preserve the tradition of the past instead of writing commentaries that might introduce anything new. M. F. Wiles (*Divine Apostle*, 8) contends that "it is to this traditionalist spirit that we owe such limited knowledge as we have of Greek exegetical writings on the Pauline Epistles between the times of Origen and Chrysostom." This does not mean, however, that there was no activity in interpreting Paul during this very important period of theological debate. There is evidence for such activity from the fragments of Acacius of Caesarea on Romans; and from Eusebius of Emesa, who doctrinally belonged to the semi-Arian camp, on Galatians. It is also probable that the best and fullest work of commentary on the Pauline Epistles after the time of Origen was the work of Theodore of Heraclea (mid-fourth century), who was also a semi-Arian, and from whom not even fragments have survived. We do have fragments, however, from two other writers of the non-orthodox camp of the late fourth century, Diodore and Apollinarius. See Wiles, *Divine Apostle*, 8–9. The complete works of these writers were not preserved by posterity because of their heretical leanings.

[8] Wiles, *Divine Apostle*, 7.

Both Chrysostom and Theodore of Mopsuestia represent a tradition different from that of Origen in the history of biblical exegesis. The roots of their approach are found in the method of their teacher Diodore,[9] who moved away from the more allegorical Origenist model (without necessarily rejecting allegory altogether). In this tradition the exegete is more concerned with the context, "inner thought development and logical, clear exposition in interpreting the text,"[10] seeking out the progression of ideas and giving to the commentary a more "unspectacular and common-sense quality which is commonly held to be one of the chief virtues of the Antiochenes."[11]

The extant fragments of Diodore's commentary on Roman's, dealing mostly with chapters 7–11,[12] make clear that Diodore's exegesis of Romans directly influenced Chrysostom's and Theodore's.[13] The commentaries of the two students of Diodore are dominated by the same themes as their teacher's work: "an emphasis on the divine οἰκονομία in the progress from the old to the new covenant of salvation and a strong focus on the problem of predestination and free will."[14] Although, undoubtedly, the shaping of Chrysostom's original thought and exegetical methodology was greatly affected by Diodore's teachings, we cannot ignore the fact that his theology, and especially his anthropology, was shaped by a broad spectrum of theologians beginning with Irenaeus and ending with the Cappadocians.[15] Even an adjusted form of Origen's legacy of the

---

9 Diodore's fragments are found in Karl Staab, ed., *Die Pauluskommentare aus der griechischen Kirche*, 113–159, Neutestamentliche Abhandlungen 15 (Munich: Aschendorff, 1933), 83ff. Peter Gorday (*Principles of Patristic Exegesis*, 305n10) notes that most of Diodore's exegesis of Romans has to be recovered by source criticism of Theodore of Mopsuestia's commentary.

10 Gorday, *Principles of Patristic Exegesis*, 104.

11 Ibid.

12 Staab, *Die Pauluskommentare*, 83ff.

13 Wiles (*Divine Apostle*, 9) agrees with this judgment. Gorday's assertion that Theodore's commentary on Romans may be a source of influence on Chrysostom cannot be adequately supported, especially because he admits ignorance as to the date of its origin. It seems more reasonable to assume that they were both influenced by a common work, that of their teacher Diodore.

14 Gorday, *Principles of Patristic Exegesis*, 104–105.

15 See my work "A Theological Analysis of Selected Themes in the Homilies of St. John Chrysostom on the Epistle of St. Paul to the Romans" (PhD diss., The Catholic

duality of man is transmitted to Chrysostom, probably through Gregory of Nyssa. One may say that as Chrysostom matured in his preaching ministry, he drew eclectically from a variety of sources, especially the authors involved in the great doctrinal debates of the fourth century. He thus formed a solid foundation of Nicene/Cappadocian theology to be his guide.[16]

The Text: Date and Provenance

Chrysostom's Commentary on Romans is comprised of a preface (Ὑπόθεσις) and thirty-two homilies (Ὁμιλίαι) that were most probably composed and delivered in Antioch between AD 386 and 397,[17] while Chrysostom was still a priest.[18] Some conclusions can be drawn from their contents: In Homily 8, he speaks of himself and his listeners as being under one bishop, and in Homily 32 he refers to the place where his hearers live as one in which St. Paul taught and was bound; both references are certainly to Antioch and not Constantinople. The sermons were probably the first commentary Chrysostom wrote on St. Paul, composed after he completed his Commentary on the Gospel of St. John.[19] Because some

---

University of America, 1995), especially chap. 2, 16ff.

16 Ibid.

17 The original texts of the *Homilies on Romans*, as most of Chrysostom's works, are not yet in critical editions. Hence the establishment of a relative chronology has only just begun (see Peter Gorday, *Principles of Patristic Exegesis*, 305n15). See also the overview of research on Chrysostom in R. E. Carter, "The Future of Chrysostom Studies," *Studia Patristica* 10, ed. F. L. Cross (Berlin: Akademie-Verlag, 1970), 14–21.

18 There is really no evidence that he preached from the pulpit during his diaconate. According to Chrysostomus Baur (*John Chrysostom and His Time*, 2 vols., trans. M. Gonzaga [Westminster, MD: Newman Press, 1959], vol. 1, pt. 1, 153) deacons did not have the right to preach at this time. The most recent biographer of Chrysostom, J. N. D. Kelly (*Golden Mouth: The Story of John Chrysostom; Ascetic, Preacher, Bishop* [London: Duckworth, 1995], 39) agrees with this, and so do Wendy Mayer and Pauline Allen (*John Chrysostom* [London and New York: Routledge, 2000], 6n10). It is more probable that his preaching ministry began with his ordination to the presbyterate. Therefore, these homilies must be from the period of AD 386–397, before he was taken by Emperor Arcadius to Constantinople, where he was consecrated archbishop of the Imperial City on February 26, 398. Kelly (*Golden Mouth*, 90) finally suggests the year 392.

19 See Baur, *John Chrysostom*, vol. 1, pt. 2, 297; cf. Johannes Quasten, *Patrology*, vol. 3, *The Golden Age of Greek Patristic Literature from the Council of Nicea to the Council of Chalcedon* (Westminster, MD: Newman Press, 1960), 442.

of these homilies are so long that it would have taken two hours to deliver them, it is possible that they could have been revised and expanded at a later time, or that they were never even delivered from the pulpit.[20]

The authenticity of the homilies is without doubt. They bear "the stamp of Chrysostom's authorship in style, language and exegetical method."[21] In addition, soon after his death eight passages of the tenth homily were quoted by St. Augustine in his *Adversus Julianum* 1.27 in an effort to clear Chrysostom of the Pelagian connection, but also to defend himself with regard to his doctrine of "original sin."[22]

The Greek text used for the purposes of this new translation is that of Henry Savile, first published in 1612 and reprinted in Patrologia Graeca 60.[23] A more recent edition of the text of the homilies was published by Frederick Field.[24] This edition was reprinted in the series Ἕλληνες Πατέρες τῆς Ἐκκλησίας,[25] accompanied by a modern Greek translation. Both Field's edition and the Modern Greek translation of the text were consulted on occasion as an aid to clarification. The English translation found in the series of The Nicene and Post-Nicene Fathers[26] was also consulted on occasion.

The Homilies on Romans as Biblical Exegesis

There have been widely differing views among scholars about Chrysostom's ability to understand and interpret the Epistles of

---

20 See Baur, *John Chrysostom*, vol. 1, pt. 2, 297.

21 Quasten, *Patrology*, 3:442.

22 For a comparison of Augustine's and Chrysostom's understanding on "original sin," see my work "Chrysostom and Augustine on the Sin of Adam and its Consequences," *St. Vladimir's Theological Quarterly* 39, no. 4 (1995): 361–378.

23 St. John Chrysostom, *Homilies on Romans* (PG 60: 386–682).

24 F. Field, *Joannis Chrysostomi Interpretatio omnium epistolarum Paulinarum*, Bibliotheca Patrum (Oxford, 1845).

25 Ἰωάννου Χρυσοστόμου Ἔργα. Ἕλληνες Πατέρες τῆς Ἐκκλησίας, τόμ. 16Β–17. Θεσσαλονίκη: Πατερικαὶ Ἐκδόσεις Γρηγόριος ὁ Παλαμᾶς, 1985.

26 St. John Chrysostom, *Homilies on Romans*, in The Nicene and Post-Nicene Fathers [henceforth NPNF], Series 1, vol. 11, trans. J. B. Morris and W. H. Simcox (reprint, Grand Rapids, Michigan: Eerdmans, 1980), 329–564.

St. Paul. On the one end of this spectrum we have critics like E. Hoffman-Aleith, who point to Chrysostom as a typical example of early Church interpreters who unconsciously failed to understand Paul in spite of their admiration for the Apostle.[27] On the other end of the spectrum we have scholars like M. J. Lagrange, who give Chrysostom high marks on his interpretation of Paul in the Homilies on Romans[28] as well as in his other Pauline commentaries.[29] Joining Lagrange in the positive view of Chrysostom is the first modern biographer of Chrysostom, Chrysostomus Baur,[30] and the prominent patrologist Johannes Quasten, who rates the Homilies on Romans as "by far the most outstanding patristic commentary on this epistle and the finest of all Chrysostom's works."[31] Quasten brings in as an early witness to his favorable judgment a contemporary of Chrysostom, Isidore of Pelusium, who, impressed with Chrysostom's exposition of the Epistle, exclaimed,

> If the divine Paul wished to expound in the Attic tongue his own writings he would not have spoken otherwise than this famous master; so remarkable is the latter's exposition for its contents, its beauty of form, and propriety of expression.[32]

---

[27] Eva Hoffman-Aleith, "Das Paulusverständnis des Johannes Chrysostomus," *Zeitschrift für die Neutestamentliche Wissenschaft* 38 (1939): 181–188. Hoffman-Aleith points primarily to the subject of divine grace and human freedom, where she sees a theology of predestination in St. Paul and the rejection of it by the Greek fathers.

[28] M. J. Lagrange, *St. Paul: Épitre aux Romains*, 7th ed. (Paris: J. Gabalda, 1950), chap. 8.

[29] See Lagrange's comments on Chrysostom's *Commentary on Galatians* in A. Merzagora, "Giovanni Chrisostomo, Commentatore di S. Paulo," *Didaskaleion* n.s. 10 (1931): 5.

[30] Chrysostomus Baur, in his monumental work *John Chrysostom and His Time*, vol. 1, pt. 2, 322, claims that "the fact is that Chrysostom's commentaries on the New Testament are considered, even in our own day, from a literary and exegetical point of view, the best and most useful that the Greek patristic age has bequeathed to us."

[31] Quasten, *Patrology*, 3:442; see also Baur, *John Chrysostom*, vol. 1, pt. 2, chap. 23, especially 297ff.

[32] Isidore of Pelusium, *Epistle 5*, 32, in Quasten, *Patrology*, 442. This statement of Isidore is also quoted by A. Merzagora, "Giovanni Chrisostomo," 1. Cf. also B. Altaner, *Patrologie*, 6th ed. (Freiburg, 1963), 291, English translation of 5th ed. by H. C. Graef (Edinburg-London, 1960), 378–379). Even more recent writers have expressed a similar opinion with regards to Chrysostom's Attic style. Ulrich von Wilamowitz-Moellendorff (*Die Kultur der Gegenwart* [Berlin, 1905], 1, 8, 212) says in

INTRODUCTION

Maurice F. Wiles, however, contends that the majority of scholars today "would steer a course somewhat between these two extremes."[33] Chrysostom's exegesis remains very close to the text, revealing a sincere effort on his part to analyze and explain to his hearers the message of Paul; following the Antiochene tradition, he avoids going into allegorical interpretations, while at the same time he "does enter with comparative thoroughness into detailed questions of the correct exegesis of the text."[34] His homiletic method may indeed be an advantage in dealing with the Letters of Paul "whose original purpose was certainly nearer to that of homiletic than to that of theological definition."[35] It becomes obvious here, as in almost all of his exegetical works, that Chrysostom had a double purpose for these homilies. As Peter Gorday notes, "He commented on as much of it [the Epistle] as he found convenient in each homily and then attached general exhortation and application."[36] He thus provided a commentary for the intellectual, along with a practical application of the Christian teachings for both the intellectual and the simple hearer.[37]

---

praise of Chrysostom, "Chrysostomus ist ein beinahe puristischer Attizist; bei ihm dominiert das reine Attisch" (quoted by Arnold Uleyn, "La doctrine morale de S. Jean Chrysostome dans le commentaire sur S. Matthieu et ses affinités avec la diatribe," *Revue de l'Université d'Ottawa* 27 [1957]: 17n42.)

33 Wiles, *Divine Apostle*, 4. Wiles points to two writers who follow this middle road: H. E. W. Turner, *The Pattern of Christian Truth* (London, 1954), 485; and K. H. Schelkle, *Paulus Lehrer der Väter: Die altkirchliche Auslegung von Römer 1–11*, 2nd ed. (Düsseldorf, 1959), 440.

34 Wiles, *Divine Apostle*, 7.

35 Ibid. Wiles sees in the Letters of St. Paul a homiletic style similar to Chrysostom's.

36 Gorday, *Principles of Patristic Exegesis*, 107.

37 This homiletical format is known as the "double audience" format and was employed extensively by previous writers, especially by Clement and Origen. See the most recent study by Jaclyn L. Maxwell, *Christianization and Communication in Late Antiquity: John Chrysostom and His Congregation in Antioch* (Cambridge: Cambridge University Press, 2006), who points out that Chrysostom's sermons "were tailor-made for their audiences" (p. 7). She also explains that "it is clear from the sermons themselves and accounts by contemporary observers that the preacher consciously attempted to communicate with different kinds of people. Moreover, his listeners responded to him and at times even adjusted their behavior according to his instructions" (p. 9).

Chrysostom's Rhetorical Style: The Application of Rhetoric to His Sermons

As it has already been demonstrated by various scholars, Chrysostom's style was formed in part by his early training under Libanius,[38] and employed many of the figures of speech of the Second Sophistic Rhetoric, though with conscious restraint.[39] It has also been pointed out that Chrysostom routinely employed the rhetorical method of the diatribe, which is a characteristic of the Second Sophistic, and his discourses are many times a διάλεξις in which he uses all the techniques of oratorical competence. For example, we find Chrysostom frequently feigning audience participation, proposing and answering objections and denials, employing popular speech, addressing children to demonstrate the juvenile behavior of their parents, and describing concrete situations in the everyday affairs of professional life, labor, sports, family ambitions and foibles, the gamut of medical experiences, clerical and monastic life, the theatre, politics, and profligacy. In each instance, he paints a concrete picture, then treats it with humor or sarcasm, withering disdain, or praise, or thundering denunciation, as he compares it with the dictates of the Christian way of life.[40] Chrysostom's *Homilies on Romans* is the only one of the early Greek commentaries on the Epistle that survives intact in its original form. Although modern scholarly opinion on its exegetical value varies, it seems that it was considered even by his

---

38 He graduated c. 367, when he was eighteen years old (see Mayer and Allen, *John Chrysostom*, 5).

39 See, for example, the study of Thomas E. Ameringer, "The Stylistic Influence of the Second Sophistic on the Panegyrical Sermons of St. John Chrysostom: A Study in Greek Rhetoric" (PhD diss., The Catholic University of America, 1921); and also the study by Mary Albania Burns, "Saint John Chrysostom's Homilies on the Statues: A Study of their Rhetorical Qualities and Form" (PhD diss., The Catholic University of America, 1930). The *Homilies on Romans* are replete with rhetorical figures of speech, as are all of his other works. It does not seem necessary that examples be given here because much has been written on the subject elsewhere. See also Jaclyn L. Maxwell's recent study *Christianization and Communication in Late Antiquity*.

40 F. X. Murphy, "The Moral Doctrine of St. John Chrysosom," *Studia Patristica* 11 (1972): 54. Murphy's comments are based on the study of Arnold Uleyn, "La doctrine morale de S. Jean Chrysostome, 100–102.

contemporaries to be one of Chrysostom's best works and was transmitted in good form to posterity. The contents and general approach to the Epistle place these homilies within the Antiochene tradition of exegesis of Diodore of Tarsus and Theodore of Mopsuestia. Although Diodore's influence on Chrysostom's approach becomes apparent when one compares his homilies to Diodore's extant fragments, Chrysostom does not limit himself to the knowledge he acquired in his youth, but utilizes the wealth of Christian tradition before him, presenting it to his audience, however, in a new way that speaks to their time and needs.

Introductory Remarks by the Late Professor Paul W. Harkins[41]

In no way does the Epistle to the Romans give a summary of Christian doctrine or a full sketch of Paul's view of Christianity.[42] It does deal with great dogmatic problems, but Chrysostom does not discuss them at length, because he was more attracted by moral and ascetical questions than by theological speculation. Many significant issues, such as the Church, the Eucharist, the resurrection of the body, and eschatology, are barely touched upon. Rather, he discusses at length his realization that our justification and salvation depend not on the deeds of the law, but on faith in Christ Jesus, the Son whom the Father's love did not spare. It is through faith that we share in the effects of the plan of salvation conceived by the Father and realized in the death and resurrection of Jesus.[43]

Biblical texts have been translated directly from Chrysostom's Greek. It seemed useful to compare Chrysostom's citations from the OT with the readings of the Septuagint as given in Rahlfs' sixth edition (2 vols., Stuttgart, 1935), which is herein designated by the abbreviation LXX.[44] In our renderings from both Testaments, we have consulted the Jerusalem Bible (JB), the New American Bible (NAB), and most recently the New Testament of the New American

---

41 This is an excerpt from the original introduction of Prof. Harkins. I have included here only what pertains to his approach to the translation process.

42 See *Jerome Biblical Commentary*, ed. Raymond E. Brown, Joseph A. Fitzmyer, and Roland E. Murphy (Englewood Cliffs, NJ: Prentice-Hall, 1968), 53:4.

43 Ibid.

44 Alfred Rahlfs, ed. *Septuaginta*. 2 vols. Stuttgart, 1935.

Bible (RNT). Wherever "cf." precedes a scriptural citation, it means either that the reader is referred to the text for confirmation of Chrysostom's argument, or that Chrysostom has quoted the text in a partial or abridged form, or that his quotation varies from Rahlfs' LXX.

Biblical proper names generally appear in the form used in NAB. Where a book of the Bible is differently designated in NAB and the Septuagint (Vulgate), both forms are given, with that from NAB first. Thus we give, for example, 2 Kgs (4 Kgdms). In the enumeration of the Psalms (or verses thereof), however, the Septuagint (Vulgate) number is given first: for example, Ps 138/139. We have made extensive use of the *Jerome Biblical Commentary* (hereafter referred to as *JBC*), edited by R. Brown, J. Fitzmyer, and R. Murphy, and references to it follow the form employed in the book itself, that is, by article and section number. The paragraphing of the homilies is our own, and we have numbered each paragraph for convenience of cross-reference. These references are given by the number of each homily in Arabic numerals, followed by the number of the paragraph(s) likewise in Arabic numerals: for example, Homily 8.16. The headings within the text are also our own. They are introduced in order to enable the reader refer back to specific topics, if necessary.

Anything like a history of exegesis would go far beyond the scope of this introduction. Suffice it to say that, among patristic writers, John Chrysostom stands in the highest rank of all who commented on the Scriptures. Like early scriptural commentaries, his are written in the form of homilies or discourses to the faithful. His explications range over almost the entire Bible, and in all Christian antiquity we find nothing to match his commentaries on Matthew's Gospel and the Pauline Epistles.

The first Reformers wrote commentaries on Paul's Letter to the Romans. But these works of men like Luther, Melanchthon, and Calvin, because they are chiefly controversial in nature, are now rarely quoted by scholars. Their successors were too energetically engaged in polemics among themselves to devote much time to regular works of exegesis.

INTRODUCTION

The twentieth century has seen what might well be called a deluge of exegesis and commentaries on Romans. At least thirty-seven works have appeared in various languages —French, German, Dutch, English, and so forth —and several of these are translations from foreign counterparts. Many of these restrict their commentaries to Romans, some to portions thereof, and still others extend to one or both Testaments. Many belong to a whole series of biblical commentaries and are still incomplete and in progress.

We have consulted many of these modern commentaries, but it seemed best to omit references to almost all of them. For the most part, they are overwhelmingly complex and actually contribute little to our approach in this translation or to the understanding of Chrysostom's thought. Therefore, we thought it best to let Chrysostom speak to his modern congregation and readers for himself.

One more question remains: Why go back to the late fourth century in search of a basis for a modern English commentary on Romans? There are many excellent reasons for this. Not only does Chrysostom quote in its original Greek almost the entire Letter to the Romans, but he also comments on the text in what amounts to a word-for-word sequence. In this he is very close to our modern method of scriptural exegesis. He furthermore uses the homily-type commentary, so commonly used in the early centuries of Christian catechesis, with the goal of spiritually edifying his audience and convincing them to come closer to God in order to transform their lives. In so doing, he is probably closer to Paul's thought and purpose than any of the modern commentators. In addition, it seemed important to us that we make available to modern readers (theologians and not) this jewel of early Christian interpretation of Scripture, especially at a time when a great number of new ways of looking at the Pauline message are being proposed. We believe that, it is necessary for modern Christians to first take a careful look at the way our early Christian fathers understood Paul before we venture into new and unsure paths of interpretation of him.

PROLOGUE

I

Whenever we observe the memorials of the martyrs, I constantly hear readings from the Epistles of the blessed Paul. And this happens twice or even three or four times a week.[1] The trumpet sound of his spiritual voice gives me a pleasure that exalts and delights my soul. Indeed, my heart grows warm with yearning as I recognize his words, which are so dear to me. I seem to imagine that he is personally present, and I feel as if my eyes are fixed on him as he converses with me.

But not everyone knows this man as we ought to know him, and this causes me grief and pain. Some people are so ignorant of him that they have no clear knowledge of the number of Epistles he wrote.[2] Nor is this the result of stupidity on their part; rather, it comes about because they have no desire for constant association with this saintly man.

As for myself, it is not because of any natural cleverness or sharpness of wit that I know as much as I know—if indeed I know anything. Rather, it is because I never cease to hold him close to me and because of my strong affection for him.

When people are loved, what is in their minds is known by those who love them before anyone else can grasp it. This is because those who experience this strong affection feel care and concern for the ones they love.[3] This saintly man pointed this out himself when he said to the Philippians, *Just as it is right that I should think in this way* Cf. Phil 1:7

---

1 Although the celebration of the Liturgy was usually limited to Sundays during Lent, Eastertide, the week of Pentecost, and other specific times, the Eucharistic sacrifice might well be celebrated every day or "as often as we wish." See Paul W. Harkins, trans., *St. John Chrysostom: Discourses against Judaizing Christians*, FOTC 68 (Washington, DC: Catholic University of America Press, 1979), xxiv, 50.

2 This would refer to the whole Pauline canon (even including Hebrews).

3 Chrysostom's love for Paul makes him Paul's alter ego and should motivate us to imitate his devotion to the Apostle.

about you, because I hold you all in my heart, both when I lie in prison and when I am defending the solid ground on which the Gospel rests.[4]

Therefore, if you are willing to be zealous in paying heed to the reading, you will need nothing more. For Christ did not lie when he said, *Seek and you shall find; knock and it will be opened to you.* But because the majority of those who are gathered here before me have undertaken the task of rearing children and caring for a wife as well as providing for a household, they could not for these reasons devote themselves entirely to this pursuit. However, you should rouse yourselves to listen to what wisdom others have gathered together; you should allot as much effort to hearing their words as you do to gathering money. Even if it shames me to demand only this much of you, still I am content if you make at least this much effort.

Cf. Matt 7:7

The Seriousness of the Evils that Come from Ignorance of the Scriptures: The Time and Order of Paul's Epistles

For evils beyond our ability to count arise from this source —I mean from ignorance of the Scriptures. From this spring the many defilements of heretical doctrines;[5] from this come sinful lifestyles; from this labors devoid of benefit arise. Just as those who are deprived of the light of day could not walk a straight path, so too those who fail to look to the Divine Scriptures are forced constantly into many sins because they are walking in the depths of the most dangerous darkness.

To prevent this from happening, let us open our eyes to the light that comes from the words of this Apostle. For what he says shines forth more brightly than the sun, and he surpasses all the others in what he recounts and teaches. Because he toiled more than those others, he drew to himself the grace of the Spirit in great abundance. And I am confident in affirming this not only from what he wrote in his Epistles, but also from the book of Acts. If anywhere there was a suitable time for preaching, in every instance others

---

4 JBC, 50:7.

5 The chief heresies current at this time were the neo-Arianism or Anomoeanism, Gnosticism and Manichaeism.

made way for him to speak. This is why among the unbelievers he was given the name of Hermes,[6] for he was the first to speak.

Because we are going to be considering this Epistle, we must mention the time when it was written. Many consider that it was written before all his others, but this is not so, although it was composed before all those that were written from Rome. Rather, it belongs to a later date than his other Epistles, although not all of them. For both Epistles to the Corinthians had been sent off earlier than the Epistle to the Romans.

This is clear from the words he wrote toward the end of this Letter to the Romans, where he said, *Now I am leaving for Jerusalem to help and support the saints. Macedonia and Achaia*[7] *have kindly decided to make a contribution to those in need among the saints in Jerusalem.*[8] And when he sent his Letter to the Corinthians, he said, *If it seems fitting that I should go myself, they will accompany me.* Here he was speaking of those who were going to carry the collected contribution to Jerusalem. Cf. Rom 15:25–26
1 Cor 16:4

From this it is clear that when he sent his Letter to the Corinthians, it was not certain that he would make this journey. When he wrote to the Romans, a sure decision had been made. If we are agreed on that, it is also clear that the Epistle to the Romans was written after both of Paul's Letters to the Corinthians.

And I also think his First Letter to the Thessalonians is earlier than this Letter to the Corinthians. For he had written to the Thessalonians about this contribution in these words: *As regards brotherly love, there is no need for me to write you. God Himself has taught you to love one another, and this you are doing to all the brothers.*[9] Cf.
1 Thess 4:9–10

---

6 Cf. Acts 14:12. In ancient Greek religion, Hermes was messenger and spokesman of the gods. By being the first to speak, Paul was fulfilling either or both of those functions.

7 Achaia was a Roman province of southern Greece.

8 The "saints," or "holy ones," is a synonym for "Christians" in Paul's Letters: for example, 1 Cor 1:2; 6:2; 16:1, 15; 2 Cor 1:1; 9:1; 13:13, etc. See W. Arndt and F. W. Gingrich, *A Greek-English Lexicon of the New Testament* (Chicago, 1957), s.v. ἅγιος.

9 Paul at times draws a distinction between φιλαδελφία and ἀγάπη. Filadelfia usually means love for one's fellow Christians; Ἀγάπη extends beyond the local community to all men and women. Cf. also 1 Thess 3:12, and see Forestell, *JBC*, 48:24. This universal love is "taught by God," who teaches men of His own nature (cf. 1 John 4:8) by the interior instruction of the Holy Spirit. Here Paul seems to

Later he wrote to the Corinthians and made this very point clear when he said, *I already know your willingness and boast about you to the Macedonians with respect to it, saying that Achaia has been ready since last year. Your zeal has stirred up most of them.*[10] By these words he showed that he had earlier spoken to the Thessalonians about this matter. This Letter to the Corinthians is later than those written to the Thessalonians but earlier than the Epistles he sent from Rome. Indeed, he had not yet set foot into the capital city when he wrote his Epistle to the Romans. Paul makes this clear when he says, *For I long to see you so that I may share with you some spiritual gift.*[11]

_{2 Cor 9:2}

_{Rom 1:11}

But it was from Rome that he sent his Epistle to the Philippians, because he says in it, *All the saints send greetings to you, especially those in Caesar's household.* The same is true for the Epistle to the Hebrews, where he says, *Those from Italy send you greetings.* Paul also sent his Letter to Timothy from Rome while he was in prison there. I think that this was the last of all his Letters. This is clear from its ending: *I for my part am already being poured out like a libation,*[12] Paul says; "the time of my dissolution is near." Surely everybody knows that he came to the end of his life in Rome.

_{Cf. Phil 4:22}

_{Heb 13:24}

_{2 Tim 4:6}

The Letter to Philemon is also among his last because Paul wrote it in his extreme old age. We know this because he says, *As Paul, an old man (πρεσβύτης) and now a prisoner for Christ Jesus.*[13] However, this Letter precedes the Epistle to the Colossians. This order of composition is clear again from the ending of the Letter to the Colossians, when Paul has this to say: *Tychicus will give you all the news. I have sent him along with Onesimus, our dear and faithful brother.*

_{Phlm 1:9}

_{Col 4:7-9}

This was the same Onesimus on whose behalf Paul composed his Letter to Philemon. That he was not another man of the same

---

mean the Gentile Christians of Thessalonika and the Jewish Christians of Jerusalem.

10 Macedonia was a Roman province in northern Greece. Its seaport was Thessalonika, on the Thermaic Gulf.

11 This verse expresses Paul's deep desire to visit Rome.

12 Paul knows his martyrdom is near. He sees that this will be an act of supreme worship in which his life will be poured out in sacrifice. Cf. Phil 2:17 and RNT n. *ad loc.*

13 NAB must have read πρεσβευτής (a conjecture of Bentley), meaning "an ambassador," for πρεσβύτης, "an old man." See Arndt and Gingrich, *Greek-English Lexicon*, s.v. πρεσβύτης.

name is made evident from the mention made of Archippus. According to the Letter to Philemon, Paul had taken Archippus as his comrade in arms and fellow worker in making his appeal for Onesimus. And in writing to the Colossians, he rouses the zeal of Archippus with these words: *And say to Archippus, 'See that you fulfill the ministry that you have received.'* Cf. Col 4:17

It seems to me that the Epistle to the Galatians is also earlier than that to the Romans.[14] But there is no need to wonder if they have a different order in the books of the Bible. In the Sacred Books the twelve prophets are put together in succession and do not follow the order of time, because they are far separated and stand at great intervals from one another. Haggai and Zechariah and others prophesied after Ezekiel and Daniel. Many gave their prophecies after Jonah and Zephaniah and all the others. Yet they are placed together with all those from whom they are so far removed in time.

But no one should think that this task is of secondary importance, or that a search of such a nature is no more than a superfluous curiosity. For the order in time of the Epistles contributes much to understanding the questions we are seeking to answer.[15] Suppose I see Paul sending off Letters to the Romans and the Colossians on the same topic but treating this topic in a different way. Suppose he writes to the Romans with considerable condescension, as when he says, *Extend a kind welcome to the man who is* Rom 14:1-2

---

14 Cf. NPNF[1] 11:336, note by G. B. Stevens, who finds it remarkable that Chrysostom's conclusions as to the order of the Pauline Letters should harmonize so well with the results of modern scholarship. This accuracy results from Chrysostom's extensive knowledge of the Pauline corpus and his careful use of internal evidence.

15 Cf. ibid., 336–337. The earliest Letters (1 and 2 Thess) are continuations of Paul's missionary preaching and teaching. Galatians 1, 2 Corinthians, and Romans reflect the doctrinal discussions of the law and grace and Paul's conflicts with the Gentiles and Judaizing Christians—questions most important for Pauline theology. The Imprisonment Epistles (Col, Phlm, Eph, and Phil) exhibit the rise and spread of Gnostic heresies that influenced the theology and life of the early Church. Finally, the Pastoral Epistles (1 and 2 Tim, Titus, Phlm) have high value as the latest Christian counsels of Paul, "now an old man."

weak in faith. Do not enter into disputes with him. A man of sound faith believes he may eat anything; one whose faith is weak eats vegetables.[16]

Col 2:20–23   But to the Colossians he does not write in the same way about the same thing. Rather, he speaks with greater freedom and boldness. For he says, *If with Christ you have died to worldly forces, why should you, as if you were still living in the world, submit to such rules and regulations as 'do not handle, do not taste, do not touch'? Such proscriptions deal with things that perish in their use, that have no honor, or that are for the indulgence of the flesh.*[17]

I find no reason for this difference other than the time of the events. At first he had to be condescending; later this was no longer necessary. And you might find him doing this in many other places. Both physicians and teachers make a practice of acting in this way: the physician does not treat those who are at the beginning of an illness in the same way as he does those who have come to the point of having their health restored for the future, nor does the teacher treat young children in the same way as he does students who need more advanced instruction.

Paul sent his Letters to the rest of his addressees because he was moved to do so by some cause or question. And he states this

1 Cor 7:1   clearly, as when he says to the Corinthians, *As regards the matters about which you wrote to me.*[18] And to the Galatians he shows this same purpose from the very beginning and throughout the entire Epistle.[19]

But for what cause or question did Paul write his Epistle to the

Rom 15:14   Romans? For certainly he testifies that they are *filled with goodness, having complete knowledge, and able to give advice to others*. Why,

Rom 15:15–16   then, does he send them a Letter? As he says, *Because God has given me the grace to be a minister of Christ Jesus*. Therefore he also said at

---

16 It would seem that there were deep differences between the converts from paganism and those from Judaism. The converts from Judaism were traumatized at the thought of giving up the old dietary rules. Paul is recommending that the pagan converts respect the consciences of the Jewish converts, even if the latter were overly scrupulous by not rejecting the Mosaic law.

17 Because in baptism we have died with Christ and hence to all worldly forces, we must pay no heed to merely human precepts and doctrines. See NAB n. *ad loc*.

18 NAB n. *ad loc*.

19 Cf. NAB, Introduction to Galatians, 220–221; and RNT, Introduction to Galatians, 283–284.

the beginning of the Epistle, *I am under obligation, and, with all my strength, I am eager to preach the gospel to you who are in Rome.*   Rom 1:14–15

And what he said—for example, that they could *give advice to oth*—*ers,* and the like—are words by which he praises and encourages the Romans. However, they stand in need of the correction that an Epistle could provide. Because he had not yet arrived in Rome, he is bringing them to order in two ways: by the help and advantage his Letter would give, and by the expectation that he himself would soon be there.   Rom 15:14

Such was the nature of that blessed soul. He embraced the entire world, and he carried all men within himself because he considered that the strongest relationship was the relationship he had with men in God. Just as if he had begotten all men, so did he love them. Rather, he showed them an affection warmer than that of any father. For such is the grace of the Spirit. It surpasses the pangs of childbirth in the flesh and displays a warmer love and yearning.

We can see this preeminently in the soul of Paul. Just as if his love had equipped him with wings, he constantly went about to all men, never stopping or standing still. Because Paul heard Christ saying, *Peter, do you love Me? Tend My sheep,* and knew that Jesus had set this task forth as the greatest measure of love, he wanted to show this love in the highest degree. Let us imitate, in our turn, this great love that Paul manifested to the world. Even if no one man can keep in order and control the entire world, nor whole cities and nations, let each of us train and correct his wife, children, friends, and neighbors.   John 21:16

Let no one say to me, "I am unskilled and ignorant." No one was less learned than Peter; no one was less skilled than Paul. Paul agreed to this himself when he said, *I may be unskilled in speech, but not in knowledge.*[20] Nonetheless, Paul, who lacked skill, and Peter, who lacked learning, overcame countless philosophers; they silenced countless orators because they did everything with their own earnestness and the grace of God. What defense will we have   2 Cor 11:6

---

20 In 2 Cor 10:10 Paul's critics admit the severity and forcefulness of his Letters but find him unimpressive as a person and lacking impact as a speaker. They feel much the same about his knowledge. But Paul can boast that he is not lacking in knowledge because his own earnestness is supported by his personal experience with God.

if we have not helped even twenty people and are unable to benefit even those who live with us?

So your alleged lack of skill and knowledge is only a pretense and an excuse. Ignorance and lack of skill do not hinder us from teaching; sluggishness and laziness do. So let us first shake off this attitude and then, with all zeal, tend to the members of our household. In this way, we shall enjoy abundant peace here on earth by controlling, in the fear of God, those who are related to us. Then we shall also share in the multitude of the blessings of heaven through the grace and loving-kindness of our Lord Jesus Christ, through whom and with whom be glory to the Father, together with the Holy Spirit, now and forever, and unto the ages of ages. Amen.

HOMILY I

Greetings from Paul, a servant of Christ Jesus, called to be an apostle and set apart to proclaim the gospel of God that He promised through His prophets, as the Holy Scriptures record.   Rom 1:1–2.

Although Moses wrote five books of the Bible, nowhere did he sign his own name.[21] Nor did subsequent authors who composed the sacred books that follow his in the Old Testament.[22] The same is true for the Gospels of Matthew, John, Mark, and Luke. But blessed Paul prefixes his name everywhere in his Epistles.

Why is this? It is because all the others were speaking for those who were present before them, and there was no need for the writers to point out that they themselves were there. But in Paul's case, he was sending what he wrote to far-off places in the form of letters. Therefore, the addition of his name was necessary.

If Paul did not prefix his name to his Epistle to the Hebrews, he did not do so because of his own prudential judgment.[23] The Hebrews were his enemies. If they heard his name at the beginning of the Letter, they would block their ears to the rest of his discourse. So he omitted his name, and, in this way, he was clever enough to win their attention.

---

21 The books referred to are the first five of the Bible, which constitute the Pentateuch, or Torah (Gen, Exod, Lev, Num, and Deut). Moses was not the author in the modern sense. Rather, these books represent at least four historical traditions and sources, referred to in modern scholarship as the Yahwist, Elohist, priestly, and Deuteronomic sources.

22 Here Chrysostom means the Historical Books. The Wisdom Books are sometimes ascribed to certain authors, but such ascriptions may only be traditional and the authors anonymous.

23 This is an interesting syllogism by Chrysostom. Modern scholarship, however, disputes the authorship of Hebrews by St. Paul.

But if the prophets and Solomon have affixed their names, I leave to you for future investigation the question as to why some did and some did not. For I must not instruct you on every point, but you must carry on the search for yourselves. Otherwise you may become more sluggish and lazy.

Rom 1:1 *Paul, a servant of Jesus Christ.* Why did God change the name and call the man who was Saul by the name of Paul? God did this so that Paul might not be considered even partially inferior, but that he might possess that distinctive something that the chief of the disciples had.[24] And God also wished Paul to have a foundation for a closer union with the other apostles.

And Paul calls himself a servant of Christ, but he is not a servant in one way only. For there are many ways one can be a servant. One way we become servants is by creation, of which the psalm-
Ps 118/119:91. ist says, *All things are your servants,* and we read also, *[I will send to]*
Jer 25:9. *Nebuchadnezzar [king of Babylon], My servant.*[25] For the work done is the servant of him who made it. Another way one can be a servant
Rom 6:17-18. is by faith. Paul says of this faith, *Thanks be to God, though once you were slaves of sin, you obeyed from your heart that form of teaching that was imparted to you; freed from your sin, you became servants of justice.*

Another way one can be a servant is by one's conduct and way of life. It was according to this way that the Lord said to Joshua,
Josh 1:2. *Moses, My servant, is dead.* Even though all the Jews were servants, Moses shone forth at the very head because of his way of life.

Because, therefore, Paul was a servant in all these ways, he put
Rom 1:1 this before that name of the greatest esteem when he said *servant of Jesus Christ.* He sets it forth before all the titles of God's plan of salvation through the Word made flesh, in this way moving from the lowest to the highest.

Surely the angel came from heaven bringing the name for Jesus when He was born[26] of the Virgin. And Jesus is called Christ by reason of His anointing, and this also pertained to the Word made

---

24 See Matt 16:18, where Simon is called Peter.
25 The words in parentheses are not necessary to Chrysostom's argument, but they are found in NAB, and in Rahlfs' Septuagint. Jeremiah is predicting the seventy years of exile the Jews will spend in Babylon for their sins against God.
26 More precisely, Chrysostom should have said "conceived." Cf. Luke 1:31.

flesh. Perhaps you will ask, "With what oil was Christ anointed?"²⁷ He was not anointed with oil, but with the Spirit. And Scripture generally calls those who have been anointed in this way *christs*.²⁸ Surely the Spirit is the most important part of anointing, because the Spirit is that for which the oil is used. And when does the sacred writer call "christs" those who have not been anointed with oil? It is when the psalmist says, *Touch not my christs, and to my prophets do no harm*.²⁹ For at that time there was no provision for anointing with oil.

*Called to be an apostle.*³⁰ In many places Paul says he was called, and in doing so he shows his candor and prudence. He also points out that he did not obtain the title by seeking after it, but that, when he was called, he was ready and obeyed the call. In the same way he calls the faithful believers *those called to be saints*. For they had been called to the point where they believed. But Paul had something else entrusted to him, namely, the apostleship,³¹ which was rich in countless blessings and was greater than all other gifts but still embraced them all.

What more need I say other than that whatever Christ used to do while he was on earth, He entrusted to His apostles when He left them? And Paul proclaimed this too when he extolled the dignity of the apostles and said, *This makes us ambassadors of Christ, just as if God were giving His exhortation through us*,³² that is, in the place of Christ.

---

27 Cf. McKenzie, DB, 34–35 (s.v. "anoint"); 624–625 (s.v. "oil"); 435–436 (s.v. "Jesus Christ").

28 Anointing brings the spirit of Yahweh first to Saul and later to David. In 1 John 2:20, 27 we read, "You have the anointing that comes from the Holy One...The anointing you have received from Him teaches you about all things." The Greek word for anointing is χρῖσμα ("chrisma"), which is usually taken to mean anointing with the Holy Spirit. Cf. Arndt and Gingrich, Greek-English Lexicon, s.v. "χρῖσμα."

29 Cf. also Isa 45:1 and NAB note ad loc.

30 Not only is Paul a servant of Christ, but his special service to the Christian community is to preach the gospel of God as an apostle. The event on the road to Damascus shows the divine origin of his call to the apostolate. The gospel he preaches is not of human origin, but divine. Cf. Gal 1:1–24.

31 Paul's apostleship implies a special charismatic call to a special charismatic service, namely, to preach the gospel.

32 As an apostle, Paul is a herald of Christ. Functioning as Christ's legate, he serves as God's instrument in carrying out the action of divine mercy.

Rom 1:1. *Set apart to proclaim the gospel of God.* Just as in a household each one is set apart for different tasks, so too in the Church the distributions of ministries are different. And I think that here Paul was hinting that he was not chosen by lot,[33] but that from the first he was appointed to this office. This is how Jeremiah reported

Jer 1:5. what God had said about his ministry: *Before you came forth from your mother, I sanctified you; I appointed you a prophet to the nations.*[34] Because Jeremiah was writing to a proud and boastful city that was proud and puffed up in every way, he showed in every way that his election was from God. For God Himself called Jeremiah and set him apart. Paul, however, speaks and acts the way he does so that he may make his Epistle worthy of belief and readily received.

Rom 1:1 *The gospel of God.* Matthew is not only an evangelist, nor is Mark, just as Paul is not only an apostle. Matthew and Mark were also apostles, but Paul is spoken of particularly as an apostle, whereas Matthew and Mark are especially considered to be evangelists. And Paul calls his Letters a "gospel" not only because of the good things they accomplish, but also for the blessings they will bring in the future.

Rom 1:1. How is it that Paul says that God preached the gospel through him? Indeed, he does say *set apart to proclaim the gospel of God.* But the Father was manifested and known before the Gospels. Yet if the Father was manifest, it was to the Jews alone, and not even to all the Jews, as would have been right and fitting. For they did not know that He was the Father, and at that time they imagined many things that were unworthy of God. It was on this account that Christ said that authentic worshippers would come and that such are the ones the Father seeks to worship Him.[35] And it was at a later date that the Father, together with the Son, was made manifest to the whole world, just as Christ had predicted. For he said,

---

33 As was the case with Matthias; see Acts 1:21–26.

34 God destined Jeremiah to be His servant even before his birth, sanctifying him and appointing him to be His prophet to the nations. Paul is perhaps recalling this verse from Jeremiah in Rom 1:5. The city to which Jeremiah refers is Jerusalem, which had fallen into idolatry. It would soon be conquered, and its people led off to captivity in Babylon.

35 John 4:23 and notes ad loc. in Confraternity ed., NAB, and RNT.

That they may know You, the only true God, and Him whom You have sent,   John 17:3.
Jesus Christ.[36]

And Paul calls it *the gospel of God* to set his audience straight at   Rom 1:1
the very start of his Epistle. For he did not come to proclaim any
gloomy tidings, as the prophets had brought accusations, indictments, and reproaches. Paul came to proclaim the good news and
the gospel of God, countless treasures of blessings that could not
be changed.

Which God promised long ago through His prophets, as the Holy   Rom 1:2.
Scriptures record. For the psalmist says, *The Lord will give a word to*   Ps 67:11 (LXX).
them who proclaim it with great power.[37] Again we read in Isaiah, *How*
beautiful are the feet of those who preach the gospel of peace![38]   Isa 52:7

II

Do you see both the name and the character of the gospel set forth
in express terms in the Old Testament? What Paul means is that
the gospel is not proclaimed by words alone, but also by deeds. For
the gospel was not the work of man alone; it is also divine, ineffable, and it transcends all nature. Because men were laying the
charge of innovation against the gospel, Paul shows that it is
older than the Greeks and is described in the prophets. Even if
God did not give the gospel from the beginning, He did not do so
because of those who were unwilling to accept it. At least those
who were willing to receive it did listen to Him. Indeed, Christ
did say, *Your father, Abraham, rejoiced that he might see my day. He*   John 8:56
saw it and was glad.[39]

How then does Jesus say, *Many a prophet and many a saint longed*   Matt 13:17
to see what you see but did not see it? This verse from Matthew's Gospel
means that they did not see it in the way you see it —I mean the
very flesh and the very miracles that are worked before your eyes
and ears. But please consider how many years ago these things
were foretold. For when God is going to prepare beforehand some

---

36 See RNT note ad loc.
37 NAB Ps 68:12 gives a different reading.
38 See also Rom 10:15.
39 Perhaps this refers back to the birth of Isaac (Gen 17:7; 21:6), which marked
the beginning of the fulfillment of God's promises concerning the seed of Abraham.

great deeds, He predicts them many years before, so as to prepare your ears to accept them when they come.

Rom 1:2 *As the Holy Scriptures record.* For the prophets not only spoke the words, but they wrote down what they had spoken. Nor did they only write the words down; they also gave examples of what they said. For instance, they show us Abraham when he led Isaac up the mountain[40] and Moses when he lifted up the serpent,[41] when he stretched forth his hands against Amalek,[42] and when he sacrificed the paschal lamb.[43]

Rom 1:3 *Concerning His Son who was descended from the seed of David according to the flesh.* What are you doing, Paul? You lifted up our souls on high. You made great and ineffable deeds appear before our eyes. You spoke of the good news and the gospel of God. You brought on stage the chorus of prophets. You showed all of them predicting many years before what would come to pass in the future. Why do you bring us down to David? Tell us, are you talking about some man, and do you give this man, the son of Jesse, as his father? In what way is this man's birth worthy of the things you were recounting?

Paul replies that this man is indeed worthy. For what Paul said to us does not concern a mere man (ἀνθρώπου ψιλοῦ).[44] This is why

Rom 1:3 he added *according to the flesh*: because he was hinting that there is a generation (γέννησις) of the same Christ according to the Spirit.[45] This is what Paul is saying.

And why did he begin from the lower generation and not from the higher? Because Matthew and Luke and Mark began from that point. For if someone is going to take our hands and lead us to heaven, he must start at the bottom and go up. That was the way it

---

40 See Gen 22:1–18 for Abraham's obedience.
41 See Num 21:4–9 and John 3:14–15 for the bronze serpent.
42 See Exod 17:8–16 for the battle with Amalek.
43 The Passover ritual is prescribed and described in Exod 12.
44 ψιλός ἄνθρωπος was a term used by the Arians with respect to Christ in denying His divinity. Chrysostom is here targeting the Arians directly and arguing that Christ is indeed God.
45 Rom 1:3–4 seems to represent an early creedal prayer that confesses Christ in both His human and divine natures. As man He died on the cross; as God He has risen from the dead.

was done in God's plan of salvation. First, men saw Him as a man on earth, and then they perceived that He was God.

In the same way that Christ Himself shaped His teaching, Paul, His disciple, paved the path leading up to heaven. And so he speaks first of His generation (γέννησιν) according to the flesh, not because it was first, but because he was leading his readers from this generation in the flesh to the generation from above.

Who was declared Son of God in power according to the Spirit of holiness by His resurrection from the dead. Rom 1:4 What Paul has said becomes obscure because of the way his words are woven together. Therefore we must divide them up. What, then, is it that Paul is saying? We are preaching Him who has His generation from David. This is quite clear. But from what source is it clear that this son of David who became flesh is also the Son of God? First, we learn this from the prophets. This is why Paul says, *Which He promised long ago through His prophets, as the Holy Scriptures record.* Rom 1:2 And this is no weak method of proof.

Second, we learn it from the very manner of His generation. Paul himself made this clear when he said *from the seed of David according to the flesh.* Rom 1:3 For thus Christ's birth broke the law of nature.[46] In the third place, Jesus worked miracles and in this way provided proof of His abundant power. This is what "in power" means. Fourth, to those who believed in Him He gave from the Spirit, through whom He made them all saints. This is why Paul says *according to the Spirit of holiness.* Rom 1:4 For to grant such gifts belongs to God alone.

In the fifth place, we learn it from the resurrection of the Lord. He was the first and only One to raise Himself. The Son Himself said that, above all else, this was a sufficient sign to stop the mouths of the shameless. For He said, *Destroy this temple and in three days I will raise it up,* John 2:19 and, *When you have lifted Me up from the earth, then you will know that I am He.* John 8:28 And again, *This generation seeks a sign, and it will not be given a sign except the sign of Jonah.*[47] Matt 12:39–40

---

46 The law of nature was "broken" in several ways by Christ's birth. He has a human and divine nature; He is Son of God and seed of David; He is Θεάνθρωπος; He is immortal God and a mortal man; He dies and then rises from the dead; His mother remains a virgin *even after His birth.*

47 Cf. John 1–2.

Rom 1:4	What does Paul mean by *who was declared* (Ὁρισθέντος)?[48] He means being shown, being made manifest, being confessed in the judgment and agreement of all—that is, by the prophets, by His marvelous birth according to the flesh, by the power shown in His miracles, by the Spirit through whom He gave sanctity, by His resurrection through which He destroyed the tyranny of death.
Rom 1:5.	*Through whom we have received grace and the apostleship for obedience to the faith.*[49] See the candor and prudence of Paul, Christ's servant. He wishes nothing to belong to himself, but everything to be the Master's. This is the gift of the Spirit, and this is why Jesus said,
John 16:12–13.	*I have much more to tell you, but you cannot bear it now. But when He comes, the Spirit of truth, He will guide you to all truth.* And again, the
Acts 13:2.	Holy Spirit said, *Set apart for Me Paul and Barnabas.* And Paul says
1 Cor 12:8.	in his Epistle to the Corinthians, *To me the Spirit has given wisdom*
1 Cor 12:11.	*in discourse, to another the power to express knowledge*, and *This same Spirit distributes all His gifts as He wills*. And to the Milesians, in the
Acts 20:28	course of a sermon, Paul said, *Over whom the Holy Spirit has made you shepherds and overseers.*[50] Do you see that Paul calls the things of the Spirit the Son's, and the things of the Son the Spirit's?
Rom 1:5	*Grace and apostleship.* That is, we have not become apostles through our own achievements, for it was not by many toils and labors that this dignity was assigned to us. But we received grace,
Rom 1:5	and this success came as the result of the gift from on high, *for obedience to the faith.*

III

For it was not the apostles who brought their deeds to a successful conclusion, but the grace that came to them beforehand to make

---

48 What Chrysostom means exactly by Ὁρισθέντος is questioned by later commentators who prefer "appointed," "installed," "set up." Fitzmyer (JBC, 53:16) points out that the contrast in Paul's words demands that, although Jesus was descended from David on the physical level, He was set up as "the Son of God with power" on the level of the Spirit. Arndt and Gingrich (*Greek-English Lexicon*, s.v. ὁρίζω) translate this locus as "declared to be the powerful Son of God."

49 Paul's role as Apostle to the Gentiles came to him through the risen Christ (see Acts 22:10). Faith begins with hearing and comes to fruition in obedience (cf. Rom 10:14–17).

50 Quoted from Paul's farewell speech to the Milesians (Acts 20:17–38).

their paths straight. Their task was to go about and preach; to persuade their hearers was the work of God. For God was operating within them and making their words effective. It was just as Luke said: *He opened their hearts,* and again, *those to whom it was given to hear the word of God.* Luke 24:45
Luke 11:28

For obedience to the faith. Paul did not say "for questioning" or "for oratorical style," but *for obedience to the faith.* What Paul is saying is that the apostles were not sent to present arguments, but to give back what had been entrusted to us. For when the Lord has revealed something, there is no need for those who hear His words to meddle with or make close inquiry into what He has said.[51] They must only accept what He has revealed. Rom 1:5
Rom 1:5

For the apostles were sent for this reason, namely, that they might repeat what they had heard and not add anything of their own, so that we, for our part, might believe. So that we might believe what? In His name. It was not that we might be busybodies and inquire into His essence (οὐσίαν),[52] but that we might believe in His name. For it was in His name that miracles were wrought. We read in the book of Acts that Peter said, *In the name of Jesus Christ, get up and walk.* And this very thing requires faith. We cannot fully grasp any of these miracles by our power of reason alone. Acts 3:6

All the nations, among whom are you who have been called to belong to Jesus Christ. What is Paul saying? Did he preach the word to all nations? It is true that he hurried from Jerusalem to Illyria. Again, from there he went forth to the very ends of the earth. This is clear from the Epistle Paul wrote to the Romans. Rom 1:5–6

But even if he did not stop at all places, what he said is not false, for he is not speaking only about himself, but also about the twelve apostles and all who preached the word after them. And in another sense, no one should look on his word as refuted if he will keep in mind Paul's zeal and the fact that even after death he continues to preach everywhere in the world.

---

51 Probably aimed at the Neo-Arian Anomoeans.

52 Here, again, Chrysostom appears to target those who dispute the "nature" of Christ and His divinity.

You must also consider how he lifts up the continuous gift of his preaching and shows us that it is far more lofty than the gift of his zealous mind. During his lifetime his preaching reached only to one nation at a time; after his death it embraced land and sea.

However, I would like you to bear in mind that Paul's soul is free from all flattery and empty adulation. The Romans were, I might say, sitting on top of the entire world. But when Paul wrote to them, even though they possessed universal power and rule, he does not for that reason grant them any more than he does to all the other nations, nor does he say that they possess any more than the rest of the world in matters of the Spirit. What he does say is "We preach to you in the same way as we preach to all nations." So he counts the Romans among the same number as he does the Scythians and the Thracians.[53]

Rom 1:6 If he had not wished to make this clear, it would have been meaningless for him to say *among whom you are counted*. He says this to put down their pride, to empty them of their haughty thoughts, and to teach them that the honor in which they were held was no greater than that to which other nations were privileged. This is Rom 1:6 why Paul went on to say, *Among whom you are counted, and you too have been called to belong to Jesus Christ*.

What Paul is saying is that you, the Romans, are counted along Gal 3:28 with the others. For if in Christ Jesus *there is neither slave nor free*, still far less is there any ruler or one without power of rule. For surely you were called; you did not come forward of yourselves.

Rom 1:7 *To all in Rome, beloved of God and called to holiness, grace and peace from God our Father and from our Lord Jesus Christ*. Do you see how constantly Paul uses the word "called"? He does so when he says Rom 1:1 *called to apostleship*, and again when he says, *Among whom are you* Rom 1:6, 7 *who have been called*, and still again when he says, *To all in Rome who have been called*. He does this not because the word is superfluous,

---

53 Scythia was a vast area in southeastern Europe, inhabited by Tartars, that bordered on the Black Sea and stretched far east into Asia. The Thracians inhabited a region in the eastern Balkan peninsula that bordered on Macedonia. It seems that Chrysostom is suggesting that both of these peoples are not on the level of the Romans with regard to civilization as well as to power and honor, yet they are on the same level with regard to God's call.

but because he wishes to remind them of God's bounty in conferring this grace of vocation.

Because it was likely that among those who believed there would be consuls and viceroys as well as poor men and those who held no public office, Paul puts aside all inequality of rank and sends a single greeting that embraces all who believe. But in all the more necessary matters of the Spirit, everything is set forth as equal for slaves and free. The love that comes from God; the calling to holiness; the Lord's gospel; the adoption as sons of God; the grace, peace, and sanctity that the Spirit sends; and all the other blessings that come from above are examples of what makes men equal. Would it not be the utmost folly, because of earthly honors, to divide and separate those whom God has joined together and made equal in sharing the greater honors?

This is why this blessed apostle from the very start has cast out this disease, which is so difficult to cure, and is leading the Romans to humility of mind (ταπεινοφροσύνην), which is the mother of blessings. This humility has made house slaves better men because from it they learn that no harm will come to them from their condition as slaves. Why? Because they really have freedom. This same virtue would incline masters to be moderate, because they have learned that being free holds no advantage for them unless their faith is leading the way.

So that you may know that Paul was not stressing this equality to mix everything up and to create confusion, but that he knew the best way to make a distinction, he did not simply write to the entire population of Rome. Rather, with the clear and proper distinction and definition, he wrote, *to all beloved of God*. For this is the best solution, and it shows the source of their sanctification. Rom 1:7

What is the source of this holiness (ἁγιασμός)? It came from love (ἀπὸ τῆς ἀγάπης). For after he said *to all beloved*, he added *called to holiness*. This shows that from this source of love comes the fountain of all our blessings. And he calls all believers holy.[54] *Grace and peace to you.* Oh, how this greeting brings countless blessings! Christ instructed His apostles to speak these words upon entering Rom 1:7
Rom 1:7

---

54 Rom 1:7.

any house.⁵⁵ This is why Paul in all his Epistles makes his beginning with the words "grace" and "peace." For it was no small war that Christ brought to a peaceful end. Rather, it was a long-standing war marked by varied tactics and strategy. And He brought this peace not through our labors, but by His own grace.

Therefore love gives us the gift of grace, and grace brings the gift of peace. So it is that Paul puts them in their proper sequence in opening his Epistle. And he prays that the Christians at Rome remain constant and steadfast, so that no other war may again be fanned into flame. He begs the God who gave these gifts to keep them firm and solid when he says, *Grace and peace to you from God our Father and the Lord Jesus Christ.*

Rom 1:7

Notice that here the word "from" is common to the Father and the Son and has the same meaning as if Paul were to have said "from the Father and from the Son." For he did not say, "Grace and peace to you from God our Father through our Lord Jesus Christ," but *from God our Father and our Lord Jesus Christ.*⁵⁶ Bless us! How mighty is the love of God! We were His enemies, dishonored and disgraced. Suddenly we have become holy; we have become sons! For when Paul calls God "our Father," he makes it clear that we are sons; when he says that we are sons, he has revealed a whole treasure-house of blessings.

Rom 1:7

Therefore let us continue to show forth a way of life worthy of God's gift. Let us keep guard over His peace and holiness. For other honors last but for a time and are gone with the end of this present life. They can be bought for a price. This is why some might say that they are honors in name only, that they have their strength and power in the wearing of fine clothes and in the fawning flattery of bodyguards.

But the dignity that comes with God's gift of holiness and adoptive sonship is not cut off by death. It makes us shine forth here on earth and makes the journey with us to the life to come. For the man who holds firm to his adoptive sonship and carefully guards his holiness shines forth more brightly and is far happier than one who wears the diadem and the purple robe of royalty. God's gifts

---

55 Matt 10:12; Luke 10:5.
56 See also 1 Cor 8:6 and RNT note *ad loc*.

bring abundant tranquility in the present life, nurture us with good hopes, and offer no grounds for worry or confusion, but provide the joy of constant pleasure.

It is only spiritual success and a good conscience that provide tranquility and joy. We will not, as a rule, find these blessings in the great power of kings, nor in abundance of wealth, nor in the pomp of power, nor in strength of body, nor in extravagance of food, nor in the adornment of dress, nor in any other thing produced by man.

The man who keeps his conscience clean—even if he wears rags for clothes and is constantly wrestling with hunger—is happier and more cheerful than those who live in the lap of luxury. On the other hand, a person who has wicked deeds on his conscience, even if he surrounds himself with all kinds of material possessions, is the most pitiful of all humans.

This is why Paul, who was in constant hunger and nakedness, who was scourged each day, rejoiced and was glad and more content than the emperors of his time.[57] Ahab was a king and enjoyed all kinds of luxurious living. When he committed that sin of his,[58] he groaned, grew despondent, and his face fell both before and after his sin. Therefore, if we wish to enjoy a pleasant life, before all else let us flee wickedness and pursue virtue. There is no other way to have a share in joy, even if we were to mount the very throne of a king.

This is why Paul said, *The fruit of the Spirit is love, joy, peace.* Let us make this fruit grow within us so that we may obtain the kingdom to come by the grace and loving-kindness of our Lord Jesus Christ, with whom be glory to the Father, together with the Holy Spirit, now and forever, world without end. Amen. Gal 5:22

---

57 Cf. 2 Cor 11:23–27, where St. Paul describes his travails. Perhaps Chrysostom is speaking metaphorically with these texts in mind. Cf. also Phil 4:10–13, especially with respect to the strength that comes from God to those who endure suffering for Him. It is also possible that Chrysostom has in mind the "thorn in the flesh" of 2 Cor 12:7, which was not scourging but probably some physical malady. Cf. O'Rourke, *JBC*, 52:42.

58 After Ahab married Jezebel, he went over to the worship of idols and built a temple and altar to Baal. See 1 Kgs (3 Kgdms) 16:29–33.

HOMILY 2

*First of all I give thanks to my God through Jesus
Christ for all of you because your faith is heralded
throughout the world.*

Rom 1:8

The greetings[59] with which Paul opened this Letter were well suited to the soul of that blessed Apostle. They also sufficed to instruct all men to offer the first-fruits of their good works and deeds to God, and to give Him thanks not only for their own good actions, but also for those of other men. For this frees the soul of envy (φθόνου) and malice (βασκανίας) and makes it clean. Furthermore, it attracts God's kindness in greater abundance to the good will of those who show their gratitude to Him. This is why Paul says in another place, *Praised be the God and Father of our Lord Jesus Christ who has bestowed on us every spiritual blessing.*[60]

Eph 1:3

Not only the rich must give thanks, but also the poor; not only those in good health, but the sick as well. Not only those who enjoy success, but those who patiently endure the opposite must also be grateful and express their thanks. It is no cause for wonder that we thank God when our business affairs are sailing along before a favorable following breeze. But also when our ship is tossed about and the waves surge high, when our ship is tossed about and runs the risk of being swamped —then is the time for giving an abundant proof of enduring patience and goodness of heart.

It was because of these virtues that Job won a crown of victory and blocked up the devil's shameless mouth. Indeed, Job gave clear proof that, when his life prospered, his gratitude was not motivated by his wealth, but by his great love for God.[61] However, you

---

59 See RNT note on Rom 1:8.
60 Cf. NAB note ad loc.
61 See McKenzie, DB, 439–442; and Michael Guinan, Job (Collegeville, MN: Liturgical Press, 1986).

must consider what caused Paul to give thanks. It was not because of the perishable things of earth, such as the glory of power and rule, for such things must be considered worthless. Rather, it was because of the things that are truly blessings, such as faith and the courage to speak freely.

And with what feeling does he give thanks! He did not say, "I give thanks to God," but *I give thanks to my God*, as the prophets do when they take what is common to all and make it their very own. But what is so strange if the prophets do this? For God himself surely does so when He is speaking privately to His servants and says that He is the God of Abraham and Isaac and Jacob. Rom 1:8

Because your faith is heralded throughout the world. What then does Paul mean? Had the whole world heard of the faith of the Romans? Had the whole world heard of it from Paul? This is in no way unlikely. For Rome was not an obscure city without distinction. I might say that, being located on a kind of summit, it was visible from every side. Rom 1:8

Consider now the power of the apostolic preaching and how, in a short time, the good news, spread by fishermen and tax gatherers,[62] took hold of the noblest of cities, and how Syrians[63] became the teachers and guides of Romans. Paul testifies to two outstanding characteristics of the Romans: namely, that they believed, and that they believed with courage. Their courageous belief was so great that their story reached the whole world. As Paul says, *Your faith is heralded throughout the world.* Rom 1:8

For it was your faith that was heralded and not your disputations, nor your discussions, nor your syllogisms. Yet there were in Rome many hindrances to the teaching of the faith. Not too long before, they had received the power of rule over the whole world. They were conceited and proud. They lived in the midst of luxury and wealth. The fishermen who brought them the gospel message were Jews from the Jewish nation—a nation hated and held in abomination by all. And the Romans were bidden to worship the Crucified One, who had been reared in Judea.

---

62 That is, the apostles: Peter, James, John, et al., were fishermen, and Matthew was a tax gatherer.
63 Again, this refers to the apostles.

And together with the doctrines of Christ, these teachers also preached a life of austerity to men who had lived the life of luxury and whose passions drove them to embrace the pleasures of the present existence. And those who were preaching the austere life were poor men of the common sort, baseborn, and sons of baseborn sires. But nothing hindered the course of their preaching. So mighty was the power of the Crucified One that it carried His message to every corner of the earth.

Rom 1:8 For Paul said, it *is heralded throughout the world*. He did not say, Rom 1:8 "It is made manifest," but *It is heralded*, just as if all men had those words on their lips. And so, when Paul was bearing witness to the Thessalonians, he added something else. After he said to them, Thess. 1:8 *The word of God has echoed forth from your mouths*, he went on to say, Thess. 1:8 *And this makes it needless for us to say anything more*. For the disciples stood in the rank of teachers. Because of their courageous freedom in speaking, they instructed all and drew to themselves those whom they taught.

Nowhere did the message come to a halt. It spread over the whole world more impetuously than fire. But here Paul says only that it is heralded. And he did well to say here that it is heralded, because he is showing that there is no need either to add to or to take away anything from what he has said. For the task of a messenger is to convey only what he has been told. This is why a priest is called a messenger: because he proclaims not his own words, but the words of the One who sent him.[64] It is true that Peter had preached at Rome. He too considered that the words he preached were the words of the One who sent him. As I said before, he was free from all grudging and envy.[65]

II

Rom 1:9 *God is my witness, whom I worship in my spirit by preaching the gospel of His Son*.[66] These words come from this apostle's innermost heart. They reveal a father's care and concern. What is it that Paul is

---

64 Cf. Mal 2:7.
65 See Homily 1.11, 31, 32.
66 Chrysostom's explication of this text might be more easily understood if he had added the rest of v. 9 ...that without ceasing I mention you always in my prayers.

saying, and why does he call on God as his witness? He was talking about his disposition and feelings toward them. Because he had never yet seen the Romans, he gives this as the reason why he calls on no man as witness to the truth of his words. Rather, he calls on God, who enters into their hearts, to guarantee the truth of what he says. What Paul was saying was "I love you," and as a pledge of this he mentions his constant prayers for them and his desire to come to them.[67] Because this explanation was not obvious, he takes refuge in the trustworthy testimony of God.

Will any one of us be able to boast that, while he is praying in the privacy of his home, he includes in his petitions all the members of the Church? I do not think so. But Paul does not pray for one city only, but sends up his petitions to God on behalf of the whole world. He does this not once or twice or three times, but continually. And if a man bears someone in mind continually, it could not be from any motive other than deep love. Note well that keeping someone in your prayers is a mark of your whole concern and love.

And when Paul says, *Whom I worship in my spirit by preaching the gospel of His Son*, he is revealing to us, on the one hand, God's grace and, on the other, his own humility. He is showing us God's grace, because God has entrusted to him a task of such importance. He is showing us his own humility because he reckons that the entire gift belongs not to his own zeal, but to the assistance that comes from the Spirit. When he adds the preaching of the gospel, he shows the kind of ministry in which he was engaged. *Rom. 1:9*

For the kinds of ministry are many and diverse. In the case of kings, all subjects are ranked under one monarch. However, all do not fulfill the same service. One serves by commanding the army, another by managing the city's affairs, and still another by keeping guard over the money in the treasuries. In the same way, in spiritual matters, one worships God and serves Him by his faith and the proper management of his own life, another by receiving strangers, and another by caring for the poor. The same was the case among the apostles themselves. Stephen and his colleagues[68] served God by protecting the widows, another group by teaching

---

67 Cf. Rom 1:9–10.
68 See Acts 6:5–15 and 7:1–60 for Stephen, his ministry, and his martyrdom.

the word, and Paul was one of those who fulfilled his service by preaching the gospel.

And this was his way of serving God, because to this he had been appointed. And this is why he not only calls on God as his witness, but also names the ministry that had been entrusted to him. In this way Paul shows that, after functions of such great importance had been put in his hands, he would not have called upon God, who had entrusted this ministry to him, to be his witness unless he were telling the truth.

Along with this, Paul also wishes to show that his love and concern for them are necessary. He must love and care for them so that they may not say, "Who are you? Where did you come from that you say you feel such great concern for this great and most imperial city of Rome?" Paul shows them that he must feel such concern if he has been enjoined to undertake this kind of ministry, namely, to preach the gospel. For one who has had this service entrusted to him must constantly keep in mind those who are to receive the word.

And he makes clear to them an additional point when he says *in my spirit*, namely, that his ministry is much more lofty than either the pagan or the Jewish worship (λατρεία), for the worship of the pagans is in error (πεπλανημένη) and of the flesh. Although the Jewish worship is true, it is also of the flesh. But the worship of the Church is quite the opposite of the pagan and, in great measure, more lofty than the Jewish. Our kind of worship comes from a spiritual soul and is not carried out with sheep, oxen, smoke, and fat. Christ made this clear when He said, *God is Spirit, and those who worship Him must worship in spirit and truth.*[69]

By preaching the gospel of His Son. Above, Paul said the gospel was the *gospel of God*. Here he says the gospel is *the gospel of His Son*. In this way, what he is saying is that there is no difference between the gospel of the Father and the gospel of the Son. For Paul had learned that what belongs to the Father also belongs to the Son, and that what belongs to the Son also belongs to the Father. For in His discourse at the Last Supper, Jesus said in His prayer to the

---

69 See NAB note on verse 23.

HOMILY 2

Father, *Just as all that belongs to Me is Yours, so all that belongs to You is Mine.* — John 17:10

That I constantly make mention of you in my prayers. This is the mark of genuine love. Paul seemed to be saying only one thing, but here he sets forth four things: that he makes mention of the Romans; that he does so constantly; that he does this in his prayers; that he prays for great things on their behalf. — Rom 1:9

Pleading that somehow, by God's will, I may at last find my way clear to come to you. For I am longing to see you. Do you see with what anguish he desires to see them? But his desire is tempered by his fear of God, for he loved them and was eager to come to them. Even though he did love them, he still did not wish to see them if it did not seem best to God that he should do so. — Rom 1:10–11

This is true and genuine love. But it is not like ours, because we fall and fail on both sides when it comes to the laws of love. Either we love no one, or, whenever we do love, we love in a way that does not meet with approval in the eyes of God. And so, in both cases, we act contrary to God's law. If talking about these things is coarse and vulgar, doing them is even more coarse and vulgar.

III

Someone might ask, "How do we love in a way that displeases God?" We do this whenever we overlook Christ, who is wasting away from hunger,[70] and provide our children and relatives and friends with more than they need. But why must I say more on this subject? If each one will examine his own conscience, he will find that this happens in many cases.

But Paul, that blessed soul, was not this kind of person. He knew how to love as he should and as was fitting for him to love. He surpassed all men in loving, but he did not transgress the proper bounds of love. See how, in his case, two things filled his heart to the bursting point: I mean the fear of God, and his desire to visit the Romans. The fact that he prayed constantly and that he did not stop praying when his prayer was not granted are marks of a

---

70 Christ is frequently identified with the poor. To give alms to the poor was to give alms to Christ.

strong and ardent love. To continue loving while he accepted the will of God is the mark of the deepest piety and reverence.

Elsewhere he called on the Lord in prayer three times, but his prayer was not answered.[71] When God's response was the opposite of what he had asked, he was most grateful that God had not heeded his request. This is the way he looked to God in all things. But in his prayer that he might visit Rome, his prayer was not granted at the time he made his request, but at a later date. And this did not displease him.

I am telling you these things so that we may not feel distressed if our prayers are not answered, or if they are heard at a later time. For we are not better than Paul, who confessed his gratitude for both, was very reasonable. After he had once given himself into the hands of Him who guides and governs all things, and after he put himself under God's control with as much submission as the clay does to the potter, wherever God led, Paul followed.

However, after he said that he prayed to see the Romans,[72] he gives his reason for his desire to visit them. And what was this reason? *That I may share with you some spiritual gift to strengthen you.* He is not simply making an idle and senseless journey as many do today. Rather, he is making the trip for necessary and very urgent reasons. Yet he does not wish to state this clearly, although he does hint at it.

For Paul does not say, "In order to teach you, in order to instruct you, in order to tell you what was left untold," but "So that I may share something with you." In this way he is showing that he is not giving them his own doctrines, but that he is sharing what he has received. And he is here observing moderation when he says *some*, that is, something small and commensurate with his ability. And what is this small something in which you are going to share? It is this, he says: something *to strengthen you*.

And this, then, is the gift of grace, namely, to not be shaken, but to stand strong and firm. But when you hear the word "grace," do not think that the reward that comes from our deliberate choice

---

[71] 2 Cor 12:8. This refers to Paul's prayers that he be freed from "the thorn in his flesh," probably some physical malady. See O'Rourke, JBC, 52:42; and RNT notes on 2 Cor 12:7–8.
[72] Rom 1:11.

HOMILY 2

has been excluded.[73] For Paul did not speak of grace to disparage the labor involved in deliberate choice, but to cut off the conceit of arrogance and pride. Nor should you lose heart because Paul called it a spiritual gift. For in his great kindness, he knows how to call even good deeds by the name of spiritual gifts, because even in these we are in great need of help and influence from above.

But when Paul said *to strengthen you*, almost without being noticed, he is showing that the Romans stood in need of considerable correction.[74] What he really wishes to say is this: "For a long time I desired and prayed to see you for no other reason but that I might strengthen you, confirm and support you, and fix you fast in the fear of God, so that you would not be constantly wavering and shaken." *Rom 1:11*

But he did not speak to them in this way because that would have shocked and upset them. But he does hint at the same message in other words and less violent terms. He made this clear when he said *to strengthen you*. Because even this sounded very arrogant, see how he softens it by the words that follow. To keep the Romans from saying, "Why? Are we wavering and shaken by the wind? Do we need your words to make us stand strong?" Paul anticipates and destroys such an objection when he adds, *But this is to be mutually encouraged and comforted by our common faith, yours and mine.* *Rom 1:11* *Rom 1:12*

This is just as if he were saying, "Do not suspect that I said this to you by way of accusation. I had no such thought in mind when I said what I did. What was it that I wished to say? You were enduring many tribulations because you were overwhelmed by those who persecuted you. So I yearned to see you so that I might console and encourage you —not only that I might console you, but that I myself might be encouraged and consoled."

---

[73] Paul never questions the freedom of the human will. Grace, in fact, strengthens this freedom.

[74] The differences between the Jewish and the pagan converts show how considerable was the correction needed by both factions.

IV

Rom 1:11 Notice the wisdom of the teacher. Paul had said *to strengthen you.* He knew that the words he spoke were harsh and burdensome to
Rom 1:12 his disciples, so he went on to say, *to console and encourage you.*[75] But this, too, was again a harsh saying, although not as harsh as what he had previously said. Nonetheless, it was harsh. Therefore, he cuts down on the harshness by smoothing his statement in every respect and making it easy to accept.

Rom 1:12 For he did not simply say *to console and encourage*, but *that we may be mutually encouraged and consoled.* Nor was he content with this,
Rom 1:12 but he softens it still more by a further addition when he says, *By our common faith, yours and mine.* God bless us! What humility! He showed that he also needed them and not only that they needed him. He put the disciples in the rank of teachers; he lets no superiority remain on his side. He points out their full equality with him. For he says that the benefit is mutual and tells them, "I need encouragement and consolation from you just as you need them from me."

Rom 1:12 And how is this to be achieved? *By our common faith, yours and mine.* Just as in the case of fire, if someone gathers together many lamps, he kindles a bright light, so too does it naturally happen in the case of the faithful. When we are left alone and by ourselves, because we have been torn away from other believers, we grow somewhat fainthearted. But when we see one another and are surrounded by our fellow members, we receive an abundance of encouragement and consolation.

However, please do not scrutinize and examine the present day, when, by God's grace, in town and city and in the very desert there are many throngs of believers and all impiety has been driven out.[76] But think of that former time when it was such a blessing for disciples to see their teacher, and for brother believers who came from another city to be seen by their brethren in the faith.

---

75 Chrysostom here plays with the words παρακληθῆναι and συμπαρακληθῆναι in order to emphasize St. Paul's desire to visit the Romans but to also show how he is looking to be encouraged and comforted by them as well.
76 Here Chrysostom directly applies his words to his own times and his Antiochene congregation.

To make what I am saying still clearer, let me offer you an example. Suppose it should ever happen and come to pass —and may God forbid that it does —that you should be carried off to the land of the Persians or the Scythians or other barbarians and be torn apart and scattered by twos and threes in those cities. Suppose then that you were suddenly to see someone from here coming to visit you. Think how great would be the consolation and encouragement that would fill your heart. If those in prison should see any of their close friends, do you not see that their spirits rise and how excited with pleasure they become?

Do not wonder that I compare those bygone times with captivity and imprisonment. In those days, people suffered far more grievous punishments than captivity and prison. They were scattered and exiled; they lived in the midst of famine and war; each day they spent in fear and trembling because they expected to die at any moment; they suspected that their friends, family members, and kinsmen might betray them. They lived in the world as if in a foreign land. They were in more difficult straits than those who were living in an alien country.

This is why Paul says, *To strengthen you, and that we may be mutually consoled and encouraged by our common faith.* And he said this not as if he were in need of assistance from them. Far from it! For how could he need their help, he who was a pillar of the Church, stronger than iron and stone, made of spiritual steel, strong enough to save countless cities? It was so as not to make his message too burdensome and his criticism too excessive that he said that he needed the consolation and encouragement the Romans could give him. _{Rom 1:12}

But if someone here should say that this consolation and encouragement was his joy at their progress in the faith and that Paul had need of that, he would not be missing Paul's meaning. But another might say, "If, then, Paul, you desire it and are praying for it, and you are going to have the benefit of receiving consolation and encouragement as well as giving them, what hinders you from coming?" To remove the suspicion underlying this question, Paul went on to say,

Rom 1:13   *My brothers, I want you to know that I have often planned to visit you and, up to now, that I have been kept from it.*[77] Notice the measure of his servant-like obedience and the display of his kindness of heart. He Rom 1:13   says, *Because I have been kept from it*. But he does not go on to say why. For he does not examine what the Lord has commanded; he only obeys.

Yet it was reasonable for a man to be puzzled as to why a city that was so famous and great, a city toward which the whole world turned its eyes, was prevented by God from having the benefit of such a teacher, and for so long a time. For the man who conquers the city that rules the world easily goes on to win over those other cities that are ruled by it. But the man who neglects the greater imperial city and lies in wait for its subject inhabitants has overlooked this most important strategy.

But still Paul meddles with none of these things, but submits to the incomprehensibility of providence. In this way he shows both the proper harmony of his own soul and teaches us all never to demand an accounting for what God has done, even if the divine actions may seem to upset many men. For to the Lord alone does it belong to command; the servants' task is to obey.

Rom 1:13   Therefore, Paul says that *he was kept from it*; he does not go on to say why. What he says is that he does not know. Therefore, do not question me about the will or mind of God. *A molded work of art* Rom 9:20   *will not say to the artist who molds it, Why did you make me like this?* Why is it, tell me, that you seek to learn the reason? Is it that you do not know that all things are under His care, that He is wise, that He does nothing without cause or reason? Surely you know that God loves you more than the father who begot you and the mother who gave you birth, that He goes far beyond a father's affection toward you and far beyond a mother's care and concern.

So ask no more questions; go not a step further. Surely this is enough to console and encourage you, because even at that time the affairs of the Romans were being wisely managed. Do not be vexed or discontented if you do not understand how all this is so. To accept the reason of providence even when you are ignorant of the way the plan of salvation works is a very strong sign of faith.

---

77   See also Homily 1.24.

V

However, Paul did succeed in doing what he was eager to do. And what was that? He was anxious to show that his failure to come was not because he scorned the Romans, but because, in spite of his strong desire to visit them, he was hindered from doing so. After he cleared himself of the charge of indifference and persuaded them that he desired to see them no less than they wished to see him, he again showed his love in other ways.

Although I was kept from coming. What he is saying is this: "I did not give up trying; I constantly kept trying, but I was always held back. Although I would not oppose the will of God, I never stopped keeping watch over my love for you." By always setting the Romans before his mind and never standing aloof from them, he kept showing his love and affection. Because he was hindered and held back, yet did not struggle against God's will, he showed all his love for his Master. [Rom 1:13]

In order to do some fruitful work among you. Although he had earlier given the reason for his desire and had shown that it was suited to him,[78] he still states it here again so as to clear away completely any suspicion they might have regarding his motives. The city of Rome was conspicuous; its beauty was unmatched over the whole expanse of land and sea; the mere desire to see it became an excuse for many to travel there. But so that they might not think anything like that about Paul, nor suspect that he wanted to be there simply because he took pride in his association with them, Paul constantly lays down the basis for his desire. [Rom 1:13]

Indeed, he said earlier, *I longed to see you in order to share with you some spiritual gift.* Here he speaks in clearer terms: *In order to do some fruitful work among you, as I have among the Gentiles.* He numbers the rulers with the subjects. For all the countless trophies, victories, and fame of consuls, he classifies them along with the barbarians. And he is quite right in doing this. For where we have the nobility of the faith, there are no barbarians, no Greeks, no foreigners, no citizens. All mount up to a single height of superiority and dignity. [Rom 1:11] [Rom 1:13]

---

78 Rom 1:11–12.

See the modesty with which Paul acts here. For he did not say, "So that I may teach and instruct you." What does he say? *So that I may do some fruitful work.* He does not simply say "fruitful work," but *some fruitful work*. Again he humbles his own part, just as he did above when he said, "So that I may share something." Then, he is humbling them, as I just mentioned, when he said, *Just as I have among the other Gentiles.*

Because you are rich and have more than other men, I am not showing less concern for the rest. We do not seek out the wealthy, but those who believe. Where, then, are the wise men of the Greeks, those who have thick beards, those who wear short tunics,[79] those who are puffed up with pride? The tentmaker[80] converted Greece and every land of the barbarians. But the famous Plato, whom they parade around and whose books they carry, went three times to Sicily with his bombastic words, with his great reputation, but failed to get the better of a single tyrant.[81] He got away from there in such miserable style that he was deprived of his freedom. The tentmaker, however, traveled not only to Sicily and Italy, but to the whole world. While he was preaching, he did not stop working at his craft, but, even then, he sewed skins together and remained in charge of his workshop.

Nor did he offend those born of consuls, and this with very good reason. For it is not trades and occupations, but lying and false doctrines, that usually make teachers contemptible and despised. This is why even the Athenians still laugh to scorn teachers who lie to them. But both barbarians as well as the foolish and the unimportant pay heed to this man Paul. For the message he preaches is set before all alike. It knows no difference of rank nor superiority

---

79 The thick beard and short tunic were the typical facial adornment and garb of the Greek teachers of philosophy.
80 The "tent maker" is, of course, Paul.
81 Plato, the student of Socrates for some seven years, founded his own school, the Academy, but also travelled widely. According to his own account in his *Seventh Letter*, he made three trips to Sicily and tried unsuccessfully to convert the tyrants Dionysius the Elder and Dionysius the Younger to his ideal system of government. He failed in this and incurred the hatred of both tyrants. For a summary of the letter and comments, see R. G. Bury, prefatory note to *Epistle VII*, in *Plato IX*, Loeb Classical Library (Cambridge, MA: Harvard University Press, 1929), 463–475.

of nation, nor any other such distinction. For what he preaches has no need of demonstrative argument.

This is why it especially deserves our admiration. Not only is Paul's preaching profitable and conducive to salvation, but it is easy to understand, readily grasped, and simple for all to comprehend. And this is the chief purpose of God's providence, because He offers His blessings to all men in common.

For God did not make the sun and moon, the land and sea, and all other things to give a greater share to the rich and wise while he gave a smaller portion of His abundant blessings to the poor. Rather, he set forth the enjoyment of these equally for all. He did this same thing with the preaching of his message. And he did this in a much greater degree, inasmuch as this message was more necessary than the gifts of nature.

This is Paul's reason for constantly saying *to all the Gentiles*.[82] Then, to show them that he is not courting their favor, but rather is fulfilling the Master's command, and because he is sending them off to give thanks to the God of all, he says, *I am under obligation to Greeks and non-Greeks, to the learned and unintelligent*. And he said the same thing to the Corinthians because he attributes everything to God.[83] *That is why I am eager to preach the gospel to you Romans as well*. Rom 1:15

Rom 1:5, 13; 11:13

Rom 1:14

VI

Oh, the noble soul of Paul! He took upon himself a task filled with so many dangers —a journey across the sea, trials and temptations, plots and intrigues, uprisings and rebellions. For it was likely, because he was going to preach in so large a city and in one under the tyrannous rule of impiety, that blizzards of trials and tests were in store for him. And so it was that he lost his life in this great city. Indeed he was beheaded there by order of the tyrant who was ruling Rome.[84]

However, even though he was expecting to endure such great sufferings, he did not become less ready to face any of them. He stood firm, he suffered pain; he was ready and eager. This is why

---

82 Cf., e.g., Gal 1:16; 1 Tim 3:16.
83 Cf. 1 Cor 9:16.
84 Paul was beheaded ca. AD 67–68 under the Emperor Nero.

Rom 1:15–16. he said, *That is why I am eager to preach the gospel to you Romans as well. I am not ashamed of the gospel.*[85]

What is this you say, Paul? The fitting thing to say was "I boast, I hold my head high, I take pride." Yet you do not say this, but you say something less exuberant, namely, that you are not ashamed. This is not the way we usually speak about things that are most glorious and outstanding.

What, then, is this that he says? Why does he speak in this way although he exulted in the gospel more than in heaven itself? At Gal 6:14 least when he sent a Letter to the Galatians, he said, *May I never boast of anything but the cross of our Lord Jesus Christ.* Why, then, does Rom. 1:16 he not say here "I boast," but *I am not ashamed?*

The Romans were most passionately excited about the things of this world because of their wealth, their ruling power, their victories, and their emperors. They considered that their rulers were equal to gods, and they even called them divine. This is why they worshipped them with temples, altars, and sacrifices. Even though they were puffed up with such pride, Paul was going to preach to them of Jesus. Yet Jesus was considered to be the son of a carpenter. He was reared in Judea in the house of a worthless woman. He had no bodyguards; he was not surrounded with wealth. He even died as a criminal between two thieves. He endured many other inglorious things.

Therefore, it was likely that the Romans were hiding themselves from Jesus because they did not yet know any of the ineffable and marvelous things about him. This is why Paul says that he is not ashamed: because he had to teach the Romans to not be ashamed. For Paul knew that if they succeeded in overcoming this shame, they would quickly move forward and come to a point where they would boast.[86]

Suppose you should hear someone ask, "Do you worship the Crucified One?" You must not be ashamed. You must not look down to the ground. Rather, boast; show your pride; and with the eyes of a free man and with head held high, profess your faith and belief. Suppose he should ask again, "Do you worship the Crucified

---

85 See note in NAB on these verses.
86 Cf. Rom 1:16–17 and see note in RNT *ad loc.*

One?" Answer him again, "Yes, but I do not worship a god who is an adulterer, nor one who slays his father, nor one who murders his children."[87] And such are all the gods of the pagans. "But I do worship Him who by His cross stopped up the mouths of demons and put an end to their tricks and snares. The cross is the work of His ineffable loving-kindness for us, the symbol of His abundant care and concern for our sake."

Such men as would ask such a question are boasting braggarts who are puffed up and think they wear the cloak of worldly wisdom. Paul would bid a long farewell to their arguments and reasoning because he came to preach the cross. Nor was he ashamed of it. *For it is the power of God leading to salvation.*[88]   Rom 1:16.

God also has the power to punish. When he punished the Egyptians, he said, *This is my great power.*[89] He also has the power to   Joel 2:25
destroy. *Fear him who can destroy both body and soul in Gehenna.*[90] But   Matt 10:28
Paul is saying that he is not coming to bring the powers of punishment or vengeance, but "the power of God leading to salvation." Why does he not speak of the former powers? Did the Gospel not speak of them? Did it not give an account of Gehenna,[91] of the exterior darkness,[92] of the venomous worm?[93] Indeed, we know of these things from no source other than the Gospel.[94] In what sense, then, does Paul say *the power of God leading to salvation*?   Rom 1:16.

Listen, then, to the words that follow: *To everyone who believes in*   Rom 1:16
it, the Jew first, then the Greek. He does not say "to everyone," but *to*   Rom 1:16
everyone who believes in it. Suppose you are a pagan Greek who has fallen into every kind of evil; suppose you are a Scythian, a barbarian, or even like a brute beast, filled with every kind of irrationality; suppose you are carrying around the burdens born of ten thousand sins. The minute you accept the account of the cross and are baptized, you have wiped out all those sins.

---

87 Prime examples of such actions are Zeus, Oedipus, and Medea.
88 Montfaucon's Greek text in Migne's PG omits "all who believe."
89 Perhaps this refers to the plagues of Egypt.
90 For "Gehenna," cf. McKenzie, DB, 300–301; cf. Matt 5:22.
91 Matt 10:28; 5:22; Mark 9:43, 45, 47.
92 Matt 8:12.
93 Mark 9:48.
94 Cf. Rom 1:16.

But why does Paul say here *the Jew first, then the Greek*? What does this difference mean? Surely, in many places he said, *Circumcision counts for nothing, nor does uncircumcision*. How is it that he makes this distinction and puts the Jew before the Greek? Why is this? For it is not that the Jew receives a greater grace because he is first, because the same grace is conferred on this one and that one. But the being first is an honor only in the order of time. The Jew does not have more because he received greater justification; he is honored only because he received it first.

Even in the case of those who are being illumined[95] —you who have been initiated know what is meant —all run to baptism, but not all at the same hour; one goes first and another second. But surely the first does not receive more than the second, nor the second more than the one who comes after him, but all enjoy the same gifts. Being first in this case is an honor in name only; there is no magnification of the grace received.

When Paul said *leading to salvation*, he again enhances the gift by showing that it is not only a gift for the present life, but that it advances still further. He makes this clear when he says, *For in the gospel is revealed the justice of God that advances from faith to faith; as Scripture says, 'The just man shall live by faith.'*

Certainly, the man who has become just shall live not only in the present life, but also in the life to come. Not only is that true, but Paul hints at something else along with that, namely, the brightness and glory of such a life. It is possible to be saved, yet not without some personal shame —as many of those who are freed from punishment by imperial kindness are saved. But so that no one, when he hears the word "salvation," may suspect this, Paul added the word "justice" —not your own but God's. In this way Paul also hints that God grants justification in abundance and of His own will. For you do not achieve justification from God by sweat and toil. You receive it by a gift from above. Of yourself you contribute one thing only —your faith.

Then, because what Paul said seemed to be beyond belief, if the adulterer, the homosexual, the grave robber, and the magician are not only suddenly freed from punishment, but also become just

---

95 That is, those to be baptized.

men —and just with the highest justification —Paul confirms what he said from the Old Testament account. At first, in a few words, he reveals the vast sea of histories to the one who has the ability to look upon it.

For after he said *from faith to faith*, Paul sends his hearers back to God's plans of salvation that were recounted in the Old Testament and that Paul explains with great wisdom in his Letter to the Hebrews.[96] For there he shows that even then both the just and sinners received justification in this way, namely by faith. This is why he makes mention of Rahab[97] and Abraham. _{Rom 1:17}

Although here Paul only hints at this justification and faith (for he was hurrying on to another urgent topic), he confirms it again by bringing before us Habakkuk, who shouts aloud and says that the man who is going to live in the future cannot live except by faith. For he says, *The just man shall live by faith*,[98] and he is speaking about the life to come. Because the gifts God gives go above and beyond all powers of reason, it is only reasonable that we must have faith. But the man who is conceited, scornful, and arrogant will achieve nothing.[99] _{Hab 2:4}

Let the heretics hear the voice of the Spirit. For the nature of our reasoning powers is as limited as I have described. It is like a labyrinth or puzzles that have no end or resolution to them anywhere. They do not let our reason stand firm on a rock. They have their beginning in vanity and pretense. For such men are ashamed to admit the existence of faith and, so as not to show their ignorance of heavenly truths, they involve themselves in the sandstorms of countless reasoning processes.

Oh, you miserable and pitiable man! You deserve ten thousand tears. If someone should ask you how the heavens and the earth came to exist —but why talk about the heavens and the earth? How did you yourself come to be born, how were you nurtured, and how did you grow? Are you not ashamed of your ignorance?[100]

---

96 Heb 11:8–31; Rom 4.
97 See Josh 2:1–21; 6:22–25; Heb 11:31.
98 Cf. Heb 10:38.
99 Because all these characteristics exclude faith, they also exclude justification.
100 Cf. Sir 11:4. Cf. also Rom 1:19–20.

But if ever there is some discussion about the Only Begotten, do you throw yourself into a pit of destruction because of your shame and because you consider it unworthy of you not to know everything? What is unworthy is your contentiousness and your ill-timed curiosity. And why do I speak of dogmas of faith? For we are not set free from the wickedness and corruption of the present life in any way other than by faith.

It was by faith that all those of bygone days shone forth, men like Abraham, Isaac, and Jacob. It was by faith that the harlot in the Old Testament was saved, and also the harlot in the New.[101]
Heb 11:31 For we read in the Letter to the Hebrews, *By faith Rahab the harlot escaped from being destroyed with the unbelievers, for she had received the spies in peace.*[102]

Rahab[103] did not say to herself, "How can these men who are captives and exiles, refugees who are living the lives of nomads, get the better of us? We have a city with walls and towers." If she had said that to herself, she would have destroyed both herself and them, just as the ancestors of those who were at that time saved had been destroyed. For when those ancestors saw men who were large and tall facing them, they questioned how they could win the battle. And so they perished to a man without marshaling their troops or engaging in conflict.

Do you see how deep is the pit of unbelief and how strong is the fortress wall of faith? For failure to believe carried countless thousands to their death. Faith not only saved a woman who was a harlot, but made her the protectress and patroness of such a great people.

Because we now know these things and more than these, let us never ask God for an accounting of what He has done. Let us accept whatever He has commanded. Let us not be busybodies by asking questions and being inquisitive—even when what God commands seems absurd in the light of our human processes of reasoning.

---

101 Cf. Luke 7.36–50; John 8:3–7.

102 See McKenzie, DB, 718.

103 Rahab was the harlot who received the Hebrew spies in Jericho and protected them, having recognized the power of the Lord God who had led them to that land (Josh 2:1–24).

HOMILY 2

Tell me, what seems more absurd than that a father slay with his own hands his only true son? Still, when the just man, Abraham, was ordered to do so, he did not meddle with the command but, because of the dignity of God who commanded him, he not only accepted what was enjoined on him, but he obeyed.[104]

Another man was commanded by God to strike a prophet. Because he thought the order was absurd, he played the busybody and simply refused to obey. For his refusal he paid the ultimate penalty by his death. But still another man did strike the prophet and was held in high esteem.[105] Saul, who had saved a man contrary to what seemed best to God, fell from his kingdom and was utterly ruined.[106]

A person could find instances other than these, and all of them would teach us never to demand an accounting of God's commands, but only to yield to them and to obey. If it is risky to be a busybody and to make idle investigations into whatever God has enjoined, and if the ultimate punishment is appointed for those whose curiosity questions His will, what excuse will they have who are meddling into matters far more secret and awesome than these? I mean such things as why and how did the Father beget the Son, and what God's essence is.[107]

---

104 Cf. Gen 22:1–18.
105 The point of these two incidents is to show that it is God's will and not the nature of things that makes the same actions good or bad. Cf. 1 Kgs (3 Kgdms) 20:35–42. See also FOTC 68:76–78.
106 Cf. 1 Sam (1 Kgdms) 15 and 31.
107 Chrysostom is chiefly aiming at the Anomoean (neo-Arian) heretics (from the Greek *Anomoios*, "unlike," referring to their belief that the Son is unlike the Father in essence). The main representatives of this group were Aetius and Eunomius. Their primary arguments were focused on the neo-Platonic idea that what is generated (γεννητός) from the One (God) who is ἀγέννητος (unbegotten) cannot be homoios to Him. Hence, the Son, begotten of the Father, cannot not of the same or even similar essence with the Father who is unbegotten. For a discussion on St. John Chrysostom and the Anomoeans, see Paul W. Harkins, introduction to the translation of Chrysostom's work *On the Incomprehensible Nature of God*, FOTC 72:19–38. The Anomoean heresy was very much active in Antioch at Chrysostom's time and produced division in the Church of Antioch. Chrysostom felt compelled to preach again their efforts to define the divine essence; he pointed to the human mind's inability to grasp the mystery of God. See also the chapter on the Anomoeans in the *Encyclopedia of Early Christianity*, ed. Everett Ferguson (New York and London: Garland Publishing, 1990), 45.

We know that the Father did beget the Son; we know that God has an essence. Therefore, let us, with all good will, accept these truths on faith, the mother of all blessings. Then we are sailing, as it were, in a tranquil harbor; we are holding to the straight course of correct doctrine; and we are guiding our lives in safety and security.

May we obtain the blessings of eternity by the grace and loving-kindness of our Lord Jesus Christ, with whom be glory, power, honor, and adoration to the Father and the Holy Spirit, forever and ever. Amen.

HOMILY 3

> *The wrath of God is being revealed from heaven against the irreligious and perverse spirit of men who, in their perversity, hinder the truth.*   Rom 1:18

Notice how wise and understanding Paul is. First he encourages by gentler arguments; now he turns to those that are calculated to arouse our fear. First he had said that the gospel is the source of salvation and eternal life, that it is the power of God, that it can save our souls through His justification. Now he tells of the things that can strike terror into those who fail to heed it and who hinder its truth.

Most men are generally not so much attracted to virtue by the gospel's promise of blessings as they are frightened by its threats of painful punishments. So Paul tries to win them over to virtue by arguments from both sources. For the same reason, God not only promised the kingdom, but also threatened men with Gehenna. And the prophets also spoke to the Jews in the same way when their words constantly mingled the accounts of evils with those of blessings.

Therefore, Paul also varies his message, not in any which way, but he puts the blessings first and, after them, the things that cause pain. In this way, he shows that the blessings flow from God's will to lead us to virtue, and the painful things come from the wickedness of those who are sluggish and indifferent. And the prophet put the blessings first in the same way when he said, *If you are willing and obey Me, you shall eat the good things of the land; but if you refuse and resist Me, the sword will consume you.*[108]   Isa 1:19–20 And this is the way that Paul here presents his discourse.

Consider what he means. Christ came and brought forgiveness, justification, and life. But He did not bring them in any which way,

---
108 Verses taken from Isaiah's indictment of Israel and Judah.

but through the cross. And this is the greatest and most marvelous thing, namely, that He not only gave them to us as gifts, but that He underwent such sufferings for men. If you outrage and insult God's gifts, then you will suffer the painful consequences.

Rom. 1:18   Notice the exalted language Paul uses. He says, *The wrath of God is being revealed from heaven.* How does Paul make this clear? If it is one of the faithful who says this, we will tell him what Christ has declared; if it is an unbeliever and a pagan who is speaking, Paul will silence him by what he will go on to say about the judgment of God. Then he will bring up an irrefutable demonstration based on the very things that he himself [the unbeliever] has done. And this is by far the most unexpected turn of events, namely, when Paul shows that those who speak against the truth itself are the very ones who prove the doctrines of the truth by their daily words and acts. But we shall discuss this a little later on;[109] for now, let us keep to the topic before us.

Rom. 1:18   *The wrath of God is being revealed from heaven.* But this happens many a time in the present life, for example, in famine, in plagues, in wars. For all of us are punished by these, both as individuals and in common. What, then, is new and strange? It will be that the chastisement[110] will be greater, that it will be common to all, that it will not be for the same reasons. What happens to us here in this world is for the purpose of correction; at that time it will be the ultimate punishment.[111]

1 Cor 11:32   This is what Paul meant when he said, *We are chastened*[112] *now to keep us from being condemned with the rest of the world.*[113] Now, many think that a great number of these things happen not because of wrath from heaven, but because of the wanton behavior of men; hereafter the punishment will clearly come from God. The Judge will then sit at the dread tribunal and order some to be dragged to

---

109 See later in this homily, §§ 9–19.
110 The Greek word used here is κόλασις, which translates to "punishment." Chrysostom utilizes different words to indicate the level of punishment that humanity suffers for our behavior.
111 The Greek word used here is τιμωρίαν.
112 The Greek word used here is παιδευόμεθα, which could also translate to "we suffer."
113 Cf. Heb 12:5–12.

the furnaces, some to the outer darkness, and some to other inexorable and intolerable punishments.[114]

Why did Paul not speak here as clearly as he did when he said that the Son of God will come with countless angels and will seek an accounting from each man?[115] Why did he say, *The wrath of God is being revealed?* Because his hearers were still newly converted, and, on this account, he at first draws them by things with which they were in complete agreement. And as well as what he said to them, I think he is also exerting his efforts toward the pagans. Therefore, he begins his Epistle from these points and later brings in his discussion about Christ's judgment.[116]   Rom 1:18

Against the irreligious and perverse spirit of men who, in this perversity of theirs, hinder the truth. Here Paul shows us that the paths of impiety are many, whereas the way of truth is one. For error takes many shapes, and these forms are intricate and confused, whereas the truth is one. And after he spoke about dogmas, he also speaks about life when he mentions the perversity of men. For perversities are also intricate. There is injustice in matters of money, as when a man does wrong to his neighbor in this regard. And there is injustice toward women, as when someone leaves his own wife and undermines the marriage of another. Surely, Paul calls this cheating when he says, *Refrain from overreaching or cheating a brother in the matter at hand.*[117]   Rom 1:18   1 Thess 4:6

Others, again, do not outrage the wife or property of their neighbor, but they do harm to his reputation. And this is injustice too. *A good name is better than much wealth.*[118] Some say that Paul   Prov 22:1

---

114 Chrysostom often enumerates the punishments of those condemned at the last judgment, where the sheep are separated from the goats; see Matt 25:31–46. In Matt 8:5–13 we read of the punishments of "weeping and gnashing of teeth" after Jesus, who has miraculously cured the centurion's servant, speaks of some Jews who will be given a place at the banquet in the kingdom of God (along with Abraham, Isaac, and Jacob). But the Jews who lacked the centurion's faith, although the natural heirs of the kingdom, will be driven out into the darkness. On that day the Son of God will come with countless angels and will seek an accounting from each man.
115 Cf. Matt 25:31–46.
116 See McKenzie, DB, 465–68 for the last judgment.
117 The "the matter at hand," according to ancient and modern commentators, refers to adultery. See Forestell, JBC, 48:23.
118 Through his reputation a man lives on after death.

said this also about doctrines. Yet there is nothing to prevent him from having said it about both a good name and good doctrines. But what he means by *In this perversity of theirs, they hinder the truth* you can learn from what follows: *Whatever can be known about God is clear to them; He Himself made it so.*[119] But they put wood and stones around this glory.

II

We have an example in the case of a man to whom the royal resources have been entrusted and who has been ordered to spend the money for the glory of the king. Suppose he instead spends the money on robbers and harlots and sorcerers. Suppose he makes them famous and illustrious from the royal resources. He is punished because he has committed the gravest injustices against the king. The same is true for those who have received knowledge of God and his glory but then bestowed this knowledge and glory on idols and, by this perversity of theirs, hindered the truth. At least, as far as they could, they acted unjustly with regard to their knowledge, because they did not direct it toward fitting objects.

Has what I said become obvious to you, or must I repeat it in clearer terms? Perhaps I must say still more. What is it that I have said? From the beginning God endowed man with knowledge of Himself. But the pagans surrounded this knowledge with wood and stones and, as far as they could, perverted the truth. Yet that truth remains unchanged because it has its own immutable glory.

But, Paul, where is the proof that God endowed men with this knowledge? Paul replies, *Whatever can be known about Him is clear to them*. But this is a statement; it is not a proof. Show me and prove to me that the knowledge of God was plain and clear to them and that, of their own volition, they passed it by. How, then, did this knowledge become plain? Did God send a voice down from heaven to men? By no means! But God did do that which, more than any voice, could draw them to this knowledge. He put before their eyes the world that He had created. In this way the wise man and the unlearned, the Scythian and the barbarian, learned through their

---

119 See Acts 14:15–17; Wis 13:1–9.

own eyes the beauty of what they beheld, so that they might mount up to God.

This is what Paul said: *Since the creation of the world, His invisible realities have become visible, recognized through the things He has made.*[120] The prophet too said this: *The heavens declare the glory of God.* What will the pagans say on that day [of judgment]? Will they say, "We did not know You"? Did you not hear the heavens sending forth a voice that served to make you see, when the well-ordered harmony of all things spoke out more clearly than a trumpet? Did you not see that the laws of night and day remain constantly unchanged? Did you not see that the disciplined order of winter, spring, and the other seasons stayed sure and immutable? Did you not see the kindness of the sea in the midst of its turbulence and waves? Did you not see that all these kept their proper order and that, by their grandeur and beauty, they heralded forth the glory of their Creator?

After taking all these together, and more than these, Paul said, *Since the creation of the world, His invisible realities, His eternal power and divinity, have become visible, recognized through the things He has made. And so they are without excuse.*[121] Yet it was not for this that God made these things, even if it was the result. For it was not to deprive them of an excuse that God set before them such great instruction and teaching. He did this so that they might come to know Him. But they acted obstinately and without good judgment; and so it was that they deprived themselves of all excuse.

Then, to show them that they were deprived of excuse, Paul said, *Although they had knowledge of God, they did not glorify Him as God or give Him thanks.* This first is the worst charge. And the second, which follows the first, is that they worshipped idols. Jeremiah accused them of this when he said, *This people has committed two wicked deeds: they have forsaken me, the fountain of the waters of life; and they have hewn out for themselves broken cisterns.*

Next, as a sign that they knew God but did not use the knowledge on fit objects, Paul brings forward this very thing, namely, that they knew gods. This is why he went on to add, *Because, although*

---

120 Cf. NAB note *ad loc.* See also Fitzmyer, JBC.
121 The Greek text omits God's "eternal power and divinity" after "invisible realities." However, the entire text is quoted in the next paragraph.

they knew God, they did not glorify Him as God. And he sets forth the reason why they fell into such senseless folly. What is this reason? They trusted the entire matter to their powers of reason. However, Paul does not put it in those words, but speaks in much sharper language. For he says, *They became futile in their thinking, and their senseless heart was darkened.*"[122]

Rom 1:21

For if someone will try to walk on a strange road or sail a strange sea on a moonless night, not only will he fail to reach his goal sooner, but he will quickly be lost. This also happens to those who try to walk the road that leads to heaven but who take away the light from themselves and then, instead of light, they entrust themselves to the darkness of their reasoning powers. They will undergo a most grievous shipwreck because they are searching for a bodiless God among bodily things, and among shapes they seek for God, who has no shape or form.

But over and above what has already been said, Paul sets forth another reason for their error when he says, *They claimed to be wise, but turned into fools instead.*[123] Because they made a show of themselves, as if they were something great; because they did not continue to go along the road that God had commanded them to follow, they were plunged into the reasoning processes of senseless folly. Then, to illustrate aloud how severe this surging sea was and how their action was beyond all pardon and excuse, Paul went on to say, *They exchanged the glory of the immortal God for images representing mortal man, birds, four-footed beasts, and snakes.*[124]

Rom 1:22

Rom 1:23

III

The first accusation is that they failed to discover God; the second is that they failed although they had great and clear signs and evidence; the third, that they said that they were wise; the fourth, that they not only failed to find God, but they even reduced God, the object of all reverential awe, to devils made of stone and wood. Paul humbles the pagans' conceit and vanity in his Letter to the

---

122 Cf. Isa 5:21.
123 Cf. Karl Barth, *Epistle to the Romans*, trans. E. C. Hoskins (Oxford, 1968), 49–50.
124 This exchange totally destroys the distinction between Creator and creature, the incorruptible and corruptible.

Corinthians, although he does not do so there in the same way he does here. For in that Letter he delivers his blow to the pagans with arguments based on the cross when he says, *For God's folly is wiser than men*.[125] But here, without any comparison to God, he ridicules the wisdom of men by itself when he shows that it is folly and only a demonstration of their own vain boasting.

1 Cor 1:25

Next, so that you may learn that although they possessed knowledge of God, so too did they betray this knowledge, Paul said that they exchanged it. Now the man who exchanges must have something to exchange. They wished to discover something more and not to be held back by the limits imposed by their human nature, and because of this they lost sight of these limits as well—for they desired innovation.

Everything that is Greek is like that, and this is why they opposed one another. Aristotle opposed Plato; the Stoics fenced themselves in against Aristotle; each was the others' foe.[126] The result of this is that one must not marvel at them for their wisdom. Rather, one should turn away from them and hate them, because by their very wisdom they became fools. If they had not entrusted what they did possess to reasoning processes, syllogisms, and sophistries, they would not have undergone the sufferings they did.

Then, in order to heighten the accusation against them, Paul ridicules their idolatries. Most of all, the fact that they made an exchange was ridiculous. Making the exchange for such things as they did is beyond all excuse. Consider, then, for what things they made the exchange, and on what they have conferred glory. Some things about God must have been manifest. For example, that He is God, that He is Lord of all, that He created men who had not existed, that He is provident, that He cares for them. For these are the glory of God.

On what did they bestow this glory? Not even on human beings, but on *an image made like to corruptible man*. Nor did they stop here, but they sank down to the worship of beasts and to images of these beasts. Please consider Paul's wisdom and note how he sets forth

1 Cor 1:25

---

125 The result is that Christ and the gospel are seen as impotent and absurd.
126 For a comparison and contrast of Aristotle and Plato, see Frederick Copleston, *A History of Philosophy*, vol. 1 (Westminster, MD: Newman Press, 1946), 2.113–120. For the Stoics, cf. ibid., 130–144.

the two extremes: God, the highest; and creeping things, the lowest. Rather, he does not put before us creeping things, but images of them, so that he might show clearly the evident madness of the pagans. For regarding the knowledge they should have had of God, who is incomparably superior to all, they bestowed this on what is incomparably more worthless than all.

Someone may ask what this has to do with the philosophers. Everything I said has to do with them above all others. Surely they had as their teachers the Egyptians, who invented these idols. And Plato, who seems to be more august and reverent than the others, takes pride and pleasure in these matters.[127] And Socrates, Plato's teacher, was all aflutter and agitated about these idols. He is the one who orders his followers to sacrifice the cock to Asclepius[128] in the temple where one might see the images of these beasts and crawling creatures. And there one might also see Apollo[129] and Dionysus[130] equally worshipped along with these crawling things.

Some of the philosophers even raised bulls, scorpions, dragons, and every other nonsense up to heaven. For the devil was eager everywhere to drag man down before the images of creeping things and to put humans beneath the most irrational of all creatures. And these were the men whom God wished to raise up above the heavens.

It was not only because of what their philosophers taught, but from other sources as well, that you will see how their chief philosopher was responsible for the things I have mentioned. For he made a collection of the poets and said that they were to be believed in their accounts of the gods, because their knowledge was accurate.[131] But all he did was to bring forward a cluster of these ab-

---

127 Plato, in the *Timaeus* 21, tells of the origin of idols in Egypt.
128 Socrates, in *Phaedo* 118, requests that his followers fulfill his vow to Asclepius with what prove to be his dying breaths after drinking the hemlock cup of execution. Asclepius was the god of medicine and healing.
129 Apollo, son of Zeus and Leto, was another god of medicine, as well as of music, archery, and prophecy; he was often identified with the sun.
130 Dionysus was the god of the vine, wine, and revelry.
131 The reference is to Plato and his collection of poets, which has not come down to us. However, see his *Ion* 533, where he maintains that poets are inspired by the gods and therefore truthful.

surdities. And then he said that this most ridiculous account must be considered as the truth.¹³²

*In consequence, God delivered them up in their hearts' lusts to unclean practices; they engaged in the mutual degradation of their bodies.*¹³³ In this way Paul shows that impiety and ungodliness caused them to pervert nature's laws. He *delivered them up* here means "He let them alone." If the commander of an army retreats and withdraws because the battle has overwhelmed him, he delivers his troops over to the enemy. He does not thrust them into the hands of the foe, but he does strip them of the help he himself might give. So too God let those alone who did not wish to accept His help, but were the first to turn away from Him, even though He had supplied everything required of Him. Rom 1:24 Rom 1:24

But consider this: God put the world before men's eyes in place of formal instruction. He gave them a mind and powers of reason that could perceive what they needed to know. Men of those times made use of none of these for their salvation, but they instead turned the gifts that they received to the opposite use. What, then, had to be done? Did God have to drag them by compulsion and force? But this could not make them virtuous. Nothing was left but to let them alone, and this God did. And He did it in the way He did so that, after they came to know by experience the things for which they lusted, they might flee from what brought shame upon them.

Suppose a king has a son who has disgraced his father and chosen to consort with highwaymen, murderers, and grave robbers. Suppose the son should prefer the way of life of these felons to his father's house. The father lets him alone so that, by actual experience, the son may learn how excessive his own madness is.

IV

How is it that Paul makes no mention of any other sin such as murder, for example, or covetousness and other such crimes? Why does he speak only of licentiousness and impurity? I think he was

---

132 Plato gives a more representative statement of his ideas about the gods in *Euthyphro* 6, which many Christian Fathers (e.g., Justin, Tertullian, Augustine) consider as a means to be used to do away with the deceits of the philosophers and poets.

133 See note in RNT. See also Col 3:5 and NAB note; and Homily 4.1–9.

Rom 1:24 — giving a hint to his audience of those times and to those who were to receive his Letter. *In their lusts for unclean practices, they engaged in the mutual degradation of their bodies.* Note the emphasis here, because it is most severe. They had no need of others to commit outrages on them. The very treatment that enemies would impose on them, this they did to themselves.

Rom 1:25 — Then, taking up the charge again, Paul says, *These men who exchanged the truth of God for a lie, who worshipped and served the creature rather than the Creator.* Things that were matters for extreme ridicule Paul sets forth specifically, but for things that seem to be more grievous than others, he uses more general terms. But by all these things he shows that to worship and serve a creature is a pagan characteristic. And see how Paul explains what he has said. He did

Rom 1:25 — not simply say *served a creature*, but he added *rather than the Creator*. Everywhere he magnifies the accusation by this comparison and deprives the sinner of any excuse.

Rom 1:25 — *Blessed be God forever. Amen.*[134] By this Paul means that God received no hurt whatsoever, for God is forever blessed. Here Paul shows that it was not to avenge Himself that God let them alone, for God Himself suffered no harm. Even if they treated Him outrageously, He was not ill-treated, nor was His glory diminished, but He remains blessed in every way. If by following his philosophy[135] a man often suffers no harm at the hands of those who insult him, much less would God suffer, because His nature is immortal and immutable, and His glory cannot be diminished or changed.

For true philosophers resemble God in this respect, namely, when they suffer nothing at the hands of those who wish to treat them insolently; nor are they ill-treated by those who commit outrages against them, nor are they beaten by those who flog them, nor are they ridiculed by others who would mock them. Someone may ask how this can be. It is possible, very possible, when you are not distressed by what is happening to you. But, how is it possible not to feel pain? Rather, how is it possible to feel pain, I would say.

---

134 This is a traditional Jewish polemic expressing abhorrence of pagan idolatry.
135 "Philosophy" here means practicing the Christian way of life. So too, in the next paragraph, "true philosophers" are those who are true Christians, who resemble God by their virtuous lives.

Tell me this. Suppose your little child should insult you. Would you consider his insult an insult? And what about this? Will you feel distressed? By no means. If you are distressed, will you not be ridiculous? Let us feel disposed toward our neighbors in the same way, and we will feel no unpleasantness or annoyance toward them. For those who treat us badly are more foolish and unreasonable than little children.

Let us not seek to avoid insults but, when we are insulted, let us endure them nobly. For this is the only secure honor. Why is this so? Because you are a master of noble endurance, whereas the other man is a master of insulting.

Do you not see that steel does not strike back when it is struck? But, you say, that is characteristic of its nature. Yet it is in your power, through your free choice, to be such as the steel happens to be by its nature. How does that come about? Did you not see that the boys were not harmed in the furnace?[136] And that Daniel in the lions' den suffered no harm?[137] It is possible for this to happen even today. Lions are standing by our side. I mean anger and lust, with dangerous fangs, ready to tear to pieces the man who falls among them. However, you must be like Daniel. Do not give those passions the chance to fix their teeth in your soul.

But someone will say that that man, Daniel, had the fullness of grace working with him. Yes, but that was because the acts of his free choice led the way for grace. If we are willing to prepare ourselves to be like Daniel, even now the grace awaits us. Even if the beasts are hungry, they will not fasten their fangs in your side. The lions saw the body of a servant, and they showed him reverence. When anger and passion see the members of Christ's body (and this is what we, the faithful, are), how can they be anything but quiet? And if they will not be still, this will happen through the fault of those who have fallen among them.

Surely there are many who spend much money on these lions of passion by keeping harlots, by undermining marriages, and by taking vengeance on their enemies. This is why they are torn to

---

[136] See Dan 3, which recounts the miraculous rescue of Shadrach, Meshach, and Abednego from the fiery furnace.
[137] See Dan 6, which recounts the story of Daniel's escape from death in the lions' den.

pieces before they reach the bottom of the den.¹³⁸ But this did not happen to Daniel. And if we should so choose, it will not happen to us. Rather, even a greater thing will happen to us than what happened in Daniel's day. For the lions did not harm Daniel. If we remain sober and exercise self-control, those who do us harm will actually help us and be of profit to us.

In this way Paul gained luster from those who insulted him and plotted against him. So too did Job from those many blows and wounds. So too did Jeremiah from the pit of mire and mud.¹³⁹ So too Noah from the flood.¹⁴⁰ So too Abel from the treachery of Cain.¹⁴¹ So too Moses from the murderous Jews.¹⁴² So too Elisha¹⁴³ and each of those great men. It was not from listlessness or luxury, but from oppression and trials, that they came to wear their shining crowns.

John 16:33 Therefore Christ, who knew that this was the foundation of good repute and esteem, said to His disciples, *You will suffer in the world. But take courage: I have overcome the world.* And what then will people say? Have many not taken flight because of these sufferings and dangers? Yes, but that was not because of the nature of the trials, but because of man's indifference and sloth.¹⁴⁴ But God, along with the trial and temptation, provides for you a way out of it so that you may be able to endure it.¹⁴⁵

---

138 Dan 6:24.
139 Jer 38:6–13.
140 Gen 6 and 7.
141 Gen 4.
142 See Exod 15–18, where we find several stories of how the Jews grumbled against Moses. Their many rebellions against him may well have involved threats to his life. See McKenzie, *DB*, 586–590.
143 Cf. McKenzie, *DB*, 232–233. The cycle of events and anecdotes about Elisha are found in 2 Kgs (4 Kgdms) 2:19–8:15. See NCE 5:386–387 for the article under "Eliseus." See also McGrath in NCE, 5:278–279.
144 The original Greek word here is ῥᾳθυμία ("laziness" and "lack of diligence," "negligence," or "carelessness"), a most favorite term of Chrysostom's in explaining our loss of connection with God and ultimate punishment. He frequently points out that if we were to be more watchful, diligent, and alert (he uses νῆψις, σπουδή and ἐγγρήγορσις), we would be able to gain the kingdom of God. For an extensive discussion on this, see P. Papageorgiou, chap. 4 of "A Theological Analysis of Selected Themes in the Homilies of St. John Chrysostom on the Epistle of St. Paul to the Romans" (PhD diss., The Catholic University of America, 1995), 256ff.
145 Cf. 1 Cor 10:13.

May He stand by all of us and reach out His hand so that, after we have been gloriously proclaimed as conquerors, we may attain eternal crowns. And we shall do this by the grace and loving-kindness of our Lord Jesus Christ, with whom to the Father, together with the Holy Spirit, be glory, honor, and power, now and always, forever and ever. Amen.

HOMILY 4

Rom 1:26–27

God therefore delivered them up to disgraceful passions. For even their women exchanged natural intercourse for that which was unnatural. And in like manner, men abandoned natural intercourse with women and burned with lust, one man toward another.

All passions are disgraceful, but especially so is the mad lust for males. For the soul suffers and is dishonored by sins more than the body is by disease. See how Paul deprives these sins of excuse just as was the case with doctrines. For in Rom 1:26 speaking about women he says, *They exchanged natural intercourse for that which was unnatural.*[146]

What Paul means here is that no one can maintain that women came to this because natural sexual intercourse was forbidden to them, nor that they were driven headlong into such monstrous madness because they could not satisfy their natural sexual desire. "Exchange" pertains to those who have something to exchange.[147] This is what Paul said when he was discussing doctrines, when he Rom 1:25 said, *They exchanged the truth about God for a lie.*

He again proves the same point, but in a different way about Rom 1:27 males, when he says, *They abandoned natural intercourse with women.* And just as he had done with the women, Paul also excludes any possibility of excuse for the men when he levels at them this accusation, namely, that they had the means for gratification but, after they put aside the means they had, they went to another gratification. Not only that, but he accused them of having dishonored the

---

146 Not only do homosexual men suffer from this perversion, but lesbian women as well, because, like the males, their acts show an exchange of the true God for lustful idolatry. See RNT note on Rom 1:24.
147 Cf. Rom 1:25 and Homily 3.22.

natural means of gratification and of rushing off to an unnatural means. But things that are contrary to nature are more irksome and less pleasurable. Hence they could not say that pleasure was their excuse. For genuine pleasure is a pleasure that is natural. And when God takes His blessing away from a pleasure, everything is upside down.

Therefore, not only was the doctrine they held spawned of the devil, but their lifestyle was diabolical. So it was that when Paul was discussing doctrine, he put before men's eyes the universe and man's power of reason when he said that men, by the intelligence with which God had endowed them, could be led to the Creator by the things they saw.[148] Then, because they were unwilling to be led to Him, they remained without excuse.

In the present case, Paul puts in place of the universe the pleasure that accords with nature. Men could have enjoyed this with more freedom from fear and greater delight, and they still could be far removed from a shameful act. But men were unwilling. And this is why they are beyond excuse and why they have heaped outrage on nature itself. And it is more disgraceful that women seek after these kinds of intercourse because they have a greater sense of shame than men do.

Here too Paul's perception deserves our admiration. Notice how he fell into two opposite matters and accomplished them both with all accuracy and exactness. For he wishes both to speak with dignity and also to sting his audience. It was not possible to do both, because one hindered the other. For if you shall speak with dignity, you will not be able to attack your audience. But if you wish to assail them vehemently, you must reveal what you are saying in clearer terms. But Paul's prudent and blessed soul had the strength to do both with exactness. In the name of nature, he gave increased strength to his accusation; he also used nature as a sort of veil to preserve the dignity of his description.

Then, after he had first assailed the women, he attacks the men when he says, "In like manner the men also, having abandoned natural intercourse with women." This is a proof of the ultimate corruption, when both sexes are corrupted. For the man was

---

148 Cf. Homily 3.11–15. There is no excuse for those who commit unnatural acts.

appointed to be master over the woman, and the woman was commanded to help the man, but their actions toward one another are such as enemies would do to each other.

Consider how forceful and vivid is Paul's use of words. For he does not say that they loved and desired one another, but that "they burned in their lusts one toward another." Do you not see that all their desire comes from a greediness that cannot stay within its proper limits? For everything that transgresses the laws established by God lusts after monstrous deeds and does not desire those things that are ordered and governed by law and custom. Many a man who abandons his desire for food will often eat earth and small stones, and others who are in the grip of excessive thirst often have a desire for mud or slime.[149] So also have these sinners rushed out after a lawless love affair.

Suppose you ask where this increase in the intensity of passion comes. It comes from this: God has let them alone.[150] And why has God let them alone? Because of the lawlessness of those who have abandoned God, *because men did shameless deeds with men.*[151]

Rom 1:27

II

Rom 1:27 When you heard Paul say that *they have burned*, do not think that the sickness is one of desire and lust alone.[152] Surely, the greater part comes from their indifference and sloth,[153] which inflamed their desire and lust. This is why Paul did not say "being swept away" or "being seized" —which he said elsewhere. What does he Rom 1:27 say? *Because men did.* They put their sin into act. And not simply into act, but they did it eagerly and in earnest. Nor did Paul call it Rom 1:27 "lust" or "desire," but *shameless deeds*, in the proper sense. For surely they treated nature shamelessly and they trampled upon its laws.

And see the great confusion that came from the one part and the other. For not only did the head alone go down, but the feet

---

149 Perhaps these perversions are intended to be indications of the madness to which lust and passion will drive a man or woman.
150 Cf. Rom 1:26–28.
151 See Homily 3.28.
152 ἐπιθυμίας μόνης.
153 ῥᾳθυμίας.

HOMILY 4

also went up, and they became enemies to themselves and to each other. Why? Because they brought in a different strife, which was divisive, varied, and more lawless than any war pitting kinsmen against kinsmen. For they divided this strife into four new and unnatural forms. For this war was not twofold or threefold, but fourfold.

Consider this: it was fitting that the two become one flesh —I mean the woman and the man. For Scripture says, *The two will be one flesh*. The desire for intercourse brought this about, and the sexes were united one with the other. The devil took this desire away and led it to another course. In this way he split the sexes from each other and made the one to become two parts, contrary to God's will. For God said, *The two will be one flesh*. But the devil divided the one into two. See there the first war. Next, the devil excited the two parts themselves to wage war against themselves and each other. For again the women outraged the women and not only the men, and the men stood against one another and against the female sex just as in a battle fought at night. Do you see the second and third war as well as the fourth and fifth? Gen 2:24 Gen 2:24

And here is another war: for along with those I have mentioned, they also treated nature itself in lawless fashion. When the devil saw that, above all, desire led the sexes together, he was eager to cut the bond so as to destroy the human race through a lack of lawful copulation. Not only this, but he also stirred up the race to wage war against each other, and he roused them to revolt.

And by receiving in themselves the fitting recompense of their perversity. See how again Paul goes to the source of the evil, namely, the impiety that comes from their doctrines. And he says that this is the recompense for that wicked conduct of theirs. If Paul were to speak of Gehenna and punishment, he did not think he would win belief in the minds of the impious and those choosing to live their lives in that fashion. Because he thought at that time that not only would these people fail to believe him, but would laugh at him as well, he shows that this punishment is found in the pleasure itself. Rom 1:27

But do not be amazed if they fail to perceive this but still take pleasure in it. Even madmen and those afflicted with inflammation of the brain hurt themselves in many ways because of their disease. They make themselves objects of pity, and others weep for them. But they themselves laugh and revel over what they have done. But we do not say on this account that they are freed from punishment. But because of this they are subject to a more serious punishment because they refuse to realize what a state they are in.[154]

But we must win the votes of those in sound health rather than of those who are sick. Yet in ancient times this practice seems to have been a law, and a certain lawgiver among them had ordered that house slaves be forbidden to make use of dry anointing[155] or to be lovers of boys,[156] although he conceded to free men this privileged place or, rather, this privilege for ill behavior.

However, they did not consider this practice to be ill behavior, but they looked on it as an honor and dignity that was too great for house slaves, but which was to be granted to men born free. And this was the judgment of the wisest of peoples, the Athenians, and of Solon, who was a great man among them. And you could find many other books of the philosophers that countenanced this disease.

Yet we do not on this account say that this practice was lawful; rather, we say that those who accepted this law are to be pitied and deserve many a tear to be wept for them. For they are enduring the same treatment that harlots undergo. Rather, the treatment they get is more pitiful. For even if intercourse with harlots is lawless, it is not contrary to nature.

Even if there were no Gehenna nor any threat of punishment, this was worse than any punishment. If they found pleasure in it, you are telling me about an additional punishment. Suppose I

---

154 As in his Baptismal Instructions (Ancient Christian Writers 31, trans. Paul W. Harkins [Mahwah, NJ: Paulist Press, 1963], 82 and passim), where Chrysostom calls drunkenness a self-chosen madness that leads to debauchery and every evil passion, so too these passions would include homosexual acts. These, then, would be both self-chosen and madness.

155 To use ointments except when bathing was called "dry anointing" and could be used only by free men.

156 House slaves were forbidden to practice pederasty. Such homosexual acts were recommended only for free men and nobles. Cf. Plutarch, Life of Solon, speaking of Pisistratus at the beginning of Solon's biography. See also Aelian, Historical Miscellanies 2.1.22; Plato, Symposium 191–192; and Aeschines, Against Timarchus 19.25.

were to see someone running around naked with his whole body smeared with mud. Suppose that he does not hide his face, but even takes pleasure in what he is doing. I would not share his pleasure. Rather, I would weep for him because he did not perceive that his action is shameful.

But so that I may show his lewdness in clearer terms, let me offer you another example. Suppose a virgin were forced to be imprisoned in her home. Suppose someone condemned her to have intercourse with irrational beasts. Suppose she were then to take pleasure in the copulation. Would she not deserve our tears especially because she could not escape from this evil and did not understand how wicked this evil was? Surely this is clear to everyone.

Certainly, if the case of the naked man was a grievous thing, the virgin's plight was no less grievous than the first. For to be treated outrageously by one's own kinsmen is more pitiable than receiving any insult from strangers. I say that those kinsmen are worse than murderers. For surely death is better than living when one is so badly treated. For the murderer separates the soul from the body; the kinsman has destroyed the soul along with the body. Whatever you would call a sin, you will say that it is in no way equal to that lawless behavior. If those who suffered these evils understood them, they would choose ten thousand deaths to avoid such treatment.

III

There cannot be, I repeat, there cannot be anything more irrational or more grievous than this outrageous treatment. When Paul was speaking about fornication, he had this to say: *Every sin a man commits is outside the body. But the fornicator sins against his own body.*[157] 1 Cor 6:18
If Paul said that, what should we say about this madness, which is so much worse than fornication that we cannot express it? Not only do I say that you have become a woman, but that you have destroyed your being as a man. You did not change into that nature that belongs to women, nor did you keep the nature that you used

---

[157] Cf. Notes in both RNT and NAB. The note in NAB suggests that the fornication referred to is probably that of religious (or temple) prostitution. See also R. Kugelman (JBC, 51:31–33), who suggests that the fornicator sins against his own body because he tears it away from the Lord and deprives it of its glorious destiny.

to have. You have become a traitor common to both natures, and you deserve to be driven out by men and women and to be stoned to death by both, because you have done wrong to both sexes.

And so that you may learn what an enormity this is, let me ask you this. If someone were to come up to you and offer to make you a dog instead of a human being, would you not flee from him like the plague? But look, you did not make yourself a dog instead of a human; you changed yourself into an animal more disgraceful than a dog. To be sure, a dog is a useful animal; he who has prostituted himself is useful for nothing.

Tell me. What about this? Suppose someone threatened to make men bear children and bring them forth. Would we not be filled with indignation? But look! Those who fell into a rage at such suggestions are treating themselves more grievously. For it is not the same thing to change into the female sex and to become a woman while staying a man but, rather, it is to be neither man nor woman.

And if you wish to learn the enormity of this evil, ask why legislators punish those who mutilate men into eunuchs. It is for no other reason than this: they cut off the nature that had made the eunuch a male. And yet the injustice they do to the eunuch is not so great [as that done by the pederast]. For those who have been castrated in many cases have been useful after their mutilation.

But there could be nothing less useful than one who has pandered himself. For not only the soul, but the body as well, of one who has experienced such acts is dishonored and disgraced. He deserves to be driven out from wherever he may be. How many hells will be enough for these sinners? If you hear the word "Gehenna" but scoff at it and refuse to believe in it, remember that fire which destroyed Sodom.[158] For we saw, yes we saw, even in the present life, an image of Gehenna.

Many will refuse to believe what is going to come after the resurrection. But if they have heard in this life that the fire is unquenchable, God here recalls them to their senses by an event that happened in the present existence. Such, then, is that conflagration

---

158 Cf. Gen 19:23–27.

and wasting with fire of Sodom. And those who have visited the site know it well; with their own eyes they have seen the damage done by the thunderbolts from on high.[159]

Consider how enormous was the sin that forced Gehenna to appear even before its time. Because many scorned God's words, it was by His deeds that He showed them an image of Gehenna in such a novel way. For that rain was incredible and unusual because the intercourse practiced by the Sodomites was contrary to nature. And this rain destroyed the land because lust had destroyed the souls of the inhabitants. Therefore, the rain was contrary to usual storms. Not only did it not stir up the womb of the earth to produce fruits, but it rendered it useless for the very receiving of seeds. For such is the intercourse of men that renders a body more useless than the land of Sodom.

What is more defiled and polluted than a man who has prostituted himself? What is more accursed? Oh the madness of it! Such derangement of mind! From what source did this lust burst forth? It has treated human nature as only an enemy would. Rather, it treats man's nature in a worse way inasmuch as the soul is superior to the body.

Oh you who are less rational than irrational beasts, you who are more shameless than dogs! For nowhere among beasts that are bereft of reason do you find such intercourse, because nature knows its proper bounds. You have made our human race more dishonorable even than irrational beasts by your outrageous deeds. From what source do these evil deeds come to birth? From wanton living and from your failure to know God. For when men cast out their fear of God, all that is good straightway goes to ruin.[160]

---

159 Cf. Jude 7.
160 Stevens points out in his note (NPNF1 11:358) that "the depravity of the heathen world, of which Paul has drawn but an outline picture, is in this homily painted in full and in dark and awful colors...The deplorable moral condition is the consequence of not following the light which God has given. It follows from the recoil of the moral law upon those who violate it. It is an example of the Savior's warning: 'If the light which is within you be darkness, how great is the darkness?' (Matt. vi. 23). The inevitable result of continued sin is a constantly increased and inveterate sinfulness which, as Chrysostom says, is itself a most bitter punishment."

IV

So that this may not come to pass, let us keep sharply before our eyes the fear of God. For nothing, I repeat, nothing, so destroys a human being as slipping away from this anchor. In the same way, nothing saves a man as does keeping his eyes fixed on this fear. For if, by keeping our eyes fixed on a man, we become more hesitant about committing sin, and if, because we are apt to blush in the presence of the gentler servants in the house, we often refrain from doing what is disgusting or out of place, consider that we will enjoy every security if we keep God before our eyes.

Nowhere will the devil assail us if such is our disposition. If he were to do so, his labor would be in vain. But if he ever sees us wandering around outside and going about with no bridle to restrain us, because we are giving him a head start, he will then be able to lead us astray in any direction. And we will experience what thoughtless house servants do in the market place. They forget the necessary services that their masters sent them to perform. And then they simply fasten themselves to those who pass their way and spend their leisure time with them.

This is what awaits us when we neglect the commandments of God. For then we stand admiring wealth and bodily beauty and the other things that are none of our business, just as those household slaves give their attention to beggars who are performing juggler's tricks. And after they have returned late, they pay the worst of penalties at home. Many have disregarded the paths prescribed for them because they were following others who were acting in such unseemly ways. But let us not do that.

For we have been sent to accomplish many urgent tasks. If we neglect these and stand around gaping at unprofitable things, because we have squandered all our time in vain and to no purpose, we shall pay the extreme penalty. For if you wish to keep yourself busy, you have things at which you ought to marvel and gape the whole time through. I mean things that do not deserve to be laughed to scorn, but which are worthy of all our wonder, amazement, and praise. The man who wonders at ridiculous things will himself be ridiculous and worse than the one who plays the buffoon. So that you may not experience this, be quick and run away from it.

Tell me this. Why do you stand gaping with eager excitement at the sight of riches? What is so wonderful about wealth that it can hold your eyes fixed on it? You keep looking at horses with gold trappings, house slaves (some barbarians, some eunuchs), extravagant and expensive garments, and an enervated soul wearing them. You fix your eyes on eyebrows raised in haughtiness, people running around in tumults.

And for what reason do these rich men deserve your wonder? Why are they better than the beggars who dance and play the pipes in the market place? For these rich men too are gripped by a great famine of virtue. They dance a dance more ridiculous than those who are beggars. They are led around at one time to costly banquets, at another to the lodging of women who are prostitutes, at another to swarms of flatterers and a throng of parasites.

Even if they wear ornaments of gold, they are especially to be pitied on this account, because the things that are nothing to them are the things they seek after and desire all the more eagerly. Please do not look at the garments they wear, but uncover their souls and see if they are not filled with countless wounds, if they are not clothed in rags, if they are not destitute, if they are not stripped of every defense.

What benefit comes from this madness for temporal things? For surely it is better to be a poor man and to live a life of virtue than to be a king and live a wicked life. The poor man enjoys every luxury of the soul; he does not even see his outward poverty because of the wealth within him. But the king, living in luxury amid things that are not proper or befitting, is punished in the things that really make the greatest difference to him and are the most important. I mean in his soul, in his reasoning powers, in his conscience —the things that will go with him to the life hereafter.

Now that we know this, let us put aside the garments ornamented with gold. Let us take up a life of virtue and the pleasure it brings. In this way, we shall, both here and hereafter, enjoy much pleasure. May we attain the blessings that have been promised by the grace and loving-kindness of our Lord Jesus Christ, with whom be to the Father and to the Holy Spirit glory, honor, and power, now and always, forever and ever. Amen.

HOMILY 5

Just as they did not choose to keep God in their knowledge,   Rom 1:28
*God gave them over to their perverse mind to do things
that were not fitting.*[161]

So that Paul might not appear to be referring in veiled terms to his Roman audience by dwelling so long in his discussion on the unnatural lust of male for male, he then passed over to other forms of sins. He turns his whole discourse to other people. Just as he always does when he is discussing sins with the faithful and he wishes to show that they must be avoided, he brings before us the Gentiles, as when he says, *Not in the passion of lust, even as the*   1 Thess 4:5
rest of the Gentiles who do not know God,[162] and again, *Do not grieve as*   1 Thess 4:13
others who have no hope.[163] Likewise in this place he shows that the sins are the sins of other Gentiles, and he deprives these sinners of every excuse.

For what Paul is saying is that sins and criminal acts are not committed through ignorance, but as a result of pursuit and practice. This is why he did not say, "Just as they did not know," but *Just as they did not choose to keep God in their knowledge.*[164] Rather, sins   Rom 1:28
come from corrupt judgment and pertinacity more than from recklessness or seizure [by an unclean spirit]. And he showed that

---

161 The opening text continues Paul's attack on those perverse Gentiles whose idolatry darkened their minds to the knowledge of God that the beauty and power of creation should have afforded to them. Instead, they turned to unnatural sins of the flesh because they ignored the distinction between Creator and creature.
162 This clearly shows that Chrysostom has not been referring to the converted Gentiles of the Christian community at Rome, but to the idolatrous Gentiles who refuse to recognize the knowledge of God that creation provides.
163 Pagan Gentile grief (especially for the dead) is devoid of Christian hope in any resurrection and eternal life of glory with Christ in heaven.
164 This is what leads to all sorts of sins. We freely choose the evil instead of the good.

sins do not come from the flesh, as some heretics maintain.[165] It is from the mind's purpose and intent for wicked desire that sins spring, and it is from this source that the fountain of evil flows.[166] For after the mind lost its nobility, everything was like a chariot that was driven from its course and overturned, because the charioteer became corrupt.[167]

Rom 1:29 *Being filled up with every kind of iniquity, malice, greed, wickedness.* See how here everything is stated with intensity and force. For surely he says that they are *filled up*, and *with every kind*. Then, after he mentioned wickedness in general, he goes on to pursue the Rom 1:29 parts, and these too in excessive fashion, when he says, *full of envy, murder*. For murder comes from envy, as was shown in the case of Abel and of Joseph.[168]

Rom 1:29-30 Then, after Paul had added, *contention, deceit, malignity, gossips, slanderers, haters of God, insolent men*, putting into different classes of accusations things that, in the eyes of many, seem to be the same, he again makes his charges stronger by rising up against the Rom 1:30 stronghold of their weaknesses when he calls them *boastful*. For when the sinner thinks haughty thoughts about his sins, it is even worse than the sinning itself. This is why Paul lays this charge on 1 Cor 5:2 the Corinthians when he says, *And you are puffed up and self-satisfied*. For if anyone is puffed up after a good deed, he has destroyed all the good. Would not the man who is self-satisfied as well as satisfied with the sins he commits —would that man not deserve every punishment? Such a man will not be able to repent in the future.

Rom 1:30 Then Paul goes on to say that they are *inventors of evils*.[169] By that he means that such sinners were not satisfied with the evils already existing, but that they even invented others. And this is the

---

165 The heretics who see all evil as coming from the flesh are the Manichaeans.
166 Paul, like Chrysostom, finds the source and seat of sin in the will, although many of sin's worst manifestations involve the body of unregenerate man. Cf. Gal 5:19–21.
167 This echoes Plato, *Phaedo* 246. The "charioteer" is the corrupt mind and will of the perverse sinner.
168 Cf. Rom 1:29. See Gen 4:1–16 for the story of Cain and Abel; The story of Joseph is told in Gen 37. His brothers plotted to kill him out of envy and did throw him into a dry cistern, but later pulled him out still alive and sold him to passing merchants who took him to Egypt (Gen. 37:28) where he was sold as a slave.
169 The perverse Gentiles misuse and abuse their minds and wills, and discover new kinds of sins to commit.

HOMILY 5

mark of those who have every purpose of sinning and are eager to do so; it does not characterize those whose chariots are driven from their course and overturned. After he had spoken of evil part by part, and after he had shown that again they had taken a stand against nature itself (for Paul said they were *disobedient to their parents*),[170] he then goes to the root of such a plague and source of ruin when he says that they are *without natural affection, without fidelity, without mercy.* — Rom 1:30 / Rom 1:31

And Christ maintained that this is the cause of wickedness when He said, *When iniquity will abound, love will grow cold.*[171] Paul too says this when he calls them *faithless, without natural affection, bound by no covenant, without mercy.* And he shows that they have betrayed the very gift of nature. — Matt 24:12 / Rom 1:31

For we have a kind of natural family feeling toward each other. Even wild beasts possess this mutual feeling. *Every beast loves his like, and every man loves his neighbor,*[172] Scripture says. But these sinners become wilder even than the wild beasts. Paul established for us through these witnesses that this evil disease came into the world from evil doctrines. He also showed clearly that the sickness in both cases came from the rashness and heedlessness of those who were suffering from this evil disease. — Sir 13:15

Just as he did in the matter of doctrines, Paul then goes on to show here too that these sinners are stripped of any excuse. This is why he says, *Although they knew the ordinance of God that those who do such things deserve to die, yet not only do they themselves do these deeds, but they also agree and sympathize with others who do them.* — Rom 1:32

Paul sets down two objections, but he takes the lead in rejecting them both. What he means is this: Why would you say that you do not know what has to be done? If you were not to know these things, you would be especially to blame because you abandoned God who pointed them out to you. But now, by many arguments, we are showing that you do know and that, when you commit an

---

170 Such disobedience shows an utter lack of respect for all authority.
171 Abundance of evil destroys love of what is good.
172 Natural law instills a family feeling between men and their fellow men, and even between wild beasts and animals of the same kind. But this principle of natural law is ignored by sinners who have a disease that makes them wilder than wild beasts. Only Christ can cure this infection, which comes from false doctrine.

offense, you do so of your own free will. But is it passion that drew you on to sin? Why then do you cooperate with it and praise it? For, as Paul said, *Not only do they do these things themselves, but they also agree and sympathize with others who do them.*

Paul put the more grievous objection first because he wished to refute what has no defense, and because he who approves of the sin is much more dangerous than the one who commits the offense. Therefore, after he spoke of this first, by means of this, he subdues the objector in what follows when he speaks these words: *That is why you, every one of you, who judges another is inexcusable. For by judging another, you condemn yourself.*[173]

Paul was denouncing the rulers of Rome[174] when he spoke these words, because that city then held in its hands rule over the whole world. Therefore, he anticipated their retort when he says, Whoever you may be, you are depriving yourself of a defense when you condemn the adulterer, while you yourself commit this same sin, even if no man judges or condemns you. By your judgment on the responsible party, you have also passed sentence against yourself. *For we know that God's judgment is according to the truth against those who do such things.*

Someone might say, "I have escaped such punishment until now." To instill fear into such a man, Paul says that things are not the same in the eyes of God as they are in this world.[175] For in this world one man is punished while another escapes, even if he has committed the same crimes. But it is not the same in the life hereafter. This is because the One who passes judgment in the life hereafter knows what is just.

Paul did not add the source from which he knows that God's judgments are just, because that would be superfluous. In the case of impiety and godlessness, Paul showed both things, namely, that the one who knows God is the impious one who acted so godlessly;

---

173 Cf. § 14 in the present homily. Paul's argument, which in Rom 2:1 seemed to switch from the Gentiles to Jews of Rome, suddenly brings in the city's rulers. However, as the argument proceeds, it becomes clear that he is attacking the Jewish world, indeed "the whole world." See also Homily 10.1–10 and Rom 5:1–15.

174 Cf. § 14 in the present homily. Paul's argument, which in Rom 2:1 seemed to switch from the Gentiles to Jews of Rome, suddenly brings in the city's rulers. However, as the argument proceeds, it becomes clear that he is attacking the Jewish world, indeed "the whole world." See also Homily 10.1–10 and Rom 5:1–15.

175 Cf. Rom 2:2–3.

HOMILY 5

and he also pointed out the source of this sinner's knowledge, that is, from creation.[176] Because this was not obvious to all, Paul also stated the cause. But here he omits mention of the source of this knowledge because it was something on which there was general agreement.

II

When Paul said, *Everyone who judges*, his words are not spoken only to those in a position of rule, but also to private citizens and subjects. For all men, even if they do not hold the throne or have no executioners or stakes [to which to chain prisoners by their feet],[177] yet they judge those who give offense in conversations and at public assemblies.[178] And they express their judgments by voting as their conscience bids them to judge. And no one would dare to say that the adulterer does not deserve to be punished. Rom 2:2–3

But, Paul says, they are judging others, not themselves. And for this reason he takes a strong stand against them when he says, *But do you think, man, that you, who are passing judgment on others who do such things as you do yourself, do you think that you will escape the judgment of God?* Paul had shown the abundance of sin in the world, an abundance that springs from doctrines and deeds. He showed that, even though men possessed wisdom, they still sinned. He showed that they had creation to lead them by the hand. But not only did they reject God, but they even preferred images of crawling things. They scorned virtue. Even though nature was pulling them away from evil, they deserted nature and turned to vice and did unnatural things.[179] Rom 2:3

Paul then went on to show that those who do such deeds are punished for them. He had already mentioned punishment when he spoke of their crime. For he said, *They received in themselves the fitting recompense of their perversity.*[180] But when they did not under- Rom 1:27

---

176 Cf. Rom 1:20. The beauties of creation, which can be known to all, are the source of knowledge of God to all who do not know Him through the law
177 Cf. Acts 16:24.
178 Perhaps as members of a jury.
179 Cf. the idolatrous Gentiles' perverted actions in Homilies 3 and 4.
180 Cf. Homily 4.13.

stand that punishment, he added for them another penalty, of which they were greatly afraid. And he had already pointed out this punishment in a special way. For when Paul said, *God's judgment is according to the truth*, he is speaking of nothing other than this.

<small>Rom 2:2</small>

But he builds this up again with further causes for fear when he says, *Do you think, man, that you, who are passing judgment on others who do such things as you do yourself, do you think you will escape the judgment of God?* You have not escaped your own judgment of yourself; are you going to escape the judgment of God? Who would say that? And yet you have judged yourself. But when the advantage of the court [of your own judgment] was so strongly on your side and you were not able to spare yourself, how will God, who can do no wrong and who is the acme of justice, fail to do the same in a much greater degree?

<small>Rom 2:3</small>

You have condemned yourself and God will receive you with praise? How could this be reasonable? Certainly, you are most deserving of a greater punishment than that man whom you judged guilty and condemned. For simply to sin is not the same thing as falling into the same evil act again after you have punished another who has committed that sin. Do you see how Paul has made the charge stronger? For what Paul means is that if you are punishing a man who has committed less grievous sins, even though you are going to bring shame on yourself, how will God fail to judge and condemn you more severely, because you have sinned more grievously? This is all the more likely because God is not going to bring shame on Himself; nor will He judge and condemn you more severely, because you have already condemned yourself by your own reckoning and judgment.

If you say, "I know that I deserve punishment," but you look upon this punishment with disdain because God is long-suffering and you feel over-confident because you did not pay the penalty on the spot, surely on this account you would be right to tremble with fear. For the fact that you did not pay the penalty only postpones your paying a more severe penalty —if you should continue to be unrepentant. And may this never happen to you!

<small>Rom 2:4</small>

This is why Paul goes on to say, *Or do you despise the riches of His goodness, His patience, and His long-suffering? Do you not know that the goodness of God is meant to lead you to repentance?* For after praising God's long-suffering and after showing that the profit that comes from it is very great for those who paid heed to it —for this was what drew sinners to repentance —Paul will give grounds for a still greater fear. For just as God's long-suffering is the basis of salvation for those who make the proper use of it, so is it the price of passage to greater vengeance for those who have looked on it with disdain.

For this is a widely circulated notion, namely, that because God is good and long-suffering, He does not exact the punishment that justice demands. But what Paul is saying is that, whenever you hold to that notion, you are only saying that the intensity of the punishment will increase. God manifests His goodness so that you may be set free from your sins, not so that you may add to them. If you will not avail yourself of His goodness in this way, your judgment will be more dreadful.[181]

Therefore, because God is long-suffering, we have the strongest reason why we must not sin and why we must not make His kindness and bounty grounds for our hardness of heart and obstinate folly. For even if God is long-suffering, He most certainly exacts punishment. What makes this clear? It becomes obvious from what follows. For if the wickedness is great and if those guilty of it have not yet received the punishment due to them, there is every need that they still be punished. If men do not overlook this need, how will God overlook it?[182]

So it is that from this point Paul goes on to his discussion about the judgment. For by showing that many are liable to give an account for their sins unless they should repent, he then brings up the subject of judgment. And he does this with increased forcefulness. This is why he says, *According to your hardness and unrepentant heart, you are storing up wrath for yourself.* For when your heart has not grown softer because of God's goodness, nor is it turned by fear of Him, what could be harder of heart than such a person as yourself? Rom 2:5

---

181 That is, on the day of judgment.
182 Cf. Rom 2:5 and RNT note *ad loc.*

After Paul has shown God's loving-kindness, he then shows His vengeance, which is unbearable for the man who has not been turned to repent. See how fittingly he has used these words. For Paul says, *You are storing up wrath for yourself,* because he is making clear what has certainly been stored up, and he is showing that it is not God who is passing judgment, but it is the one who is being condemned who is responsible for this. For Paul says that *you are storing up for yourself,* not that "God is storing up for you."

For God did everything He could and equipped you with the power to distinguish what was good from what was not. He showed you that He is long-suffering, that He called you to repentance and threatened you with the dreadful day because He was in every way drawing you to convert yourself. But if you continue to be stubborn and unyielding, *you are storing up wrath for yourself on the day of wrath and of the revelation and of the just judgment of God.*

So that you would not think it was passion when you heard the word *wrath,* Paul went on to add *of the just judgment of God.* And it was well that he also said *of the revelation,* because that is the time when each one receives what he deserves. For here on earth many a man often deals maliciously with others and plots unjustly against them. But this is not so in the world to come; there *God will render to every man according to his deeds; to those who by patience in good works [seek glory and honor and immortality, He will give eternal life].*[183]

III

Paul filled them with fear by his harsh severity while he was talking about punishment. But he did not, as we might have expected, go immediately into the matter of vengeance. Rather, he turns to a more pleasant topic, namely, to the reward given in return for good works. What he says is this: *Life eternal will He give to those who by patience in good works seek glory and honor and immortality.*[184] Here he also rouses up those whose courage has failed in the midst of trials and temptations; he shows that it is not right to put one's

---

183 Chrysostom here omits the portion of the text within the brackets. Cf. notes on Rom 2:1–11 and Rom 2:6 in RNT.
184 The omitted words of the text as cited in § 26 are included except for "He will give eternal life."

HOMILY 5

trust and confidence in faith alone.[185] For surely that tribunal can inquire into deeds as well.

Notice that, when he is speaking about the things to come, he cannot speak too clearly about the future blessings, but he mentions only "glory and honor." Because these future blessings transcend all that is human, he has no image of them to show what they are in human terms. So he sets them before us as best he can by things that we see as bright and shining, such as glory, honor, and life. For these are things that are most eagerly sought after by men. But those blessings of the life to come are not like these inasmuch as they are incorruptible and immortal.

Do you see how he has also opened for us the doors regarding the resurrection of our bodies when he speaks of incorruptibility and immortality? For incorruptibility will belong to the corruptible body. Then, because this was not sufficient, he added glory and honor. For we shall all arise incorruptible, but not all will rise to glory, because some will go to punishment, and others to glory.[186] For Paul says, *To those who out of selfishness*. So again Paul deprives of pardon and excuse those who live evil lives; he shows that they have fallen into wickedness because of a kind of contentiousness and careless lack of concern. These are the ones *who do not submit to the truth, but assent to iniquity*. Rom 2:8

Again, see another accusation. What kind of a defense would a man have who flees from the light and seeks the darkness? Paul did not say, "who are forced to or who are driven by a tyrant," but who *assent to iniquity*. What he means is that their fall was of their own choosing. It was not a crime forced on them by necessity. *Affliction and tribulation will be visited upon the soul of every man who does evil*. That is, even if a man is wealthy, if he is a consul, if he is the emperor himself, the word of the judgment is not ashamed to condemn any one of these. Here there is no place for positions of dignity.[187] Rom 2:8

Rom 2:8

Rom 2:9

---

185 A clear statement that neither Paul nor Chrysostom opposes the position on justification found in Jas 2:17, 20–24.
186 Cf. Rom 2:7–8.
187 All men must answer for their sinful actions on the day of judgment. Earthly honors will excuse no one.

So Paul has shown how excessive their disease is. He has given the reason why they are sick, namely, their carelessness and lack of concern for their ailment. He has pointed out how it will end: ruin is waiting to receive them. Even though amendment and reconciliation were easy, in the matter of punishment Paul comes down heavily on the Jew. *The Jew first, and then the Greek.*[188]

Rom 2:9

Because the Jew had enjoyed a larger share of teaching and instruction, he would deserve to endure a greater punishment for his transgressions of the law. So it is that the wiser and more powerful we are, by so much more are we punished if we sin. And surely if you are rich, more money will be demanded of you than from a man who is poor. If you are wiser, a stricter obedience. If you have surrounded yourself with authority and power, more illustrious good works will be expected of you. And so, in the case of all other things, you will contribute measures to match your resources. *There will be glory and honor and peace for everyone who has done good, first to the Jew, and then to the Greek.*

Rom 2:10

What Jew does Paul mean, and about what Gentile is he speaking here? He means those who lived before the coming of Christ. For his discussion had not yet arrived at the times of grace;[189] he was still lingering on earlier days. And from those times long gone he was clearing away and abolishing the difference between the Gentile Greek and the Jew. Then, when he will remove this difference between them in the time of grace, he will not appear to be doing something new and burdensome.

For in those earlier days,[190] when so great a grace had not yet shone forth, the religious culture of the Jews was solemn, famous, and glorious in the eyes of all. If there were no difference at that earlier time, what could they say for themselves now after so great a manifestation of grace? It was on this account that Paul probes this very point with such great earnestness. For surely, when a

---

188 The Greeks, of course, are Gentiles of whatever race or nation.
189 The "times of grace" refers to Christ's incarnation and earthly life.
190 The "earlier days" refers to the times before Abraham and circumcision, the giving of the law, and the coming of Christ. Chrysostom realizes that he must clarify these periods to show that during those times there was no real difference between those who were circumcised and those who were not.

hearer learned that this lack of difference prevailed in former times, he will accept it all the more after the faith had come.

Here Paul does not call Greeks those who worshipped idols, but those Gentiles who adored God, those who obeyed the natural law, those who faithfully kept all the sacred rituals that contribute to piety —except the religious observances of the Jews. Such men were Melchisedek,[191] Job,[192] the Ninevites,[193] and Cornelius.[194] Here, then, Paul is already breaking through the difference between circumcision and uncircumcision.[195] At a distance in time, he is assailing this distinction long beforehand, so as to do so without arousing suspicion. He will strike a blow against it when another occasion forces him to do so. And this is, as always, a mark of his prudence as an apostle.

For if he had located this in the times of grace, what he said would appear to offer grounds for much suspicion. But because he is describing the evil and wickedness gripping the world and what follows from that, the step he takes into his discussion of these matters frees his teaching from all suspicion.

IV

Here Paul makes it clear that this was his intention and this was why he stated his argument the way he did. For if he had not been eager to establish this point, it would have been enough when he said, *According to your hardness and unrepentant heart, you are storing up wrath for yourself on the day of wrath.* Rom 2:5 At that point he could have dropped that subject, because his argument would have been complete. But that was not Paul's purpose, namely, to speak only about the future judgment, but he also wished to show that the Jew had no advantage over the kind of Gentile I have described.[196] Paul does this so that the Jew might not be proud and haughty.

---

191 For Melchisedek see McKenzie, *DB*, 563; and Gen 14:18–20.
192 For Job see McKenzie, *DB*, 439–42; and the book of Job.
193 For the Ninevites see McKenzie, *DB*, 618.
194 For Cornelius see McKenzie, *DB*, 152; and Acts 10.
195 The point in mentioning Melchisedek, Job, the Ninevites, and Cornelius is that they were all non-Jews and hence uncircumcised, but still worthy of justification.
196 Cf. § 34 of this homily.

This is why he goes further and has availed himself of this order and arrangement.

But consider this. Paul frightened his audience; he re-echoed in their ears the dread day; he told them how great an evil it was to live one's life in wickedness; he pointed out that no one commits sin through ignorance nor without paying the penalty; even if he does not pay it now, he certainly will pay it.[197] Next he wishes to prepare them to accept the fact that the teaching of the law was not a matter of excessive urgency. Punishment and reward depend on deeds, not on circumcision or uncircumcision.

Because, therefore, he said that the Greek will by no means escape punishment and took this as a matter of general agreement, he also established from this the fact that the Gentile will receive honor. He next showed that the law and circumcision were superfluous. For it is the Jews whom he is chiefly opposing here. Why was this so? First, because the Jews were rather contentious in disposition and fond of quarreling; because of their vanity, they did not think they deserved to be classified along with the Gentiles. Secondly, they considered anyone ridiculous who thought that faith did away with all sins.

Therefore, Paul first accused the Greeks, on whose behalf he is making his argument, so that he may attack the Jews without suspicion and with a boldness born of confidence. Then, when he came to a close scrutiny of the question of punishment, he shows that in no way is the Jew helped by the law, but he even finds it a heavy burden. And he had started to establish this earlier.[198]

The Greek was left without excuse or defense because he did not become a better man, even though creation and his powers of reasoning were leading him by the hand. All the more will this be true of the Jew who, along with these aids, had also received the instruction that came from the law. Therefore, after Paul had persuaded the Jew to be willing to accept this reasoning in regard to the sins of other people, he then forces the Jew, even against his will, to do the same in the case of his own sins. And so that his argument may become acceptable to the Jew, Paul then leads him

---

[197] That is, unless he repents and is converted to an upright life.
[198] Cf. Rom 2:9 and §§ 28–32 of this homily.

to rewards that he will find more beneficial. For he says, *Glory and honor and peace will be awarded to everyone who does good, to the Jew first and then to the Greek.* Rom 2:10

For in this world, as many good things as a man possesses he holds on to with many troubles, whether he is wealthy, powerful, or a king. Even if he is not at variance with someone else, at least he is often at variance with himself and, in his own thoughts, he fights many a battle. But there is nothing like this in the life hereafter. There he finds everything tranquil, free from trouble, and possessing genuine peace.

And so, because Paul has established from what was said above, namely, that those who do not possess the law will enjoy the same blessings, he adds the reason for this when he says, *With God there is no partiality.*[199] When he said that both the Jew and the Greek are punished if they sin, there was no reason for giving reasons. But when he wishes to prove that the Greek is also honored, he must prepare a foundation for his assertion. For such honor gave reason for wonder and was contrary to expectation if one who had not heard either the law or the prophets should receive this honor because he had performed good works. Rom 2:11

Therefore, as I said before,[200] Paul is making them grow accustomed to the reports predating the times of grace so that then he might, along with the faith, more easily bring them to approve and accept those reports. For here he is in no way suspected of establishing his own position. Therefore, after he said, *Glory and honor and peace will be awarded to everyone who does good, to the Jew first, and then to the Greek,* he added, *With God there is no partiality.* Bless us! How much more than a victory has he gained! For he showed, by reducing the argument to an absurdity, that for this to be untrue would not be according to God's will. For it is a matter involving partiality, and such is not God's nature. Rom 2:10
Rom 2:11

Paul did not say that if this were not so, God would be a respecter of persons. His statement is more dignified. *With God there is no partiality,* that is, God does not examine the quality of persons, but the difference of their actions. So, when Paul said what he did, Rom 2:11

---

199 See RNT note *ad loc.*
200 Cf. § 33 of this homily.

he showed that the Jew differs from the Greek not in actions, but in person only. The consequence of this would be to say, "Because the one man is a Jew and the other a Greek, it is not on this account that the one is honored and the other disgraced. The honor and the disgrace come from the deeds of each."

But Paul did not say that. For he would have stirred up the wrath of the Jew. But he sets down something further that pulled the Jew down lower still and checked his haughtiness, so that he was forced to admit it. And what was that? It is what Paul says next: *As many as have sinned without the law will perish without the law. And as many as have sinned under the law will be judged by the law.*[201] For here, as I said before, Paul shows not only the equality of honor of the Jew and the Greek, but also that the Jew is heavily weighted down by the gift of the law.

For the Greek is judged without the burden of the law. For the words *without the law* here mean not what is more burdensome, but what is less a burden. That is, the Greek does not have the law to accuse him. For *without the law*, that is, apart from the condemnation that comes from the law, means that the Greek is condemned without the punishment that comes from the law. His condemnation comes only from the reasoning powers given to him by nature. But the Jew is condemned *in the law*, that is, he has both nature and the law to accuse him. Inasmuch as the Jew had enjoyed greater care and concern, the greater will be the penalty he pays.

V

Do you see by how much Paul has imposed on the Jews a greater need to rush to the recourse of grace? Because they said that they had no need of grace because they are justified by the law alone, Paul shows that the Jews are in greater need of grace than the Greeks. Why? Because they are going to receive a greater punishment. Then Paul again brings in another argument to contend with what the Jews have said. *For it is not they who hear the law who are just in the sight of God.* Paul did well to add, *in the sight of God.* For perhaps in the sight of men they can appear to be holy and

---

201 See RNT note on Rom 2:12–16.

august and to boast about their greatness. But in the sight of God it is altogether the opposite, because *only those who fulfill the law are justified*. Do you see what a wealth of reasons he uses as he turns what the Jews had said to mean the opposite? For what he is saying to the Jew is this: "If you deem yourselves deserving of salvation because of the law, the Greek will stand before you in this respect, because the Greek has been seen as a doer of what has been written in the law." Rom 2:13

The Jew will say, "And how is it possible for one who has not been a hearer of the law to become a doer of it?" Paul replies, "Not only is this possible, but what is much more than this. For not only is it possible to become a doer without hearing the law, but even after hearing it, it is possible not to be a doer." And Paul sets forth this last point more clearly and with greater force when he says, *When you teach another, do you not teach yourself?* But here Paul is still proving only the former point. Rom 2:21

For he says, *When the Gentiles, who have no law, do by nature what the law prescribes, these, who have no law, are a law unto themselves.*²⁰² What Paul is saying is this. "I am not throwing out the law, but I am justifying the Gentiles from that source."²⁰³ Do you see how, by weakening the glorious boast of Judaism, he gives no handle or opportunity for any accusation against himself, as if he were dishonoring the law? Quite the opposite. He establishes his whole argument by exalting the law and by showing how great it is. Rom 2:14

Whenever Paul says "by nature," he means *according to natural reasoning*. And he shows that there are others who are better than the Jews and, what is of greater importance, who are better for the very reason that they had not received the law and do not have that by which the Jews seem to lord it over the Gentiles. Therefore, Paul says, the Gentiles are objects of admiration because they did not need the law and yet they still showed forth everything the law enjoined, namely, deeds. And they did this without having the letters engraved on their minds. Rom 2:14

---

202 See RNT note on Rom 2:12–16.
203 The Gentiles observe the law even though they have never heard it. But they do act as their conscience dictates.

Rom 2:15–16 For this is what Paul says: *They show the demands of the law written in their hearts. Their conscience alone bears witness to them, even when conflicting thoughts accuse or defend them on the day when, according to my gospel, God will judge the hidden secrets of men through Jesus Christ.* Do you see how again Paul puts that day before the Jews and brings it close to them, shaking their minds and showing that those Gentiles must be held in higher honor because they were eager to accomplish what the law demanded, even though they did not have the law?

What really deserves our admiration is Paul's apostolic prudence, and this is what we must speak of now. After he has shown from what he has established that the Greek is superior to the Jew, both by inference and by the conclusion from his reasoning, he still does not state this so as not to anger the Jew. To make clearer what I have said, I shall use the apostle's own words. For Paul had Rom 2:13 said, *It is not those who hear the law, but those who follow it, who will* Rom 2:14 *be justified.* In the following verse he continues, *When the Gentiles, who have no law, do by nature what the law prescribes.* The inference from this is that the Gentiles are far better than those who are instructed in the law.

But Paul does not say this. Instead, he stays on the topic of praise for the Gentiles; for the time being he does not pursue his discourse by comparing Jews and Gentiles. And his reason for this is so that the Jews would accept what he was saying. And so, as I said, he did not speak in this fashion. But how does he continue Rom 2:14–15 his discourse? *When the Gentiles, who have no law, do by nature what the law prescribes, these who have no law are a law unto themselves. They show the demands of the law written in their hearts. Their conscience bears witness to them.*[204]

Instead of the law, conscience and reason are enough. In this way Paul shows again that God made man independent for choosing the good and avoiding the evil. And do not be surprised if he proves this point once, twice, and many times. It was a topic that was extremely necessary for him to prove because of those who were saying, "Why did Christ come at this time, and where, during times before this, was the plan of providence at work?"

---

204 See also Jer 31:33 and Wis 17:11.

HOMILY 5

Therefore, because he was now doing battle against these men and their questions as secondary opponents, he shows that both in bygone days and before God gave the law, human nature fully enjoyed His providence. For surely *whatever can be known about God is clear to them*[205]; they knew what was good and what was evil, and it was by their knowledge of these that they judged others. And it was by way of reproaching them for this that Paul said, *Wherein you judge another, you are judging yourself.*[206] But in the case of the Jews, in addition to what has been said, they also had the law, and not merely reason and conscience. Rom 1:19
Rom 2:1

Why does Paul say *accuse or defend*? For if they have a written law and they know what the law demands, how is it that reason can still accuse them?[207] But Paul is no longer saying *accuse* only about the Jews, but he says it about the whole human race. At that time, our reasoning powers stand before the Judge; sometimes they accuse us, and sometimes they defend us. And a man has no need of another accuser before that tribunal.[208] Rom 2:15
Rom 2:15

Next, to make men's fear greater, Paul did not say "the sins of men," *but the hidden secrets of men*. For Paul said, *Do you think, you who judge those who do such things while you do the same things yourself, that you will escape the judgment of God?* So that you may not receive a vote of condemnation such as you are casting yourself, but so that you may see that God's judgment is much more exacting than your own, Paul added *the hidden secrets of men*. And he went on to say, *according to my gospel through Jesus Christ*. For humans sit in judgment over overt acts only. Rom 2:16, 3

Rom 2:16

Above Paul spoke only of the Father.[209] But later, after he had ground them down with fear, he added the mention of Christ as well. And he did not speak of Christ alone, but even here he brings in the Son in the way he does, namely, after he has made mention of the Father. And through these things he exalts the value of his message. What he is saying is that his message is proclaiming openly what nature had taught by anticipation.

---

205 See Homily 3.10–14.
206 Cf. Rom 2:1. See also Matt 7:2.
207 Cf. Rom 2:15.
208 Cf. Rom 2:15–16.
209 See § 52 of this homily.

VI

Do you see how wisely Paul brought them and bound them to the gospel and to Christ, and how he also showed that what we are does not come to a halt with this life on earth, but continues to a life beyond. Above, Paul laid the foundation for this when he said, *You are storing up for yourself wrath on the day of wrath*, and here again: *God will judge the hidden secrets of men.* Each one, therefore, must go to his own conscience and, after pondering over his sins, must seek an accurate accounting from himself, so that we may not be judged worthy of condemnation along with the world.[210]

That court is a dreadful one; awful is that tribunal; the accounts rendered are filled with trembling; a river of fire rolls along. *A brother shall not redeem, shall a man redeem?*[211] Recall what is said in the Gospel of the angels running to and fro,[212] of the locked door to the bridal chamber,[213] of the lamps that had not gone out,[214] of the powers dragging people into the furnaces.[215]

And consider this too. If the secret sin of any one of us were revealed today only to those here in the church, how would the one who is guilty pray that he might perish and the earth gape open for him rather than that he have so many witnesses to his wickedness? What will we suffer on judgment day, when everything is brought before the eyes of the whole world, when those we know and those we do not know are looking on in a theater so vast and bright?

But, alas, why am I forced to frighten you? Is it because of the judgment of men, when I should be doing this because of the fear of God and His condemnation? For, tell me, what will happen to us on that day when we have been bound and, gnashing our teeth, we are led into the outer darkness?[216]

Rather, what will we do —and this is of all things the most frightening —when we give offense to God? For if a man has any

---

210 Cf. 1 Cor 11:32.
211 The meaning seems to be that no man can buy God off to gain salvation, no matter how wealthy he is.
212 See Matt 13:41 (explaining the parable of the weeds).
213 See Matt 25:10 (explaining the parable of the ten virgins).
214 See Matt 25:10 (explaining the parable of the ten virgins).
215 See Matt 13:42 (explaining the parable of the weeds).
216 See Matt 13:41-42 (explaining the parable of the weeds).

sense and reason, he has already endured Gehenna whenever he falls from before the face of God. But because this causes the sinner no immediate pain, on this account God threatens him with fire. But we ought to feel pain not when we are punished, but when we commit sin.

Listen to Paul when he weeps and grieves over his sins for which he will not pay the penalty. *I am not worthy to be called an apostle because I persecuted the Church,* he said. Then also listen to David when he had been freed from punishment but, because he thought he had offended God, when he called out and said, *Let your hand be upon me and upon my father's house.* For to offend God is more serious than being punished. But now we are in such a miserable state that, unless there were the fear of Gehenna, we would not quickly choose to do anything good. Therefore, even if for no other reason, we would be deserving of Gehenna on this account, namely, because we fear Gehenna rather than loving Christ.

1 Cor 15:9

2 Sam (2 Kgdms) 24:17

But the blessed Paul does not feel this is the case, but quite the opposite. It is because we feel otherwise that we are condemned to Gehenna. At least, if we were to love Christ as we ought to love Him, we should have known that to offend the Christ we love will cause greater pain than the pains of Gehenna. But because we do not love Christ as we ought to love Him, we do not know how great this punishment is. And this is what most grieves and makes me moan.

And yet what has God failed to do to make us love Him? What has He not contrived? What has He left undone? We sinned against Him, although He had done us no wrong, but even had blessed us with countless and ineffable benefits. When He was calling us and drawing us to Himself by every means, we have turned away from Him. Yet he did not punish us for this, but He personally ran to us and held us back when we were fleeing from Him. But we shook Him off and leaped over to the devil's side. Not even at this did He stand far away from us, but He sent countless messengers to summon us again and console us —the prophets, the angels, the patriarchs. However, we not only did not receive His ambassadors, but even scorned and insulted them when they came.

Despite our reactions to His kindness, He did not reject us but, like the most ardent lovers who have been scorned, He went about and entreated all He chanced to meet on earth or in heaven. He went to Jeremiah[217] and to Micah[218] along with all the others, not so that he might burden us, but so that he might offer a defense for what He was doing. And along with the prophets, He went around Himself to those who had turned away from Him because He was ready to render to them an account. He wished to ask them to enter into a discussion with Him and to draw those who had turned a deaf ear to His appeals into a conversation with Him.

Mic 6:3 *O, My people, what have I done to you? Wherein have I grieved you? Answer Me.* These were His words to them. And after all that, we slew the prophets. We stoned them. We did them other cruel wrongs beyond counting. What did He send in place of these? No longer did He send prophets, no longer angels, no longer patriarchs. But He sent His own Son in person. After the Son came, He too was killed. Yet this did not quench God's love, but kindled it into a brighter flame.

And God continues to beseech us, even after His Son was slain. He continues to entreat us and to do everything to turn us
2 Cor 5:20 to Himself. And Paul proclaimed this when he said, *On behalf of Christ, we are acting as ambassadors, God, as it were, appealing through us. Be reconciled to God.*

VII

But none of these things has reconciled us. Yet even so, God did not abandon us. He continued to threaten us with Gehenna and He continued to promise us the Kingdom, so that He might attract us to Himself in this way. But we still continue to remain in our callous and unfeeling frame of mind. What could be worse than this savage and brutal cruelty? If a human being were to have done the things that God has done, would we not, time and time again, have become slaves to such a man? Will we turn away from God when He treats us in this way?

---

217 See, e.g., Jer 13:17.
218 See, e.g., Mic 6:3.

O, how rash and unfeeling we are! We live our whole lives through in sin and wickedness. If we ever do some slight and insignificant good, like unfeeling house slaves, we examine it with a mercenary spirit and we are precise in computing the reward if our good action has some recompense coming to it. And yet the recompense is greater if you do not do the good act if your only motive is your hope that it will bring a reward. For to think this way and to be exact in your computation is more characteristic of a hired man than of a prudent house slave.

For we ought to be doing everything for the sake of Christ, not for the sake of recompense or reward. And surely, this is why He has threatened us with Gehenna and has promised us the kingdom, namely, so that we may love him. Therefore, let us love Him as we ought to love Him. For this is the great reward, this is the kingdom, this is pleasure and enjoyment, this is the delight, this is the glory, this is the honor, this is the blessedness beyond description,[219] which no word can set before us, which no mind can grasp.[220]

know not how I was led into this discussion when I was exhorting men who do not scorn the power and glory of the present life to scorn the kingdom here on earth for the sake of Christ. Yet those great and noble men [of the past] achieved this measure of love. At any rate, hear how Peter burned with love for Christ and put Him before soul and life and everything else. When he denied Christ,

---

219 μυριομακαριώτης. In "Being Transformed: Chrysostom's Exegesis of the Epistle to the Romans," *Greek Orthodox Theological Review* 36, nos. 3–4 (Fall/Winter 1991): 221n31, Demetrios Trakatellis points out that this is a neologism introduced by Chrysostom, one that indicates his profound understanding of love. In Homily 8.14 (PG 60:456), Chrysostom defines the term Μακαριώτης in this way: "Μακαριώτητα δὲ ὅταν εἴπω, τὴν κορυφὴν λέγω τῶν ἀγαθῶν ἁπάντων. Ὥσπερ γὰρ μισθοῦ πλέον ἡ δικαιοσύνη, οὕτω δικαιοσύνης, πλέον ὁ μακαρισμός" ("When I speak of blessedness, I mean the peak of all blessings. Just as justification is greater than the reward of wages, so blessedness is greater than justification"). Therefore, it seems to me that when he speaks of muriomakariovth" he is using a new word construction to emphasize the ultimate bliss of the kingdom of God.

220 This text of Chrysostom and the one in Homily 9.50–52 are some of his most emphatic statements about God's love for us and the need to love Him in return. Cf. Homily 7.61–62. For more discussion on "love" as used by Chrysostom, see Papageorgiou, chap. 2 of "A Theological Analysis of Selected Themes in the Homilies of St. John Chrysostom on the Epistle of St. Paul to the Romans" (PhD diss., The Catholic University of America, 1995), 106–113.

he did not grieve because of the punishment. He wept because he had denied the One he longed for, and that was to him more bitter than any punishment. And he showed his great sorrow and love before the grace of the Spirit came upon him.

<small>John 13:36; John 6:68; Matt 8:19 & Luke 9:57</small> And Peter constantly kept asking, *Where are You going?* and *To whom shall we go?* And again he said, *I will follow You wherever You will go.*²²¹ For Christ was everything to him. Nor did he make heaven or the kingdom of greater account than Christ, the One for whom he longed. For you, Christ, are all those things to me. That is what Paul means.

<small>Ps 72/73:25</small> And why do you wonder if Peter's feelings are so disposed? Listen to what the prophet says: *For what have I in heaven but You? And what have I desired on earth besides You?* What the psalmist is saying is this: "I desire nothing of the things in heaven above or on earth below other than You alone." This is the love of desire; this is the love of friendship. If we love in this way, not only things in the present life, but even things in the world to come, will we consider to be nothing in comparison to our love for Christ. From this love we will enjoy the fruits of the kingdom, because we are finding delight in our love for Christ.

Someone will ask, "How will this be?" How many times did we heap opprobrium on Him after He had given us countless blessings? Yet He stood firm and called us to Him. How many times did we run away from Him? Yet He did not forsake us. Rather, He ran after us and drew us to Himself. If we consider these things and others like them, we will be able to fan this desire for Him into flame.

If an ordinary man were the one who loved in this way, and a king the one who was loved as we are loved, would not the king feel respect for the greatness of such love? He most certainly

---

221 In Matthew the words are spoken by a scribe who turns out to be a would-be follower of Jesus and who must have been frightened off by Jesus' reply that He lives a life of hardship and has nowhere to rest His head. In Luke the same words are spoken by another would-be follower, who is not identified; Jesus' answer is the same as in Matthew. For a reference to Peter's dedication to Jesus see Luke 22:33 as well as John 13:37. Chrysostom spoke extemporaneously in some of his sermons and it would be possible that he confused the words of the scribe in Matthew or the other man in Luke with Peter's affirmation of his willingness to suffer and even die for Christ as in Luke 22:33 or John 13:37.

would. But here the situation is reversed. The ineffable beauty and the glory and the wealth belong to Him who loves us, and we are the ordinary men. How will we not be deserving of punishments beyond number, we who are the worthless and negligent ones, because we are loved with such excessive love by so great and wonderful a lover, and yet we reject His love?[222]

He has no need of any one of us; even so, He does not stop loving us. We stand in the greatest need of what is His; even so, we do not cling to His love. To Him we prefer wealth, human friendships, and bodily indulgence. We value power and glory above Him who values nothing more than He values us.

For God had one only begotten and true Son. Yet He did not spare Him because of us. But we value many things above Him. Would there not be good reason for the punishment of Gehenna, even if it were twice, three times, or countless times as grievous as it is? For what could we say when we value the precepts of Satan above the laws of Christ, when we neglect our own salvation so that we may value the works of wickedness above Him who took upon Himself every suffering on our account?

And what pardon do such actions deserve? What defense can they offer? There is none. Let us take a stand in the future so that we may not be swept down from the cliffs. Let us return to sobriety of mind. Reckoning up all these things, let us send up glory to Him by our deeds —for words are not enough —so that we may enjoy glory from Him. May all of us attain to this by the grace and loving-kindness of our Lord Jesus Christ, with whom be to the Father, together with the Holy Spirit, glory, power, and honor, now and always, world without end. Amen.

---

[222] Chrysostom here points to the love of God and the joys that come from His blessings, but he immediately follows with strong words to emphasize the ultimate pain and suffering of Gehenna. This is a technique he applies throughout his homilies in his effort to win his hearers over to the Christian life by promising them bliss on the one hand, but also threatening them with punishments on the other.

HOMILY 6

Rom 2:17–18

Behold, you are called 'Jew,' and you rely upon the law, and you glory in God, and you know His will, and you approve the better things because you are instructed by the law.[223]

After Paul had said that nothing that pertains to salvation is missing for the Greek if he is a doer of the law; and after he made that wonderful comparison,[224] he goes on to also set down the glories of the Jews, because of which they looked down upon the Greeks. First, there is the very name of "Jew," which was exceedingly glorious, as today the name of "Christian" is. For surely from the name of "Jew" there arose a great distinction even in those days. So Paul starts from this bygone time. But see how he destroys that name.

Rom 2:17 For Paul did not say, "You are a Jew," but *You are called Jew, and you glory in God,*[225] that is, just as if you were loved by Him and were valued above other men. Here Paul seems to me to be gently making a mockery of their arrogance and their great madness for glory, because they did not use this gift for their own salvation, but abused it to rise up against others and to hold them in scorn.

Rom 2:18 *And you know His will, and you approve the better things.*[226] Indeed this is a disadvantage if this knowledge is not accompanied by

---

223 Cf. RNT note on vv. 17–29, which points out that mere possession of the law does not prove virtue. Circumcision is not an elitist moral sign. Paul is preparing to present his argument for justification through faith.
224 Cf. Homily 5.32–59. Chrysostom makes clear that the Jew possesses no advantage over the Greek because of circumcision.
225 "Glory in God" means that the Jews boast loudly of God for making them a chosen people that has received the law and has been favored by God over other men.
226 The Jews' knowledge of God's will and approval cannot help them to salvation because their abuse of this knowledge and approval do not result in virtuous deeds. Hence these are really a disadvantage.

deeds; yet it seemed to be an advantage. So on this account Paul is making an accurate statement. For he did not say, "You are doing," but *You know and approve*, not "You follow and do." Rom 2:18

You are confident that you are a guide for the blind.[227] Here again he did not say that you are a guide for the blind, but *You are confident.* Therefore, what he says is that you are boasting. For the arrogance of the Jews was great. This is why Paul uses almost the same words as the braggart Jews did. At any rate, see what the Jews said in the Gospels: *You were altogether born in sins, and you teach us?*[228] Rom 2:19
Rom 2:19

John 9:34

For they looked down on all men. To convince them of this, Paul continued to extol them and to demean the other races, so that in this way he might get a stronger hold on them and also make his accusation against them a more weighty one. Therefore, he goes on to add to such charges and to increase them by reporting them in different ways. *For you are confident that you are a guide for the blind, a light for those in darkness, an instructor of the foolish, a teacher of children, having in the law the pattern of knowledge and truth.* Rom 2:19–20

Again, he did not say "in conscience and in deeds and in right actions," but *in the law*. And when he had said "in the law," Paul does here what he did also in the case of the Gentiles. As he said there, *For wherein you judge another, you condemn yourself,* so also he says here: *Therefore, you who teach another, do you not teach yourself?* There he used sharper language; here his words are milder. For he did not say, "Surely on this account you deserve a greater punishment because when you were entrusted with such important matters, you did not use any of them as you should have." Rather, Paul continues his discourse in the form of a question, altering what he had said. Instead he asks, *So you who teach another, do you not teach yourself?* Rom 2:18

Rom 2:1
Rom 2:21

Rom 2:21

Please consider Paul's prudence and discretion from another case. For he sets down the advantages that came to the Jews not from their zeal, but through a gift from above. He then shows that these advantages had no value for them if they neglected them; instead, they then brought an increase in punishment. The fact that

---

227 Their confidence is another indication of their boasting.
228 This is a pertinent citation because the Jews speak these words to the man born blind whom Jesus cured: see John 9:6.

they are called Jews comes not from any of their good works, nor does the fact that they received the law, nor the other advantages that Paul has just enumerated; they came from grace from above. Paul said toward the beginning of his Letter that hearing the law is no help unless doing what the law commands is added to mere hearing. Paul said, *For it is not they who hear the law who are just in the sight of God.*[229] But now he shows in greater detail that not only the hearing, but what was more important than the hearing, the teaching itself of the law, will not be able to protect the teacher if he does not fulfill in act what he teaches. This is what Paul means. And not only will the fact of his having taught the law fail to protect him, but it will serve to bring to him a greater punishment.

And Paul has used his words well. For he did not say, "You have received the law," but *You rely upon the law.* For the Jew did not work hard and grow weary by going about and looking for what he must do; he was content to have a law that pointed out the road that led to a virtuous life. For even if the Gentiles have a reasoning power given by nature and it is from this that they have some advantage over the Jews, inasmuch as their reason does everything the law requires without hearing it, still the Jews had a greater ease and facility in observing the law.

But if you, a Jew, say, "Not only do I hear the law, but I also teach it," this very thing adds to your punishment. Because in this matter the Jews were haughty in their thoughts, it is especially from this that Paul shows that they are ridiculous. For when he says *guide for the blind, instructor of the foolish, teacher of children,* he is speaking of their conceit. For they heaped great abuse on their proselytes and called them blind, foolish, and children.

II

This is why Paul illustrates more richly things that were thought to be praises of the Jews. He did so because he knew that what he said would give a foundation for a stronger accusation. *Having in the law the pattern of knowledge and of truth.* This is just as if someone had a picture of the king and would paint nothing comparable to it, but

---

229 See Homily 5.48, 53.

HOMILY 6

those who were not entrusted with the painting were to imitate it exactly even without the original [to use as a model].[230]

Then, after Paul recounted the advantages of the Jews, which they had from God, he speaks of their failures and brings before us the accusations made by the prophets. *You who teach another, do you not teach yourself? You who preach that men must not steal, do you steal? You who say that men must not commit adultery, do you commit adultery? You who abominate idols, do you commit sacrilege?* For they were strictly forbidden to touch the wealth in the temples of the idols because of the defilement. But, Paul says, the tyranny of avarice persuaded them to trample this law underfoot. Rom 2:21–22

Paul then goes on to bring in next a much more grievous charge when he says, *You who glory and pride yourself in the law, do you dishonor God by transgressing the law?"* Paul has laid down two charges —rather, three. The Jews dishonor, and they dishonor that by which they were honored, and they dishonor Him who honored them. This last went far beyond the ultimate folly, pride, arrogance, obstinacy, and ingratitude. Rom 2:23

He goes on, then, to bring in the prophet as their accuser, so that he may not seem to be charging the Jews from his own personal motives. First he does this briefly, in a few words, and, as it were, in summary; afterward he does this in greater detail. First he brings in Isaiah; afterward he cites David when he has shown that there are several reproaches.

What Paul means is this: "To show you that I am not saying these things to reproach and revile you, listen to what Isaiah says." For Isaiah says, *On your account my name is continually blasphemed among the Gentiles.*[231] See here another accusation. Not only does Isaiah say that the Jews outrage God, but they cause others to do so as Isa 52:5 (LXX)

---

230 Cf. Rom 2:21–22. See Fitzmyer, *JBC*, 53:31; and Deut 7:25–26. Josephus, in his *Antiquities* (4.8.10, paragraph 207), is at pains to answer a charge suggested in Acts 19:37, where the people of Ephesus seem to have accused the Jewish converts of being temple robbers. Josephus also mentions a strange etymology for the Greek name for Jerusalem (Hierosolyma): that it is supposedly derived from the Greek verb hierosylein ("rob a temple"). However, on the matters of abomination of idols and sacrilege, Paul may have been thinking of Isa 52:5 (LXX) or even the reason given by Chrysostom, that such looting of pagan temples involved defilement for the Jew. Fitzmyer suggests that Ezek 36:20 might be a more suitable text. Cf. also RNT note on Rom 2:24.
231 Cf. Rom 2:24; Ezek 36:20, 23.

well. What benefit can come from your teaching when you do not teach yourselves?

Earlier Paul had merely said this; here he has even turned it around to the opposite. Not only do you Jews fail to teach yourselves, but you fail to teach others what must be done. And what is far worse, you not only fail to teach the law, but you do teach the opposite, namely, to blaspheme, and that is opposed to the law.

But circumcision is important, the Jews will say. I agree, but it is important at the time when it also has the circumcision within.[232] Notice Paul's prudent judgment. See how he brought in the mention of circumcision at an opportune time. He did not begin with it right off, when there was considerable public opinion in favor of it. But he had shown that the Jews had offended God in a more grievous way and had been the cause of blasphemy against God. Therefore, he then had an audience that had already condemned them. Because he had stripped them of their position of dignity and because he felt confident that no one would cast a vote in their favor, he introduces his discussion on circumcision.

Rom 2:25

So Paul says, *Circumcision is profitable if you keep the law.* Still, a man could reject it and say, "What is circumcision? It is not a virtuous deed for the man who has it, is it? For it is performed at an untimely age.[233] Those who have lived in the desert wilderness a long time have remained uncircumcised." And from many other points of view a man might look upon it as not being very necessary.

And yet it is not upon these grounds that Paul rejects it, but for a reason that was most necessary, namely, from the case of Abraham. For the greater force of victory is this, namely, to show that circumcision can easily be despised because of the very source from which it became venerable in the eyes of the Jews. And it would have been possible to say that even the prophets call the Jews uncircumcised. Yet this is not a defect of circumcision, but of those who follow it badly.

What Paul was looking for was to show that, even in the best life, it has no force or power. This is what he next proposes to do. And here he does not bring in the patriarch Abraham, but, because

---

232 Paul agrees if it also is circumcision of the heart.
233 Eight days after birth.

Paul had previously rejected circumcision on other grounds, he keeps Abraham for later, when he brings in his discussion of faith and speaks in this way: *How then was faith credited to Abraham? Was it when he was in the state of circumcision or in the state of uncircumcision?* As long as circumcision is struggling with the Gentile and uncircumcision, Paul does not wish to say anything about these things for fear that his Letter may become overly burdensome. When circumcision is fighting against faith, then he prepares himself more completely to do battle with it. Rom 4:10

However, up to now, the battle has been against uncircumcision. On this account, Paul pursues his discussion less violently and says, *Circumcision is profitable if you keep the law; but if you are a transgressor of the law, your circumcision has become uncircumcision.* What Paul is saying is that there are two uncircumcisions and two circumcisions, just as there are two laws. For there is the law of nature and there is the written law. And there is also a law between these two, namely, the law that is shown through deeds. Consider how he points out these three laws and brings them before our eyes. Rom 2:25

He says, *When the Gentiles, who have no law.* Tell me, what law does he mean? He means the written law. *Do by nature what the law prescribes.* Of what law does he speak here? *Those who have no law.* What law is that? The written law. *They are a law unto themselves.* How? By making use of their nature and its law. *Those who show the work of the law.* Of what law? The law that is shown through deeds. The law that is written in letters lies outside; the law that lies within comes from nature; and the third is shown in deeds. Letters dictate the first, nature dictates the second, and deeds dictate the third. This third law is necessary, and it is on account of this law that the other two exist, namely, the one that comes from nature and the one that is written in letters. And if the third law is not present, no good comes from the other two, but even the greatest harm. Rom 2:14
Rom 2:14
Rom 2:14
Rom 2:14
Rom 2:15

Paul demonstrates this in the case of the law that comes from nature when he says, *Wherein you judge another, you condemn yourself.* In the case of the written law, he says, *You who preach that men should not steal, do you steal?* So also there are two uncircumcisions; one is natural, the second comes from act. And there is Rom 2:1
Rom 2:21

one circumcision that is in the flesh, and there is a second that comes from freedom of choice. This is an example of what I mean. A man has been circumcised when he was eight days old. This is a circumcision of the flesh. Another man has done everything that the law prescribes. This is a circumcision of the mind's intention. It is this latter circumcision that Paul requires above all, and the law requires it even more.

III

See, therefore, how Paul has agreed to circumcision in word but puts an end to it in deed. For he did not say, "Circumcision is superfluous, circumcision is unprofitable, is of no use." But what did he say? *Circumcision is profitable if you keep the law.* He accepted it up to this point when he says, "I agree and do not deny that circumcision is honorable." But when is it honorable? When, along with circumcision, the law is observed. *But if you are a transgressor of the law, your circumcision has become uncircumcision.*

Rom 2:25

Rom 2:25

Paul did not say that circumcision is no longer profitable so that he would not seem to be insulting or reviling it. But after he has stripped the Jew of his circumcision, he then deals him a blow. However, this was no longer an insult to circumcision; rather, it was an assault on the man who, by his thoughtless indifference, had utterly destroyed his circumcision. It is the same as when men who were in positions of dignity are later caught and convicted on most grievous charges. The judges remove them from the honor of their rank, and then they punish them. That is what Paul did. For after he said, *If you are a transgressor of the law,* he went on to add, *Your circumcision has become uncircumcision.* And once he has shown that the transgressor is now uncircumcised, he then condemns him without fear.

Rom 2:25

Therefore, when the uncircumcised keep the precepts of the law, will not their uncircumcision be turned into circumcision? See what Paul is doing. He is not saying that uncircumcision overcomes circumcision, for this would be very difficult for those who were then listening to his Letter to understand and accept. But he does say that "circumcision has become uncircumcision." And he then asks what

Rom 2:26

circumcision is and what uncircumcision is. And he says that circumcision is a good deed and uncircumcision is an evil one. And after he has changed the uncircumcised man who had done good deeds into the circumcision, and after he had thrust the circumcised man who lived a corrupt life into uncircumcision, in this way he gives the victory to the uncircumcised.

Still, he does not say "to the uncircumcised," but he goes back to the topic itself when he speaks as follows: "Will not his uncircumcision be turned into circumcision?" Nor did he say, "be credited," but rather "be turned into," which is a more vivid and impressive term. This is what he did above when he did not say, "Your circumcision is credited as uncircumcision," but "has become."

And the uncircumcision that is from nature will judge. Do you see that Rom 2:27
Paul recognizes two uncircumcisions, the one from nature and the other from free choice? Here Paul speaks of that which comes from nature; but he does not stop here, but goes on to say, *If he fulfills the* Rom 2:27
law, will he not judge you who, with the letter [of the law] and circumcision, are a transgressor of the law?

See how very subtle Paul's sagacious judgment is. He did not say that natural uncircumcision will judge circumcision, but he brings in uncircumcision, to which the victory belonged. But he does not yet show that circumcision was worsted, but that the Jew who had been circumcised had lost the battle. He does this because he is sparing his audience and does not wish to offend them by what he says.

Nor did he say, "You who have the law and circumcision," but he puts it still more mildly when he says, *You who, with the letter and cir-* Rom 2:27
cumcision, are a transgressor of the law. That is, such uncircumcision defends circumcision, because circumcision has been wronged; and it comes to the aid of the law because the law has been abused. And so this uncircumcision sets up a glorious monument of triumph. For then the victory is a brilliant one because the Jew is not judged by a Jew, but by the uncircumcised. It is the same as when Matthew says, *The men of Nineveh will rise up in the judgment with this* Matt 12:41
generation and condemn it.

Therefore, Paul does not dishonor the law; indeed, he has great reverence for it. Rather, he dishonors the man who brings disgrace upon the law. Then, after he has established this clearly, he goes on with confidence to define what the Jew really is. And he points out that he rejects neither the Jew nor circumcision, but rather the one who is not a Jew and has become uncircumcised. On the one hand Paul seems to defend circumcision, but on the other he destroys the opinion people held about it because he wins their agreement from the conclusion he draws.

For he shows that not only is there no difference between the Jew and the uncircumcised, but also that the uncircumcised man is the better one if he gives heed to himself, and that this man is the one who is really the Jew. This is why Paul says, *He is not a Jew who is so outwardly, nor is that circumcision that is so outwardly in the flesh.* Here Paul attacks them because they do everything for show. *But he is a Jew who is so inwardly, and circumcision is a matter of the heart in the spirit, not in the letter.*

Rom 2:28

Rom 2:29

IV

When Paul said this, he has cast out everything that is bodily. For surely circumcision is outward, as are the Sabbaths, the sacrifices, and the purifications. Paul hinted at all this by a single statement when he said, *For he is not a Jew who is so outwardly.* But because there was much discussion about circumcision because even the Sabbath yielded to it,[234] there was good reason for Paul to aim and prolong more arguments against it. For when he said, *in the spirit,* he was preparing beforehand the road for the way of life of the Christian Church. And so, he brings in the faith. For it, too, is in the heart and in the spirit and has praise from God.[235]

Rom 2:29

Rom 2:29

And why did Paul not show that the Greek who lives a good life is not inferior to the Jew who lives a good life, but that the Greek who lives a good life is better than the Jew who transgresses the law? His reason was to make the victory one that there could be no doubt about. For when there is agreement on this matter, circumcision of the flesh is necessarily rejected and the need for a good life is everywhere proved.

---

234 Cf. John 7:22–23.
235 Cf. Rom 2:29.

HOMILY 6

For when the Greek finds salvation without these[236] but the Jew who has them is punished, Judaism stands idly by. But again Paul does not mean the Greek who is sunk in idolatry, but that the one who fears God is virtuous and stands free from the pagan observances established by law. *What advantage, then, remains for the Jew?* Because Paul has rejected them all —the hearing [of the law], the teaching, the name of "Jew," the circumcision, all the other things —when he said, *He is not a Jew who is so outwardly, but he who is so inwardly,* he sees next that an objection is coming up, and he makes a stand against it. Rom 3:1

What is this objection? If these things are of no benefit, what reason was there for the nation to be called, and why was circumcision given to them? What then does Paul do, and how does he answer it? The same way he answered previous objections. Just as he said in those other cases that the praises did not belong to them but were benefits given by God, so too when they were successful, it was God's doing —for to be called a Jew, and to know God's will, and to approve the better things were not the result of some good work of theirs, but came to them by the grace of God.

And the prophet reproached them in the same way when he said, *He has not done so to any other nation, and He has not shown them His judgments.* And again, Moses had said, *Ask now whether anything has happened like this event, if a nation has heard the voice of the living God out of the midst of the fire and has lived.* Ps 146/147:20
Deut 4:32–33

And Paul did the same thing here. When he was speaking about circumcision, he did not say that circumcision was of no profit apart from a good life, but that circumcision does profit with a good life. This means the same thing, but he expresses it in milder terms. And, again, he says, "If you be a transgressor of the law." But he did not say that you who have been circumcised gain no profit, but "Your circumcision has become uncircumcision." Again, after that, he does not say that uncircumcision will judge circumcision, but that uncircumcision will judge you, the transgressor of the law.[237] In this way he spares what pertains to the law but strikes those who transgress it. And this is what he does here.

---

236 That is, the law and circumcision.
237 Cf. Rom 2:27.

For after he had stated this objection to his own statement when he said, *What advantage, then, remains for the Jew?* Paul did not say, "None," but he went along with what was said. And in what he goes on to say in the following verses, he again refuted it and shows that the Jews were even punished for the position of importance that they claimed. How did he do this? Let me tell you by bringing the objection into the full light.

Paul said, *What advantage, then, remains for the Jew, or what is the use of circumcision? Much, in every respect. First, indeed, because the oracle of God was entrusted to them.*[238] Do you see, as I said before, that in no way is it their good deeds, but the benefits given by God, that Paul counts up? But what does he mean by *was entrusted to them?* It means that they had the law placed in their hands because God considered them so deserving that He entrusted to them the oracles that were brought down from heaven.

I know that there are some who say that the word "entrusted" does not apply to the Jews, but to the oracles, that is, that the law was "believed in." But what follows does not permit us to accept this interpretation. In the first place, Paul is saying this by way of accusing them, and he is showing that, although they enjoyed many benefits from above, they still gave evidence of great ingratitude. And what follows makes this clear. For Paul goes on to say, *For what if some of them did not believe?*[239] If some of them did not believe, how is it that some say that the oracles were believed in? What does Paul mean? He means that God entrusted these to them, not that they believed in God's words in the oracles. How else will what follows make sense? For surely Paul did say, *For what if some of them did not believe?*

What he says after that makes the same point clear. For again Paul goes on to add, *Their unbelief will not make void the fidelity of God, will it? God forbid!* Therefore, Paul is proclaiming that what was entrusted to them was a gift from God. Please also consider in this place the prudence of Paul. Again, he does not bring in the accusation against the Jews as coming from himself, but rather from

---

238 "τὰ λόγια τοῦ θεοῦ", in other words, "The oracle of God," is the utterance of God.
239 That is, they were unfaithful to the utterances of God. In 1 Tim 3:16 the same word for unfaithful is used but seems to mean unbelieving.

the objection. It is just as if he were to say, "But perhaps you will say, 'What is the profit of this circumcision?' For they did not avail themselves of it as they should have done. They had the law entrusted to them, and they were unfaithful to this trust."

Up to this point, Paul has not been overly severe in his accusation. But just as if he was setting God free from these charges, Paul in this way turns the entire accusation against the Jews. For he says, "Why do you make the complaint that the Jews did not believe? What has this to do with God? The ingratitude of those who received a benefit does not overturn the benefit God gave, does it? It does not make an honor cease to be an honor, does it?" This is what Paul means when he says, *Their unbelief will not make void the fidelity of God, will it? God forbid!*

It would be just as if someone should say, "I honored so-and-so. But if that man did not concern himself with the honor, this does not bring an accusation against me, nor does it do harm to my loving-kindness, but it does show his insensibility." Paul not only says this, but much more. What he means is that their unbelief not only fails to inflict a complaint on God, but even shows that God's honor and loving-kindness are greater, because he is certainly honoring one who is going to dishonor him.

V

Did you see how he made them accountable for the charges by means of the benefits in which they gloried? God treated them with such great honor that He did not hold back His good will toward them, even if He foresaw what would come of it. But they committed outrages against the God who honored them —outrages through the very benefactions with which they had been honored. Then, when Paul said, *For what if some of them did not believe* —but it was clear that they all did not believe —even though he was saying no more than their history proved, so that he might not seem to be overly severe in his accusation, as an enemy might be, he puts what was historical truth in the mold of a reasoning process and a logical demonstration.

Rom 3:3

For this is what Paul said: *Let God be true, but every man a liar.*[240] What he is saying is something like this: "I do not mean that some did not believe but, if you wish, put down that all were unbelieving." In the face of the tumultuous crowd, he yields on the historical fact, so that he may not seem to be overbearing or open to suspicion. Indeed, Paul says that in this way God is more justified. What does he mean by "is justified"? He means that if there could be a trial and an examination of the things God had done for the Jews and of the things the Jews had done to Him, the victory would be with God and all the court's decrees of justification would belong to Him.

And after he had proved this clearly from what he had just said, Paul then brought in the prophet who also gave his assent to these things when he said, *That You may be justified in Your sayings, and may overcome when You are judged.*[241] For God himself did all things for His part, but the Jews did not become better even for all that God did. Then, arising from this, Paul brings forward another objection to our attention and says, *But if our wickedness shows forth the justice of God, what shall we say? The God who inflicts His wrath is not unjust, is He? (I speak in a purely human way.) God forbid*"[242]

Ps 50:6 (LXX)

Rom 3:5–6

Paul is solving one absurd objection with another. Because this is not too clear, I must state it in less ambiguous terms. What, then, is it that Paul means? God honored the Jews; the Jews heaped insults on Him. This makes God the victor and proves His great love for men because He honored them even though they were the sort of men they were. So what Paul means is that we heaped insults on Him and treated him wickedly; for this reason God becomes victorious, and His righteousness shone forth brightly. Why, then, am I being punished, someone might say, because I was the cause of His victory because of the outrageous things I did to Him?

How does Paul solve this? Again, as I said, he solves it by another absurdity. For if you were the cause of God's victory but after that you are punished, then an act of injustice has been done. But if God is not unjust, and you are still punished, then you are

---

240 This seems to mean "God must be true even though every human being is a liar," as it is translated in RNT. Cf. Ps 115:2 (LXX).
241 Cf. Rom 3:5–6.
242 Cf. Ps 50:6 (LXX).

no longer the cause of His victory. Note the pious caution of the Apostle. For when he said, *The God who inflicts His wrath is not unjust,* *is He?* he went on to add, *I speak in a purely human way.* What Paul means is this: "How could anyone argue with the way men reason? For God's righteous judgment far surpasses the things that seem to be just in the eyes of men, and God has certain other ineffable reasons for it." Rom 3:5 Rom 3:5

Then, because this was not altogether clear, Paul again says the same thing a second time. *But if my falsehood makes God's truth abound to His glory, why am I still judged as a sinner?* What Paul means is this: "If God loves mankind and is certainly shown as just and good from the things in which you have failed to heed Him, not only should you not be punished, but you should have kindness done to you." Rom 3:7

But if that were the case, we will find as a result that absurdity that is circulated among many, namely, that good comes from evil and that evil is the cause of good.[243] Then one of these two must follow: either that God is unjust in punishing us; or that if He does not punish us, it is from our evil deeds that God gains the victory. But both of these are exceedingly absurd. And when Paul is demonstrating this, he brought in the Greeks as the ones who sired such opinions.

Paul does this because he thought that the quality of the persons who were saying these things was a sufficient charge against what they said. For they were the ones who ridiculed us and used to say, *Let us do evil so that good may come from it.* And this is why Paul stated it clearly when he asked, *And why should we not —just as we are slandered and as some maintain that we say —why should we not do evil that good may come from it? Because the condemnation of those who do this is just.* Rom 3:8 Rom 3:8

Because Paul said, *Where offense abounded, grace abounded still more,* to ridicule him and to pervert what he said to another meaning, his Gentile foes said, "We must hold fast to wickedness so that we may enjoy the good things." But Paul did not say that. In fact, to correct it, he does say this: *What then? Shall we continue in sin so that grace may abound? God forbid!* What does he mean? What he is Rom 5:20 Rom 6:1–2

---

243 Cf. Rom 3:8.

saying is this: "I was speaking of bygone days. I did not mean that we should make this a practice." He was leading them away from this suspicion, and he even said that this was impossible in future times. *How shall we, who are dead to sin, live any longer in sin?*

Rom 6:2

VI

Paul had no difficulty in assailing the Greeks, for their life had become very corrupt. Even if the life of the Jews seems to have been careless, still they had strong ways of covering it up, namely, the law and circumcision, the fact that God had associated with them, and that they were the teachers of all. But Paul has stripped them of these benefits and has shown that, because of these, they are being punished all the more. And this is the conclusion with which he here brings his discussion to a close.

For if they are not punished when they do such things, that blasphemous saying, *Let us do evil that good may come from it*, must be spread abroad. But if this is impious, and if those who spread it abroad by repeating it are impious too, they will pay the penalty. Paul makes this clear when he says, *The condemnation of those who do this is just.* And it is very obvious that they are punished. And if those who repeat this saying deserve vengeance, much more will those who put it into act. If these deserve vengeance, it is because they have sinned. For it is not man who inflicts the punishment so that anyone might suspect the sentence given, but it is God, who is just in everything He does.

Rom 3:8

Rom 3:8

If their punishment is just, then those who spread that maxim abroad acted unjustly when they slandered and ridiculed us. For God has done and does everything so that our way of life may shine forth brightly and be upright in every way. Therefore, let us not be idle and unconcerned. If we are not, we will be able to make the Greeks abandon their error. However, when we express our love of wisdom in our words but act shamelessly in our deeds, with what expression in our eyes will we look at them? With what sort of tongues will we discuss doctrines with them?

For the Greek will say to each of us, "You have failed to carry out God's commands in a lesser matter. How do you consider yourself worthy to teach me in a matter of greater importance? You who have not yet learned that avarice and greed are evils, how can you speak with wisdom about the things in heaven? Do you not know that avarice is evil?" Therefore, my charge is more grievous because you are guilty of sin when you know that what you are doing is wrong.

But why do I speak of the Greek? For our laws do not allow us to enjoy this boldness and freedom of speech when our lives have become corrupt. For the psalmist says, *But to the sinner God has said, 'Why do you declare My ordinances?'*[244] Once the Jews were carried off as captives. When the Persians were pressing them and asking them to sing for them their hymns to God, the Jews replied, *How will we sing the Lord's song in a foreign land?*[245] And if it was not lawful for them to sing the oracles of the Lord in a strange land, all the more was it forbidden for the estranged soul to do this. For the estranged soul [of the sinner] knows no mercy.

Ps 49/50:16

Ps 136/137:4

If the law made them sit in silence because they were captives and had become slaves of men in an alien land, much more is it right for those who are slaves to sin and have come to be in an alien state to curb their mouths. And yet the Jews did have their harps at that time. For the psalmist says, *We hung our harps on the willows in the midst of it.* But neither were they allowed to sing with the harp. Therefore, neither is it lawful for us to speak boldly and freely even if we have a mouth and tongue, which are the harps and instruments of speech, as long as we are slaves to sin. For sin is more tyrannical than any barbarian.

Ps 136/137:2

Tell me: What will you say to the Greek if you are guilty of plunder and avarice? Will you say, "Put away your idolatry? Recognize and acknowledge God? Do not seek silver and gold?" Will he not laugh at you and say, "Tell that first to yourself"? For it is not the same thing for one who is a Greek to worship idols and for one who is a Christian to commit the same sin. How will we be able to lead others away from worshipping idols if we do not lead ourselves away from this same thing? For we are closer to ourselves than

---

244 The ordinances are especially those against theft and adultery.
245 The foreign land is Babylon, where the Jews were held in captivity. This captivity cut them off from Sion and cultic worship.

to our neighbors. Therefore, when we do not persuade ourselves, how will we persuade others? For when a man does not manage his own household well, he will not take care of the Church either.[246] How then will a man who does not manage his own soul be able to set others on the right path?

Do not tell me that you do not worship an idol of gold. Rather, show me that you do not do those things that gold bids you to do. For there are different kinds of idolatry. One looks on wealth as his lord, another makes his belly his god, still another makes a god of some other most grievous lust. But do you not sacrifice oxen to them as the Greeks do? What is far more grievous, you slaughter your own soul for these. You do not bend your knees and worship them? But with greater obedience you do everything that your belly and gold and the tyranny of lust command you.

It is on this very account that the pagans are loathsome, because they turn their passions into gods; they call lust Aphrodite, anger Ares, and drunkenness Dionysus.[247] You do not carve out idols as they do. Yet, with great eagerness, you bow down to the very same passions when you make the members of Christ members of a harlot[248] and when you plunge yourself into other acts of iniquity.

Therefore, I urge you to take to heart the excess of this absurdity and to flee from this idolatry. For such is the name Paul gives to avarice.[249] I further urge you to flee not only from the avarice that has to do with money and possessions, but also from the avarice that shows itself in evil lust and clothing and at the table and in all things. For we shall pay a much more grievous penalty if we fail to heed the laws of the Lord. Jesus said, *For the servant who knew the will of his Lord and did not do it will receive many blows.* (Luke 12:47)

So that we may escape this punishment and be useful to others as well as to ourselves, let us cast all wickedness from our souls and choose virtue. For in this way we shall attain to the blessings that are to come. May all of us find these blessings by the grace and

---

246 Cf. 1 Tim 3:5.
247 Aphrodite is the Greek goddess of love (lust); Ares is the Greek god of war (anger); and Dionysus is the Greek god of wine, revelry, and drunkenness.
248 Cf. 1 Cor 6:15 and RNT note *ad loc.*
249 Cf. Col 3:5.

loving-kindness of our Lord Jesus Christ, whom with the Father, together with the Holy Spirit, be glory, honor, and power, now and always, world without end. Amen.

HOMILY 7

Rom 3:9–18	*What then? Are we better off than they are? Not at all. For we have already brought the charge against both Jews and Gentiles that all are under the domination of sin.*
Eccl 7:20	*But it is written: 'There is no just man, not even one; there is none who understands; there is none who seeks after God; all have gone astray; together they have become*
Ps 13/14:1–3	*unprofitable; there is none who does good, not even one.*
Ps 5:9; Jer 5:16	*Their throat is an open sepulcher; they deal treacherously*
Ps 139/140:3	*with their tongues; the venom of asps is behind their lips;*
Ps 9/10:7	*their mouth abounds in curses and bitterness; their feet*
Isa 59:7–8	*are swift to shed blood; destruction and misery are in their paths, and they have not known the road of peace,*
Ps 35/36	*there is no fear of God before their eyes.'*[250]

Paul accused the Gentiles, and he accused the Jews. What follows next was to speak of the justification that comes through faith. If the law of nature did not help, nor did the written law do any more, but if both weighed heavy on those who did not use them as they should and showed that those who failed to follow them deserved greater punishment, then for the future the salvation that comes from grace was the necessary course.[251] Therefore, Paul, tell us of this salvation and make it clear to us.

---

250 In this long opening text Paul raises the question as to whether the Gentiles enjoy an advantage over the Jews. This cannot be entirely the case because both are dominated by sin. The Jews are still privileged because God is faithful to His promises to them. But the Jews have failed to do their part, and all humanity shares the common burden of sin. Jews and Gentiles are linked together in a chain of texts from Rom (1:18–2:25; 3:9) and from the OT. Cf. RNT note on Rom 3:9–20, which also links together all men. Here Paul joins texts that mention the parts of the human body that contribute to man's infidelity: throat, tongue, lips, mouth, feet, and eyes.

251 Neither natural law nor the written law can of themselves win salvation for sinful man. Justification and salvation can come only from grace and faith.

HOMILY 7

But Paul does not yet make bold to do this because he views with suspicion the reckless violence of the Jews. Rather, he again leads his discussion into an accusation of them and again he brings in David to level the charges against them. David had spoken at length about these charges,²⁵² which Isaiah put briefly when he was furnishing a strong checkrein for the Jews.²⁵³ And Paul did this so that none of his hearers, because they were sufficiently shackled by enough accusations of the prophets, might bound off or skip away while the subject of faith was being discussed and made clear.

And surely the prophet set down three excesses: he said that all of them together were doing evil deeds; that they were not interspersing good deeds with the evil, but that they sought after wickedness alone; and that they did this with all their strength and intensity. Then, to prevent them from objecting by asking, "What, then, if these same things were said to others?" Paul went on to add, *But we know that whatever the law says, it is speaking to those who are under the law.* Rom 3:19

This is why, next to Isaiah, who admittedly was aiming at the Jews, Paul brought in David to show that these things should be attributed to them. For what need was there, he means, for a prophet who was sent for your correction to accuse other people? For the law was not given to others, but to you. Why, then, did Paul not say "we know that whatever the prophet says" instead of *whatever the law says*? Because Paul usually gives the name of "the law" to the entire Old Testament. Indeed, in another place he says, *Do you not hear in the law that Abraham had two sons?*²⁵⁴ And here he calls the Psalms "the law" when he says, *We know that whatever the law says, it is speaking to those who are under the law.*²⁵⁵ Rom 3:19

Next, he shows that what he said was not simply for the sake of making an accusation; rather, it was in order to smooth the road for faith. Such is the harmony between the two Testaments, the Old and the New, that both the accusations and the reproofs

---

252 See the opening text for this homily.
253 See, e.g., Isa 59:1–15.
254 See also Gen 16:15 and 21:2–3.
255 Paul's inclusion of the Psalms within "the law" (for him, the entire OT) contrasts with the system of other Jewish writers, who usually excluded the Psalms from the general classification of "the law."

were entirely for this purpose, namely, that the door of faith might open and enlighten those who hear them. This was what chiefly destroyed the Jews, namely, their proud and haughty conceit in themselves. And Paul mentions this later in this Epistle when he says, *Being ignorant of the justice of God, and seeking to establish their own, they have not submitted to the justice of God.*²⁵⁶

<small>Rom 10:3</small>

But the law and the prophet anticipated this and overthrew their arrogant thoughts and put down their conceit. Why? So that the Jews might come to a realization of their own sins and that, after they had emptied themselves of all their madness and saw that they were running the risk of receiving the ultimate punishment, they might run with all zeal to Christ, who is offering them forgiveness of their sins, and so might receive His grace through faith.

Certainly Paul was hinting at this when he said, *Whatever the law says, it is speaking to those who are under the law, in order that every mouth may be shut and the whole world may be accountable to God.*²⁵⁷ Here Paul shows that they are stripped bare of the boldness of speech that comes from works, that their words are only shameless and false pretensions. And this is why he used the expression properly when he said *In order that every mouth may be shut,*²⁵⁸ because he is showing their impudent and uncontrollable boasting and that their tongues were literally being stopped up. For their words had swept along like an intolerable flood. But the prophet stayed the torrent.²⁵⁹

<small>Rom 3:19</small>

<small>Rom 3:19</small>

But when Paul said *In order that every mouth may be shut,* he did not mean that the reason for their sinning was so that their mouth might be shut, but that the reason why they were being reproved was so that they might not fail to perceive that they were committing this very sin.

<small>Cf. Rom 3:19</small>

And the whole world may be accountable to God. Paul did not say "the Jew," but "all nature," that is, *the whole world.* When he says, *In order that every mouth may be shut,* his words hint at the Jews, even if he has not stated this clearly, so that what he says may not be overly

<small>Rom 3:19</small>
<small>Rom 3:19</small>

---

256 See RNT note *ad loc.*
257 A taunt against the complacent attitude of the Jews and all other sinners.
258 This verse is aimed chiefly at the boastings of the Jews; it also indicates God's victory over the universal bondage of sin.
259 "The prophet" is the psalmist.

harsh. But when he says, *That the whole world may be accountable to God*, these words were spoken of both Jews and Gentiles at the same time.²⁶⁰   Rom 3:19

But this is no small motive for the Jews to repress their arrogance. Why? Because even in this they have no advantage over the Gentiles, but, in the same way as the Gentiles, they have been abandoned as far as salvation is concerned. For that man would quite properly be said to be accountable because he cannot of himself have a sufficient reason to defend or help himself, but needs another to lend him aid and assistance. And such was the case with the whole human race because we had lost what we needed for salvation.²⁶¹

*For through the law comes the recognition of sin.*²⁶² Again Paul assails the law, but with moderation. For what he says is not an accusation of the law, but of the sluggish indifference of the Jews. Nevertheless, he is still eager and earnest at this point to show the great weakness of the law, because he is about to bring in his discussion on faith. What Paul means to say is: "If you Jews boast about the law, you are bringing more shame upon yourselves. For the law puts your sins on parade." But again he does not say this too sharply. Rather, he softens the tone of his reproof.   Rom 3:20

For through the law comes the recognition of sin. And so the punishment is even greater [not because the law is feeble, but] because of the Jews. For the law has been able to reveal your sin to you, but it was up to you to flee from it. Therefore, by not avoiding the sin, you have drawn on yourselves a greater punishment, and the good work of the law has become for you a source of more severe reprisal.   Rom 3:20

---

260 Cf. Rom 3:19. Both Jews and Gentiles are accountable to God; neither has an advantage over the other in this respect.
261 A loose echo of Ps 142/143:2. No living man is just, and therefore all need justification to be saved.
262 Cf. Rom 3:20. The commandments catalogue what is sinful. But, after learning from the law what is wrong, the sinner still pursues and embraces it. Cf. Rom 7:7–8.

II

Therefore, after he had increased their fear, Paul then brings in the matter of grace. After he had established in them an abundant desire to have their sins forgiven, Paul says, *Now the justification of God has been made manifest apart from the law.*[263] Here he has uttered an important statement, one that required much preparation and proof. For if those who lived under the law not only did not escape punishment, but even were all the more weighed down under its precepts, how is it possible apart from the law not only to escape vengeance, but also to be justified?

And so Paul has set forth two important concepts, namely, "to be justified" and "to obtain these blessings apart from the law." Therefore, Paul did not simply say "justification," but "the justification of God," because he is showing from the dignity of the divine person the greater and higher degree of the gift. He is also making it clear that the promise can be kept, for all things are possible to God. Nor did he say that the justification was given, but that it *had been made manifest.*[264] He said this to cut off any accusation that he was a doctrinal innovator. For a thing that has been made manifest is said to be such because, even though it is old, it has been hidden.

Not only this, but also what follows, shows that this is not something new. For after Paul said *has been made manifest,*[265] he went on to add *being attested by the law and the prophets.*[266] He means this: "You do not feel troubled because it has only now been given, do you? You are not frightened as you would be at a new and strange phenomenon, are you? Both the law and the prophets foretold it long before this." Some of the passages he had pointed out in the course of this argument, and others he will presently cite.

Among the earlier witnesses he brought in Habakkuk, who said, *The just man will live by faith.*[267] In what follows he introduces

---

263 Cf. Isa 51:6–8.
264 Rom 3:21–26 gives consolation that balances the frightening language of vv. 9–20 by showing what was known was known from the law and the prophets but was not realized by the Jews.
265 Here begins the central argument of Romans, namely, the development of the doctrine of justification by faith in our redemption through Christ.
266 Therefore this doctrine is neither new nor novel.
267 See NAB note *ad loc.* Paul also cites this text in Gal 2:16 and 3:11, as does the au-

HOMILY 7

Abraham and David and shows them as they spoke to us about these matters. For Abraham was a patriarch and a prophet; David was a king and a prophet. And the promises about these matters had been made to both of them. And this is why Matthew, at the beginning of his Gospel,[268] mentions both of them in the first place, and then, in order, the forefathers.[269]

For after Matthew said *the book of the origin of Jesus Christ*, he did not wait, after mentioning Abraham, in order to name Isaac and Jacob, but he did mention David along with Abraham. Indeed, the strange thing is that he put David before Abraham when he said *the son of David, the son of Abraham*, and then began to list Isaac and Jacob and all the rest in order. This is why the Apostle Paul here keeps naming them in turn and says, *The justification of God being attested by the law and the prophets*. Matt 1:1
Matt 1:1
Rom 3:21

But so that no one may say, "How are we to be saved if we contribute nothing on our part to what is set before us, namely, our salvation?" Paul shows that we make no small contribution to this —I mean by our faith. After Paul had said *the justification of God*, he adds *through faith to all and upon all who believe*. Again the Jew is upset and disturbed by this because he has no special honor compared to the rest of men, because he is counted in with the whole world. Therefore, so that the Jew may not feel this way, Paul again humbles him with fear when he goes on to say, *For there is no distinction, as all have sinned*. Rom 3:21
Rom 3:22
3:22–23

Do not say to me, "This man is a Greek; another is a Scythian; still another is a Thracian," for all are in the same state. If you have received the law, you have learned only one thing from the law, namely, to know sin. But you have not learned how to flee from it. Next, so that they may not say, "Even if we have sinned, we have not sinned in the same way as those men have sinned," Paul went on to add, *All are deprived of the glory of God*. Even if you have not committed the same sins as the others, you are deprived of glory just as the others are, because you are one of those who have offended God. But one who has committed offense does not belong Rom 3:23

---

thor of Heb in 10:38 —all to the same purpose.
268 Cf. Matt 1:1.
269 Cf. Matt 1:2–16.

with those who are glorified, but with those who have been put to shame and disgrace.

But be not afraid. The reason why I said these things was not that I might drive you to despair, but that I might show you the loving-kindness of our Master. This is why Paul went on to say, *They are justified as a free gift by His grace through the redemption that is in Christ Jesus, whom God has set forth as a propitiation by His blood through faith, to manifest His justice.* [Rom 3:24–25]

See by how many proofs Paul establishes what he has said. His first proof comes from the dignity and worthiness of the Person. For it is not man who is accomplishing these things in which he might fail. Rather, it is God, who can do all things. For as Paul says, justification belongs to God.[270] Second, we have proof from the law and the prophets. Do not be afraid because you have heard the words *apart from the law*, for surely the law itself approves of this. [Rom 3:21] Third, we have another proof from the sacrifices in the Old Testament. For it was on this account that Paul said *by His blood*, to recall to their minds those sheep and calves. [Rom 3:25] What Paul means is that if the slaughter of irrational animals removed sin, all the more will this blood of Christ do so. Nor did he simply say "through the ransoming," but *through the redemption*, so that we might never again return to that slavery. [Rom 3:24]

And for this same reason he calls it *forgiveness*,[271] so as to show that if the type possessed such great power, all the more will the reality show the same. Again, when Paul is making it clear that this is neither something new nor strange, he says *has set forth*. [Rom 3:25] And after Paul said *God has set forth*, and after he had shown that this was the work of the Father, Paul makes it clear that it is also the work [Rom 3:25]

---

270 Cf. Rom 3:4.
271 Cf. Rom 3:25. The Greek word is ἱλαστήριον. According to Louw and Nida, *Biblical Dictionary*, 40.12, ἱλασμός and ἱλαστήριον are the means by which sins are forgiven. See also 1 John 2:2: "αὐτὸς ἱλασμός ἐστιν περὶ τῶν ἁμαρτιῶν ἡμῶν" ("[Christ] Himself is the means by which our sins are forgiven"). This is the primary patristic use of the term. Some translations render ἱλαστήριον as "propitiation," which leads to a wrong interpretation of the term. Propitiation is essentially a process by which one does a favor to a person in order to make him or her favorably disposed, but in the NT God is never the object of propitiation. Unlike pagan sacrifices, the Jews offered sacrifice not in an attempt to gain the favor of God, but rather as a process of personal transformation that led to the forgiveness of their sins.

of the Son. For the Father foreordained it, but Christ, by His blood, successfully accomplished the whole redemption.

To manifest His justice. What is the manifestation of His justice? The manifestation of God's riches means that not only is God Himself rich, but also that He makes others rich. The manifestation of His life means that not only is He alive, but also that He makes the dead to live. And the manifestation of God's power means not only that He is powerful, but that He also makes the weak and feeble powerful. So also the manifestation of God's justice means not only that He Himself is just, but also that He suddenly makes others just, even when they have been corrupted by sin. Therefore, by way of explaining "manifestation," Paul himself went on to add, *So that God Himself is just and justifies him who believes in Jesus.* Rom 3:25

Rom 3:26

III

Therefore, feel no doubt. For justification comes not from works, but from faith. Do not flee from the justification of God, for it is a double blessing. Why? Because it is easy, and it lies open to all. Do not blush or feel ashamed. For if God Himself is shown as accomplishing this and, as someone might say, if He finds pride and takes pleasure in doing so, why do you slink away and hide yourself from that in which your Master is glorified? Therefore, after Paul raised the expectations of his hearers by saying that what has happened is a manifestation of God's justice, he again uses fear to urge anyone who is listening to him but who hesitates to come forward when he says *by remitting former sins.* Rom 3:25

Do you see how he constantly reminds them of their sins? He did this before when he said *For through the law comes the recognition of sin,*[272] and after that *Since all have sinned.*[273] But here his words are stronger. For Paul does not say "for your sins," but *by the remission,* that is, by the cessation of vital energy. For no longer was there hope for a return to a life that is healthy, but, like a paralyzed body, Rom 3:20

Rom 3:23

Rom 3:26

---

272 See §§ 11–12 of this homily.
273 See §§ 18–19 of this homily.

there was need for a helping hand from above. Such too was the state of a soul that was dead.

And what was indeed worse is that Paul laid this down as a charge and shows that it is a still stronger accusation. What is that accusation? The fact that the remission came through the long-suffering forbearance of God. What Paul means is this. You could not say that you did not find abundant forbearance and goodness. But the words *at the present time* point to One who is showing great forbearance and loving-kindness. For after we had despaired, Paul says, "and the time for sentencing had come, and our evils had increased, and our sins were seen in their fullness, at that moment God showed His power, so that you might learn how great is the abundance of His justice."

For if this had taken place in the beginning, it would not have seemed so wonderful and unexpected as it does now, when every manner of cure had been brought to the test and failed. Paul says, Rom 3:27 *Where then is your boasting? It has been shut out. By what law? The law of works? No, but by the law of faith.*[274] Paul is at pains to show that faith possesses such strength as was never even assumed for the law. For when he said that God justified man by faith, he is again attacking the law.

And he does not say, "Where, then, are the right actions of the Rom 3:27 Jews? Where is their just dealing?" Rather, he says, *Where is your boasting?* Everywhere he shows that they only talk big and boast as if they possessed something more than other men, even if they show no work to prove it. And after he said "Where then is your boasting?" Paul did not say "It has been put out of sight and is Rom 3:27 gone," but *It has been shut out*. And this being shut out expresses the idea that they boasted at the wrong time because such boasting no longer has a proper place or a suitable time.

After the judgment day has been set, those who wish to repent no longer have a proper time to repent. So now, when the sentence has been passed for the future, and all are about to perish, and He who would have freed them from these terrible things by His grace is present, they no longer have a proper time to put forward an amendment for reform based on the law. For if they had need

---

274 See RNT note ad loc.

to strengthen themselves, it should have been done before Christ's coming. But once He who would save by faith had come, the proper time for these efforts had been taken away. Because all had been found guilty, it is Christ, then, who saves by grace.

And this is why Christ came at the time He did, namely, so that they might not say that if He had come in the beginning, it would have been possible to find salvation through the law by their own efforts and good works. It was to stop up their shameless mouths that Christ delayed His coming for a long time so that, after it had been proved by every argument that they could not achieve salvation by themselves, He might save them by His grace. And this is also the reason why, after Paul had said before *to manifest his justice*,[275] he went on to add *at the present time*. Rom 3:25

But if some should contradict this, they are acting just as a man would act if he had committed a grievous wrong and had failed in his defense in court. But then, after he had been judged guilty and was about to be punished, he was set free by a royal pardon. He would be shameless if, after he was pardoned, he was to boast and say that he had done nothing wrong. The time to prove this was before he had received the pardon. Once it had come, the time would not have been a proper one for making such a boast. Indeed, this is what happened in the case of the Jews.

The Jews had betrayed themselves, and this was the reason why Christ came. And by His very coming, He took from them any reason for boasting. For it is the Jew who says that he is the teacher of children, who boasts in the law, and who calls himself an instructor of the unwise.[276] But he needs a Teacher and a Savior as much as the children and the unwise do. Therefore, he would have no excuse for boasting. For if even before this circumcision became uncircumcision, this is all the more true now, because it has been banished from both periods of time. But when Paul said *It has been shut out*, he shows how this was done. How was it shut out? "By what law? The law of works? No, but by the law of faith." Rom 3:27

---

275 See § 23 of this homily.
276 Cf. Rom 2:20. See Homily 5.4, 9–11.

IV

Rom 3:27 Notice that Paul also calls faith a law, because he is fond of dwelling on familiar words so as to soften any expression that might appear to be novel or strange. But what is *the law of faith?* It is to be saved by grace.[277] Here Paul also shows the power of God, because not only did God save, but He also justified and led men to boast[278] and exult. Nor did God have need of works, but looked only for faith. Paul tells us this because he is preparing the believing Jew to live a life of moderation, and he is calming down the unbelieving Jew in such a way as to attract him to the faith.

The man who has been saved was proud because he had observed the law. But now he will listen because he himself has stopped up his mouth, he has accused himself, he has renounced claims to his own salvation [based on the law], he has shut out and excluded boasting. And the man who has not believed will have been humbled because he has not rid himself of these same obstacles; and so he will be able to be brought over to the faith. Do you see how great is the superiority of faith, how it has removed us from the obstacles of old, how it does not permit us to boast of them?

Rom 3:28 *Therefore, we come to the conclusion that man is justified by faith, apart from the works of the law.* After Paul had shown that by faith they were superior to the Jews, he then goes on to discuss faith with great freedom and confidence. And again he offers a cure for what seemed at this point to upset the Jews. For these two things were disturbing them: first, that those who had not been saved by their works could be saved apart from works; and second, that justice was still served if the uncircumcised were to enjoy the same blessings as those who, for so long a time, had been nurtured in the law.

The second was far more upsetting to the Jews than the first difficulty. Therefore, because Paul had already established the truth of the first, he then went on to establish the second. This problem disturbed the Jews so much that, even after they had accepted the faith, they complained against Peter because of this question in

---

277 As opposed to being saved by the law.
278 "Boast" is here used in a good sense, not as in Rom 2:17, where "glory in God" means "boast loudly of God." See Homily 6.2.

HOMILY 7

the case of Cornelius and the events connected with his conversion.[279] So what does Paul say? *Therefore, we come to the conclusion that man is justified by faith, apart from the works of the law.* Rom 3:28

Paul did not say "a Jew," or "one subject to the law," but after he brought his discourse into a much broader scope and opened the doors of salvation to the whole world, he said *man*, using a name common to human nature. Taking his start from this, he answers a question that had not been brought forward. For it was likely that the Jews would take it in bad grace and be scandalized when they heard that faith justifies all men. So Paul went on to ask, *Is God the God of the Jews only?* This was just as if he were to say, "Why do you think it strange that every man be saved? God does not play favorites, does He?"[280] Rom 3:28, Rom 3:29

He showed from this that if they wished to threaten and abuse the Gentiles, they would be insulting the glory of God if they would not allow Him to be the God of all men. But if God is the God of all men, His providence extends to all. If His providence extends to all, in like manner, He saves all through faith. This is why Paul says, *Is God the God of the Jews only, and not the God of the Gentiles also? Indeed, He is also the God of the Gentiles.* For God does not play favorites, as the Greek myths say, but He is the one God common to all men. Therefore, Paul goes on to say, *For there is but one God.*[281] That is, the same God is the Master of Jews and Gentiles. Rom 3:29, Rom 3:30

But if you are speaking to me of the old times, even then God's providence was common to all, even if God exercised it in different ways. To you Jews a written law was given; the Gentiles had a law from nature. And the Gentiles had no less than you if, at least, they were willing to follow their law. In fact, they could have surpassed you. And Paul was hinting at this very thing when he went on to say, *who will justify the circumcised by faith and the uncircumcised through faith.* Rom 3:30

Paul was reminding them of what he had said earlier about uncircumcision and circumcision, where he showed that there was no difference. If there was no difference then, all the more is this

---

279 See Acts 10:11–18.
280 Cf. Rom 2:11. See Homily 5.43–45.
281 Therefore, the one God is the one way of salvation open to all men.

true now. And to establish this more clearly now, he shows that both states alike require faith. So Paul says, *Do we then abolish the law through faith? By no means! Rather, we establish the law.*[282]

Do you see how varied and indescribable Paul's judgment is? By the very words "we establish," he showed that the law was not then standing, but had been destroyed. Also note Paul's exceeding power and with what ease he proves what he wishes to prove. For here he shows that faith does not destroy the law, but even lends it a helping hand, just as the law itself had paved the way for faith. For just as the law bore witness to the faith by anticipating it —for Paul said, *being witnessed by the law and the prophets* —so faith established and confirmed the law when it had grown slack and weak.

How did the faith establish the law? This is a question you might ask. What was the work the law was to achieve? Why did this work cover everything? It was to make man just and righteous. But the law lacked the power to do this. As Paul put it, *For all have sinned*. But faith came and succeeded in making man just. For as soon as a man believed, he was also justified. Therefore, faith established the purpose of the law, and it brought to accomplishment that for which the law proposed to do all things. Therefore, faith did not make the law void, but brought it to completion.

So Paul here showed three things: first, that it was possible to be justified apart from the law; second, that the law lacked the power to do this; and third, that faith does not oppose the law. Because this especially upset the Jews, namely, that the faith seemed to be opposed to the law, Paul shows more than the Jew wished, namely, that not only was faith not opposed to the law, but even was a staunch ally of the law and worked hand in hand with it. And this was what the Jews especially wanted to hear.

V

But even after this grace by which we have been justified, we must still live a good life. So let us show our earnestness, an earnestness that is worthy of so great a gift. We shall show this if we keep watch

---

[282] That is, the law of faith does not annul the law, but rather confirms and upholds it. See RNT note on Rom 3:31.

over charity, the mother of all blessings, and do so with abundant zeal. This love for our fellow human beings is shown by more than mere words or greetings. It means guarding them and proving itself in deeds. For example, by easing poverty and want, by lending aid to the sick, by rescuing men from dangers, by standing by those in trouble, by weeping with those who mourn, by rejoicing with those who are glad.[283] For even this last is also a mark of fraternal love. Still, this rejoicing with those who rejoice seems to be a little thing; however, it is a very great thing and requires the spirit of true wisdom.

We might find many who accomplish the more irksome tasks but who are remiss when it comes to this rejoicing. Many weep with those who weep but no longer rejoice when others are glad. Instead, they shed tears when others are rejoicing. But this is because they feel malice and envy toward the man who is glad. So it is not a small duty to rejoice when your brother rejoices, but it is surely greater than shedding tears when he is sad. Perhaps it is not only greater than weeping with those who weep, but even greater than standing by those in danger.

In any event, there are many who have shared dangers with those who were in danger, but when their companions won esteem and fame, they felt the bite of envy. Such is the tyranny of a grudging heart. Although the dangers are a matter of toil and sweat, the envy is a matter of intent and free choice. Nevertheless, many who have endured the more irksome task have failed to accomplish a task that is easier than the one they endured. They waste away and are consumed when they see others held in honor, when they see an entire Church being of service either by preaching or in some other ministry.

What could be worse than this? No longer is such a person fighting against his brother; he is fighting against the will of God. When you have pondered this, rid yourself of this sickness. Even if you are unwilling to set your neighbor free, at least free yourself of these countless evils. Why do you wage war in your thoughts? Why do you fill your soul with tumult? Why do you stir up a storm? Why do you turn everything upside down? If your disposition is such,

---

283 Cf. Rom 12:15–21, a passage that summarizes the obligations of fraternal charity.

how will you ask for your sins to be forgiven? For if God does not forgive those who refuse to forgive the wrongs done to them, what kind of forgiveness will He grant to those who try to injure others who have done them no harm?

For this is a proof of the ultimate wickedness. Such men are fighting against the Church with the devil at their side. Perhaps [they are] even worse than the devil. For it is possible to be on one's guard against the devil. But these men have put on the mask of friendship; they are throwing themselves headfirst into the furnace, because they are sick with a disease that not only fails to rouse our pity, but even rouses us to ridicule them.

Why, tell me, do you turn pale? Why do you tremble? Why do you stand there timid and afraid? What dreadful thing has happened? Is it because your brother is honored, renowned, and esteemed? Then you should honor him, rejoice with him, and give glory to God, because a member of your own body is honored and esteemed. But you are grieving because God receives glory. Do you see the direction your war is taking? But the envious man says that it is not because God is receiving glory, but because my brother is. Yet it is through him that glory rises up to God, and so too will the war you are waging rise up against God. No, he says, this does not grieve me, but I did wish God to be glorified through me.

Therefore, rejoice with your brother because he is being esteemed. Then God receives glory a second time, and this second time he receives it through you. Everyone will say, "Blessed be God, who has servants of such a disposition that they are free from all envy and that they rejoice together over one another's blessings." And why do I speak of your brother? If he were both hostile to you and your foe, but if God were receiving glory from him, for this reason you should make him your friend. But you are making your friend an enemy because of the esteem in which he is held. Suppose someone should cure your body when you are sick—even if he were an enemy of yours, you would consider him one of your best friends thereafter. If there is someone who brings beauty to the body of Christ, that is, the Church, and who is a friend, will you count him as an enemy?

How could you show more clearly that you are waging war against Christ? On this account, even if someone works miracles; shows himself as a pattern for celibacy, for fasting, for making his bed on the bare ground; and all but outstrips the angels by these virtues, he will be more accursed than all men as long as he is in the grip of the vice of envy. He will be more a breaker of the law than the adulterer, the fornicator, and the robber of tombs.

VI

So that no one may charge me with excess in what I say, I would be glad to put this question to you. Suppose someone took up a burning torch and a mattock and then tore down and set fire to this church building and demolished this altar. Would not each one of those here present hurl stones at him because he was sacrilegious and a lawbreaker? Suppose, then, that someone carries in a flame that is much more destructive than the fire of the torch —I mean the flame of envy. This flame does not destroy buildings of stone, nor does it demolish an altar of gold.[284] But it does overthrow and destroy the instruction built up by the teachers, [an instruction] that is far more precious than walls and altars. What kind of forgiveness does this man deserve?

Let no one tell me that, even though he had often tried, he lacked the strength to succeed. For deeds are judged by the intention behind them. Saul did kill David, even though his intention to do so failed to be carried out.[285] Tell me, do you not think that you are plotting against the sheep of Christ when you wage war against the Shepherd? Are they not the sheep for whom Christ shed His blood and for whom He commanded us to do and suffer all things? Do you not remind yourself that your Master sought your glory and not His own?

If you were to seek His glory, then you would also find your own. But if you seek your own glory before His, then you will never enjoy a glory of your own. What then will be the remedy for this? Let us all pray together and let us lift up our voices as one in their behalf,

---

284 This probably means an altar adorned with decorations inlaid with gold.
285 Cf. 1 Sam (1 Kgdms) 19:10.

just as we would for the possessed. For surely these are in a more miserable state than those dwelling with demons within them, inasmuch as their madness is a self-chosen one.[286]

For this sickness stands in need of much prayer and supplication. If a man does not love his brother, even though he empties out his wealth, even though he is made shining by martyrdom, he wins no advantage from these. Consider how great a punishment that man would deserve if he waged war against another who has done him no harm. This man is worse than the Gentiles. For if loving those who love us does not give us any advantage over the Gentiles, on what level will we put the man who envies those who love him? Tell me that.

Surely being envious is worse than waging war. Why? Because once the reason for the war has been removed, he who was waging it puts aside his hatred. But the envious man would never become a friend. The warrior shows himself in open battle; the envious man fights his foe under cover. The one who wages war can often assign a reasonable cause for the conflict; the man who is eaten with envy can give no other reason than his madness and an intention inspired by Satan.

To what, then, could such a soul be compared? To what kind of viper? To what kind of asp? To what kind of worm? To what kind of beetle? For there is nothing more accursed, nothing more pernicious, than a soul of this sort. For envy has subverted churches; it has begotten heresies. It has put weapons in the hands of a brother;[287] it has caused those hands to be dipped in the blood of a just man.[288] It has torn away the laws of nature; it has opened the doors to death. It brought God's curse into action. It did not allow that miserable man to recall his mother's birth pangs, or his parents, or anything else. But it brought him to such a pitch of frenzy and led

---

286 See Harkins, *St. John Chrysostom: Baptismal Instructions*, ACW 31, pp. 84, 85, 256, 258, 272. In speaking of possession by demons and in comparing it to the evil of drunkenness, the many involuntary evils of mind and body that result from diabolic possession deserve our pity and tears, but we scoff at the drunkard because his evil is self-chosen. So too envy is a self-chosen madness and a pernicious curse that warrants no pardon or excuse.

287 The "brother" whom Chrysostom chooses to exemplify envy is Cain.

288 The "just man" is Cain's younger brother, Abel, whom Cain murdered because he envied him.

him to such madness that he did not even give in when God called him and said, *To you shall he submit, and you shall rule over him.*[289]   Gen 4:7 (LXX)

Yet God did not remit the charge against him, nor did he subject his brother to him. But still his disease was so incurable that even though countless medications were applied, the putrefaction continued to gush forth. Why, you most miserable of all men, does your ailment keep harassing you? Is it because God has received honor? Rather, this is a mark of a mind possessed by Satan. Is it because your brother surpassed you in esteem? But it is possible for you in turn to surpass him. So if you wish to win out, do not kill him, do not destroy him.

Rather, let him go and keep on living, so that the basis for your struggle may continue; surpass him while he still lives. For in this way the crown of glory is going to be yours. But if you slay him now, you are passing a sentence of defeat against yourself. But envy recognizes none of these arguments. Why do you love glory in the midst of so vast a solitude? For they were the only ones dwelling upon the earth at that time. But not even that held him back. He threw everything out of his soul. He took his stand with the devil and stationed himself in Satan's ranks. For the devil led the forces on the side of Cain.

Because it did not satisfy Satan that man was subject to death, he tried to make it a greater tragedy by the way man died. So he persuaded Cain to slay his own brother. For he was in haste and in anguish to see the sentence carried into act, because he was never satisfied with our human ills. For at that time the devil was just like a man who had his enemy in prison. Even after he had seen this enemy sentenced to death, but before he was taken outside the city for execution, Satan would hurry to see him slaughtered within the walls because he could not wait for the suitable time for the sentence to be carried out. Even though the devil had heard that man will return to dust,[290] he was in anguish to see something worse, namely, a son dying before his father died, a brother slaying his brother, and an untimely and violent slaughter.

---

289 Here God even assures Cain of his right of primogeniture. Cain's envious action shows us that we must not envy our brothers, by which he means not only kinsmen, but also fellow members of Christ's mystical body.
290 Cf. Gen 3:19.

VII

Do you see to what great evils envy lends its aid? Do you see how it filled to the full the insatiable heart of the devil? Do you see what sort of banquet table it set before Satan? Do you see how enormous a feast he desired to see? Let us flee from this sickness of envy. For it is not possible —no, it cannot be —that we will escape that fire prepared for the devil unless we are set free from this disease. But we shall be set free if we keep in mind how much Christ has loved us and how He commanded us to love one another.

How much did Christ love us? He gave His precious blood on our behalf, even though we were His enemies and had done the greatest wrongs to Him. You must also do this to your brother. This is why Christ said, *A new commandment I give you, that you love one another just as I have loved you.* Indeed, the measure of His love did not stop here. For Christ did this on behalf of His enemies. Are you unwilling to shed your blood on your brother's behalf?[291]

Why is it then that you shed even your brother's blood,[292] because you are disobeying Christ's commandment in a way diametrically opposed to it? Christ did not do what He did as if it were a debt He owed. But if you do it, you are fulfilling an obligation. When that servant who had contracted a debt of ten thousand talents then demanded the one hundred denarii owed to him, he was punished.[293] It was not only because he made this demand of his fellow servant, but because, even in spite of the kindness done to him, he had not become a better man and he failed to follow the example of his master, who led the way and forgave his debt.

After all, it was a debt that the servant owed, if indeed it was a debt. Surely all that we do, we do in payment of a debt. So it was that Christ said, *When you have done everything, say, 'We are unprofitable servants: we have done what we were under an obligation to do.'* If, then, we will show our love, if we give money to those in need, we

---

291 We must not envy our brothers as Cain did. In fact, we must not envy our neighbors, whom we must love as we love ourselves. All Christians are our brothers in Christ. Therefore we must be ready to shed our blood for them and our neighbors, not because they are enemies, but because they are kinsmen.
292 Your brother is not only a kinsman (as Cain was to Abel), but also a fellow member of Christ's mystical body.
293 Cf. Matt 18:24–34.

are satisfying a debt, not only because Christ led the way in doing good, but also, if ever we do give, we are distributing the goods that are His.

Why then do you deprive yourself of the goods over which He wished you to be the master? For He commanded you to give these goods to another, so that you might have them yourself. As long as you alone possess them, you do not have them yourself. But when you give them to another, then you yourself receive them. There is nothing that could match this token of love, is there? Christ himself poured out His blood on behalf of His enemies; but we do not pour out our money on behalf of our Benefactor. He poured out His own blood; but we do not pour out the money that is not our own. He did so before us; we fail to do so even after He gave us an example. He did so for our salvation; we fail to do so even for our own benefit and advantage. No profit comes to Christ from our love for mankind, but the entire advantage accrues to us.

This is the reason why we are commanded to give our goods away, namely, so that we may not be deprived of them. For it is just as if someone should give a silver piece to a little child; he bids the child to hold on to it tightly, or to give it to a servant to keep and guard, so that it cannot be snatched away by anyone who wishes to steal it. So it is that God does with us. For Christ is telling us, "Give your goods to someone in need so that no one may steal them from you —for example, no calumniator; no devil; no thief; nor, after all the others, death. For as long as you hold on to it yourself, you are not safe in holding on to it. But if you give your goods to Me through the poor, I will guard them all carefully for you and, at the fitting time, I will restore them to you with an abundant increase. I do not receive your goods to take them away from you. Rather, I receive them to increase them, to guard them more carefully, and to save them for you until that time when there is no one who lends at interest or can be moved by pity."

What then would be crueler than we would be if after such promises we did not permit ourselves to lend our goods to Christ? Indeed, this is why we would go to Him destitute, naked and, poor, without the goods committed to us. Why is that? It is because we did not entrust our goods to Him who would guard them more carefully than anyone else. And so we shall pay the ultimate penalty.

For when we are accused, what shall we be able to say to avoid our own self-destruction? What pretext can we put forward? What defense can we offer? For what reason did you refuse to give? Did you not believe that you would get it back again? How could this make sense? Because Christ has given to one who has given nothing, how much more will He give after He has received?

Does the sight of your possessions give you pleasure? Give them away all the more on this account, because in heaven they will give you greater delight, because in heaven no one will take them away. But if you hold on to them here on earth, you will suffer countless evils. The devil leaps upon rich men just as a dog jumps on a child who is holding a morsel or a cake to tear it away from him.

Therefore, let us give our possessions to the Father. If the devil sees this happening, he will immediately retreat. Then, when the devil is gone, the Father will give all these goods back to you safe and sound, because the devil cannot cause a disturbance in the world to come. For the rich are no different from little children who are being troubled and disturbed by little dogs. The puppies are all yapping around the youngsters, and they keep snapping and tearing at their clothes. Only the rich are troubled not only by men, but also by their baser passions, by gluttony, drunkenness, fawning flattery, and every sort of licentiousness.

If we have to lend money, we search with the greatest care for those who pay good interest and are fair in their dealings. But when it comes to squandering our goods, we do quite the opposite. We pass God by, even though He is fair in His dealings and offers in return not a hundredth part, but rather gives a hundred times as much. Instead, we seek out those who will not even pay back the principal.

VIII

Our belly uses up the larger portion of our resources. But what does it give back? Dung and corruption. What does vainglory give back? Envy and malice. What do stinginess and thrift give back?

Care and worry. What does licentiousness give back? Gehenna and the venomous worm. These are the debtors of the rich, and, as interest on the principal, they pay off with evils in this world and with dread things to be expected in the next. Tell me, shall we make a loan to them with such punishment as interest? Shall we not entrust our possessions to Christ, who holds out to us heaven, immortal life, and ineffable blessings?

What excuse will we have? Why do you not give to Him who will by all means give to us and who will give back in greater abundance? Perhaps it is because a long time will pass before He repays. However, He surely repays us in this life too. For He is not lying when He says, *Seek the kingdom of heaven and all these things shall be given you besides.* Matt 6:33 Do you see His excessive liberality? For He is saying that those goods have been kept and do not become less; these goods on earth I give by way of an increase and addition. But, besides these gifts, the fact that you will not receive the others for a long time is going to make your wealth greater, because the interest increases it.

Surely we see this in the case of those who borrow money. A moneylender makes the loan more readily to those who pay it back after a long time. For a borrower who pays off a loan quickly cuts off the progressive increase of the interest. But when a man holds on to the money that he has borrowed for a longer time, this then makes the profit from it grow larger. So we are not offended at the delay in the case of men; we even contrive to make the delay longer. Shall we, in the case of God, be so small-minded in our disposition that, because we must wait for heaven, we shrink back and avoid giving of our goods?

And yet, as I said, God does give a return here on earth and, along with the reason of which I spoke, because He is arranging for another and still greater return, the entire amount is being stored up in heaven. For the abundance of what is given and the beauty of that gift far transcend the worthless life we live on earth. Why? Because while we are in a corruptible and perishable body, we cannot receive those crowns that never fade. Nor in the present course of life, which is turbulent, confused, and open to many changes, can we receive that rest that cannot change and cannot know confusion.

Suppose someone owed you money but at the time you were living in a foreign land. Suppose you had no servants who could transport the money to where you were then living. If your debtor promised to repay the loan, would you not have exhorted him in countless ways not to pay it off while you were in the foreign land rather than in your own country? But do you think it is right to receive those ineffable spiritual blessings here on earth? What madness this would be! If you receive them in this world, you will receive what is certainly corruptible. If you wait for the time that is suitable, God will give you goods that are incorruptible and cannot be contaminated. If you receive them on earth, you will have gotten lead; if you receive them in heaven, you will get pure gold.

But God has not deprived you of all the blessings of this life. For along with that promise of which I spoke, He made another promise when He said, *Everyone who loves the things of heaven will receive a hundredfold in this life and will inherit life eternal.* If we do not receive the hundredfold, we are the ones to blame, because we did not give a loan to Him who can give back so much. For as many as give have received that much, even though what they give is little.

<small>Matt 19:29</small>

Tell me this. What great amount did Peter give? Was it not only a broken net, a fishing rod, and a fish hook? But still God opened to him the houses of the whole world, spread before him land and sea, and all men invited him to share their possessions. Rather, they sold what they had and brought what they had gotten, and laid it at his feet.[294] They did not put it in his hands—they were not so bold as to do that—because they showed him such great honor along with their munificence.

"But that was Peter," you will say. So what does that mean, sir? For this promise was not made to Peter alone. Christ did not say, "You alone, Peter, shall receive the hundredfold," but *Everyone who has left his home or his brothers shall receive a hundredfold.* For Christ did not recognize any distinction of persons, but only the merits of deeds rightly done. Someone may say that the throng of his children stands around him. "I wish to leave them well off. Why

<small>Matt 19:29</small>

---

294 Cf. Acts 4:34–36; 5:1–11. See RNT note on Acts 5:1–11.

should I make them paupers?" If you leave them all you have, again you are turning over all you possess to precarious guards. But if you leave God as their joint heir and trustee, you have left them countless treasures.

When we seek vengeance for ourselves, God does not come to our aid. But when we entrust ourselves to His hands, we receive more than we expect. The same thing happens in the case of possessions. If we are overly concerned about them, God will stop having concern for them. But if we throw our whole concern on God, He will set both our possessions and our children in all security.

And why do you wonder if this happens in the case of God? For you might see it happen even with men. If you are dying and do not ask any of your relatives to take care of your children, it often happens that a kinsman, who is more than willing to step forward of his own accord, is apt to blush and feel ashamed to do so. But if you put the care of your children upon him, just as if he had been highly honored, he will of himself give the greatest recompense in return.

IX

If, then, you wish to leave great wealth to your children, leave them the care that God gives. While you did nothing, God gave you a soul, shaped your body, and favored you with life. When He sees that you are showing such good character and conduct by apportioning their possessions to the Lord Himself along with them, how will God fail to open to them the door to every kind of riches? After Elijah was nourished with a little bit of meal, he then saw that the woman honored him before her children. So he made threshing floors and oil presses appear in the little house of the widow.[295] Think how much kindliness and friendliness the Lord of Elijah will show forth and make manifest.

Therefore, let us not consider how we may leave our children rich, but how we may leave them virtuous. For if they put their confidence in their wealth, they will care about nothing else, because they can cover up the wickedness of their ways with the abundance

---

295 1 Kgs (3 Kgdms) 17:10–16.

of their riches. But if they see themselves stripped of the comfort that comes from wealth, they will do everything so that they may find for themselves much consolation in poverty, because they are virtuous. Therefore, do not leave them wealth, so that you may leave them virtue.

For it would be a mark of the greatest madness not to make them masters of our wealth while we are still alive, but, after we have died, to give full freedom to the easy-going nature of the young. Surely, while we are still alive, we will be able to demand an accounting, to correct them, and to curb them if they are making bad use of their possessions. But after our death, when they have lost us, and while they are still young, we would be giving them the power that wealth brings. We would be pushing our unfortunate and miserable children over countless precipices, we would be heaping fire on fire, and we would be letting oil drip into a fierce furnace.

So, if you wish to leave them your wealth with safety, leave them God as their debtor and put in His hands what you have written in your will as their bequests. If they receive your money, they do not know to whom they will give it. But they will find many scheming and unfeeling people. If you take your possessions before you die and lend them to God, your treasure remains free from plunder, and repayment will be made with great ease. For when God pays back to us what He owes, He is pleased with us, well pleased. He looks with a more favorable eye on those who have made loans to Him than on those who have not done so. And He loves most those to whom He owes the most.

So if you wish to have God as your constant friend, make Him your debtor for many loans. For a lender does not rejoice as much because he has debtors as Christ is glad because He has those who lend to Him. Christ flees from those to whom He owes nothing, but He runs after those to whom He owes debts. Therefore let us do everything so that we may have Him as our Debtor. For this is the suitable time for those who make loans to Him, and Christ now stands in need.[296]

---

296 In the persons of the poor and the needy.

For if you will not give to Him now, Christ will not ask of you after you leave this life. For it is here on earth that He thirsts; it is here on earth that He hungers. He is thirsty because He thirsts for your salvation. For this is the reason why He begs, this is the reason why He goes about naked: He is working to bring immortal life to you. Therefore, do not ignore Him. He does not wish to be nourished, but to nourish; He does not wish to be clothed, but to clothe and to furnish you with that golden garment, the robe of royalty.

Do you not see that the more caring kind of physicians, when washing the sick, also wash themselves, even if they do not need cleansing? In the same way, Christ does everything for you because you are sick. On this account, when He makes a demand of you, He uses no violence, so that He may give you an abundant return and so that you may learn that He does not ask of you because He has need of you, but because He is attending to your need for Him. And so He comes to you dressed in cheap garb and with outstretched hand. If you should give Him a small coin, He would not turn away; even if you scorn Him, He does not leave you, but He comes back to you again. For He loves us and strongly desires our salvation.

Therefore, let us hold money in scorn so that we may not be scorned by Christ. Let us hold money in scorn so that we may gain the money itself. For if we keep careful guard over it in this world, we shall lose it entirely, both here and hereafter. If we are very generous in lending it out, we shall enjoy plentiful wealth in both lives. If a man wishes to become rich, let him become poor so that he may become rich. Let him spend so that he may collect. Let him scatter so that he may gather.

If this sounds strange and unexpected, look at the sower of seeds. Consider that he will not be able, in any other way, to gather more if he will not scatter what he has and if he will not give freely of what is ready at hand. And so let us sow our seed and cultivate heaven, so that we may reap with great profit and find eternal blessings by the grace and loving-kindness of our Lord Jesus Christ, with whom be to the Father, together with the Holy Spirit, glory, power, and honor, now and forever, world without end. Amen.

HOMILY 8

Rom 4:1–2

*What then shall we say that Abraham,
our father in faith according to the flesh, found?
For if Abraham was justified by works, he has reason for
boasting, but not in relation to God.*[297]

When Paul said that the world had become guilty before God, that all had sinned, and that it was possible to be saved only through faith, he was eager to show that this salvation was not a matter for feeling shame, but rather a cause for shining glory, a glory that is greater than that which comes from deeds. Because a salvation that involves any feeling of shame brings with it some despondency, Paul removes any suspicion of this for the future, although he had already hinted at this when he called it not only salvation, but also justification. Indeed he said,

Rom 1:17 *For in it the justification of God is revealed.*[298]

For he who is saved in this way has confidence along with salvation because he is just. And Paul speaks not only of justification, but also of the manifestation of God; for God is revealed in things that are glorious, shining, and great. Paul also establishes this from the topic that he is now discussing, using questions to advance his argument. This was his usual method, because it makes his point clear and shows his confidence in what he is saying. Surely he did

Rom 3:1; 9 this earlier when he said, *What advantage then remains to the Jew?*[299]
Rom 3:27 And: *Are we better off than they are?* And again: *Where then is your boast-*
Rom 4:1–2 *ing? It has been shut out.*[300] And here he says, *What then shall we say of Abraham, our father?*

---

[297] In this homily Chrysostom will expand on Paul's treatment of the significance of the faith of Abraham. Paul also discusses this significance in Gal 3:6–18.
[298] See Homily 2.62–65.
[299] See. Homily 6.34.
[300] See Homily 7.27–28.

Because the Jews kept constantly turning over in their minds the fact that this patriarch and friend of God was the first to receive circumcision, Paul also wishes to point out that Abraham received justification from faith. And this provided Paul with a great advantage for winning a victory over the Jews. For it was not unlikely that a man who had done no good works might receive justification from faith. But when a man who is adorned with good deeds is justified not from his works, but by his faith, this is a source of wonder and is also a very strong proof of the power of faith.

Therefore, Paul passed by all the others and brought his discussion back to this man. And he called him "our father according to the flesh." In this way he casts the Jews out of genuine relationship with Abraham and paves the way for the Gentiles to have the rights of kinship with him. For Paul then says, *For if Abraham was justified by works, he has reason for boasting, but not in relation to God.* Rom 4:2

Therefore, after Paul said that *God justifies the circumcision by faith and the uncircumcision through faith,*"[301] and after he had given sufficient proof of this earlier, he now gives through Abraham a stronger proof than he had promised; he wages the battle for faith as opposed to works and makes this just man the subject of the whole contest. And Paul had a reason for doing this. Therefore, he sets Abraham on a lofty level when he calls him *our father* by putting on the Jews the obligation of heeding him in all things. Rom 3:30 · Rom 4:1

For, Paul says, do not tell me about the Jewish people, and do not bring forward this one and that one. For I will go to the head of all Jews, the one from whom circumcision took its beginning. For Paul goes on to say, *If Abraham was justified by works, he has reason for boasting, but not in relation to God.* What is said here is not clear, so we must make it clearer. For there are two kinds of boasting: one from works, and the other from faith. Rom 4:2

Therefore, after Paul said, *If Abraham was justified by works, he had reason for boasting, but not in relation to God,* he showed that Abraham could have a reason for boasting from faith, which is a much stronger reason. For Paul's great power is shown in the fact that he turned the objection to the opposite meaning. For he shows that what belonged to salvation by works, namely, reason for boasting Rom 4:2

---

301 See Homily 7.39.

and the free expression of it, belongs much more to salvation by faith. For the man who boasts in his good works can set before himself his own labors. But the man who prides himself on his faith in God shows forth a much greater basis for boasting inasmuch as he is glorifying and magnifying the Lord.

For when he accepted on faith in God things that the visible world did not suggest to him, he showed genuine love for God and heralded forth the splendors of God's power. But this is a mark of a most generous soul, of a philosophical spirit,[302] and of a lofty mind. For to avoid stealing and murdering marks the ordinary man. But to believe that God can do the impossible requires a soul of a noble nature and one that is earnestly disposed toward God. And this is also a sign of genuine love. The man who keeps the commandments surely honors God, but he who seeks and follows wisdom through faith, and who has accepted the correct judgment about God, has glorified Him and has revealed a greater esteem than that which is shown through works.

Therefore, the boasting that comes from obedience is the boasting of one who does the right thing; the boasting that is rooted in faith glorifies God and belongs entirely to God. For the man who believes bases his boasting on the great things he holds in his mind about God, things that redound to the glory of God. This is why Paul says that the man of faith has reason for boasting in relation to God. This is not the only reason, but there is also another. Not only does the man of faith boast because he sincerely loves God, but also because he has enjoyed great honor and love from God.

For just as this man has loved God because he held in his mind great thoughts about God —for this is a proof of love —so also has God loved him, even though the man is accountable for countless sins, because God has not only freed him from punishment, but has also made him just. Therefore, the man of faith has reason to boast because he was deemed deserving of great love.

Rom 4:3–4; See Gen. 15:6; Gal. 3:6

For what does Scripture say? 'Abraham believed God, and it was credited to him as justice.' Now to him who works, the reward is not credited to

---

302 In Christian writings the "philosophical spirit" means the spirit of the man who chooses the Christian way to guide his life.

him as a favor, but as something due.[303] Is not that which is credited as a debt, therefore, the greater? Someone might ask this question. My answer would be: "By no means!" Why? Because the greater reward is credited to the one who believes. But it would not have been credited unless he had made some contribution himself.

II

And so this man too has God as his debtor —not because God owes him ordinary things, but rather things that are great and lofty. For to show his sublimity of mind and spiritual understanding, Paul does not simply say "to the man who believes," but *to the man who believes in Him who justifies the impious.*[304] It is the faith of such a man that is credited as justification. For consider how great a blessing it is to believe and to be fully assured that God can not only immediately free from punishment that man who has lived in impiety, but can even make him just and deem him deserving of those immortal honors. [Rom 4:5]

Therefore, do not think that this man is less deserving because this gift was not credited by grace to the other man —the man of works. For this is the very reason that makes the man of faith glorious, namely, the fact that he is enjoying such a great grace and manifesting such great faith. And see too that the recompense is greater. Wages and rewards are given to the man of works; justification is given to the man of faith.[305] And justification is a recompense that embraces most fully many rewards.

After Paul showed this from the case of Abraham, he brings in David to support with his vote what has been said. What then does David say? Whom does he call blessed? Is it the man who toiled in doing works? Or is it the man who had received grace, the man who had rejoiced in forgiveness and won this gift?[306] When I speak of blessedness, I mean the peak of all blessings. Just as justification

---

303 See RNT note on vv. 2–5.
304 Cf. RNT note *ad loc.*
305 Cf. Rom 4:6–8. The absence of meritorious deeds presents no obstacle to justification by God. See Fitzmyer, *JBC*, 53:45.
306 I.e., through baptism.

is greater than the reward of wages, so blessedness is greater than justification.[307]

After Paul had shown that justification was better not only because Abraham had received it, but also by reasoning (for Paul says, *He has reason for boasting, but not in relation to God*), again Paul makes clear in another way that justification is more august and sublime. He did this when he brought in David, who supported this position by his vote. For David calls the man who has been justified "blessed" when he says, *Blessed are they whose iniquities are forgiven*.[308] And Paul seems to be bringing in a witness who gives a testimony that does not suit his purpose. For David did not say, "Blessed are they whose faith was credited as justification."

But Paul brings in this verse from the Psalm on purpose, not by mistake, so that he may show the greater superiority of justification. For if he is blessed who has received forgiveness from grace, much more so is the man who has received justification and has manifested his faith. But where there is blessedness, from there all shame has been taken away, and glory is there in abundance. For blessedness increases rewards and glory.[309]

What then is the advantage of the man of works? Paul does state this, but without writing it down. For he says, *Now to him who works, the reward of wages is not credited to him as a favor*.[310] But what gives the man of faith priority in rank Paul proves by a written testimony when he quotes David as his witness by saying, *Blessed are they whose iniquities are forgiven and whose sins are covered over*.[311]

Someone may ask, "Why do you say that you receive forgiveness not as something owed, but according to grace?" See my reason. I say this because it is this person who is called blessed. And David would not have called him blessed unless he saw that this person was enjoying grace in abundance.[312] And Paul did not say, "This

---

307 Cf. Rom 4:9 and RNT note *ad loc*. See also § 20 of this homily. Cf. also Homily 5.73, Homily 7.61–62, and Hom 9.50-52. See also discussion on "love" as used by Chrysostom in Papageorgiou, "A Theological Analysis," chap. 2, pp. 106–113.
308 Cf. Rom 4:7.
309 Cf. § 20 of this homily.
310 The laborer working for wages has a strict right to his pay.
311 Cf. Rom 4:7.
312 Cf. Rom 4:6–7.

HOMILY 8

forgiveness, then, does not hold good for the circumcision." What does he say? *Does this blessedness (which was greater) hold good only for the circumcision, or also for the uncircumcised?* [Rom 4:9]

For the question that Paul is now asking is with whom this good and great thing is to be found. Is it with the circumcision or with the uncircumcision? And see how superior it is. For Paul is showing not only that it does not shun the uncircumcision, but was even happy to dwell with the uncircumcision before the circumcision began to exist. Because David, who called the forgiven sinner blessed, was himself circumcised and was speaking to those who were circumcised, see how pertinacious Paul was in his effort to apply David's words to the uncircumcised.

For after Paul had joined blessedness to justification and had shown that both are one and the same, he asks how Abraham had received justification. For if blessedness belongs to the just man, and Abraham had received justification, let us see how Abraham had received it. Was it while he was still uncircumcised, or after he was circumcised? Paul says that Abraham was still uncircumcised.[313]

How then was justification credited to him? When he was in the state of circumcision, or in that of uncircumcision? Not in circumcision, but in uncircumcision. For we say that to Abraham *faith was credited as justice.* [Rom 4:3] After Paul had just mentioned the Scripture (for he had said, *For what does Scripture say? 'Abraham believed God, and it was credited to him as justification'*),[314] here he goes on to accept the judgment of the speakers, and to show that justification came to Abraham when he was still uncircumcised. [Rom 4:3]

Next, from this Paul solves another objection that was lifting its head. For someone might say that if Abraham was justified while he was still uncircumcised, why was circumcision brought in? Paul says, *He received the sign and seal of the justification of the faith, which he had when he was uncircumcised.*[315] Do you see how Paul showed that the Jews, rather than the uncircumcised, were in the ranks of parasites[316] and that they were added to the uncircumcised [Rom 4:11]

---

313 Cf. Rom 4:10–11.
314 See Gen 15:6.
315 For baptism as the seal of the Christian soldier, cf. Jean Daniélou, *The Bible and the Liturgy* (Notre Dame, IN: University of Notre Dame Press, 1956), 58–59.
316 "Parasites" were flatterers who stayed as dinner guests at a host's table —wheth-

Gentiles? For if Abraham, while he was still uncircumcised, received justification and a crown, but later received circumcision, then the Jews came in later. Therefore, Abraham is the father of the uncircumcised who belong to him by faith, and then the father of those in the circumcision.[317] And so Abraham is the ancestor of two families.

Do you see how faith brings light? Until faith came the patriarch did not receive justification. Do you see that uncircumcision posed no hindrance? Surely he was not hindered from being justified before he was circumcised. Therefore, circumcision is later than faith.

III

And why do you wonder if circumcision is later than faith when it is certainly later than uncircumcision? Not only is circumcision later than faith, but it is also far inferior to faith. It is as far inferior as is the sign to the reality of which it is the sign, for example, as the seal is to the soldier.[318] You may ask why Abraham needed a seal. He did not need one himself. Why then did he receive it? So as to be the common father both of those who believed in uncircumcision and of those who believed in circumcision.

But it is not without qualification that Paul says this of those who believe in circumcision. This is why he went on to say, *Not merely of those who are circumcised*. For if Abraham is father of the uncircumcised, he is not father because he was uncircumcised, even though he received justification while he was still uncircumcised, but because they emulated his faith. And so much less will he be forefather of the circumcised because he was circumcised, unless faith should be added. For as Paul says, Abraham received circumcision so that both of us might have him as our ancestor, and so that the uncircumcised might not cast aside the circumcised.[319]

Rom 4:12

---

er invited to share his hospitality or not.
317 Cf. Rom 4:11–12.
318 See Harkins, *John Chrysostom: Baptismal Instructions*, 338. The sign of the cross is not only the brand that marks us as belonging to the flock of Christ, but it is also the seal that shows that we are enlisted in His army.
319 Several manuscripts read, "So that the circumcised might not cast aside the un-

Do you see how the uncircumcised had him as an ancestor first? But if circumcision is something august and holy because it preaches justice, the uncircumcision still has no small preeminence, because it received justice before the circumcision did. Therefore, you Jews will be able to have Abraham as your forefather at the time when you walk in the footsteps of faith,[320] when you are not contentious or obstinate, and when you do not start quarrels by bringing in the law. Tell me, Paul, of what faith are you speaking? *Of the faith that was Abraham's while he was still uncircumcised.*   Rom 4:12

Again Paul tries to calm down the haughtiness of the Jews by reminding them of the time of Abraham's justification. And he does well to remind them of "the footsteps," so that, just as Abraham did, you Jews may believe in the resurrection of the bodies of those who have died. For Abraham surely showed that he believed in this. So if you Jews reject uncircumcision, learn for sure that neither do you gain any help from circumcision. Unless you follow in the footsteps of faith, even if you have been circumcised ten thousand times, you will not be a descendant of Abraham. For he too received circumcision for this reason, namely, that a man who was circumcised might not cast you out. So do not demand this of him too.[321] For this was to be a help for you, not for Abraham.

But, someone objects, this was a sign of justification. At that time you were in need of bodily signs; now there is no need for these. Then the objection is raised: "Was it not possible to learn the virtue of his soul from his faith?" Yes, it was possible, but you needed this additional sign. Because you did not imitate his virtue, nor could you see it, circumcision was given to you as a visible sign. The reason for this was so that, once you grew accustomed to this seal on the body, you might also, little by little, be led to the true love of wisdom in the soul. Also, when you had zealously accepted this as a great privilege, you might learn to imitate and revere your ancestor.

Not only did God prepare you for this in the matter of circumcision, but also in all the other things. I mean, for example, the

---

circumcised, nor the uncircumcised cast aside the circumcised."
320 Cf. Rom 4:12.
321 Cf. the variant reading mentioned in note 27 above.

sacrifices, the Sabbaths, and the festivals.[322] To show that it was for your sake that Abraham received circumcision, listen to what follows. After Paul said that Abraham received it as a sign and a seal, he also set down the reason when he said, *That he might become the father of the circumcised*, that is, of those who received circumcision of the spirit as well. So that if you have only the circumcision of the flesh, nothing more will come to you.

For this circumcision of the flesh is only a sign when the reality of which this is the sign appears on you, that is, faith. If you do not have faith, this sign cannot be a sign. For of what will it be a sign, of what will it be a seal, since there is nothing to be sealed? It is much as if you show us a purse with a seal on it when there is nothing inside the purse. That kind of circumcision is ridiculous if there is no faith inside. For if it is the sign of justification but you do not have justification, neither then do you have the sign of justification.

For the reason why you received this sign was so that you might seek the reality of which you have the sign. But if you were going to seek only the sign and not the reality, you would have no need for a sign. Circumcision, however, is a sign of justification not only for the circumcised, but for the uncircumcised as well. Therefore it is a sign of nothing other than that there is no need for circumcision. *For if they who are of the law are heirs, faith is made empty, the promise is made void.*[323]

Paul has proved that faith is necessary, that it is older than circumcision, that it is stronger than the law, and that it establishes the law. For if all have sinned, faith is necessary; if Abraham received justification before he was circumcised, faith is older; if knowledge of sin comes through the law but was made evident apart from the law, faith is stronger; if the law has borne testimony to faith, and if faith established the law, faith is not opposed to the law, but is a friend and ally of the law.

Paul showed again and from another source that it was also impossible to receive the inheritance through the law. For after he

---

322 All these were most important in Jewish cultic worship.
323 According to verses 14–17, the promise cannot be through the law. That would annul faith and completely destroy the promise.

HOMILY 8

compared the inheritance with the law and after carrying off the prizes of victory, he again brings it into contrast with the law when he says, *For if they who are of the law are heirs, faith is made empty.* So that no one may say that it is possible to have faith and to observe the law, he shows that it cannot be done. For the man who clings to the law as if it has the power to save him dishonors the strength and force of faith. That is why he says, *Faith is made empty*, that is, there is no need for salvation through grace. For then it cannot show the power that belongs to it. *And the promise is made void.* Perhaps the Jew might say, "Why do I need faith?" If, then, this were true, the things that were promised would be taken away along with faith.[324]   Rom 4:14

IV

See how Paul is doing battle with the Jews in everything that came from the patriarch in the days of old. For after he showed from this source that justification was joined to faith in the inheritance, he also shows that the promise was joined to them in like manner. Paul wanted to keep the Jew from saying, "What do I care if Abraham received justification through faith?"[325] So Paul says, "Then what does make a difference to you, I mean the promise of the inheritance, cannot come into act apart from justification through faith." And that caused them the greatest fright.

The Jew may ask of what promise Paul is speaking. Of the promise that Abraham will be the heir of the world and that in him all his posterity will be blessed. And how is this promise made void? Paul says, *Because the law works wrath, for where there is no law, neither is there transgression.*[326] But if the law works wrath and makes   Rom 4:15

---

324 Cf. Homily 4.14.
325 Paul wishes to emphasize that Abraham received justification, but not through any dependence on the law. If the Jew should insist that to him Paul's position makes no difference, Paul frightens him by further insisting that justification through faith is required for the validity of the promise (cf. Rom 4:13–14). The promise was for an heir born to Sarah (cf. Gen 15:4; 17:16, 19) and for numerous posterity (cf. Gen 12:2; 13:14–17; 17:8; 22:16–18), who would spread to all the nations of the earth (cf. Gen 12:2–3). Paul has set this cardinal tenet against the claim of circumcision; now he is pitting it against the law. Cf. Fitzmyer, *JBC*, 53:47.
326 See RNT notes on Rom 4:15 and Rom 1:18–32. See also Rom 2 and 3; Gal 3:10–14, 19; and Rom 7:7–12 and RNT notes ad loc.

men responsible for transgressing it, quite clearly it also makes them subject to a curse.³²⁷ But those who are subject to a curse and punishment, those who are responsible for transgression, do not deserve to inherit. Rather, they deserve to pay a penalty and to be rejected.

What happens then? Faith comes, drawn on by grace, so that the promise comes into effect. Where there is grace, there is forgiveness; where there is forgiveness, there is no punishment. But when the punishment is removed and the justification follows from faith, nothing hinders us from being heirs to the promise, the promise that comes from faith. And so Paul says, *Therefore the promise was the outcome of faith, that it might be a favor of grace, so that the promise of God might be secure for all the offspring, not only for the descendants who are of the law, but also for those who are of the faith of Abraham, who is the father of us all.* You see that faith not only establishes the law, but also prevents the promise of God from falling to the ground. On the other hand, when the law is observed beyond its proper time, it makes faith useless and hinders the promise from being fulfilled.³²⁸

By these arguments Paul shows not only that faith is not superfluous, but is even so necessary that without it salvation is impossible. *For the law works wrath*, because all have transgressed it. But faith does not permit wrath to have even a beginning. As Paul says, *Where there is no law, neither is there transgression.*³²⁹ Did you see how he not only obliterates sin after it has come into existence, but does not even permit it to come into being? This is why he says *by a favor of grace*.³³⁰ Why? Not to shame us, but *so that the promise might be secure for all the offspring.*³³¹

Here Paul sets down two blessings: that the things given are secure, and that they are for all the offspring. In this way he gathers together the Gentiles and he shows that the Jews are excluded if they contend against the faith. For faith is more secure than the law because faith does no damage and hence you must not contend

---

327 Cf. Gal 3:10–19 and note in RNT.
328 NPNF¹ 11:389n2.
329 The law must yield to faith and grace.
330 Cf. Rom 4:16. The man who lives his faith lives by grace.
331 I.e., all who share Abraham's faith, whether Jew or Gentile.

HOMILY 8

against it. It even saves you when you are in danger from the law. Next, after he said *for all the offspring*, he defines what offspring he means when he says for the offspring *of faith*.³³² By these words he attaches this relationship to the Gentiles and shows that those who do not believe as Abraham cannot be in accord with Abraham. Rom 4:16
Rom 4:16

And see a third thing that faith has accomplished. It has made the relationship with that just man more precise and definite and showed that he is the ancestor of more numerous descendants. Therefore, Paul did not simply say "Abraham," but *the father of us who believe*. Next, to seal what he said by a testimony, Paul said, *As it is written, 'I have appointed you the father of many nations.'*³³³ Rom 4:11
Rom 4:17

Did you see that these things were already planned from of old? What then, someone may say, if the Scripture says this of the Ishmaelites³³⁴ or of the Amalekites³³⁵ or of the Hagarenes?³³⁶ As Paul goes on, he shows more clearly that this was not said about them. But in the meantime, he hurries on to another point by which he proves this very thing. For he defines the manner of such a relationship and establishes its truth by his great intellect. What does Paul say? *In the sight of God, in whom he believed*. Rom 4:17

What Paul is saying is this: just as God is not the God of one portion, but is the Father of all, so also is this man Abraham. And again, just as God is not the Father according to a relationship of nature, but according to a relationship of faith, so too is Abraham, because his obedience makes him the father of all of us [who believe]. Because the Jews had no idea of this relationship because they clung fast to that crasser notion, Paul shows that the relationship of faith is the more valid and stronger one as he leads his discourse up to God.

And along with this, Paul also makes it plain that Abraham received this as a reward for his faith. Thus if this were not so and if he is the father of all who dwell on the earth, the phrase *in the sight of God* would be out of place, and God's gift would be curtailed and cut off. For the phrase *in the sight of* is equivalent to "alike with." Rom 4:17
Rom 4:17

---

332 Cf. Rom 4:16.
333 Here is quoting Gen 17:5. See NAB note on Gen 17:5.
334 See McKenzie, *DB*, 403.
335 See McKenzie, *DB*, 23–24.
336 See McKenzie, *DB*, 331.

Tell me, what is so wonderful about being the father of those who are born from oneself? Every man possesses this power. The unexpected thing is this: that Abraham received by the gift of God those descendants whom he did not have from nature.

V

So, if you are willing to believe that the patriarch was honored, believe that he is the father of all. But when he said *in the sight of God, in whom he believed,* Paul did not stop at this, but went on to add, *Who gives life to the dead and calls things that are not as though they were.*[337] For Paul was already laying the foundation for his discussion of the resurrection. And this was also useful for the topic at hand. If it was possible for God to give life to the dead and to bring in things that are not as if they were, it was also possible for God to make those who were not born of him [Abraham] to be his children.

And this is why Paul did not say "brings in things that are not as though they were," but *calls,* because he is showing what is far easier. For just as it is easy for us to call the things that are, so for God it is easy —and easier by far —to give subsistence to things that are not. But after Paul said that the gift of God was great and ineffable and after he had discoursed about God's power, he shows that the faith of Abraham was deserving of God's gift, so that you would not think that Abraham was honored without sound reason.

And after Paul had roused the attention of his audience, so that the Jew might not grasp hold of him and say, "And how is it possible for those who are not children to become children?" Paul changes the course of his discussion to the patriarch and says, *Hoping against hope, Abraham believed, so that he became the father of many nations according to what was said: 'So shall your offspring be.'*[338]

How was it that *Hoping against hope, Abraham believed?* By a hope that comes from God, one that is against human hope. For he is showing the greatness of the action and permitting no disbelief in what is said. The two hopes are contrary to one another, but faith

---

337 That is, "calls into being what does not exist."
338 See Gen 15:5.

has mingled them and blended them together. But if Paul were talking about the descendants of Ishmael,[339] this discussion would have been superfluous, for they were not born according to faith, but according to nature. But Paul also brings Isaac[340] before our eyes; for Abraham did not believe on behalf of those nations, but on behalf of the one who would be born of his barren wife.[341]

Therefore, if the reward is that Abraham was the father of many nations, it is clear that he was to become father of those nations on whose behalf he did believe. So that you may know that he is speaking of those nations, listen to what follows. *And without weakening in faith, he did not think of his own body, which was as good as dead because he was nearly a hundred years old, nor of the dead womb of Sarah.*   Rom 4:19

Did you see how he sets down the obstacles as well as the just man's lofty spirit, which surmounts all problems? He said that what was promised was *against hope*, and this is the first obstacle.   Rom 4:18 For Abraham had no other to look to who had gotten a child under such circumstances. Those who came after him looked to him, but he looked to no man but to God alone. And this is why he said *against hope*.   Rom 4:19

Next, his body was as good as dead, and this was the second obstacle. The third and fourth were the dead womb of Sarah. *But in view of the promise made by God, he did not waver through unbelief.*[342]   Rom 4:20 For God offered no proof, nor did He give a sign; His mere words were unsupported by evidence, words that promised what nature did not promise. But still Paul says that *he was not weakened*. He did not   Rom 4:19 say that Abraham did not believe, but that he was not weakened, that is, he did not doubt, nor did he hesitate, even though the hindrances were so great.

From this we learn that even if God promises impossibilities beyond number, and if one who hears God's promises does not receive the fulfillment, it is not the nature of things that is to blame, but the folly and want of understanding of him who did not receive what was promised. But Abraham *was strengthened in faith*.   Rom 4:20

---

339 See McKenzie, *DB*, 403.
340 See McKenzie, *DB*, 396–397.
341 Cf. Rom 4:19.
342 See RNT note *ad loc.*

See Paul's wisdom.[343] Because his discussion was about those who perform works and those who believe, Paul is showing that the man of faith performs more works than those who rely on works, and that the man of faith needs more power and much strength, and endures no small amount of labor.

For those who relied on works counted faith as worthless, because it involved no difficult task. So Paul took a firm stand against this and showed that not only the man who is successful in practicing temperance or any other similar virtue, but also the man who manifests faith, needs even greater power. For just as the man of temperance needs strength to fend off the reasons for intemperate excess, so the man of faith must have a powerful soul in order that he may thrust aside the thoughts and designs that lead to disbelief.

How then did Abraham become strong? Paul shows that this strength came from turning the matter over to faith and not to reasoning. Otherwise he would have fallen. But how did he keep his faith straight? Paul tells us, *By giving glory to God and by being fully persuaded that whatever God has promised, He is able also to perform.* Therefore, to refrain from idle and curious questions is to give glory to God, just as by asking them we are transgressing. If our curious questions and searching into things of this world bring about our failure to glorify God, all the more is this true if we are overly curious in the matter of our Lord's generation, and the result is that we will suffer the utmost penalty for our insolence. For if we must not search into the figure and type of His resurrection, all the more must we not raise curious questions on those subjects that are secret and awesome.[344]

And Paul did not merely say that Abraham believed, but that he was *fully persuaded*.[345] For faith is such a thing that it is clearer than proof by reasoning, and it persuades us more fully. For it is not possible for another reasoning process to come along afterward to shake and destroy our faith. For if a man is persuaded by words, he can also have words change his persuasion. But the man who is

---

343 See NPNF¹ 11:391n1.
344 These words seem aimed at the Neo-Arian Anomoeans.
345 These convictions that rest on faith are far stronger than those which rely on logic.

strengthened by faith has fortified his hearing against arguments that would destroy that faith.

Therefore, after Paul said that Abraham was justified by faith, he shows that he also gives glory to God by his faith. And this is especially characteristic of a good life. *For let your light shine before men so that they may see your good works and give glory to your Father who is in heaven.* Notice that this was seen as belonging to faith. Just as the good works are in need of power, so also does faith require it. For here, in the matter of good works, as in many other things, the body takes part in and shares in the sweat of toil. But there, in the matter of faith, success depends on the soul, without the body's help. So the labor is greater because the soul has nothing to divide and share the toil with it. ^{Matt 5:16}

VI

Do you see how Paul showed that everything that belonged to works is attached to faith in greater abundance, for example, boasting in relation to God,[346] the need for power and toil,[347] and, again, giving glory to God?[348] For after Paul said that *whatever God has promised, He is also able to perform*, it seems to me that he is proclaiming beforehand what will come to be. For God's promise embraced not only the present, but the future as well. For things of the present are a type of things to come. Therefore, failure to believe is a mark of a weak, small, and pitiful mind. ^{Rom 4:21}

Thus when people accuse us of believing, let us make against them a counteraccusation of not believing, because they are pitiful, small-minded, foolish, and weak, with a disposition no better than that of asses. For just as believing is a characteristic of a lofty and noble-natured soul, so failure to believe is a characteristic of a soul that is unreasonable and worthless, one that has sunken to the senselessness of sheep. So let us leave these unbelievers behind us; let us imitate the patriarch; let us give glory to God as Abraham did.

---

346 Cf. §§ 1–10 of this homily.
347 Cf. § 51 of this homily.
348 Cf. § 54 of this homily

By giving glory to God. What does this mean? It means that Abraham reflected on God's justice and limitless power. And after he had received a correct concept of God, he was fully persuaded about the things God had promised. Therefore, let us too give glory to God, both through our faith and through our good works, so that we may also receive the reward of being glorified by God. For God said, *I shall glorify those who give glory to Me.* And yet, even if no reward is set before us, this very thing would be a glory, namely, to be deemed deserving of giving glory to God.

For if men who speak words of praise to kings take pride in this very fact alone, even if there is no other reward, consider how great a glory there would be that our Master is glorified by us, just as we should consider how great a punishment it would be to cause God to be blasphemed because of us. And yet, as for His glorification, God wishes this very thing to be brought about for our sake. He has no need of it for Himself. For how great do you think the distance between God and man is? Is it as great as the distance between men and worms?

But I have not yet begun to say how great the distance is even if I set down as great a distance as I can, for it is impossible to say how great it is. Would you wish to have great and brilliant glory among worms? Of course not! Therefore, if you, who are a lover of glory, would not wish this, how could God —who is so free from this passion for glory and is so far above it —how, I say, could He have need of glory from you?

But still, even if God has no need of it, He says He desires it for your sake. If God endured becoming a slave for your sake, why do you wonder that He clings to other things for the same reason? For God considers that nothing is beneath His dignity if it will contribute to our salvation. Because we know this, let us shun every sin, seeing that it is because of sin that God is blasphemed. *Flee from sin as from the face of a serpent. If you come too near it, it will bite you,* says the prophet.

For the serpent does not come to us, but we draw near to it of our own accord. For God has seen to it that the devil[349] does not

---

349 The devil is the serpent, "the most cunning of all the animals that the Lord God had made" (Gen 3:1).

overcome us by his own tyranny; otherwise no one could make a stand against his strength. On this account, God has sent the devil away and exiled him like some robber or tyrant. Unless he catches someone naked[350] and alone in his hiding place, the devil does not dare to attack. Unless he sees us journeying through the desert, he does not have the boldness to assail us.

But the desert and dwelling place of the devil is nothing other than sin. Therefore, we are in need of *the shield of faith and the helmet of salvation.*[351] We need the sword of the Spirit, not only that we may suffer no evil, but that we may cut off the devil's head if he should be of a mind to leap upon us. We have need of constant prayer so that he may be crushed under our feet. For he is shameless and brutal because he fights with weapons from below. Yet even with this strategy, he wins the battle. The reason for this is that we are not eager to raise ourselves above the blows with which he strikes us. Eph 6:13–17;

For the devil cannot lift himself up very high, but he crawls on the ground. And the serpent is the type of which he is the reality. And if God imposed this punishment on the devil from the beginning,[352] much more does He do so now. And if you do not know what it means to fight with weapons from below, I shall try to explain this manner of doing battle. What then is this fighting with weapons from below? It is to strike us with the things from below, the things of this world: with pleasure, with wealth, and all the goods of this life.

Therefore, if the devil sees someone flying up toward heaven, first of all he will not be able to leap up to catch him. Second, if he tries to do so, he will speedily fall. So fear not, because the devil has no feet. Be not afraid, because he has no wings. He crawls upon the earth and among the things on earth. Therefore, you must have nothing in common with earth and you will have no need to toil or labor. For the devil knows nothing of fighting face to face, but, like a serpent, he hides himself among the thornbushes and lurks constantly in the deceit of riches and wealth.[353]

---

350 I.e., unarmed against his foe.
351 Cf. 1 Thess 5:8.
352 Cf. Gen 3:14.
353 Cf. Matt 13:32.

If you cut down the thorns, he will easily be put to flight, because he is a coward. And if you know how to charm him with divine incantations, he will be overpowered without delay. For we certainly do have spiritual incantations, such as the name of our Lord Jesus Christ and the power of the cross. This charm not only drives the serpent from where he is lurking and casts him into the fire,[354] but it even cures wounds.[355]

VII

Even if there are many who invoked the Lord's name but have not been cured, this came from their paucity of faith and not from the weakness of the name they invoked. Even when they pushed and pressed around Jesus, they gained no benefit. But the woman with the hemorrhage did not even touch his body, but only the hem of his garment, and stopped the flow of blood that had assailed her for so many years.[356] This name is a fearful force against devils, passions, and diseases.

Therefore, let us glory in the name of Jesus, let us fortify ourselves by it. It was in this way that Paul became great even though he was of the same nature as we are, but his faith had made him an entirely different man. So great was the abundance of his faith that even garments [that had touched him] had great power.[357] What excuse would we deserve to have if even the shadow and garments of those men[358] drove off death, whereas our prayers do not even keep our passions in check?

What is the reason for this? The difference between our will and purpose and theirs is great, although we have an equal and common nature. Paul was born and raised in a way similar to that in which we were born and raised. He lived on the same earth and breathed the same air. But in other respects he was much greater and much better —in his zeal, his faith, and in his love. Let us imitate him; let us allow Christ to speak through us. Christ desires

---

354 Cf. Acts 28:5.
355 Cf. Mark 16:18; Acts 3:6; 9:34.
356 Luke 8:43–44.
357 Cf. Acts 19:12.
358 Paul and the other apostles.

this more than we do. It was for this reason that Christ made ready this musical instrument [of our persons], and He does not wish it to remain useless and idle. He desires always to hold it in his hand.

Why then do you not keep it ready and serviceable for the hand of your Maker? Why do you let its strings grow loose and, by your luxurious living, make the instrument inharmonious? Why do you make the whole lyre unfit for Him to use when you should be tightening the strings to tune them to play melodies? Why do you not keep them in harmony with spiritual salt?[359] If Christ will see that our instruments are properly tuned and harmonized, He will make them resound through our souls. When this has taken place, you will see angels and cherubim dancing with joy.

Therefore, let us become worthy of His blameless hands. Let us invite Him to strum the strings of our hearts. But He needs no invitation. Only make your hearts worthy of His touch, and He will run to you before you ask. When Christ considers the heights to which a man will attain in days to come, He rushes to him. Indeed, He composed a panegyric for Paul before Paul had become the great apostle he was going to be. What then will Christ not do when He sees a man reach the peaks of perfection? For Christ will make our hearts resound with music, and the Spirit will indeed come to rest upon us. We shall be more luminous than the heavens. The sun and moon will not be fixed in our bodies. Indeed, we shall have the Lord of the sun and moon and the angels dwelling and walking about within us.

I do not say this so that we may bring the dead back to life or cleanse lepers. I say it so that we may show forth a sign greater than these miracles. I mean the sign of love. For in whatever place this beautiful virtue may be found, there immediately the Son is present together with the Father, and the grace of the Spirit comes again and again. *Where two or three are gathered in My name, there am I* Matt 18:20 *in the midst of them.* For this is a sign of great affection and a mark of those who love dearly, namely, to have their loved ones surrounding them on every side. What I mean is this. Is there any group of men who do not wish to have Christ in their midst? Perhaps a group of men who are quarreling with one another.

---

359 The strings of musical instruments were soaked in brine.

Perhaps someone will laugh at me and say, "What do you mean? Do you not see that we are all within the same walls and in the same sacred enclosure of the church, standing in the same fold in unanimity? Do you not see that no one is fighting, that we are under the same common shepherd,[360] that we are shouting the responses together, that we are all listening to what is said, that we are sending up our prayers with one voice? And do you talk about fighting and quarreling?"

I did speak of quarrels, and I am neither out of my mind nor have I lost my wits. For I see what I see, and I know that we are in the same fold and under the same shepherd. This is why I am especially stricken by grief, because we are at odds although so many things are bringing us together. Someone may ask, "What kind of discord do you see here?" Here I see none; but when our gathering has broken up, one man levels an accusation at another; another hurls open insults at his neighbor; and still another speaks slander, is greedy and grasping and violent; and still another is gripped by an unlawful love affair; and still another is devising countless plots. If it were possible to reveal our souls, then you would see all these things in sharp focus, and you would know that I have not lost my mind.

VIII

In peacetime, do you not see that armies lay aside their weapons and cross over into the camp of the enemy unarmed and off their guard? But when they are protected by their weapons and outposts, when they spend the nights awake and alert and keep the campfires continually burning, such a situation is no longer a sign of peace, but of war. For we are on our guard against one another; we fear each other; each of us whispers into his neighbor's ear. When we see anyone else draw near, we fall silent and gird ourselves for action in every way. And this is not a mark of those who feel confident, but of those who are very carefully on their guard.

But someone will say, "We do this not in order to do harm, but in order to not be harmed." This is why I am grieving. Why? Because

---

360 The shepherd, of course, is the bishop.

HOMILY 8

we are living amongst our brothers but still must be on our guard in order to not suffer harm. This is why we burn such large campfires. This is why we set up guards and outposts. And the reason for this is the widespread lying, the considerable treachery, the wholesale destruction of love, and the war without truce. And this is why we might find many men who have greater confidence in pagans than in Christians.

Therefore, how great a feeling of shame must we have? How much weeping, how much groaning, do these actions deserve? Someone might ask, "What will happen to me? So-and-so is a harsh and stubborn villain." Where are the principles of your Christian way of life? Where are the rules given to us by the Apostle, that we must bear each other's burdens?[361] For if you do not know how to deal well with your brother, when will you be able to deal well with a stranger? If you have not learned how to treat a member of your own body, when will you be able to draw a foreigner to you and unite him to yourself?

But how should I feel? I am very amazed and upset. I am even at the point of tears, and I could send forth abundant fountains from my eyes, as that prophet said,[362] when I see countless enemies on that plain who are more dangerous than those whom the prophet saw. For when he saw the enemy approaching, he said, *I am pained in my bowels*. When I see men drawn up in ranks under one general, men who then make a stand against one another, biting and tearing each other's members, some for money, others for glory, some ridiculing and mocking and inflicting wounds at random on one another; when I see corpses slain with greater hostility than casualties in battle, where now only the mere name of brothers is left, I can think of no dirge that could describe this tragedy as it deserves. Jer 4:19 (LXX)

Show reverence, therefore, show reverence for this table in which we all share.[363] Show reverence for Christ, who was slain for our sake, who is the sacrifice lying on this altar.[364] Robbers who

---

361 Cf. Gal 6:2.
362 Cf. Jer 9:1.
363 Cf. 1 Cor 10:16–18 and RNT note on 10:14–22.
364 In Heb 13:10, "We have an altar" does not refer to the Eucharist, but to the sacrifice of Christ. In fact, the Eucharist is never clearly mentioned in Hebrews. Cf. note

have shared in salt are no longer robbers in the eyes of those with whom they have shared the salt. The table makes those who were crueler than wild beasts gentler than lambs.[365] But after we share in such a table and such food as is on this altar, we arm ourselves against each other. Instead we should be doing this against the devil, who is waging war against all of us.

This surely is why with each passing day we become weaker and he becomes stronger. We do not help one another in building a wall to defend ourselves against him. Instead we stand by his side and take him as our commander while we wound each other. But it is against him alone that we ought to be waging war. Yet now we let him escape as we aim our arrows against our brothers. "What kind of arrows?" someone may ask. The arrows of our tongue and mouth. For it is not only javelins and darts, but also words, which are much sharper than spears, that inflict wounds.

Someone will ask, "And how will we be able to end this war?" Only perceive that when you speak ill of your brother, you are pouring forth slime from your mouth. Only see that it is a member of Christ whom you are slandering. Only see that you are eating your own flesh.[366] Only see that you are making judgment day — frightening and beyond bribery as it is — more bitter for yourself. Only see that the arrow is killing not the one who was struck with it, but you, who aimed the bow and shot the dart. Only then will you be able to end this war.

Did he do you some wrong? Did he treat you badly? Groan for him, but do not speak ill of him. Weep not for the wrong done to you, but for your brother's perdition. Weep as your Master wept for Judas, not because your Master was crucified, but because Judas betrayed him. Did your brother insult you; did he abuse you? Pray to God that he may win His mercy and graciousness. He is your brother; he was born with the same birth pangs as yourself; he is a member of your body; he has been called to the same table.[367]

---

ad loc. in RNT. The text means that the notion of intermingling Judaism and Christianity cannot be entertained. Cf. NAB notes on Gal 2:11–14 and Gal 2:15–21.
365 "Sharing salt" means eating together and thus proving a friendship far removed from their usual criminal acts.
366 Cf. Ps 26/27:2.
367 The table here is the Eucharistic altar, where we receive Christ's Body and Blood

You may say that he assaulted you again and again. Therefore, your reward will be greater and richer. For this reason it is especially right that you dismiss your anger, because he received a mortal hurt when the devil wounded him.

IX

Therefore, you must not strike him; you must not dash yourself down together with him. For as long as you can stand, you can save him too. But if you tear yourself apart by returning his abuses, who will then raise both of you up? Will it be the one who was wounded? But he will not be able to do so, because he is lying on the ground. Will you do it after you have fallen along with him? Because you cannot lend a helping hand to yourself, how will you have the strength to help another?

Show your nobility, therefore, and stand up with courage. Hold your shield before you and with patience and forbearance drag your fallen brother from the battle. Did not anger deal him his wound? You must not add to his wound, but you must tear out the dart that struck him earlier. If we associate with one another in this way, we all will quickly be healthy and sound. But if we take up arms against each other, then there is no need thereafter for the devil to achieve our destruction.

All war is destructive, but civil war is especially so. And this war is even more destructive than civil war, inasmuch as our just claims [as Christians] are greater than the claims of citizenship, yes, and even of kindred blood itself. In olden times, Cain slew his brother Abel and shed the blood of his kinsman.[368] But this murder of Christians is more lawless than that, inasmuch as the rights of relationship in faith are stronger, and the evil manner of death more bitter.

For Cain wounded the body, but you sharpened your sword against the soul. Were you the first to suffer hurt? Yet it is not the suffering of hurt, but the doing of evil, that really puts a curse on the suffering of injury. Consider this: Cain slew Abel. Abel was the

---

as our food and drink.
368 Cf. Gen 4:8.

one slain. Which one, then, was the one who died? Was it the one Gen 4:10 who shouted aloud after death? For God said, *The voice of the blood of Abel, your brother, cries out to me.* Or was it the one who still lived in fear and trembling? For he, Cain, was more pitiable than any dead man.[369]

Do you see how it is better to have a wrong done to you, even if you come to the point of being murdered? Learn then how doing wrong is worse, especially if the wrongdoer has the strength to shed blood. That wrongdoer struck and slew his brother. But the brother received a crown; the slayer was punished. Abel was unjustly done away with and slain, but even in death he accused, did away with, and subdued his murderer. Yet Cain still lived but was mute, was ashamed, was convicted, and got the opposite of what he intended.

Cain did away with Abel because he saw that Abel was beloved, and Cain expected to drive him out of that love. But he only made God's love greater, and God sought after Abel all the more, even af- Gen 4:9 ter he died. For God said, *Where is Abel, your brother?* For Cain's envy did not quench God's love, but rather inflamed it the more. Cain did not lessen Abel's honor by murdering him, but he increased it. Before Cain slew him, God had made Abel subject to Cain. But because Cain did away with him, even though Abel was dead, he will take vengeance on Cain. So great was God's love for him.

Who then was the one who was condemned? Was it the one who punished, or the one who was punished? Was it he who enjoyed such great honor from God, or the one who was given over to a new and unexpected punishment? "You did not fear him while he was still alive," God says. "Therefore, fear him now that he is dead. You did not tremble when you were about to thrust your sword into him. After you shed his blood, you will be gripped with a continual shivering. While he lived he was your servant, and you did not endure him, nor were you patient with him. Therefore, now that he is dead, he has become your master, and you must fear him."[370]

My beloved, bear these things in mind, and let us flee from envy; let us quench the fires of evil. Return love for love to one another,

369 Cf. Gen 4:13–15.

370 Cf. Gen 4:10–12; Harkins, *St. John Chrysostom: Discourses*, 210–213.

so that we may reap the blessings love brings both in the present life and in the life to come, by the grace and loving-kindness of our Lord Jesus Christ, to whom be glory and power, world without end. Amen.

HOMILY 9

Rom 4:23–24

Now not only for his [Abraham's] sake only was it written that 'it was credited to him,' but also for the sake of us, to whom it will be credited if we believe in Him who raised Jesus our Lord from the dead.[371]

Paul had said many great things about Abraham: about his faith, his justification, and the honor he had received from God. But Paul wished to keep his hearers from saying, "And what does that have to do with us? For Abraham was the one who was justified." So Paul sets us again close to the patriarch, because the power of spiritual discussions is so great. For Paul said that the Gentile who has just come to believe, even if he has done no good work, has no less than the Jew who believes, nor than the patriarch himself. Rather, if I must speak a marvelous truth, he even has much more.

Our nobility is so great that the faith of that patriarch is a type of our faith. Paul did not say "If it was credited to Abraham, it is likely that it is credited to us too" so as to make this a matter of inference. Paul speaks from the authority of the divine laws and makes the whole matter a statement of Scripture. For why was it written, he is saying, except that we may learn that we too receive justification in this way?[372] For we have believed in the same God and about the same things, even if not in the case of the same persons. And after he spoke of our faith, by bringing in the cross he speaks of God's ineffable kindness, with which He always surrounds us. Paul now

Rom 4:25

makes this clear when he says, *who was delivered up for our sins, and rose again for our justification.*[373]

See how, after he mentioned the cause of Christ's death, he makes the same cause also a proof of His resurrection. For why

---

[371] Cf. Rom 8:11; 10:9; 1 Pet 1:3, 21; 1 Cor 15:17; Isa 53:4–5, 12.
[372] As Abraham did, i.e., by grace, faith, and justification. Cf. Rom 4:25.
[373] See also Isa 53:4–5, 12; 1 Cor 15:17; Rom 8:11.

was Christ crucified? Paul is telling us that it was not because of any sin that Christ Himself had committed. This is made clear from His resurrection. For if Christ were a sinner, how did He rise from the dead? But if He rose from the dead, it is obvious that He was not guilty of sin. But if He was not guilty of sin, why was He crucified? He was crucified for the sake of others.

But if He was crucified for the sake of others, then certainly He did rise again. He rose again so that you may not say, "If we are accountable for such great sins, how were we able to receive justification?" Paul pointed out that Christ blotted out all sins so that he might guarantee his word both by the faith of Abraham, by which Abraham received justification; and by the passion of our Savior, by which we were freed from our sins.

After Paul made mention of Christ's death, he also speaks of His resurrection. For Christ did not die so that He might hold us accountable for punishment and condemnation, but so that He might show His loving-kindness and do a good service for us. For this reason Christ both died and rose again in order to bring about our justification. *Therefore, having been justified by faith, let us have peace with God through our Lord Jesus Christ.* Rom 5:1

What does Paul mean when he says, *Let us have peace?* Some say that he means "Let us not quarrel in our obstinate striving to bring in the law." But to me it seems that Paul is now speaking to us about our way of life. For Paul had much to say about faith, and he put it before the justification that comes from works. To prevent anyone from thinking that what he had said was an argument for sluggishness and indifference, he says, *Let us have peace,* that is, let us sin no more, let us not return to our former ways, for that is making war against God. Rom 5:1

Someone will say, "How is it possible to sin no more?" How was our former state possible? For if, when we were accountable for so many sins, we were set free from all of them through Christ, all the more will we be able, through Him, to remain in the state in which we are. For it is not the same thing to receive peace when there is no peace and to keep it after it has been given to us. Acquiring it is more difficult than keeping it.

Nonetheless, the more difficult has become easy, and it did come into effect. Therefore, what is easier becomes easily effected if we cling to Christ, who has accomplished even those other things for us. But here I do not think that Paul is hinting only at what is easy, but also at what is reasonable. For if Christ set us free after we had waged war against Him, it is reasonable that we remain in a state of reconciliation and give to Him this recompense for His forgiveness, so that He may not seem to have reconciled to the Father uncouth and unfeeling creatures. For Paul says, *Through whom we also have access by faith*. Therefore, if Christ gave us access when we were far away, much more will He keep us now that we are near.

II

Please consider how everywhere Paul sets down these two points: both what Christ does, and what we do. The things that Christ does are varied, numerous, and different. For surely He died for us, He freed us from sin, He led us near to Himself, and He gave us grace beyond description, whereas we contributed our faith alone. And so it is that Paul says, *Access by faith to that grace in which we stand*.

Tell me, to what kind of grace? It is the grace of being deemed worthy of the knowledge of God, the grace of being freed from error, the grace of knowing the truth, the grace of obtaining all the blessings that come to us through baptism. Christ has given us access to this grace so that we may receive these gifts. Christ gave us this grace not merely so that remission and freedom from our sins might be ours, but also so that we might receive countless benefits and dignities. Nor did He stop with these. Christ also promised those ineffable blessings that surpass our powers of mind and speech.

This is why Paul put down the two points of present and future. When he said *that grace*, he made clear what we have received here and now. But when he said, *And we exult in the hope of the glory of God*, he unveiled all the blessings that are to come. And Paul did well to say *in which we stand*. For such is the grace of God: it has no end, it knows no limit, but it always moves forward to greater things. And this is impossible for men.

Let me give you an example. A man has received the rule, the glory, and the power. But he does not remain in these forever, but quickly he falls from his place. Even if someone does not take them away, death comes on and will remove him from all his sovereignty. It is not the same with God's gifts. For neither man, nor time, nor circumstances, nor the devil himself, nor death, can come and cast us out of these blessings. But when we die, we cling to them more firmly and continue to enjoy more and more of them. And so, if you do not believe in the gifts to come hereafter, put your faith in those to come from the gifts you have already received in this life.

For this is why Paul said, *And we exult in the hope of the glory of God.* Rom 5:2 He said this so that you may learn what kind of soul the man of faith must have. For we must be filled with certainty not only for what has been given, but also for the blessings that will be given just as if they had already been granted. For we exult in gifts that have already been given. So what Paul means is that because the hope for the gifts of the future life is as strong and sure as for the gifts already granted, it is in that hope that we exult in the same way. And for this reason he has also called those gifts a glory. For if they contribute to God's glory, they will surely come to pass —for God's glory, if not for ours.

What Paul means is this. Why am I saying that the blessings of the future life deserve that we exult in them? The very evils of the present life are enough to brighten our faces and to make us feel proud. This is why Paul added, *And not only that, but we also exult* Rom 5:3 *in tribulations.* Consider, then, how great are the future blessings when we can even be elated about things that seem to be painful and distressing. This is how great God's gifts are and how free [they are] from anything that causes unpleasantness or annoyance.

For in the case of external matters of this world, struggles for them involve toil, pain, and affliction; crowns and rewards provide pleasure. But in the case of tribulations this is not so; in fact, the struggles are just as pleasurable as the rewards. Why is this? Because when we were undergoing tribulations, the temptations were many, but the kingdom of heaven was our hope; the dread things were in our hands, the good things were our expectation.

This freed the weaker ones even before they received the crowns. Paul gives them prizes when he says, *We also exult in tribulations.*

Paul did not say that you must exult. He says *we exult;* he brings us encouragement in his own person. Next, because what he said seemed strange and unexpected —if a man who is struggling because of hunger, who is in chains and being tortured, who is being insulted and reviled, still must exult —Paul then confirms what he had said. And what is more, he said that these torments deserve that we exult in them not only because of the blessings in the world to come, but because of our present plights.

Certainly, these tribulations are a good thing in themselves. Why? Because they anoint us with the oil of endurance. And so, after Paul said, *We exult in tribulations,* he also set forth the reason when he added, *Knowing that tribulation makes for endurance.* Again, notice Paul's argumentative spirit and how he turns his discussion in the opposite direction. Because it was tribulations above all that made these men give up on the future blessings and drove them to despair, Paul tells them that it is for these very reasons that they must be confident and not give up hope in the future blessings.

For he says, *Tribulation makes for endurance, and endurance makes for tested virtue, and tested virtue makes for hope. And hope does not disappoint.* For not only are tribulations not destructive of such hope, but they are well suited for providing it. Even before the blessings of the future life, tribulation provides the very great benefit of endurance, and it can make the man who is undergoing trial and temptation a person of tested virtue. Also, tribulation makes some contribution to the blessings yet to come, because it makes hope come to full strength in us. For nothing prepares us to hope for blessings as much as a good conscience does.

III

And so no one who has lived an upright life despairs about the future. By the same token, many who have followed a careless lifestyle are crushed by a bad conscience and wish that there were no judgment and no recompense to be made. Why is this? Do our blessings lie in hopes? In hopes, yes, but not in human hopes.

Human hopes are often dashed to the ground and bring shame on the one who hoped. Suppose the one in whom he expected to find protection either dies or he still lives but has changed his mind. Our situations are not like those, because our hope is strong and cannot be moved or changed.

For the One who has made the promises to us lives forever. And even if we die, we who are going to enjoy the fulfillment of God's promise will rise again. And there is absolutely nothing that can put us to shame, because we have not been lifted up heedlessly and in vain by unsound and ill-founded hopes. And so after Paul had freed them of all doubt by these words, he does not stop his discourse with the present, but he again moves on to the future. He does this because he knows that the weaker souls, even though they are seeking the goods of the present life, are not satisfied with them.

However, he gives them a guarantee of future blessings through those blessings that have already been given, to prevent anyone from saying, "What about this? Suppose God is unwilling to grant these future blessings to us." We all know that God is willing because we all know that He can grant them, that He keeps his promises, and that He lives. "But how do we know that He is also willing?" From the things that He has already done. "From what things that He has already done?" From the love that He has shown for us. "By doing what?" By giving us the Holy Spirit.

And so after Paul said, *Hope does not disappoint*, he added a proof of this when he said, *Because the love of God is poured forth in our hearts*. Paul did not say that God's love has been given to us, but *is poured forth in our hearts*, to show the lavishness of His love. For God gave this love, which was the greatest gift —not heaven and earth and sea, but that which was more precious than all these. God gave a love that has made men into angels, sons of God, and brothers of Christ. And what is this gift? It is the Holy Spirit.[374]

If God were not willing to grant us great crowns after our labors, He would not have given us such great blessings before our toils and trials were over. But now the warmth of God's love is proved by this, namely, that He did not honor us slowly and little by little,

---

374 Cf. Rom 8:14–17.

but He poured forth suddenly a fountain of blessings and did this before our struggles were over. Even if you are not very deserving, you must not despair. You have the love of God, who is your Judge, as a mighty advocate to support you.

Rom 5:5 This is why, after Paul had said, *Hope does not disappoint,* he attributed everything not to our right actions, but to the love of God. And after he mentioned the gift of the Spirit, he again turns to the Rom 5:6–8 cross when he says, *For while we were still weak, at the set time, Christ died for the wicked. For scarcely in behalf of a just man does one die; yet perhaps one might bring himself to die for a good man.*[375] *But God is proving His love for us.*

What Paul is saying is something such as this. If a man would not be quick to choose to die for a virtuous fellow human being, ponder on the love of your Master when, not for virtuous men, but for sinners and enemies, He was seen hanging on the cross. And Rom 5:8–10 this is what Paul says next, *Because if, when we were still sinners, Christ died for us, much more, now that we have been justified by his blood, will we be saved through Him from wrath. For if, when we were enemies, we were reconciled to God by the death of His Son, much more, now that we have been reconciled, shall we be saved by His life.*

What Paul has said seems to be repetitious. But this is not the case if anyone carefully attends to his words. Consider this: Paul wishes to give his audience a guarantee about the future blessings. First he reproves them by the statement of Abraham, the just man, when he said that Abraham was fully persuaded that God could do whatever He promised.[376] Next his guarantee rests on the grace that has been given; then on the tribulations, because they could lead us to hope; and again on the Spirit whom we have received; and finally on Christ's death and the wickedness of our former lives.

And as I said before, what Paul says appears to be a single thing, but we find that it is two, three, and many more things. First, Paul tells us that Christ died; second, that He died for the wicked; third, that He reconciled, that He saved, that He justified, that He made us immortal, that He made us sons and heirs. Therefore, it is not by

---

375 See Stevens' note in NPNF[1] 11:398.
376 Cf. Homily 8.48–52 and Rom 4:20–21.

Christ's death alone that Paul's statement must gain greater force, but also from what was given to us by Christ's death. Indeed, if He died only for the sort of people we are, what He had done would be the greatest proof of His love.

But when Christ is seen giving such great gifts to such people as ourselves at the hour of his death, what occurred overshadows every excess and leads even the very dullest to believe. There is no other who is going to save us except the Christ who loves us so much, sinners though we are, that He even gave Himself up for us. Do you see how strong a proof this topic provides for hope in the future blessings?

Before this, there were two difficulties with regard to our salvation: the fact that we are sinners, and our need to be saved by the death of the Master. This second was incredible before it happened. It required an abundance of love so that it might come to pass. But now that it has occurred, the rest are easier. For we have become friends, and there is no further need for Christ to die. Shall God, who spared His enemies to such an extent that He did not spare His own Son, shall God fail to protect those who are now His friends, and at a time when there is no further need to hand His Son over to death?

When a man fails to rescue and save another, it is either because he does not wish to do it or because he cannot do it even if he should wish to do so. Neither of these can be said about God. [That God wished to save us is clear] because He handed over His Son to death. That He was also able to save is proved from the fact that He justified those who were sinners. What is there, then, to hinder us from obtaining the blessings of the world to come? Nothing!

Then, again, to keep you from blushing and feeling ashamed when you hear of sinners, enemies, the weak, and the impious, listen to what Paul says. *And not this only, but we exult also in God through our Lord Jesus Christ, through whom we have now received reconciliation.* Rom 5:11
What does Paul mean by *and not this only?* He means that not only were we saved, but we even glory for this very reason — a reason for which some think that we should feel ashamed and hide our faces. Rom 5:11

For the fact that we were saved when we were living in the midst of such great wickedness is the strongest sign of how greatly we were loved by Him who saved us. For God did not save us by angels or archangels, but by His only begotten Son Himself. So the fact that He saved us, and that He saved us when we were the kind of men we were, and that He did this by the Only Begotten (and not only by the Only Begotten, but by His blood) all weave for us countless crowns in which we can exult. Nothing we can claim matches in glory and confidence the fact that we are loved by God and that we have a friend in Him who loves us.

This is what makes the angels, the principalities, and the powers glorious. This is greater than the kingdom. This is why Paul sets it before the kingdom. This is why I count as blessed the spiritual powers, namely, because they love God and obey Him in all things. It was for this reason that the prophet marveled at them when he said, *Mighty in strength, doing His bidding.* Isaiah also extolled the seraphim. He showed the greatness of their virtue from the fact that they stood close to that glory,[377] and this was a sign of the greatest love.

Ps 102/103:20

IV

Therefore, let us imitate the powers above. Let us not only be eager to stand close to the throne, but also to have Him who is seated upon the throne dwelling within us. For He loved us even when we hated Him. And He continues to love us. For surely *He makes the sun to rise on the wicked and the good, and sends rain on the just and the unjust.* For you must love Him, because He loves us. And He does love us.

Matt 5:45

Someone might say, "How does a God who loves us threaten us with Gehenna and punishment and vengeance?" He does so for this very reason, namely, because He loves us. He does all this in an effort to cut out your tendency toward evil. He frightens you as if this fear were a kind of bridle to restrain you from rushing on to a worse way of acting. He gives blessings and pains to send you up from your downward path, to lead you to Himself and away from all evil, which is a worse state than Gehenna. But if you sneer at everything that has been said and wish to live a life of continuous

---

377 Cf. Isa 6:1–2.

wickedness rather than to suffer a single day of punishment, this is no cause for wonder.

For this is a sign of your imperfect judgment, of your drunken state, and of your incurable disease. Little children too, when they see the physician bringing to them cauterizing fire or a scalpel, leap up and run away, shrieking and tearing their hair. They choose to destroy themselves by a continuous putrefaction of their body rather than, by enduring a timely pain, to enjoy the healthy state that the pain would bring.

But those with a discerning mind know that the sickness is worse than the pain of the scalpel's cut, just as being wicked is worse than being punished. For the one leads to cure and a return to health; the other destroys one's health and leaves the patient continually ailing. Surely it is clear to everyone that health is better than sickness. Therefore, thieves should weep not when their sides are dug through, but when they dig through the walls of a house and commit murder.

For if the soul is of greater value than the body—and it certainly is—when the soul is destroyed, there is more reason for groaning and lament. If the soul should lack all feeling and perception, on that account we must grieve for it all the more. For we ought to feel more sorrow for those who love with unbridled passion than for those who are tossed by a violent fever, and more sorrow for drunkards than for those being put to torture. But if such passionate love and drunkenness are worse than fever and torture, someone may say, why is it that we show them greater preference?

As the proverb puts it, the reason is that many men are pleased with what is worse and choose it, while they turn aside from what is better.[378] And we can see this in the case of foods, of governments, of this life's desires, of the enjoyment of pleasure, of wives, of houses, of slaves, of fields, and of everything else. Tell me this. What is a more pleasant experience? Is it to have intercourse with women or with males, with females or with mules?

Nonetheless, we shall find many who pass women by but have intercourse with irrational animals and commit outrages on the

---

378 Cf. Prov 22:14a (LXX): "εἰσὶν ὁδοὶ κακαὶ ἐνώπιον ἀνδρός, καὶ οὐκ ἀγαπᾷ τοῦ ἀποστρέψαι ἀπ' αὐτῶν."

bodies of males. Yet natural pleasures are more enjoyable than unnatural ones. Still, there are many who pursue things that are ridiculous, unpleasant, and that involve punishment as if they were enjoyable and brought pleasure. Someone will say, "Yes, because to them these things seem to bring pleasure." But for this very reason, then, they would be miserable, because they think that what brings no pleasure is a source of pleasure and joy.

And so it is that they reckon that the punishment is worse than the sin. But this is not so. Quite the opposite is true. For if the punishment were an evil for the sinners, God would not have added evils to evils, nor would He have wished to make the sinners worse men. For God, who does everything to quench evil, would not have increased it. Therefore, being punished is not an evil for the sinner. But it is an evil for one in the state of sin not to be punished, just as not being cured is an evil for one who is sick.[379]

For, there is nothing as evil as absurd desire. And when I say "absurd," I mean the desire for luxury, for unseasonable glory, for power, and for all things that go beyond need or necessity. For such is the man who lives a soft and dissolute life. He seems to be happier than anyone else, but he is more miserable because he is bringing upon his soul harsh and tyrannical rulers.

This is why God made our present life one of labor. He did this so that He might free us from that slavery and bring us into genuine and perfect freedom. This is why God threatened punishment and made toils our lot in life by putting bonds on our conceited minds. So too, when the Jews were bound to the mud and the making of bricks,[380] they lived moderately and constantly called upon God. But when they got their freedom, they murmured and provoked the Master and pierced themselves with countless evils.

Someone might ask, "What would you say of the many times that men have been changed for the worse by tribulation?" I would say that the change and reversal are not the effect of tribulation, but of the weakness of those men. If someone has a weak stomach and has to purge himself with a bitter medicine that upsets his stomach, we will not put the blame on the medication, but on

---

379 Cf. Plato, *Gorgias* 478–479.
380 During their exile in Egypt; see Exod 1:14.

the weakness of his stomach. So also here we will put the blame on a mind that is prone to evil. Surely a person who undergoes a change for the worse because of tribulation will suffer this all the more because of his laxity and licentious living.

If he falls after he has been tied up and bound (for this is what tribulation is), he will do so all the more when his bonds are loosened. If he suffers a reversal when he is bound, he will do so all the more when he is relaxed. Again my objector asks, "And how will I be able to avoid being changed for the worse when tribulation comes?" You will be able to do so if you realize that, whether you wish it or not, you will have to endure what has afflicted you. If you bear it with gratitude, you will reap the greatest profit. But if you bear it with impatience, with passionate rage and blasphemy, you will not in that way make your misfortune less, but you will make the waves of pain greater.

Because of these considerations, then, let us make what is a matter of necessity a matter of our free choice. I mean something such as this: Suppose one man has lost his only son; suppose another man has lost his entire fortune. Consider that what has occurred cannot be undone, but that benefit can be derived from an incurable disaster. How? By bearing it with a generous spirit. Instead of curses and blasphemies, offer thanksgiving to your Master and, in this way, the evils brought upon you against your will become good deeds that you have freely chosen.

Do you see that your son was snatched from you at an early age? Say, *The Lord has given; the Lord has taken away.* [Job 1:21] Do you see that your fortune is gone? Say, *I came forth naked from my mother's womb, and there naked shall I return.* [Job 1:21] Do you see wicked men prospering and just men faring badly and suffering countless dreadful ills? Do you not know how to discover the cause of what has happened? Say, *I became brutish before You. Yet I am continually with You.* [Ps 72/73: 22–23]

But if you are seeking the cause, consider that God has set the day on which He will judge the whole world, and so you will cast aside your doubt. For on that day each one will receive what he deserves, even as Lazarus and the rich man.[381] Recall the apostles. For even though they were scourged and driven into exile and suffered

---

381 Cf. Luke 16:19–31.

ten thousand tortures, they rejoiced because they were deemed worthy to suffer disgrace for the name of Jesus Christ.[382] Therefore, even if you are weak, endure it bravely, give thanks to God, and so you will receive the same reward as the apostles did.

But if you are weak and in pain, how will you be able to feel grateful to the Master? You can if you truly love Him. For the three boys who were thrown into the fiery furnace,[383] and others who were imprisoned and faced with countless other trials, never stopped giving thanks. Much more will those who are in the grip of disease and feeling the pangs of sickness be able to do this. For there is nothing —surely there is nothing —that love[384] cannot conquer.[385]

When the love is the love of God,[386] it is the loftiest of all loves. Neither fire, nor sword, nor poverty, nor sickness, nor death, nor any other such thing will seem terrible to the one who possesses such love as this. He laughs all these dread things to scorn; he will fly up to heaven; he will be in a state in no way inferior to those who dwell there. For he sees nothing else, neither sky, nor earth, nor sea, but he looks to one beauty alone, the beauty of the glory of God. Neither will the pains of the present life be able to discourage him, nor will the goods and things that bring pleasure here be able to arouse or elate him.

Let us, therefore, love this love of God (for there is nothing that can match it) both for the sake of things of this world and those of the world to come. Rather, more than this, let us love it because of the nature of this love itself. For it will free us from the punishments of this world and those of the ages to come, and we shall enjoy God's kingdom. Yet neither freedom from Gehenna nor enjoyment of the kingdom is anything in comparison to what we are going to say. For it is greater than all these to have Christ as our beloved and our lover[387] at the same time.

---

382 E.g., Acts 5:40–41.
383 Cf. Dan 3:19–24.
384 πόθος: A passionate yearning.
385 Cf. Rom 8:35–39.
386 "Ἐρασθῶμεν τοίνυν τοῦτον τὸ ἔρωτα τούτου." The term "eros" is utilized here to show the powerful love we are called to develop for God.
387 "τούτων γὰρ ἁπάντων μεῖζον τὸ τὸν Χριστὸν ἐρώμενον ἔχειν ὁμοῦ καὶ ἐραστήν." Chrysostom uses some strong and colorful terms and images to express his understanding of this love. Instead of ἀγάπη, ἀγαπῶ or φιλία, φιλῶ, he uses πόθος, ποθῶ,

When this happens with men, it is loftier than any pleasure. When God is both lover and beloved, what word, what thought will be able to express the blessedness of the soul? Nothing else but the experience can do so. In order, therefore, that we may learn through our own experience[388] of this spiritual joy, this blessed life, and this treasure of untold blessings, let us put aside all things and cling to that love so that we may see our own joy and the glory of the God whom we desire and love. For to Him belong the glory and the power, together with His only begotten Son and the Holy Spirit, forever and ever. Amen.

ἔρως, and ἐρῶμαι, a terminology that reveals an understanding of love as not only more dynamic and intense but also more intimate, pulling the human toward the divine with a powerful force. See discussion in Papageorgiou, "A Theological Analysis," 110–113. Trakatellis, "Being Transformed," 222–223, notes, "What is particular in Chrysostom's exegesis of Romans, is this emphasis on a consuming, vibrant and total love which in turn becomes a central anthropological concept. A love leading to a transformation of the human being and, at the same time, becoming a sign of such a transformation. Here, love seems to be both cause and effect in the process of a radical human change, and Chrysostom appears to make no distinction between the two, perhaps deliberately so."

388 πεῖρα. Chrysostom points to "experience" as the only way to explain God's love. This concept is at the foundation of the Eastern monastic mysticism; the Christian life is developed in man's loving relationship with God, as experienced in prayer and worship.

HOMILY 10

Rom 5:12
Therefore, as through one man sin entered into the world and, through sin, death, and thus death has passed unto all men inasmuch as all have sinned.[389]

Paul does just what the best physicians do when they inquire closely into the root cause of diseases and come to the source of the trouble. First he said that we had received justification, and then he showed this by the patriarch, Abraham; and by the Spirit; and from the death of Christ. For Christ would not have died unless He were going to justify us. Next Paul confirms what he had shown by these witnesses, but from another source. While confirming his topic from opposite arguments, namely, from death and sin, he asks how, and in what way, and from what source death entered the world and how it conquered man.

How then did death come in and conquer? Through the sin of Rom 5:12 one man. But what does he mean when he says *inasmuch as all have sinned*? After Adam fell into sin, all became mortal because of him, Rom 5:13 even those who had not eaten of the tree. *Until the law, sin was in the world, but sin is not taken into account when there is no law.*[390] Some Rom 5:13 consider that Paul used the words *until the law* to mean the time before the law was given, such as the time of Abel, of Noah, or of Abraham, the time until Moses was born.

---

389 Paul is about to establish that God's love assures salvation for those whom He has justified despite the fact that in Adam all men have sinned. Through Adam sin entered the world and, through sin, men must suffer death, because Adam's sin brought with it mortality for all. But God's love will bring a new and unending life hereafter. See the notes on Romans 5:12–21 in NAB and RNT. Also ponder the penetrating remarks of Fitzmyer (JBC, 53:50–60) on this difficult chapter. See also my study on original sin: "Chrysostom and Augustine on the Sin of Adam and Its Consequences," *St. Vladimir's Theological Quarterly* 39, no. 4 (1995): 361–378.

390 The same principle as is stated in Rom 4:15. Before the law was given, evil deeds were committed, but the sinners were not legally charged. Cf. Fitzmyer, *JBC*, 53:58.

What sort of thing was sin at that time? Some say that Paul was speaking of the sin in paradise. Paul would then be saying that sin had not yet been done away with, but the fruit of it was still flourishing. For that sin [in paradise] brought in the death common to all, the death that has conquered and tyrannized us. Why then did Paul add, *Sin is not taken into account when there is no law?* Those who think and speak as we do say that Paul put these words in because of an objection on the part of the Jews. If sin does not exist apart from the law, how did death destroy all those men before the law was given? I think that what I am going to say is more reasonable and fits in better with the Apostle's thought. *Rom 5:13*

And what is this? When Paul said, *Until the law, sin was in the world*, I think he means this, namely, that after the law was given, the sin that came from the transgression of the law prevailed and continued to prevail as long as the law existed. For sin can have no existence, Paul says, when there is no law. What he means is this. If this sin that comes from transgression of the law produced death, how is it that all those died who were born before the law was given? If death had its origin from sin, but sin was not taken into account when there was no law, how is it that death conquered and prevailed? *Rom 5:13*

From this it becomes clear that it was not the sin that comes from transgression of the law, but the sin that came from Adam's disobedience, that destroyed all things. And what proves this? The fact that all men died before the law was given. For Paul says, *For death reigned from Adam to Moses, even over those who did not sin.* And how did death reign? *After the likeness of the transgression of Adam, who is the type of Him who was to come.* This is why Adam is a type of Jesus Christ. *Rom 5:14* *Rom 5:14*

Someone will ask, "How is Adam a type of Christ?" He is a type because Adam became the cause of death for his descendants, even though they had not eaten of the tree, because death came into the world when Adam ate of it. So too Christ became, for those sprung from Him, the One who gained that justification that, by His cross, He graciously granted to all of us, even though our acts were unjust.

This is why Paul constantly stresses "the one" and everywhere brings him to our attention, as when he says, *Just as through one man death entered the world,* and *By the offense of the one many died,* and *Nor was the gift as it was in the case of one man's sin,* and *Judgment was from one man unto condemnation,* and again *And if by one man's offense, death reigned through the one man,* and *Therefore, if by the offense of one man,* and again *Just as by the disobedience of one man the many became sinners.*

_{Rom 5:12}
_{Rom 5:15; 16}
_{Rom 5:17}
_{Rom 5:18; 19}

Nor does Paul let go of the "one man" theme. He holds fast to it so that when a Jew says to you, "How is it that by the good action of the one man, Christ, the world was saved?" you would be able to say to him, "How is it that by the disobedience of the one man, Adam, the world was condemned?" However, sin and grace are not equivalent to each other, nor are death and life the same, nor are the devil and God equals. The distance between them is without limit.

Therefore, both from the nature of the task, from the power of Him who undertook it, and from the very fitness of what was done (for this is much more suited to God, namely, to save rather than to punish), the supremacy and victory are on God's side. If this is so, what reason would you have for failing to believe? Tell me that! Paul showed that what had occurred was reasonable when he said, *But the gift is not like the offense. For if by the offense of the one the many died, much more has the grace of God and the gracious gift of the one man, Jesus Christ, abounded for the many.*[391]

_{Rom 5:15}

What Paul is saying is something like this. If the sin is so strong and is the sin of one man, how can grace, and that the grace of God—not only the grace of the Father, but also the grace of the Son—fail to surpass in every way the power of sin? It is much more reasonable that God's grace is far stronger than sin. For one man to be punished on account of another man does not seem to be very reasonable. But for one man to be saved by another is both much more fitting and more reasonable. Therefore, if the first of the two took place, the second may all the more be likely to happen.

---

[391] Cf. RNT note on Rom 5:12–21. "The gift" is the grace of justification through faith in Jesus Christ.

II

Therefore, from his comparison of the strength of sin and the greater strength of God's grace, Paul has shown that man's justification is both likely and logical. For after Paul had proved the strength of sin, the greater strength of grace would then be more readily accepted. He establishes that this was also necessary from what follows. How then does he prove this? Paul says, *The gift was not at all like the sin committed by the one man. For the judgment from the one sin led to condemnation. But grace led from many offenses to justification.* [Rom 5:16]

What is it that Paul is saying here? He is saying that a single sin had the power to bring on death and condemnation. But grace not only took away that one sin, but also the sins that came into our souls after that one. So that the comparison of "the gift" and "the sin" might not bring in an equal measure for the blessings of grace and the evils of sin, and so that when you heard of Adam's sin, you might not think that it was only that sin that Adam brought in that was taken away, Paul says that the remission applied to many offenses.[392]

What makes this clear? It becomes obvious because, after the sins beyond counting that were committed after Adam's sin in paradise, the result was justification. Where there is justification, it follows by all means and of necessity that there is life, as well as countless blessings—just as death follows where there is sin. For justification is more than life because it is the source of life.

Therefore, it is clear that very many blessings came into men's souls and that not only was Adam's sin taken away, but all the other sins as well. Paul proved this when he said, *Grace led from many offenses to justification.* [Rom 5:16] From this, of necessity, we have a joint proof that death was torn out by the roots. Because he had said that grace and justification were stronger than sin and death, Paul must now prove this very thing again.

Paul had just said that if the sin of one man destroyed all, much more would the grace of one man have the power to save. And he showed that not only that one sin was taken away by grace, but all the other sins as well. And he showed that not only were sins taken

---

392 Cf. Rom 5:19.

away, but that justification was also given. He also proved that Christ not only did the same amount of good as Adam had done of harm, but also that the good that Christ did was much greater and more abundant. Therefore, because Paul had revealed such lofty truths, he felt it was necessary here to give fuller proof for what he had said.

Rom 5:17　How then does he give this proof? He says, *If death reigned through one man because of his offense, much more shall those who received the overflowing grace and gift of justification live and reign through the one man, Jesus Christ.* What Paul is saying here means something such as this. What gave death its weapons against the world? It was that only the one man ate of the fruit of the tree. If, then, death received such power and strength from the one sin, when some men were found who had received grace and justification far greater than sin, how can they thereafter be subject to death?[393]

Rom 5:17　This is why Paul did not say here "grace," but *overflowing grace*. For from that grace we received not only as much as was required for removing that sin, but much more. For surely we were both freed from punishment and we rid ourselves of all evil; we were born again from above;[394] and when the old man was buried, we rose again. We were redeemed and sanctified; we were brought into adoption and justification. We became brothers of the Only Begotten, His joint heirs, and of one body with Him. Indeed, we were counted as His flesh and were joined to Him as a body to its head.

Rom 5:17　All of these, then, were what Paul gave the name of *overflowing grace*, showing that not only did we receive a medication that would compensate for the wound inflicted by sin, but also one that would bring us health, beauty, honor, glory, and dignities far surpassing our nature. Each one of these was enough to destroy death. But when all of them obviously run together as one, not even a trace of death is left, nor can even a shadow of it remain to be seen.

Suppose someone threw into jail a man who owed him a few cents—not only the man himself, but his wife, children, and

---

[393] Paul seems here to mean not only physical death, but also spiritual death, which is the separation of man from God, who is the unique source of life. Cf. Rom 5:21; 6:21, 23; 8:2, 6.
[394] Cf. John 3:3.

servants too, because of the man who owed the money. Suppose, then, that another man should pay off not only the few cents, but should add a free gift of ten thousand dollars to the debtor, and bring him from prison into the royal palace, and to the throne of the highest power. Suppose this benefactor should make the debtor share in the loftiest honor and every kind of magnificence. Suppose this benefactor would never thereafter remind him of the few pennies he had owed. Such was the situation in which we were.

For Christ paid off much more than we owed —as much more as a limitless ocean compared to a small drop of water. My friend, do not be doubtful when you see so great a wealth of blessings, do not inquire how that spark of death and sin was quenched when so great a torrent of graces rushed down upon it. Paul hinted at that when he said, *Those who received the overflowing grace and justification live and reign.* [Rom 5:17]

Because he had now clearly demonstrated this, he again made use of his first argument, and he strengthens it by repetition when he says that if through that offense all were punished, then they could also be justified by these means.[395] This is why Paul says, *Therefore, as from the offense of one man the result was condemnation for all men, so from the justice of the one man the result was justification of life for all men.* [Rom 5:18]

And again he insists upon this when he says, *For just as by the disobedience of the one man the many were constituted sinners, so by the obedience of the one man the many will be constituted just.* [Rom 5:19] Yet what Paul says seems to involve no small question. But if anyone pays careful attention, the question is easily answered. What, then, is the question? It is that he says that through one man's disobedience the many were made sinners. For the fact that when Adam sinned and became mortal those who were his descendants also became mortal is not improbable. But how would it be logical that from

---

395 Cf. Rom 5:15–17. See Stevens' note in NPNF[1] 11:403. Chrysostom grasps the fact that these verses constitute an argument *a fortiori*. There are three contrasts between sin and grace that show the superior power of grace: (1) It is much more reasonable that many should find life in one man's act than that many should suffer death because of one man's sin. (2) The condemnation has in it only the power of one sin; the power of grace overcomes countless transgressions. (3) Life in Christ must be greater than death in Adam.

Adam's disobedience another man would become a sinner? For such another man will not be found as owing a penalty on this account unless he became a sinner of his own accord.[396]

III

Rom 5:19 What, then, does the word *sinners* mean here? I think it means "subject to punishment and condemned to die." Paul has shown clearly and at length that when Adam died we all became mortal. The question now is "Why did this happen?" But Paul is no longer posing this question, because it does not contribute to his present theme. He is now doing battle against the Jew, who doubts and laughs to scorn the question of justification through one man.

For this reason, after he has shown that the punishment was carried over from one man to all, he no longer addresses the question as to why this was done. It is not a superfluous question, but Paul focuses only on things necessary to his argument. For the rules governing disputations forced him to not discuss this, but rather to refute his Jewish opponent. Therefore he leaves the question without a solution. But if any of you are seeking to learn the answer, we will say this by way of solution to the question.

Not only have we been in no way harmed by this death and condemnation if we will live a sober life, but we will even benefit, despite the fact that we have become mortal and subject to death. The first reason for this is the fact that we do not sin in a body that is immortal. The second is that we have countless grounds for following a religious way of life. Surely, the presence of death and the expectation of dying ourselves persuade us to be moderate, to practice self-control, to be subdued, and to keep ourselves away from all wickedness and evil.

Together with these virtuous acts, or even before them, death has brought in other and greater blessings. For it is from death that the crowns of the martyrs came, as did the rewards of the apostles. It was by death that Abel received justification, as did

---

[396] Section 22 of this homily shows the reason why "all men sinned" even before the law. Because Adam's disobedience brought in sin and physical death, his descendants who became sinners of their own accord received the penalty of spiritual death and separation from God, as well as of physical death.

Abraham after his son was slain, as was John [the Baptist] when he was beheaded for the sake of Christ, as were the three youths and Daniel.[397] For if we should will it so, neither death nor the devil will be able to do us harm.

Over and above these examples, we can also say this: Immortality will await us and, after a brief period of chastisement, we will enjoy without fear the blessings to come. It will be just as if we were under instruction in a kind of school in the present life where we learned from disease, tribulations, trials, poverty, and other things that seem to be deserving of dread, so that we might become suited to receive the blessings of the world to come.[398]

Now the law intervened that the offense might abound.[399] After Paul showed that the world was condemned by Adam's sin but was saved and set free from condemnation by Christ,[400] now, at the proper time, Paul raises the question about the law. And here, again, he undermines its glorious reputation. For he tells us that not only was the law far from doing any good and that it did not in any way prove helpful, but he shows that it even increased the malady of sin when it intervened. *(Rom 5:20)*

But the word *that* in the text quoted here does not give the cause, but the effect. For the reason why the law was given was not *so that the offense might abound*, but so that it might diminish and take away the offense. But the result was quite the opposite. Nor was this the case because of the nature of the law, but because of the carelessness and sluggishness of those who had received it. But why did Paul not say "the law was given," but *the law intervened*? It was to show that the need for the law was temporary but not absolute or necessary. And he says this in his Letter to the Galatians, *(Rom 5:20)*

---

397 Death is not an unmixed evil, as is seen from the examples of Abel (cf. Gen 4:3–8), Abraham (cf. Gen 22:1–13), and John the Baptist (cf. Matt 14:1–12). Although Abel and John were actually slain, Abraham, on God's command, slew a ram in place of Isaac. Also, Shadrach, Meshach, and Abednego (cf. Dan 3:19–24), as well as Daniel himself (Dan 6:21–23), all avoided death although they were ready to lay down their lives rather than offend God.

398 In § 27, it is tempting to see a veiled reference to the doctrine of purgatory; however, it seems safer to see three references to the travails of life on earth.

399 With the introduction of the law comes a second period, which Paul sees as posing a hindrance to justification.

400 Cf. Rom 5:19.

where he makes the same point clear, but in another way. For there he says, *Before the faith came, we were imprisoned by the law, shut up for the faith that was to be revealed.*[401]

<small>Gal 3:23</small>

Therefore, the law was guarding the flock not for itself, but for another law. Because the Jews were vulgar, dissolute, and indifferent to the very gifts that were bestowed on them, the law was given to them for this very reason, namely, that it might convict them the more, and teach them clearly in what a state they were, and, after increasing the accusation against them, might repress them all the more.

But you must not be afraid, for this was not to make the punishment greater, but so that the gift of grace might be seen to be greater. This is why Paul went on to say, "Where the offense has abounded, grace has abounded still more." Paul did not say "Grace has abounded," but *Grace has abounded still more*. For grace not only freed us from punishment, but also gave us remission from our sins, as well as life and other blessings, which we have mentioned many a time.

<small>Rom 5:20</small>

It is just as if someone should free a man suffering with fever from his illness, but also should make him handsome and strong, and endow him with honor. Or, again, not only would he give food to one who was hungry, but also make him master of great wealth and lead him to the highest post of authority and rule. But someone will ask, "How did sin abound?" The law gave countless commands. Therefore, because they transgressed them all, sins abounded. Do you see how great is the difference between grace and the law? For the law added to their condemnation; grace gave its gifts in superabundance.

IV

After Paul had spoken of God's ineffable liberality to us, he again seeks out the beginning and the source of death and life. What then is the source of death? It is sin. It was on this account that Paul said, *So that as sin has reigned through death, so also grace may reign by way of justification, leading to eternal life through Jesus Christ,*

<small>Rom 5:21</small>

---

401 Also see Gal 3:9.

our Lord. He said this to show that sin was a sort of king, and death was a kind of soldier standing in the ranks of sin, armed with weapons supplied by that king.

If, then, sin has armed death, it is quite clear that the justification, which takes away sin and which has been brought in by grace, not only disarms death, but also takes it away and destroys its entire dominion, inasmuch as justification is mightier than the dominion of death. For neither man nor the devil confers justification. Rather, it comes to us from God and His grace. And it leads our life to a better state and to infinite good.

This life will have no end, and from this you may come to know its fullness. Sin came and drove us from our present life. But when grace came, it presented us not with our present life on earth, but with a life that is immortal and eternal. However, it is Christ who is the cause of all these blessings for us. So have no doubts about your life if you have justification. For justification is greater than life on earth, because it is the mother of life hereafter.

What then shall we say? Shall we continue in sin so that grace may abound? By no means! Again Paul is turning his argument to a moral discussion. He does not make the transition directly so as not to seem to be burdensome and vexing to many in his audience. Rather, he makes the transition from the sequence of his doctrinal teaching. For by varying his discourse in this way, he avoids giving displeasure to his hearers by what he will say. It was on this account that later in this letter he says, *But I have written rather boldly here and there.* But if he had not done so, they would have thought that he was rather harsh. Rom 6:1

Rom 15:15

And so he had shown the greatness of the grace by the greatness of the sins that it healed. But for this reason, in the eyes of the unthinking, what he said seemed to be an encouragement to commit sin.[402] For they would say that if a greater grace was seen because we committed great sins, let us not give up sinning so that a greater grace may be shown to us. So that they might not say this or even think it, see now how Paul turns the objection around.

First he does it by a prohibition when he says, *By no means!* And he usually does this when people admit that the question is most Rom 6:2

---

402 Rom 5:20.

Rom 6:2 absurd. Then he sets forth an argument that cannot be opposed. What is this argument? He says, *How shall we who are dead to sin still live in it?* What does he mean by *we who are dead?* Does it mean that as far as sin goes, we have all received the sentence of death? Or does it mean that we are dead to sin because we believed and were baptized? Surely it is the latter reason that we should give, and what follows makes this perfectly clear.

Rom 6:2 And what does Paul mean when he says, *We became dead to sin?* He means that we must not obey sin in anything any more. Baptism did this once and for all; it made us dead to sin. However, by our own zeal after baptism, we must continually go on doing this successfully, so that even if sin gives us ten thousand commands, we refuse to obey any. We remain as motionless as a corpse. It is true that elsewhere Paul says that sin itself is dead.[403] But he says that because he wishes to show that virtue is easy. But here, because he is eager to rouse his audience, he applies death to sin to us.

Rom 6:3 Because what he had said was not yet clear, Paul again explains it and speaks in a rebuking fashion. For he says, *Do you not know, my brothers, that all of us who have been baptized into Christ have been baptized into His death? Therefore, we were buried with Him by means of baptism into death.* What does Paul mean when he says that we have been baptized into His death? He means that it is with a view to our dying as Christ died. For baptism is the cross. What the cross and burial were to Christ, that is what baptism has become for us, even if not in the same way.

Rom 6:5 For Christ died and was buried in the flesh, but our death and burial are death and burial to sin. This is why Paul does not say "united with Him in death," but *united with Him in the likeness of His death.* For His death and ours are both deaths, but not of the same subject. For one death, death in the flesh, was Christ's. Ours is death to sin. Therefore, just as His death was a true death, so also is ours. If ours is truly a death, we again must contribute our fair share.

Rom 6:4 This is why Paul went on to say, *So that, just as Christ has risen from the dead through the glory of the Father, so we also may walk in newness*

---

403 Cf. Rom 7:8, and see notes *ad loc.* in Confraternity edition and NAB. See also note on Rom 7:7–12 in RNT.

of life. Here, along with the attention we must pay to our new life, Paul is also hinting at the subject of our resurrection. How is this so? What he is saying is that if you have believed that Christ died and that He was raised up, therefore you must believe in your own death and resurrection.[404] For yours is like His because yours is also a cross and burial. If you shared in His death and burial, much more will you share in His resurrection and life. If the greater thing —I mean sin —has been destroyed, you must no longer doubt about the lesser —I mean about the destruction of death.

But for the time being Paul leaves these questions to be pondered by the consciences of his hearers. After the future resurrection has been set before our eyes, he demands of us another resurrection, the new way of life, which is brought about in our present existence on earth by a change in our habits. For when the fornicator becomes chaste, the covetous man merciful, and the harsh man mild, a resurrection marking a beginning of the future resurrection has taken place.

How is this a resurrection? It is a resurrection because sin is dead, justification has arisen, the old life has disappeared, and we are living in that new and angelic life. And when you hear of a new life, look for a great alteration and a considerable change.

V

But I burst into tears and groan deeply when I think of how great is the change of life and habits that Paul demands, and of how deep a sluggishness we have given ourselves over to by returning, after baptism, to our former old age, by going back to Egypt, and by recalling the garlic stalks after we had eaten manna.[405] We do undergo a change for ten or twenty days at the time of our baptism, but then we again take up our former ways. But Paul demands that this change in our way of living last not for a set number of days, but for our whole life.

But we return to our former vomit[406] although we have received the youth that came from grace. Again we are building up the old

---
404 Cf. Rom 6:5.
405 Cf. Num 11:4–6.
406 Cf. Prov 26:11; 2 Pet 2:22.

age that comes from sin. For it is the love of money, the slavery to unsuitable desires and to sins of whatever sort, that usually makes an old man of the one who pursues them. And what has become decayed and has grown old is near its end.[407] Yet we cannot see a body so enfeebled and palsied by age as is a soul that is decayed and corrupted by many sins.

For in this state a soul is driven to the ultimate stage of dotage. It utters inarticulate sounds such as men do who have grown very old and delirious. Such a soul is filled up and running at the nose. It is greatly deranged and forgetful. It has scales before its eyes. It is disgusting and is an easy prey for the devil. And surely the souls of sinners are such. Not so are the souls of the just: they are youthful, well favored, and totally in the flower of their prime. They are fully prepared for any fight or struggle.

But the souls of sinners, even if they are subjected to a slight assault, immediately fall and perish, as the prophet declared when he said, *But rather as the chaff that the wind scatters away from the face of the earth*. In such a way are those who live in sin driven here and there. They lie unprotected for all to abuse. For neither do they see with clear vision, nor do they hear distinctly, nor do they speak articulately. Their throats are filled with hiccups. They carry about a vast amount of saliva floating around in their mouths. I wish it were saliva, and not something still more disgusting.

Ps 1:4

But as it is, they utter words more malodorous than any slime. And what is still worse, they lack the strength to spit their saliva-soaked words away, but, much to our disgust, they catch the saliva in their hands and smear it upon themselves, where it hardens and becomes difficult to remove. Perhaps you grow squeamish as you listen to this description. You should do so all the more at the facts described. If you are disgusted when these unpleasant things happen in the body, you should be much more disgusted when they are happening in the soul.

Such a one was the young man who wasted all his possessions and had fallen to the lowest level of evil.[408] His condition was weaker than that which any imbecile or invalid has suffered. But after he

---

407 Cf. Heb 8:13.
408 The story of the prodigal son is found in Luke 15:11–32.

made up his mind, he suddenly became a new man by changing his mind and by a single resolve. For when he said, *I shall return to my father*, this one sentence provided him with every blessing. Rather, it was not the simple words, but the deed that was added to the words. For he did not say, "I shall return," and then stayed where he was. He said, *I shall return*, and he went back and made the entire journey.

Luke 15:18

Luke 15:18

Let us do the same. Even if we have been carried into a foreign land, let us return to our Father's house, and let us not fear the length of the journey. If we make up our minds, the way back again is easy and very quick. Only let us leave the strange and foreign land, for that is what sin is, and it leads us far away from our Father's house. Therefore, let us leave this land, so that we may quickly return to our Father's house.

For our Father loves us dearly. Because we have changed, He loves us no less than those whose good repute has earned His love. He will even love us more, just as the father in the parable poured great honors on his son. For he felt great pleasure when he got his son back. Someone may say, "How am I to come back?" Only make a beginning and the whole task is completed. Stay away from evil and go no further into it, and you have already taken hold of the problem.

In the case of sick people, just as getting no sicker could be the beginning of getting better, so too does it happen in the matter of evil. Do not fall any deeper into sin, and your wickedness will come to an end. Even if you do this for two days, you will stay away from sin more easily on the third day. And after three days, you will add ten days, then twenty, then a hundred, and then your whole life. For the further you go on, the more easily will you see that the road is easy. And soon you will stand at the top of the hill, and all at once you will enjoy many blessings.

For so it was at the time when that prodigal son returned. There were flutes, harps, dances, banquets, and festivals. And the father, who ought to have demanded an accounting from his son because of his untimely extravagance and his flight to such a faraway place, made no such demands. Rather, he looked on his son as a lad of good reputation. He could not find it in himself to reproach him even with a word, nor did he mention his former deeds. Rather, he embraced him, kissed him, and killed the fatted calf. He put a robe on him and added many an adornment.

Because we have these examples, let us take heart and not despair. For God does not rejoice so much when He is called Master as when He is called Father. Nor does He find as much pleasure in having a servant as when He has a son. He does not wish to be called Master or to have a servant rather than being called Father and adopting a son. Surely this is why He did all that He has done, this is why He did not spare His Only Begotten[409] so that we might receive the adoption as sons, so that we might love Him not only as Master, but as our Father.

And if He obtains this love from us, just like one who has been glorified, He takes delight in it and broadcasts it to all the world. And He does this even though He needs nothing of what we have to give. Surely He did this in the case of Abraham when He said for all the world to hear, *I am the God of Abraham and Isaac and Jacob.*[410] His servants should have found glory in this, but now it is the Master who clearly does so.

This is why Jesus says to Peter, *Do you love me more than these?* to show that He looks for nothing from us before love. It was also for this reason that the Father ordered Abraham to sacrifice his son,[411] so that He might show to all that the patriarch loved Him exceedingly. This desire to be loved exceedingly comes from God's exceeding love. This is the reason why Christ said to the apostles, *Whoever loves father or mother more than Me is not worthy of Me.*

VI

This is why Christ commands us to put our soul, which is more closely united to us than all else, second to our love for Him. He does this because He wishes to be loved by us above and beyond all else.[412] For when we have no great feelings for a person, we do not have any excessive need for his friendship and love, even if he is

---

409 Cf. Rom 8:32.
410 Cf. NAB note; Matt 22:32; Mark 12:26; Luke 20:37.
411 Cf. Gen 22:2.
412 Cf. Matt 10:39; John 12:25.

a great and illustrious man. But when we feel a warm and genuine love for someone, even if the person we love is of low rank and humble station, we consider his love to be a great honor. On this account, Christ Himself called it glory not only to be loved by us, but also to undergo those shameful sufferings on our behalf. But those sufferings were a glory only because of His love. But when we suffer on His behalf, it is not only because of love, but also because of the greatness and dignity of Him whom we long for, that these sufferings could reasonably be called a glory and in fact be a glory.

Therefore, let us run to face the greatest dangers on His behalf just as if we were running to seek crowns of victory. Let us not think that poverty or sickness or insults or slanders or death itself is burdensome or oppressive when we endure these things for His sake. If we are living a sober life, we are the ones who profit most from these sufferings. But if we are not living a sober life, even the pleasures that are the opposites of these sufferings will bring no benefits to us.

Consider this. Is someone insulting you and fighting with you? Then he is making you ready to be watchful and on your guard. He is affording you an opportunity to become like God. If you love the one who is plotting against you, you will be like Him who *makes the sun to rise on the wicked and the good*. Does another man steal your possessions? If you endure this with nobility, you will receive the same reward as do those who give everything to the poor. For we read in the Letter to the Hebrews, *You have joyfully accepted the plundering of your belongings because you know that you have a better possession in heaven and a lasting one.* [Matt 5:45] [Heb 10:34]

Did someone revile you and reproach you? Whether his words were true or lies, he has woven for you a very great crown if you endure his abuse with mildness. The man who slanders also provides us with an abundant reward. For Jesus said, *Rejoice and exult when men will falsely speak every wicked word against you, because your reward is great in heaven.* And again, even if he is speaking the truth, it is also of the greatest advantage, but only if we endure with mildness what he says about us. [Matt 5:11–12]

For the Pharisee was telling the truth when he was speaking evil about the publican. But still he made a just man out of the publican.[413] But what need is there to talk about them one by one? If we go through all the trials of Job, we can get an accurate account of all of them. This is why Paul also said, *If God is for us, who is against us?*

Rom 8:31

Therefore, just as our zeal brings us profit even from things that cause us pain and distress, so too, when we are sluggish and lazy, we do not become better men because of these things, which could help and profit us. Tell me this. What help did Judas get from his association with Christ? How did the law help the Jews? How did paradise help Adam? How did Moses help those in the desert?

Therefore, putting aside all else, we must look to one thing only, namely, how we may properly manage our own affairs. If we do this, the devil himself will never be superior to us, but he will be a great help to us if he prepares us to be watchful and to live a sober life. This is the way Paul aroused the Ephesians when he was describing how fierce the devil is.[414] But we slumber and snore even though we have to deal with an enemy who is so wicked.

If we were aware that a serpent was lurking next to our bed, we would have roused up our energy and zeal to slay it. When the devil is lurking in our souls, we think we are suffering no dire harm, and we fall back to sleep. The reason for this is that we do not see him with our bodily eyes. And yet this is why we must rouse ourselves the more and live the sober life. For if a man might easily guard himself against an enemy whom he can see, we cannot readily escape an unseen enemy unless we are constantly armed for battle. This is all the more true because the devil does not know how to make a straightforward attack. If he did, he would quickly be defeated.

But often it is under the appearance of friendship and love that he injects his cruel poison. It was in this way that the devil induced Job's wife to give him that wicked advice after she had put on the mask of love.[415] So too, while speaking with Adam, Satan played the part of an actor who was protecting Adam and was concerned

---

413 Cf. Luke 18:10–14.
414 Cf. Eph 6:11–13.
415 Cf. Job 2:9.

about him when he said, *Your eyes will be opened on the day you eat* — Gen 3:5
of the tree. The devil also put on a pretense of piety and persuaded Jephthah to slay his daughter and to offer an unlawful sacrifice.[416]

Did you see his artifices and craft? Did you see his varied and changeful methods of waging war? Be on your guard and on every side defend yourselves with spiritual weapons,[417] so that you may accurately learn his devices. Do this so that he may not make you his captive, but that you may easily make him yours. It was in this way that Paul got the better of him, namely, by learning these things with exactness. This is why he said, *For we are not unaware of* — 2 Cor 2:11
his devices.

Therefore, let us take care to learn and avoid his treacherous plots so that, after we have carried off our victory over him, we may be proclaimed as victors both in the present life and in the age to come. And may we attain to eternal blessings by the grace and loving-kindness of our Lord Jesus Christ, with whom be glory, power, and honor to the Father, together with the Holy Spirit, now and forever, world without end. Amen.

---

416 Cf. Judg 11:29–40.
417 Cf. Eph 6:11–17.

HOMILY 11

Rom 6:5

If we have been united with Him through the likeness to His death, so also shall we be through a likeness to His resurrection. [418]

What I said before I shall now say again, namely, that Paul frequently turns his discourse into moral application. In his other Epistles he does not do this, but separates them into two sections: the first part he limits to dogmatic questions, and in the second he concerns himself with moral matters. But he does not do this here. Throughout this whole letter he mingles the two, and he treats of the one and the other so that his discussion may be readily received.[419]

Here, then, Paul says that there are two dyings, and two deaths. The first is accomplished by Christ in baptism; the other should be accomplished by ourselves through the zeal of our lives after baptism. That our former sins were buried came about through the gift of Christ. That we remain dead to sin after baptism must be the work of our own earnestness and zeal, however much we see that God is helping us here. For baptism possesses the power not only to do away with our former sins, but also to strengthen us against future falls. Just as in the case of your former sins you contributed your faith so that they were destroyed, so in the case of your sins after baptism you must show the change in your earnest zeal so that you do not defile yourselves again.[420]

---

418 Paul continues his exposition of how freedom from sin, which comes from the grace of justification, leads to new life in God through Jesus Christ.
419 Cf. Homily 10.36.
420 Justification often involves two deaths: the one is the death to sin accomplished by Christ in baptism; the other, which involves death to sins committed after bap-

For it is this, and counsel like it, that Paul is giving you when he says, *For if we have been united with him through the likeness to his death, so shall we be through the likeness of his resurrection also.*[421] Do you see how he roused his audience by immediately leading them to his Master and by his effort to show them their great likeness to Christ? This is why Paul did not say "united by his death," so that you might not contradict him, but "through the likeness of his death." For our substance itself did not die, but the man of sins, that is, wickedness, died. — Rom 6:5

Nor did Paul say, "For if we had a share of (or took part in) the likeness of His death." What did he say? *If we have been united (or grown together) with the likeness of His death*, because he was hinting by the word *united* or *growing together*[422] that the fruit of this likeness is found in us. For just as Christ's body, when buried in the earth, bore as its fruit the salvation of the world, so also our bodies, when buried in baptism, bore as their fruit justification, sanctity, adoption, and countless blessings. And our bodies will hereafter bear as fruit the gift of resurrection. — Rom 6:5

Because, then, we were buried in water while Christ was buried in the earth — we in regard to sin and Christ in regard to His body — this is why Paul did not say "united in death," but *united in the likeness of death*. For the one and the other are death, but not of the same subject. If, therefore, Paul is saying, we have been united in death,[423] we will be united in the resurrection. And here he is speaking of the future resurrection. — Rom 6:5

When Paul spoke earlier about death and said, *Do you not know, my brothers, that all we who have been baptized into Christ were baptized* — Rom 6:3

---

tism, involves more than just faith, such as the earnestness and zeal of our lives after baptism to avoid the defilement of sin that would destroy our life in God by future falls. Such falls are prevented or repented for through the help that comes to us by Christ's resurrection.

421 Verses 5, 6, and 7 affirm of the baptized Christian what Paul will say about Christ Himself in verses 8, 9, and 10, which supply the Christological foundation for the new Christian way of life. See Fitzmyer, JBC, 53:64.

422 Paul here uses the bold image of "growing together" to express the communication of Christ-life to the Christian in the way a young branch grafted on a tree is nourished by the main stock. See Fitzmyer, JBC, 53:64.

423 The construction here is harsh and seems to require "in the likeness of death." See NPNF1 11:408n1.

into his death,[424] he gave no clear explanation about resurrection. Rather, he spoke about the way of life after baptism and bade us to walk in the newness of life. This is why he here takes up the same discussion and now proceeds to foretell to us the resurrection. And so that you may learn that he is not speaking of the resurrection that comes from baptism, but about that other resurrection, he goes on to say, *For if we have been united through the likeness of his death.* But he does not then say, "We shall be in the likeness of His resurrection." What he does say is *We shall be of the resurrection also.*

Rom 6:5

Paul does not wish you to say, "If we do not die as he died, how are we to rise as he rose?" For when he mentioned the death, he did not say "united by death," but *by the likeness of death.* But when he spoke of the resurrection, he did not say that we shall be in the likeness of his resurrection, but that we shall be of the resurrection itself. He did not say that we *have been*, but that we *shall be.* By these words he makes it clear that he is referring to the resurrection that has not yet occurred but that will take place in the future.

Rom 6:5

Next, because he wished to make what he said worthy of belief, Paul shows that there is another resurrection here in this world and prior to the future resurrection, so that from the present resurrection you may believe in the one that will come hereafter. For after he said that we will be united in the resurrection, he went on to add, *For we know that our old self has been crucified with Him in order that the body of sin may be destroyed.*[425] In this way Paul puts together both the cause and the proof of the resurrection to come. He did not say "has been crucified," but *has been crucified with Him.* In this way he brings baptism close to the cross.

Cf. Rom 6:6

So Paul had just said, *We have been united with Him in the likeness of His death in order that the body of sin may be destroyed.* But he is not calling this body of ours by that name, but he is giving the name

Cf. Rom 6:5–6

---

424 Chrysostom cited this text (Rom 6:3) in Homily 10.40. See the Confraternity edition's note on Rom 6:3, which states that in baptism by immersion, the descent into the water suggests the descent of the initiate's body into the grave, and the ascent suggests his resurrection to a new life as a Christian.

425 Chrysostom takes the "body of sin" to indicate sin in general; it might also mean the body as subject to concupiscence (ἐπιθυμία: "desire/sexual desire/lust") and all the other passions that make it an instrument of sin. For an extensive discussion of the various forms and expressions of ἐπιθυμία, see Papageorgiou, "A Theological Analysis," chap. 4, pp. 226–245.

body of sin to all iniquity. Just as he called the whole sum of wickedness *the old man*, so again he also calls the wickedness that is made up of the different parts of iniquity the body of that *old man*. And so that [you may see that] what I have said is not the result of conjecture, listen to Paul as he interprets this very point in what follows. Cf. Col 3:9.

After Paul said, *So that the body of sin may be destroyed*, he added, *That we may no longer be slaves to sin.* For he wishes this body to be dead in this way, not so that it die and disappear, but so that you sin no more. And as Paul goes on, he makes this still clearer when he says, *For he who is dead has been freed of sin.*⁴²⁶ Paul says this about every man, namely, that just as he who is dead is freed from sinning for the future because he is now a corpse, so also is the man who comes up from the waters of baptism. Because he died there once and for all, he must remain dead to sin altogether. Rom. 6:7

II

Therefore, if you have died in baptism, remain dead. For no man who has died can commit sin any longer. But if you do commit sin, you are destroying the gift of God. Therefore, after Paul has demanded of us to live the Christian way of life, he is quick to bring up the crowns when he says, *But if we have died with Christ.* Indeed, this is the greatest crown and comes before the others because we share it with Christ. But he says that he gives you another reward too. What sort of reward is this? It is life eternal. For Paul says, *For we believe that we shall also live together with Christ.* What makes this clear? *For we know that Christ, having risen from the dead, dies now no more.* Cf. Rom 6:8

Cf. Rom 6:8

Cf. Rom 6:9

Consider again Paul's determination and see how he establishes this point from opposite grounds. Because it was natural for some to be upset because he mentioned the cross and death, he shows that for the future they must feel confidence because of both the cross and death. For Paul tells you that, because Christ died once, you must not consider that He is dead. Surely, from the very fact that He died, He remains immortal. How can this be true? Because His death became the death of death. He did die, but for this very

---

426 Probably referring to those who are justified and hence freed from sin.

Cf. Rom 6:10 reason He does not die. *For the death He died, He died to sin*. What does Paul mean by *to sin*? He means that Christ was not subject to that death, but that He died because of our sin. The reason that Christ died was so that He might take away that sin and cut off its sinews and its power.

Do you see how he frightened them? For if He does not die a second time, then neither is there a second bath of baptism. But if there is no second bath of baptism, then do not incline the scale of your lives towards sin. Paul argues all these things because he is taking a stand against what some have held, namely, *Let us do evil that good may come*,[427] and *Shall we continue in sin so that grace may abound?* So he sets down all these arguments because he is tearing out such opinions by their roots. So Paul says, *The life that Christ lives, He lives for God*, that is, a life incapable of dissolution, so that *death no longer has dominion over Him*. For if it was not because He was subject to it, but because of the sins of others, that He died that death, much less will He die again, because He has destroyed that death.

Cf. Rom 3:8
Cf. Rom 6:1
Cf. Rom 6:10
Cf. Rom 6:9

Cf. Heb 9:26–28 Paul also said this in his Epistle to the Hebrews: *But as it is, once and for all at the end of the ages, He has appeared for the destruction of sin by the sacrifice of Himself. And just as it is appointed that men die once, and after this comes the judgment, so also was Christ offered up once to take away the sins of many; the second time He will appear not to take away sin, but to bring salvation to those who await him.*

Paul also shows both the strength of the life that is lived according to God and the power of sin. As for the life lived according to God, he shows that Christ will die no more. As for the power of sin, if it brought about the death of Him who is without sin, how can it fail to destroy those who are subject to it?

Then, after he had discussed the life of Christ, so that no one might ask, "What then does what you have been talking about have to do with us?" he went on to add *So must you consider yourselves to be dead to sin but alive to God*. And he did well to say *you must consider*. For it is not possible to put before our bodily eyes what he is talking about. He goes on to ask what we must consider. *That you are dead to sin but alive in God in Christ Jesus, our Lord*. For the one who lives in

Cf. Rom 6:11
Cf. Rom 6:11

---

427 See Homily 10.36–37.

this way will lay hold of every virtue because he has Jesus Himself as his ally. For that is what Paul means by *in Christ*. For if Christ raised the dead to life, much more will He be able to keep them alive when they are not dead.

Therefore, do not let sin rule in your mortal body so that you obey its lusts. Paul did not say, "Let not the flesh live or act," but *Do not let sin rule*.[428] Christ did not come to destroy our nature; He came to set aright our power of free choice. Then, to show that wickedness does not hold us in its grip by force or necessity, but only when we will it so, Paul did not say, "Let sin not tyrannize," because that would imply necessity, but *Do not let sin rule*. Cf. Rom 6:12

For surely it would be absurd for those who are being led into the kingdom of heaven to have sin ruling over them as their queen,[429] and for those who are being summoned to reign with Christ to choose to be the captives of sin. This would be just as if a man should tear the diadem from his head and choose to be a slave to a woman possessed by an evil spirit, who came to him as a beggar clothed in rags.

Next, because it is a difficult task to overcome sin, see how Paul shows that the labor is even easy. See how he exhorts and encourages us when he tells us not to let sin rule *in our mortal bodies*. For this shows that our struggles are temporary and quickly over and done. But at the same time he reminds us of our former evil state and the source of death. For it was from sin that the human body became mortal, although it was not prone to death in the beginning. Cf. Rom 6:12

But it is possible for one who has a mortal body not to sin. Do you see how abundant the grace of Christ is? For Adam slipped and fell even though he had a body that was not yet mortal. Yet although you have a body subject to death, you will be able to receive a crown. Someone will ask how it is, then, that sin rules? It does not rule of its own power, but because of your indifference and sluggishness.

---

428 Perhaps we have here an argument against the Manichaeans and their tenet that material things are intrinsically evil and that sin is unavoidable.

429 The Greek word for sin is ἁμαρτία (*hamartia*), a feminine noun, which may be why the ruler here is a queen.

This is why, after he said, *Do not let sin rule,* Paul showed what manner of sovereignty sin possessed. For he went on to add, *So that you obey its lusts.* For it is no honor to indulge the body with power in all things. Rather, to do so is the highest degree of slavery, and this stretches dishonor to its utmost extreme. For when the body does whatever it wishes, it is then robbed of all freedom; when it is held in check, then it especially preserves its proper value. *Do not offer the members of your body to sin as weapons of iniquity any longer. Rather, offer yourselves to God as weapons for justice.*

Cf. Rom 6:12

Cf. Rom 6:13

III

Therefore, your body stands midway between evil and virtue, just as its weapons do. The man who puts these weapons to use accomplishes either evil or virtue. An example would be if two men had the same kinds of weapons to defend themselves. One of the men was a soldier doing battle to defend his country; the other was a soldier turned robber who carried his weapons against the country's inhabitants. No accusation would be leveled against the weapons, but against the crime committed by the one who uses them.

We can say this of the body that becomes evil or virtuous according to the intention of the soul and not according to the body's nature. Take the eye as an example. If the eye ogles the beauty of another person, it then becomes a weapon of wickedness, but not because of its own operation. For the operation of the eye is to see, not to see with wicked intent. The wickedness comes from the mind of him who commands the eye. If you bridle and curb your eye, it becomes a weapon for justice. The same is true of the tongue, the hands, and all the body's other members.

Paul did well to call sin unrighteousness. For when a man commits sin, he commits an injustice either to himself or his neighbor — rather, to himself more than to his neighbor. Therefore, now that Paul has led us away from wickedness, he leads us to virtue when he says, *But offer yourselves to God as those who have come back to life from the dead.* See how, from his unadorned words, in this verse he speaks of God after having spoken of sin in the preceding verse.

Cf. Rom 6:13

For after he showed how great the difference between the two rulers was, he shuts off from every excuse the soldier who rejected God and chose to serve in the ranks of the kingdom of sin. And Paul proves this not only by what he has said, but by the words that followed, when he said, "As those who have come back to life from the dead." By these words he shows the destruction of sin and the greatness of God's gift.[430] For consider, Paul is saying, who you were and what you have become.

Who, then, were you before? You were dead and ruined by a destruction that could not be set aright by any means. For there was no one who could lend you aid. And who did you come to be from among those whom death had destroyed? You came back to live an immortal life. And who did this for you? God, who can do all things. Therefore, it is right and just for you to join the ranks that God commands and to present yourselves with as much zeal as would those *who have come back to life from the dead, and whose members are weapons of justice for God.* Cf. Rom 6:13

Therefore, the body is not evil if it can at least become a weapon for justice. For when Paul called it a weapon, he made it clear that there is a harsh warfare awaiting us. We need strong armor and a noble spirit that understands the nature of these battles well. And before all else, we need one to command us. But the Commander is close at hand. He is ever ready for the fray; He is ever invincible. He has prepared for us strong weapons. But we must have the firm resolve to use these weapons as we should, so that we may obey our Commander and take up the fray for our fatherland.

Therefore, after Paul had given us this great exhortation and reminded us of weapons, fighting, and wars, see how again he encourages the soldier and anoints his zeal when he says, *No longer shall sin have dominion over you, because you are not under the law, but under grace.* If, then, sin no longer has dominion over us, why does he impose such commands as when he said, *Do not let sin rule in your mortal body,* and *No more offer your members to sin as weapons for iniquity?* Cf. Rom 6:14

What does Paul mean when he gives these commands? When he said these words, he was, as it were, sowing here a kind of seed

---

430 The "gift" is the grace of justification and baptism.

in his discourse, a seed that later he is going to unfold and develop with extended argument. What then is this statement? Before the coming of Christ, our body was easily overcome by sin. For after Adam's sin brought death, a great swarm of passions entered into man. And for this reason he was not very nimble in the race for virtue. Neither was the Spirit yet present to help, nor was baptism, which could deaden these passions.

Man was like a resistant and ill-bridled horse that ran but often went astray. The law stated what must be done and what must not be done, but it did not propose to those in the contest anything more than counsel and advice through its words. After Christ's coming, the struggles became easier, but greater goals were set for us because we had a greater share of help. This is why Christ said, *Unless your justice exceeds that of the scribes and Pharisees, you will not enter the kingdom of heaven.*

Cf. Matt 5:20

But Paul will say this more clearly later on; meanwhile, he here hints at it briefly by showing that sin will not get the better of us unless we bend very low and submit ourselves to it like slaves. For it is not only the law that commands us, but also grace, which took away our former sins and fortifies us against future transgressions. For the law promised the crowns after the trials, but grace gave us the crowns first, and then drew us into the struggles.

It seems to me that Paul is not here alluding to the whole life of a believer, but that he is making a comparison between baptism and the law. And he states this also in another place when he says, *The letter kills, but the spirit gives life.* For the law convicts one of transgression; grace frees him from it. Just as the law establishes the sin by convicting man, so grace, by forgiving the sin, does not permit us to be sin's subject and slave. The result is that you have been freed from this tyranny in two ways: because you are not subject to the law, and because you have enjoyed grace.

Cf. 2 Cor 3:6

IV

So after Paul has given his audience a chance to catch their breath, he again gives them grounds to feel secure by bringing in an exhortation in reply to an objection. This is what he says. *What then?*

Cf. Rom 6:15

Are we to commit sin because we are not under the law, but under grace? By no means! First he denies it because it is so absurd. Next he turns his discourse into an exhortation. For he shows that there is great ease in the struggle when he has this to say: *Do you not know that when you offer yourselves as obedient slaves to someone, you are the slaves of the one whom you obey, whether yours is the slavery of sin, which leads to death, or of obedience, which leads to justification?* Cf. Rom 6:16

What Paul means is this: "I am not speaking of Gehenna, nor of the great punishment it brings. I am speaking of the disgrace it is in this world when you become slaves, slaves by your own choice, slaves of sin. And the price you pay is so great that you die a second death. For before baptism, this slavery brought death to your body. Your wound required such great medical care that the Lord of all things came down to die and, in this way, to destroy the evil. If, after such a great gift and freedom, sin again takes hold of you with your full consent — because you again bend down low before it as its slave — what is there that sin will not do? Therefore, do not rush into so deep a pit; do not willingly give yourselves up in surrender."

In times of war soldiers are often forced to surrender even against their wills. But here no one will overcome you unless you choose to desert. And after Paul tried to shame them out of a sense of duty, he fills them with alarm by the different consequences. He puts before them the wages of both kinds of slavery: death or justification. And the death is not such as the mortal body undergoes — it is one that is far worse.

For if Christ is to die no more, who will destroy death? No one. Therefore we must be punished and suffer vengeance forever. For the death that men can perceive by their senses is not the death still to come. In this life death gives rest to the body by separating it from the soul. *The last enemy to be destroyed will be death.*[431] And for this reason the punishment will last forever. Cf. 1 Cor 15:26

But this will not be so for those who obey God; justification and the blessings that spring from it will be their reward. *But thanks be to God that you who were the slaves of sin have now given obedience from* Cf. Rom 6:17

---

431 The argument found in §§ 22–32 of this homily is clarified in the RNT and NAB notes on Rom 7:13–25.

your hearts to that form of doctrine into which you were delivered.[432] So, after Paul turned them away from slavery to sin and frightened them by the consequences that followed it, he exhorted them by the rewards awaiting those obedient to God, and he again sets them on the right road by reminding them of the benefits to come.

In this way, he shows that they have been set free from great evils, that this was not accomplished by any toils and labors of their own, and that what comes in the future would be easier to manage. Just as a man who has rescued a captive from a cruel tyrant encourages the captive not to run back again to his master by reminding him of the difficulties of that tyranny, so does Paul show us most vividly the evils of the past by giving thanks to God.

For, as Paul says, to set us free from all those evils was beyond any human power, but he thanks God, who was willing and able to accomplish such things. And he did well when he said, *You gave obedience from your hearts.* For you were subject to neither necessity nor force, but you came to Him of your own accord and zeal. And this is the statement of a man who is praising and rebuking at the same time. For if you came forward of your own accord and had to endure neither necessity nor force, what pardon or defense would you have if you ran back again to your former ways?

Next, so that you may learn that all this occurred not so much because of their prudence, but also because of God's grace, after Paul said, *You gave obedience from your hearts,* he went on to add, *to that form of doctrine into which you were delivered.* For their obedience from the heart reveals their free will. But that they were delivered hints at the help that came from God. But what is the "orm of doctrine? It is to live rightly and in conformity with the best mode of conduct. *Freed from your sin, you became slaves of justice.*

Cf. Rom 6:18

He [Paul] shows here two of God's gifts: that He freed us from sin; and that He enslaved us to righteousness, which is a state better than any kind of freedom. This is what God has done, just like one who, receiving an orphan from the barbarians in the land of exile, not only redeems him from captivity, but also makes himself

---

[432] The Confraternity edition explains "you were delivered" as meaning "you were instructed"; NAB as "which was imparted to you"; and RNT as "to which you were entrusted." All would refer to the teaching of the Holy Spirit.

his adopted father, bringing him to a position of the greatest dignity. This is what God has done for us also.

For not only have we been set free from our former evils, but God has led us to the life of angels and paved for us the road to the best conduct and way of life. God did this by handing us over to the safekeeping of justice, by killing off our former evils, by bringing the old man in us to death and leading us by the hand to immortal life. Therefore, let us continue to lead this life. For many a man who seems to breathe and walk is in a more miserable state than those who have died.

V

For there are various ways of being in the state of death. One is the death of the body, in which Abraham was alive even though he was dead. For Abraham said, *God is not the God of the dead, but of the living.* Another is the death of the soul to which Christ alluded when He said, *And leave the dead to bury their dead.*[433] Another form is one that deserves our praise, the death that is brought about by Christian living and good conduct, of which Paul said, *Put to death the parts of you that are rooted in earth.*[434] Another, which is the cause of this, is the death that takes place in baptism. For, as Paul said, *The old man in us has been crucified,* that is, has been put to death. Cf. Matt 22:32
Cf. Matt 8:22
Col 3:5;
Cf. Rom 6:6

Therefore, because we know these various ways, let us flee that death in which we die even though we are still alive.[435] But let us not fear that death by which it is common to our nature that all men die. As for the other two deaths, one is given by God and is most happy and blessed; the other is praiseworthy because it is accomplished by ourselves together with God. Let us choose and strive after both of these.

Of these two forms of death, David calls the one blessed when he says, *Blessed are they whose transgressions are forgiven*; and the other causes Paul to marvel in his Letter to the Galatians, where he says, *They who belong to Christ have crucified their flesh.* Of the other two, Christ held that one deserved to be despised when he said, *Do not* Psalm 31/32:1
Gal 5:24
Cf. Matt 10:28

---

433 Confraternity and NAB notes *ad loc.*
434 Cf. Gal and notes *ad loc.* in Confraternity and NAB.
435 I.e., death through sin.

be afraid of those who kill the body but cannot kill the soul, but the other he called worthy of fear when he added, *But rather be afraid of him who is able to destroy both soul and body in hell.* [Cf. Matt 10:28]

Therefore, flee from that state of death that destroys the soul and the body. Let us choose the kinds that David called blessed and that caused Paul to marvel, so that, of the other two, we may escape the one and fear the other. For there would be no benefit for us in seeing the light of day and in eating and drinking if the life within us would not be made manifest through good works.

Tell me: What would it profit a king to be clothed in a purple robe and to be wearing a sword if he had not a single subject, but was without defense against anyone who was bent on insulting and attacking him? In the same way, it will be no benefit to a Christian if he has the faith and has received the gift of baptism but is subject to every passion. For in this way, his impetuous acts will be more violent and his shame all the greater. For just as the man who wears the diadem and the purple robe gains nothing from this garb to enhance his own honor, but wantonly insults his robe and crown because of his own shame, so also the believer who lives a corrupt life will not only fail to be an object of respect because of his faith and baptism, but rather will be a greater object of scorn. *For whoever has sinned without the law will perish without the law, and whoever has sinned under the law will be judged under the law.*[436] [Cf. Rom 2:12]

In his Letter to the Hebrews, Paul said, *Whoever makes void the law of Moses dies without any mercy on the word of two or three witnesses. How much greater a punishment will he deserve who has trodden underfoot the Son of God?* And this is very reasonable. For Christ might say, "I have put under subjection to you all the passions by your baptism. Therefore, how does it happen that by violating such a great gift, you have become an entirely different person? I slew and buried your former transgressions like worms. Why then did you beget other sins?" [Heb 10:28–29]

For sins are worse than worms. Worms destroy the body, but sins destroy the soul and give rise to a greater stench. Yet we do not smell the stench of sin, and therefore we make no effort to get rid of it. For the drunkard does not know how disgusting is the

---

436 See Homily 5.46.

smell of soured wine, but one who does not drink perceives the stench acutely.

And so it is in the case of sins. The man who lives a strict life knows the mire and stain in which those others live; but the man who has given himself up to wickedness, like the man who has become stupefied with wine, does not know that he is sick. And this is the most difficult and worst part of wickedness, namely, that it does not allow those who have fallen into it to see how great is their own disgrace, but while they are wallowing in mud, they think that they are enjoying the scent of perfume. And so they cannot free themselves, but even though they are overrun with worms, they feed their vanity on them, just as men pride themselves on a store of precious stones.

And this is why these sinners do not even desire to do away with these worms. They even nurture and increase them in themselves until they send them to join the worms of the world to come. The worms of this world are not only patrons and protectors of those worms that belong to the afterlife; they are the sires of those that never die. As Jesus said, *Their worm shall not die*. These kindle the Gehenna that is never quenched. To prevent this from happening, let us destroy this fountain of evils, let us put out the fires in the furnace, and let us tear out the roots of wickedness from the very bottom. You will do no good by cutting off the tree of evil above the roots. If the root remains in the soil, it will send forth the same shameful shoots. Cf. Mark 9:44, 46

What then is the root of the evils? Learn from the good vinedresser,[437] who has exact knowledge of these matters, who tends the spiritual vine, and who tills and cultivates the entire world. What then does Paul tell us is the cause of all evils? It is the lust for money and possessions. *Covetousness (φιλαργυρία) is the root of all evils*, he says. From this come quarrels, enmities, and wars; from this come rivalries, abuses, suspicions, and violence; from this come murders, robberies, and desecrations of tombs. Because of this vice, not only cities and countrysides, but also roads and places that are inhabited and uninhabited, mountains, groves, hills — in a word, all places — reek with blood and murder. Cf. 1 Tim 6:10

---

437 I.e., St. Paul; see, e.g., 1 Cor 3:6–9.

Nor has this evil kept its hands off the sea. Even there too it has burst in with great madness, because pirates besiege it on all sides, because they have devised a new method of highway robbery. By covetousness, the laws of nature have been overturned, the laws governing blood relationships have been thrust aside, and the rights of our very being have been destroyed.

VI

For the absolute power of possessions has put into the hands of covetous men weapons to be used against the living and the dead. For they do not make peace with them even after death, but they break open graves and stretch out their impious hands even against the corpses of the dead. They do not permit those who have passed from life to be free from their treacherous plotting. And you will find all evils rooted in this source, whether they occur in the home, the marketplace, the courts of law, the senate houses, the royal palaces, or any other place. You will see that they all burst forth from this lust for money and possessions.

For this is the evil that has filled all places with blood and murder. This ignites the fire of Gehenna. This has made cities no better off than deserts, but even in a much worse condition. You can protect yourselves against those robbers who lie in wait beside the highways more easily, because they are not setting upon you at every hour and from every place. But the robbers in the midst of the cities, who imitate the highwaymen, are much worse. They are harder to watch out for than robbers on the road. They have the boldness to commit their crimes in the open, whereas the road agents rob you from where they lie in wait and hide.

For the criminals in the cities have made allies of those laws that were passed to put an end to this wickedness, and they have filled the cities with their crimes and murders. For is it not murder and worse than murder, I ask you, to hand over a poor man to a life of hunger, to throw him into jail, and, along with starving him, to expose him to tortures and ten thousand torments? Even if you do not do these things to him with your own hands, you are still the reason why he is treated this way, and you are committing these outrages more than those servants who carry out your orders.

The executioner who slays the poor victim plunges his sword into him just once. He causes him pain for a brief moment, but he does not continue to inflict further torture. But you, by your calumnies, by your wanton insults, by your treacherous plotting, turn light into darkness for him and cause him to die ten thousand deaths. Consider how many times you slay him, instead of only once. And what is worst of all is that you are plundering and grasping for wealth not because you are driven by poverty nor because hunger forces you to do so, but so that your horse's bridle, the roof of your house, and the capitals of your pillars may be covered with an abundance of gold.

And how great a punishment in Gehenna would these actions deserve? For you are casting into ten thousand calamities one who is your brother, who has shared with you in ineffable blessings, who has been so honored by your Master. And you are abusing him in this way so that you may beautify stones and floors and the bodies of irrational beasts, even though none of these can perceive the beauty with which it is adorned. Your dog receives great care and attention. But because of your dog and all the things I mentioned, a man — rather, Christ — is locked into a life of utmost poverty and famine.

What is worse than this confusion of priorities? What is more grievous than this lawlessness? How many rivers of fire are punishment enough for such a soul? This man, made in the image of God, stands in unseemly shame because of your inhumanity to man. But the faces of the mules that draw your wife's carriage shine with an abundance of gold, as do the skins and the wood that make a canopy for her as she rides in it. If there is need for a throne or a footstool, they are all made of gold and silver.

Because of your avarice, the member of Christ's body, the one on whose account Christ came down from heaven and shed His precious blood, does not have the food he needs to stay alive. But couches are adorned with silver on every side, while the bodies of the saints lack the covering they need. In your eyes, Christ is held in less honor than all things, whether they be servants, mules, a couch, a throne, or a footstool. I make no mention of vessels meant for a still less honorable and meaner use than these things; I leave them to your imagination.

If these words that you hear from me make you shrink back in dread, then do not do the deeds they describe, and what I have said will do you no harm. Refrain from such actions and put an end to the madness of living such a life. For the desire for these possessions is clearly a form of madness. Therefore, put these aside and, although it is late, let us at long last look up to heaven; let us call to mind that day that is coming; let us turn our thoughts to that dread tribunal, and the accounts that must be settled with exact payments, and the sentence that no bribery can change.[438]

Let us consider that, even though God sees all these things, He does not hurl a thunderbolt from on high, even if these sinful acts deserve much more than thunderbolts to punish them with calamities. But God does not do this. He does not send a tidal wave to wash us away, nor does He burst open the land with an earthquake to swallow us up. He does not quench the light of the sun nor hurl down the heavens, stars and all. He does not remove everything from where it belongs, but He leaves all things in their proper places so that all creation may continue to serve us.

Therefore, as we ponder on this, let us stand in awe of how great His loving-kindness is. Let us return to the noble origin that is ours, even if now our condition is no better than that of irrational creatures. Indeed, we are now in a state far worse than wild beasts. At least they love the creatures of the same nature as themselves, and their common nature is enough to make them feel a warm affection toward each other.

But you, besides your common human nature, have countless other reasons that bring you together and bind you to your own members. You have been honored with the power of reason; you are united in religion; you share in ten thousand blessings. Yet you have become fiercer than wild beasts. You show great eagerness

---

438 The sentence passed on the day of judgment.

for useless things. You look down upon God's temples[439] and let them perish from hunger and nakedness. Many a time you even surround them with evils beyond number.

Even if your love for glory and reputation makes you do these things, you have a far greater need to attend to your brother than to your horse. For the better the creature that enjoys your act of kindness, so much the brighter is the crown that is woven for you for your eagerness to be kind. But now, when you fall into the opposite actions, you fail to perceive that you are drawing countless accusations upon yourself.

For who is there who will not speak ill of you? Who will not bring an indictment against you for the utmost cruelty and hatred of humankind when he sees that you are dishonoring the race of men by putting irrational animals before human beings — and not only the race of brutes, but even your house and furniture? Were you not listening when the apostles told how the first Christians who received the word they preached sold both houses and lands to support the brethren?[440]

But you are grabbing up houses and lands so as to adorn your horse, your woodwork, your animal skins, your walls, and your floors. And what is worse is that not only men, but women too, share in this madness. They encourage their husbands to such vain labor and force them to spend their money everywhere rather than on what is truly necessary. And if anybody accuses them on these accounts, they have practiced a defense that is open to many an accusation.

Someone will say that you are caring both for the unnecessary adornments and for the things necessary for your lifestyle. What is this that you are saying? Are you not afraid to make such a statement? Are you not afraid to reckon Christ's hunger along with horses, mules, couches, and footstools? Instead, you do not number Him with these luxuries, but you distribute the greater portion of your wealth on these externals while you scarcely give a scant portion to Him.[441]

---

439 The victims of these crimes are temples of the Holy Spirit.
440 Cf. Acts 4:34.
441 By contributions to the poor, who, as so often in Chrysostom, are identified with Christ.

Do you not know that all things belong to Him? Do you not know that this includes yourself and all you possess? Do you not know that He fashioned your body and gave you your soul as a gift and that He apportioned out the whole world? Do you give only a small recompense in return? If you rent out a small hut, you demand back the rent money to the exact penny. Even though you are reaping the fruit of His whole creation and are living in so wide a world, you do not let yourself pay out a scant amount of rent because you have given yourself and all your possessions to vainglory, as if everything depends on that.

As regards its natural excellence, your horse would not be a better horse because it is wearing this adornment, nor is the rider mounted on it a better man. Indeed, sometimes the rider is held in less esteem than the horse. For many men forget the rider as they turn their eyes to the adornment of the horse and to the attendants who strut before it and behind it. But they hate the rider whom this entourage is guarding. They turn from him as from a common foe.[442]

This does not happen when you adorn your own soul. Then men and angels and the Lord of angels are all weaving a crown for you. And so, if you are in love with glory, stop doing what you are now doing. Stop making your horse beautiful. Beautify your soul so that you may shine forth and be seen from every side. As it is now, nothing could be meaner and cheaper than you, because your soul is a desert, and you have only the beauty of your horse and house to protect you.

But if you cannot endure to listen to what I am saying, lend an ear to what some foreigner did and be ashamed when you see the kind of life these aliens live. The story goes that this foreign man entered a magnificent house that was gleaming with an abundance of gold and glittered with the great beauty of its marble pillars. When he saw that the floor was covered with carpets strewn in every direction, he spat in the face of the master of the house. When he was censured for his action, he said that he had done what he did because there was no other place in the house where

---

442 The rider is probably the master of the wealth that his sinful greed has amassed for him.

he could spit. And so it was that he was forced to offer this affront to the face of the master of the house.[443]

Do you see how ridiculous is the man who adorns external things and how easy it is for all reasonable men to despise him? And it is very reasonable. Suppose someone would let your wife be clothed in rags and go neglected while he gave your maidservants bright robes to wear. You would not endure this meekly. You would be inflamed with anger and say that this was an outrage and the gravest insult.

Consider, then, how this applies to your own soul. When you beautify your walls, floors, furnishings, and everything else but you do not give alms generously or practice your religious life in other ways, this is exactly what you are doing. Rather, what you do is far worse. For there is no difference between your wife and your maidservant, but there is a great difference between the soul and the flesh. If this is the case with regard to the flesh, the difference is much greater between your soul and your house, and between your soul and your couch or your footstool.

What defense would you deserve if you adorn those things with an abundance of inlaid silver while you disregard your soul and leave it clothed in rags, squalid, starving, filled with sores, and torn to pieces by countless dogs?[444] And after all that, do you consider that you will win glory because you have beautified the externals with which you are surrounded? Surely, this is the very height of madness. Even when you are being ridiculed and reproached, when you are acting shamefully and with dishonor, when you are exposing yourself to the ultimate punishment, do you still find pleasure in these things?

Therefore, I beg you, as we ponder these thoughts, let us return to our senses, even though it is late. Let us become our own masters; let us transfer this adornment from external things to our own souls. For in this way, the adornment itself remains inviolate and unharmed. It will make us equal to the angels and will furnish us with blessings that can never change. May it come to pass that we attain these blessings through the grace and

---

443 See Diogenes Laertius, *Vita Aristippi*.
444 Cf. the parable of the rich man and Lazarus in Luke 16:19–31, esp. vv. 20–21.

loving-kindness of our Lord Jesus Christ, to whom be glory forever and ever. Amen.

HOMILY 12

I speak in a human way because of the weakness   Rom 6:19
of your flesh. Just as you yielded your members
as slaves to uncleanness and iniquity for lawlessness,
so now yield your members as servants
to righteousness for your sanctification.

Paul had demanded great strictness of life when he ordered us to be dead to the world and wickedness, and to remain unmoved in the face of the working of sins. It seemed that he was asking for something great and burdensome, something that was beyond the power of human nature. But when he asked this, he wished to show that what he demanded was not excessive, nor even as much as should be expected from a man who had enjoyed so great a gift.[445] Rather, it was light and quite in due proportion, and Paul proves this by arguing from contraries.

For Paul says, *I speak in a human way*,[446] just as if he were to say   Cf. Rom 6:19 "from human reasoning," or "from things that are usual." By the phrase *in a human way*, he means either this or the limitation that it requires. For elsewhere he says, *May no temptation take hold of you ex-*   Cf. 1 Cor 10:13 *cept such as is common to man*, that is, "in due proportion" and small.

Just as you yielded your members as slaves to uncleanness and iniquity   Rom. 6:19 *for lawlessness, so now yield your members as servants to righteousness for your sanctification.*[447] So there is a great difference between the

---

445 The gift of justification through baptism.
446 Chrysostom will speak in such a way as to be understood by his hearers.
447 There are two masters to whom man can be a slave: iniquity is the master that leads to lawlessness, but righteousness is the master that leads to sanctification (which is the end result of being consecrated to God in Jesus Christ). Obviously, the Christian must serve righteousness.

masters, but the amount of servitude he asks for is still equal. Yet men should contribute much more, and more by as much as sanctification is greater and better than the power of lawlessness. But he asks for no more because of your weakness.

But he did not speak of the weakness of your free will or of your earnest zeal, but *of your flesh*. And this makes his demand less severe. And yet on the one side there is uncleanness, and on the other there is sanctification. On the one side is lawlessness, and on the other righteousness. And who is so miserable and in such distress that he does not contribute as much earnestness to the service of Christ as he does to the service of sin and the devil? Listen, then, to what follows and you will see clearly that we do not even make this slight contribution.

For when it is stated in such bald terms, it seems hard to believe and difficult to accept. For no one would endure hearing that he does not serve Christ as much as he serves the devil. So Paul proves this by what follows and makes it believable when he brings before their eyes their service to Christ and when he tells them how they have fulfilled that task. For he says, When you were slaves to sin, you had freedom from justice.[448]

Cf. Rom 6:20.

What Paul is saying is something like this. When you were living in wickedness, impiety, and the worst kinds of evil, your obedience to evil was such that no action of yours was in any way good. This is what Paul means when he says, You had freedom from justice. That is, you were not subject to justice, but you were entirely estranged and alienated from it. For you did not divide the manner of your servitude by giving some of it to justice and some of it to sin, for you devoted yourselves entirely to wickedness.

Now, therefore, because you have removed yourselves from sin and have gone over to the side of justice, devote your whole selves to virtue and do nothing at all that is evil, so that you may show a measure that is at least equal to your former servitude to sin. And yet not only is the difference great in the absolute sway of the two masters, evil and justice, but also the slavery to lawlessness and to

---

448 But the freedom from justice is a false freedom because it leads to enslavement to sin and punishment by death. Freedom from sin begets sanctification and eternal life in Christ, our Lord.

sanctification are worlds apart. And Paul explains this very point with great clarity. He shows under what conditions they formerly were slaves to evil and under what conditions they are now servants of justice. He does not speak of the harm that came from the evil action but, for a while, he speaks of the shame it brought.

For Paul says, *But what fruit did you have from those things of which you are now ashamed?* Your slavery was so great that even the recollection of it makes you blush. But if the recollection makes you ashamed, the deed itself must do so all the more. So now you have gained a double profit: you have been freed from this shame, and you have learned in what a state you were. And at the time you sinned, you received a double hurt: you did things that merited shame, and you did not even know that you should be ashamed. And this is worse than doing what you did. Nevertheless, you still remained in your state of servitude. Cf. Rom 6:21

And so, after Paul gave abundant proof of the harm that came from the things you had done at that time from the shame they brought with them, he now comes to the point in question. What is that point? *For the end of those things is death.* Because shame does not seem to be beyond endurance, Paul comes to that which is most to be feared — I mean death — even though what he had said before was enough to rouse us to fear. Consider how excessive an evil sin is, because sinners could not be freed from shame even though they had been freed from punishment. What Paul is saying is this: What wages do you expect from the sinful deed when you hide your face in shame and blush at the mere recollection of what you did, when you feel this shame even after you have been freed from punishment, and even when you are in the state of so great a grace? Cf. Rom 6:21

But this is not the way things are when they pertain to God. Paul says, *But now that you have been set free from sin and you have become slaves to God, you have sanctification as your fruit and life everlasting as your end.* The fruit of sin and evil was shame, even after the sins were forgiven. The fruit of freedom from sin and slavery to God is sanctification. And where we have sanctification, there we have much confidence. The end of sin and evil is death. The end of sanctification is life everlasting.[449] Cf. Rom 6:22

---

449 Cf. Rom 6:23.

II

Do you see how Paul shows that some blessings have already been given to us, whereas others are still objects of our hopes? And from those already given, he finds a guarantee for those to come. From sanctification he finds proof of eternal life. To forestall the objection that all blessings exist as the objects of hope, he shows that you have already reaped these fruits. In the first place, you were set free from wickedness and such evils of which even the recollection brings shame. Second, you have become the servants of justice. Third, you have enjoyed sanctification. And fourth, you have attained life, and a life that is not temporary, but everlasting.

However, Paul says, you must be a servant of these blessings to the same degree as you were servants to sin. And for the present, Paul makes no greater demand,[450] even if the Master of these blessings is far superior and the difference in the kind of slavery is great, as too are the rewards for which you serve.

Next, because Paul had mentioned weapons and a king, he continues in the same vein when he says, *For the wages*[451] *of sin is death, but the gift of God is life everlasting in Christ Jesus our Lord.* Although he mentioned the wages of sin, he did not keep to the same order. For he did not say "the reward for your good deeds," but "the gift of God." In this way Paul shows that they were not set free by their own efforts, nor did they receive what was due to them or repayment for their work and toils, but that all things came to them as a gift of grace.[452]

And so the superiority comes from this gift of grace, not only because God set them free and improved their condition, but because He did this with no toil or labor on their part. And he not only set them free, but He gave them far greater gifts, and He gave them through His Son. Paul inserts all these points in his argument because he has already spoken about grace and next he is going to reject the law. To prevent both these topics from making his

---

See Rom 6:23

450 Cf. § 3 of this homily.
451 A term used for payment for service in the army.
452 Here Paul closes his argument on sin and death vs. justification and life in Christ much in the same way as he closed the argument based on the parallel between Adam and Christ. Cf. Rom 5:21.

hearers rather listless and indifferent, he inserted the part about strictness of life, because everywhere he strives to rouse his audience to the practice of virtue.

When he calls death the wages of sin, he again stirs them to fear and strengthens them against the dangers that are to come. For the words he speaks both remind them of what they were and also make them thankful and stronger against everything that will happen to them. Here, then, he brings to an end his exhortations and returns again to matters of doctrine when he says, *Do you fail to recognize this, my brethren? For I am speaking to those who know the law.* Cf. Rom 7:1

Because Paul had said that we are dead to sin, he shows here that not only does sin have no dominion over them,[453] but neither does the law. But if the law has no dominion, much less does sin. And to make what he says easier to accept, he clarifies his point by using a human example. It seems that he is stating one thing, but he sets forth two arguments for his proposition. One is that when a husband has died, his wife is no longer legally subject to her husband, and there is nothing to prevent her from becoming the wife of another man.[454] The other is that in this case not only has the husband died, but the wife has died as well, so that she enjoys a double freedom.[455]

For if after her husband has died she has been freed from his authority, when she too is certainly seen to have died she has been freed all the more. For if the one event frees her from his authority, all the more does the death of both occurring at the same time. And so, when Paul is about to enter upon the proof of these points, he begins with an encomium of his audience by saying, "Do you fail to recognize this, my brothers? For I am speaking to those who know the law." That is, I am saying something that is clear and on which we are agreed, because I am speaking to those who have accurate knowledge of these matters, namely, *That the law has dominion over a man as long as he lives.* Cf. Rom 7:1

---

453 Cf. Rom 6:14.
454 Cf. Rom 7:2–3.
455 As a widow, she is no longer a wife. Therefore she dies to the law that subjects her to her dead husband. Cf. Homily 7.19. See also RNT note on Rom 7:1–8; and Charles Homer Giblin, *In Hope of God's Glory: Pauline Theological Perspectives* (New York: Herder and Herder, 1970), 382–383.

Paul did not say "over a male" or "over a female," but *over a man* (ἀνθρώπου), which is the name common to either person. For, as Paul says, *The man who is dead is justified from sin.* The law, then, is given for the living; for the dead it no longer has any commands. Do you see how Paul sets forth a twofold freedom? And next, after he has hinted at this as he opens his argument, he carries on his proof in the case of the woman. This is what he says, *For the married woman is bound to her husband by the law as long as he lives. But if her husband dies, she is set free from the law of the husband. Therefore, while her husband is alive, she will be called an adulteress if she gives herself to another man. But if her husband dies, she is freed from that law and she does not commit adultery if she gives herself to another man [in marriage].*

Cf. Rom 6:7

Cf. Rom 7:2–3

Paul constantly stresses this point, and he does so with great accuracy because he is very sure of the proof derived from it. He puts the law in the husband's place, and, in the place of the wife, he includes all who believe. Next he draws a conclusion that does not follow from the premises. For the conclusion would be to say, "Therefore, my brothers, the law has no dominion over you, because it is dead."[456] Even though he hinted at this in his premise, it is not what he said. Later, in the inference he does draw, so as not to make what he says offensive, he brings in the wife as having also died when he says, *Therefore, my brothers, you also died to the law.*[457]

Cf. Rom 7:4

When the death of one or the other partner has occurred, it grants the same freedom. What, then, is there to prevent Paul from showing favor to the law when no harm is done to the subject he is discussing? *For the married woman is bound by the law to her husband as long as he lives.* Where now are those who bring false accusations against the law?[458] Let them listen to Paul and hear how, even when he finds it necessary, he does not destroy the dignity of the law, but has great things to say about its power. While it is still in effect, the Jew is bound to it, and they who transgress it and reject it while it is still alive bear the name of adulterers. But if they let go of it once it has died, that is no cause for wonder. For in human affairs, one

Cf. Rom. 7:2

---

456 Cf. Stevens' note in NPNF¹ 11:418.
457 See Confraternity note *ad loc.*, and see RNT and NAB notes on Rom 7:4.
458 The false accusers are the Manichaeans, who said that the law was given by an evil being.

who does this is subject to no accusation. *But if the husband dies, the wife is set free from the law of the husband.* Cf. Rom. 7:3

III

Do you see how in the example Paul shows that the law is dead? But he does not do this in his inference. *Therefore, while the husband is alive, the wife will be called an adulteress if she gives herself to another man.* See how he spends time on accusations against those who transgress the law while it is still alive. But after the law has been abrogated, Paul then shows favor to it with all certainty and, by doing so, he does no harm to the faith. For he says, *While the husband is alive, the wife will be called an adulteress if she gives herself to another man. Therefore, my brothers, you also.*[459] The suitable conclusion would be for him to go on and say, "Because the husband is dead, you will not be judged guilty of adultery if you give yourselves to another man." Cf. Rom. 7:3
Cf. Rom 7:3–4

But Paul did not say that. What did he say? *You are dead to the law.* If you are dead, you are no longer subject to the law. For if after her husband has died the wife is not subject to him, all the more is she freed from him when she herself has died. Do you see Paul's wisdom and how the purpose of the law is that we be divorced from it and married to another? For Paul says that there is nothing to prevent marriage to a second husband after the first husband has died. How could the law prohibit a second marriage when, even while the first husband was still living, it permits a wife who has received a bill of divorce to marry another?[460] Cf. Rom. 7:4

But Paul does not set down this fact because it was rather a charge against wives. For even if the law were to make a concession to them, it still was not free from blame.[461] And in the cases where Paul has won his victory by the necessary proofs, he does not seek for what is superfluous, for he is not one to quibble. This, then, is no cause for wonder, because the law itself frees from any charges those of us who are divorced from it, because its purpose was that we should belong to Christ. The law itself has died, and

---

459 See Confraternity note *ad loc.*, as well as notes in RNT and NAB.
460 See Deut 24:1–4 and note in NAB.
461 Matt 19:7–8. See NAB note on Matt 19:3–8.

we have died. Hence the basis of its power over us has been removed for two reasons.

But Paul is not satisfied with these arguments alone. He also adds the basis for them. For he has not simply set down death; he again brings in the cross, which has accomplished these things. And in this way, he puts us under a responsibility. For he does not merely say that you have been set free, but that you have been set free through the death of the Master. For he says, *You have been made to die to the law through the body of Christ*. Nor does he base his exhortation on this alone, but also on the superior excellence of the second Spouse. Therefore, he goes on to add, *So as to belong to another, who has risen from the dead*.

Cf. Rom 7:4

Cf. Rom 7:4

Next, to prevent them from saying, "What about this? Suppose we do not wish to consort with a second husband. For the law does not make an adulteress of the widow who lives in a second marriage, nor does it force her to do so." To prevent them from saying this, Paul shows that, from what has already been done for us, we are obliged to choose this second marriage.[462] He sets this forth more clearly in other Letters, where, for example, he says, *You are not your own*, and *You have been bought at a great price*, and *Do not become the slaves of men*, and again *One man died for all, in order that they who are alive may live no longer for themselves, but for Him who died for them*. And so Paul was alluding to such statements when he says here *through His body*.

Cf. 1 Cor 6:19; 20;
Cf. 1 Cor 7:23;
Cf. 2 Cor 5:15

Cf. Rom 7:4

And next Paul exhorts us to better hopes when he says, *So that we may bring forth fruit to God*. What he suggests is that before we were bringing forth fruit for death, but now we are bringing forth fruit for God. *For when we were in the flesh, the sinful passions roused by the law worked in our members, and we bore fruit for death*. Do you see the wages to be gained from your former husband?[463] Paul did not say, "When we were under the law," because he everywhere avoids giving the heretics an opportunity for argument, but he says, *When we were in the flesh*, that is, in evil deeds, in the carnal life.

Cf. Rom 7:4

Cf. Rom 7:5

For Paul is not saying that Christians were in the flesh at an earlier time but are now going around as disembodied spirits. Nor

---

462 I.e., the marriage to Christ.
463 I.e., the law.

when he said *in the flesh* did he mean that the law was the cause of sins, nor yet was he freeing it from odium. For it held the role of a bitter accuser because it laid bare the sins of men. For that which multiplies commandments for a man who is in no way willing to obey multiplies his transgressions. This is why Paul did not say "the sinful passions that were produced by the law," but *the sinful passions that were aroused by the law*. So he did not add "produced by the law," but simply said *by the law*. By this he meant the sinful passions that appeared or became known through the law.   Cf. Rom 7:5

And in order to not lay the accusation on the flesh, he did not then say "the sinful passions that our members made active," but *the sinful passions that were at work in our members*. By this he showed that the source of the evil had its beginning elsewhere, namely, in the evil thoughts that were working in us, and not from the members that had these evil thoughts working in them. For the soul plays the part of a musician, while our flesh plays the part of the lyre, which gives forth the sounds that the musician forces it to echo. Therefore we must impute the blame for the discordant strains to the musician and not to the lyre.[464]   Cf. Rom 7:5

Next Paul says, *But now we have been set free from the law*. Do you see how here again he spares both the flesh and the law? For he does not say that the law produced no effect, nor that the flesh produced no effect, that is, that they were set free. What he says is that we were set free. And how were we set free? We were set free because the old man, who was held down by sin, has died and been buried. Paul showed this when he said, *Having died to that by which we were held down*. It is just as if he had said that the bonds by which we were held down had died and were broken, so that what was holding us down, that is, sin, no longer held us down.   Cf. Rom 7:6   Cf. Rom 7:6

But do not fall back or grow sluggish to an extreme. You were set free so that you might become servants, but not in the same sort of slavery. Rather, we have been set free *so that we may serve in the new spirit and not in the antiquated letter of the law*. But what is it that Paul is saying here? We must reveal what he means here, so that   Cf. Rom 7:6

---

[464] For an extensive discussion on Chrysostom's understanding of the dynamics between soul and body, and of human responsibility for sin and evil, see Papageorgiou, "A Theological Analysis," chap. 2, pp. 62–71.

when we come upon this text we may not be upset or perplexed. What Paul means is that when Adam sinned and his body became subject to suffering and death, he received many physical defects. The horse became less active and less obedient to the rein.[465] But after Christ came, He made the body more nimble for us through baptism, because He roused it by the wings of the Spirit.

IV

On this account, the racecourses laid out for us and for those men of old are not the same. In those olden days the race was not as easy as it is now. Because our course is an easier one, Christ demands not only that we be free from murders, as was demanded of the men of old, but we must also be free from anger.[466] Nor did Christ command us only to be free from acts of adultery, but even from adultery of the eyes.[467] Furthermore, we are commanded not only to not swear false oaths, but even [to not swear] true ones.[468] And Christ also orders us to love our enemies as well as those friends who love us. And in all His other mandates, Christ has also made the racecourse longer for us.[469]

And if we do not obey these commands, Christ has also threatened us with Gehenna. This shows that the objectives we must seek are not matters of honor or distinction for those entered in the race, such as celibacy and poverty are. Rather, they are things that must by all means be fulfilled and attained. For these are matters of necessity and great urgency, and the man who fails to fulfill them pays the ultimate penalty. This is why Christ said, *Unless your justice exceeds that of the scribes and Pharisees, you shall not enter the kingdom of heaven.* But he who does not see the kingdom will certainly fall into Gehenna. [Cf. Matt 5:20]

This is why Paul said, *For sin will not have dominion over you, because you are not under the law, but under grace.*[470] And here he says again, *So* [Cf. Rom 6:14; Cf. Rom 7:6]

---

465 Cf. Plato, *Phaedrus* 246–247.
466 Cf. Matt 5:21–22.
467 Cf. Matt 5:27–28.
468 Cf. Matt 5:33–37.
469 Cf. Matt 5:43–48.
470 See Homily 11.28.

that we may serve in the new spirit and not in the antiquated law. For it is not the letter, that is, the old law, that condemns us, but it is the Spirit that is helping us. This is why among the ancients, if someone was seen practicing virginity, it was a matter for great amazement, but now the practice has spread all over the world. And in those days, some few men despised death, and did so with great difficulty; but now, both in villages and cities, countless hosts of martyrs, both men and women, are eager to lay down their lives.

Next, after Paul had said these things about the law and the Spirit, he again answers an objection that is beginning to emerge. And in answering it, he establishes the point he wishes to prove. And so he does not bring in his solution as something leading up to his main argument, but as something that is opposed to it. He does this so that from the need to answer the objection he may grasp an occasion for saying what he wishes to say. And in this way he makes his accusation less offensive to his hearers.

For after he said, *In a new spirit and not according to the antiquated letter,* he went on to say, *What then shall we say? Is the law sin? By no means!* But earlier he had said, *The sinful passions that were aroused by the law were at work in our members,*[471] and *Sin will not have dominion over you, because you are not under the law, but under grace,* and *Where there is no law, neither is there transgression,*[472] and *But the law intervened that the offense might abound,*[473] and *The law works wrath.*[474] Cf. Rom 7:7
Cf. Rom 7:5.
Cf. Rom 6:14
Cf. Rom 4:15;
Rom 5:20; 4:15

Because all these statements seem to be slandering the law, he sets forth the objection so that he may correct the suspicion arising from them. So Paul says, *What then shall we say? Is the law sin? By no means!* So before he comes to his proof, he makes this appeal to win the favor of his audience and to soothe any who were offended by the things he had said. For after they had heard this and had become fully satisfied with Paul's disposition, they would join him in investigating the difficulty and would not be suspicious of what he was saying. This is why he first stated the objection. Cf. Rom 7:7

For he did not ask, "What then would I say?" Rather, his question is *What then shall we say?* Paul speaks just as though a deliberation

---

471 See Homilies 9.28; 11.28; 12.26, 33.
472 See Homily 7.35, 39.
473 See Homily 10.28.
474 See Homily 7.35, 39.

and a judgment were before the court and he was discussing the question before a general assembly that had been organized and gathered together. He makes his statement as if the objection arose not from him, but from the course of the discussion and from the real circumstances of the case.

Cf. 2 Cor 3:6 What Paul is saying is that no one will deny that *the letter kills, but the spirit gives life.* This is clear, and no one will dispute it. Therefore, if we are agreed on this, what would we say about the law? That it is sin? By no means! Explain the difficulty then. Do you see how Paul supposes that he has his opponent standing next to him? Do you see how he has assumed the dignity of the teacher and how he comes to the solution? What then is the solution? The law is not Cf. Rom 7:7 sin, he says. *I did not know sin except through the law.*[475]

See how wise Paul is. By way of an objection, he has set down what the law is not. By removing this objection, he is winning the favor of the Jews, and now he may persuade them to accept the lesser alternative. And what is that lesser alternative? *I did not know sin except through the law. For I would not have known what evil desire* Cf. Rom 7:7 *was unless the law had said, 'Thou shalt not covet.'*

Do you see how, little by little, Paul shows not only that the law is the accuser of sin, but also how, in a measure, it produces sin? However, it does not do this through its own fault. Paul shows that this happens because of the lack of judgment on the part of the Jews. And surely he was eager to stop up the mouths of the Manichaeans when they leveled their accusations against the law. For after he said, *I did not know sin except through the law,* and *I would not have known what evil desire was unless the law had said, 'Thou shalt not covet,'* Paul went on to add, *But sin, having taken an occasion from* Cf. Rom 7:8 *the commandment, roused in me all manner of lust.*

V

Do you see how he freed the law from blame? For Paul says that it Cf. Rom 7:8 is not the law, *but sin, having taken an occasion,* that increased lust and brought about the opposite of what the law intended. But this came from weakness, not from depravity. For whenever we lust

---

475 See Confraternity and RNT notes on Rom 7:7–26.

for something and are hindered from having it, the flame of our evil desire is increased all the more. But this is not contrary to the law. For the law itself hindered us in order to keep us away from lust. But sin, that is, your own sluggishness and evil intention, put what was good to a purpose opposed to it. It is not the fault of the physician, but of the patient, if the patient puts his medicine to a bad use. God did not give the law to rouse your evil desire, but to quench it, even if the opposite resulted. But the law is not to blame for this; rather, we should blame ourselves.

Suppose a man is suffering from a fever and desires a drink of cold water, even if his condition makes the time for this all wrong. Even if the physician should increase the patient's desire for this ruinous pleasure by refusing to let him have his fill, it would not be right to blame him for refusing. For the physician's task was only to prohibit him; the patient had the obligation to abstain from drinking the water.

Suppose, then, that sin did find an occasion from the law itself. Surely there are many evil men who increase their wickedness because of good precepts. For this was the way the devil destroyed Judas when he plunged him into his greed for money and made him steal what belonged to the poor. Still, it was not the fact that the purse was entrusted to him that brought this about. Rather, it was the wickedness of his own will. And when Eve caused Adam to eat of the tree, she had him expelled from paradise. But not even in that case was the tree the cause, even if through it the occasion for his sin was given.

But do not wonder that Paul has made his discussion regarding the law a rather vehement one. For he is taking a stand against an urgent necessity. He is preventing what he has to say from providing an argument for those who suspect otherwise. So he takes great pains to make his present statement correct. Therefore, do not examine what he is now going to say by itself, but put beside it the purpose that leads him to say what he does. Consider too the madness of the Jews and their vigorous spirit of contention, because Paul is anxious to do away with these. He does seem to breathe out many heated words against the law, but his purpose is not to slander it. Rather, he wishes to weaken the strong contentiousness of the Jews.

For if there is a charge to be made against the law, namely, that sin has found an occasion in it, this occurs in the New Testament as well. For certainly, we find there too countless laws covering many more important matters. And we may see there the same thing happening not only regarding lust and evil desires, but simply about all wickedness. For Christ said, *If I had not come and spoken to them, they would have no sin.* Therefore, from this text, sin found an occasion and a greater punishment. And again, when Paul was discussing grace, he said, *How much worse punishment do you think he who has trodden underfoot the Son of God deserves?*

John 15:22

Heb 10:29

Therefore, the more severe punishment finds its source from this, namely, from the greater benefit given. But Paul also said that the reason the Greeks were without excuse was because, even though they had been honored with the gift of reason and had gained a knowledge of the beauty of creation, and from that were able to be led to the Creator, they did not make use of this wisdom about God in the way they should have done. Do you see that in the case of the wicked, in every way, the occasions for greater punishment come from good things?

But surely we shall not on this account lay any accusation at the door of the benefits that come from God. Rather, we shall marvel at them the more. But we shall put the blame on the spirit of those who abuse these blessings and turn them to a contrary purpose. Therefore, let us do this also in the case of the law. And this is an easy and simple thing to do. But the other is difficult. How is it that Paul says, *I would not have known lust unless the law had said, 'Thou shalt not covet'?* For if man had not known lust before he had received the law, what was the reason for the flood? Why was Sodom burned to the ground? What then did Paul mean? He meant that lust that was stretched to its uttermost. And this is why he did not say "worked lust in me," but *all manner of lust*, hinting there at how violent the lust was.

Cf. Rom 7:7

Cf. Rom 7:8

What then is the profit of the law if it has increased our passions? So someone will object, "It brought us no profit, but it did bring much harm." Yes, but that is not the fault of the law; the blame lies with the carelessness of those who received it. For sin produced this blame even if it did so through the law. But this was not the purpose of the law; rather, the law intended the opposite. And so sin became violent and stronger. But again, this was not the fault of the law. Rather, it was the fault of the arrogance and senseless obstinacy of those who sinned.

For without the law, sin was dead,[476] that is, it was not clearly recognized as sin. For those who lived before the law knew that they sinned. But after the law was given, they came to a more exact knowledge of sin. On this account they were subject to a stronger accusation. For it was not the same thing to have nature accuse them as, along with nature, to have the law plainly declare every charge against them. Cf. Rom 7:8

Paul also said, *I was living without the law at one time.*[477] Tell me, when was that? "Before Moses." See how Paul makes haste to show, both by what it did and by what it did not do, that the law weighed heavily on human nature. For when he said, *I was living without the law*, he meant that judgment was not given against him in the same way as with the law. *When the commandment came, sin came to life, and I died.*[478] Cf. Rom 7:9.

Cf. Rom 7:9.

This seems to be an accusation against the law, but if you should submit it to careful examination, it is also seen as an encomium of the law. For it did not propose as sin what was not a sin, but it did point out sins whose true nature as sins was concealed. And this was praise for the law if, at least before the law, men were committing sins without perceiving that their actions were sinful. But after the law came, even if they reaped no other benefit, they had precise knowledge of this very fact, namely, that they were sinning. This would be no small help for freeing themselves from wickedness. And if this did not free them from evil acts, this

---

476 See Confraternity note *ad loc.*

477 Paul does not mean he lived before Moses, but that before Moses the law had not been given.

478 See NPNF¹ 11:422n1, which finds the last two sentences somewhat strange even for the corrupt spirit of sinners, because their corruption destroys all hope of recovery. Certainly, one use of the law was to make sinners aware of their sorry state. But Chrysostom's words may well be taken in the sense of the parable of the fig tree that bore no fruit. See Isa 5:4; Matt 21:19; and Luke 13:6.

had nothing to do with the law, which had done everything it could do to achieve this end. The entire accusation lies with the spirit of those sinners — a spirit that has been corrupted beyond all hope of recovery.

VI

What did happen was not according to reason, namely, that they received harm from things that were intended for their profit. This is why Paul also said, *The commandment that should have brought me life was found to bring me to death.* He did not say "became death" or "brought forth death," but *was found to bring death.* In this way he explains the novel and unexpected absurdity and turns the whole thing back onto the sinner's head. For if, he is saying, you were willing to see the purpose of the law, it was leading to life and was given for this reason. But if death resulted from it, the blame belonged to those who received the commandment, and not to the commandment, which was leading to life.

Cf. Rom 7:10

Also, he made this very thing still clearer by what follows when he said, *For sin, having taken its occasion and opportunity through the commandment, deceived me and, through it, killed me.* Do you see how in every instance he attacks sin and frees the law of every charge? This is why Paul went on to say, *So the law is holy, and the commandment is holy, just, and good.*

Cf. Rom 7:11

Cf. Rom 7:12

But if you wish, let us bring before you the language of those who falsify these explanations and interpretations. For in this way the statements that I have made will become still clearer. Some people say that Paul's statements here do not speak of the law of Moses. Some say he is speaking of the natural law, others of the commandment given in paradise. But everywhere Paul's objective is to abrogate the law of Moses, whereas he never has a word to say against the other laws.

And this is very reasonable. For it was because the Jews stood in fear and horror that the Mosaic law would be abrogated that they were so obstinate in opposing grace. As for the commandment given in paradise, it is clear that neither Paul nor anyone else gave it the name of "law." And so that this may become clearer from

HOMILY 12

his own words, let us run through them and retrace the argument he used a little earlier. After he had spoken in precise terms about their way of life, he went on to say, *Do you fail to recognize this, my brothers: that the law has dominion over a man as long as he lives?...So you are dead to the law.*[479]   Cf. Rom 7:1, 4

Therefore, if these words are spoken about the natural law, we will be found as having no natural law. And if this is true, we are more senseless than beasts without reason. But this is not true; certainly it is not. As regards the law in paradise, there is no need to be obstinate and contentious, so that we may not be starting up an idle battle and arming ourselves on issues on which we are agreed. And how is it that Paul said, *I did not know sin except through the law?*[480] He is not talking about a complete lack of knowledge, but of more precise and accurate knowledge.   Cf. Rom 7:7

For if this was said about the natural law, how would the words that follow make sense? For Paul says, *At one time I was living without the law.* Now certainly, neither Adam nor any other human being lived without the natural law. As soon as God formed Adam, the Lord put in him the law of nature and established it firmly to dwell in the whole human race. And apart from these facts, it is nowhere clear that Paul called the law of nature a commandment. But he does call the Mosaic law both a commandment and just and holy, as well as a spiritual law.[481] But the law of nature was not given to us by the Spirit,[482] because barbarians and Greeks and all human beings have this natural law. Hence it is clear that Paul is discussing the Mosaic law above, as well as afterward, and in all the other passages.   Cf. Rom 7:9

And this is why Paul calls this law holy when he says, *So the law is holy, and the commandment is holy, just, and good.* For even though after the law was given the Jews have become unclean and unjust and greedy, this does not make void the goodness of the law, just as their unbelief does not destroy the faithfulness of God. And so   Cf. Rom 7:12

---

479 See §§ 17 and 22 of this homily.
480 See §§ 38–41 of this homily.
481 Cf. Rom 7:12.
482 This does not contradict Gen 6:3 or Psalm 94/95:10, because Chrysostom here uses the term "Spirit" in a limited sense, as in John 7:39.

it is clear from all these reasons that Paul is discussing the Mosaic law.

Cf. Rom 7:13 And Paul says, *Did this good thing, then, become death for me? By no means! Rather, it was sin, so that it might be seen as sin*, that is, so that it might be shown how great an evil sin is. I mean the careless will, the inclination to what is worse, the very act, and the perverted judgment. For these are the causes of all things that are evil. But Paul goes even further than this when he shows how the grace of Christ was beyond all measure and when he teaches us how excessive the evil from which Christ set the human race free was. Indeed, this evil became worse because of the medicines used to cure it; it was increased by the things that tried to hinder it.

Cf. Rom 7:13 This is why Paul went on to say, *In order that sin, by reason of the commandment, might become immeasurably sinful*. Do you see how everywhere Paul intertwines these things, namely, sin and the law? And by the very things that he uses to bring his accusations against sin, he again shows still more the goodness of the law. Nor did he accomplish little by showing how great an evil sin is and revealing all its poison and bringing it before our eyes. And he made this clear when he said, *In order that sin, by reason of the commandment, might become immeasurably sinful*. That is, so that it might become clear how great an evil, how great a source of destruction, sin is. But this is shown by the commandment.

By this Paul also shows the preeminence of grace above the law — the preeminence above, not in conflict with, the law. For you must not look to this, namely, that those who received the law became worse. Consider, rather, the other side, namely, that the law not only had no desire to make evil go to greater lengths, but that it was even eager to cut out the evil that existed before. If it lacked the strength to do this, give it a prize for its good intentions. But give greater worship to the power of Christ. For by tearing up its roots and pulling it out of the ground, His power destroyed an evil so varied and so difficult to wrestle with.

But when you hear me speak of sin, do not think of it as a really existing force, but think of it as an evil action that constantly comes upon men and departs from them, which does not exist before it takes place, and which vanishes again after it has occurred. This, then, is why the law was given. However, no law was ever given to destroy natural things but, rather, to correct a way of acting that is purposely wicked.

VII

Lawgivers of foreign nations know this too, as does the whole of human nature. For they repress only the evils that arise from carelessness; they do not profess to cut out those which are allotted to us by nature, for they cannot do that. The things given by nature remain unchangeable,[483] as I have told you in other discourses on many occasions. Therefore, let us put aside these contests and again turn our efforts to moral exhortation. Rather, I should say that this part—the moral exhortation—belongs to those contests.

If we cast out wickedness, we should also bring in virtue. And by these means we shall clearly teach you that wickedness is not a natural evil. In this way we shall easily be able to also stop up the mouths of those who seek after the source of evil, not by words alone, but also by actions.[484] And we can do this because we share the same human nature with them, even if we have been freed from their wickedness. So let us not look at how much labor is involved in seeking virtue, but rather look to the possibility that our search will succeed. But if we are earnest in our search, the labor will be light and easy.

If you tell of the pleasure you find in evil deeds, tell me also of how a life of vice ends. For that life of wickedness ends in death. But virtue takes us by the hand and leads us to life. If you wish, let us examine both of them—the evil life and the life of virtue—before they come to their ends. For we shall see that wickedness has much pain attached to it, but virtue brings much pleasure. Tell me this. What is more painful than a bad conscience? And what brings more pleasure than a good hope? For there is nothing, absolutely nothing, that is likely to cut us so deeply or to press so hard upon us as the expectation of evil. And there is nothing that raises us up and all but gives us wings as much as a good conscience does.

---

483 Aristotle makes the same point in his *Nicomachean Ethics* (bk. 2, chap. 1).
484 The Manichaens.

And we can learn this from things that happen before our own eyes. Those who are shut up in prison and are waiting for sentence to be passed against them, even if they enjoy food in great abundance, live a more painful life than those who go begging through the alleys but have nothing on their consciences to trouble them. For the expectation of a dreadful punishment does not permit the prisoner to notice the pleasure of the food he holds in his hands.

And why do I speak of those in prison? There are men who are not in jail and who possess wealth, even though their consciences are weighed down with wicked deeds. But craftsmen who work and spend the whole day in labor are in a far better state than they. It is for this reason that we call gladiators unhappy. Even though we see them drinking, living in luxury, and filling their bellies in the taverns, we say that they are the most miserable of men. Why? Because the disastrous end they must expect is much greater than the pleasure they are enjoying. So if to them a life of this sort seems to be pleasing, you must not forget the word I am constantly saying to you.

But what would you say about adulterers who, for the sake of a little pleasure, endure a disgraceful slavery, a loss of money, and constant fear?[485] They undergo a life just like Cain's, or rather a life more difficult than Cain's, because they are filled with fear for the present and with trembling at the future. They are suspicious of their friends as well as their enemies, of those who know of their evil deeds as well as those who are unaware of them. When they fall asleep, they are not free from struggles, because their bad conscience shapes for them dreams filled with many terrors to frighten them.

But this is not so with the man who is chaste and sober. He spends this life in great tranquility and freedom. So then, compare the many surging waves of those fears, which come from a moment of pleasure, with the peace and tranquility of an entire life that was lived with the brief labor of self-control and continence. Then you will see that the peaceful life of purity was more pleasurable than the turbulent life of sin.

---

485 Cf. Horace, *Satires* II.7, lines 56–67.

Take the man whose mind is set on snatching the possessions of others and making them his own. Tell me this. Does he not endure countless toils as he runs here and there, as he flatters slaves, freemen, and doorkeepers? He must frighten here and threaten there. He must act shamelessly. He must keep watch and tremble. He must contend with and be suspicious of everything. But the man who holds wealth and possessions in scorn is not like that. For he enjoys great pleasure, because he lives his life in all tranquility and perfect security. And if anyone should go through the other kinds of vice, he will see much tumult and many rocky places.

And what is more important is that, in the case of virtue, the laborious parts come first and after that comes the pleasure, so that in this way the toilsome parts become easier. But in the case of the evil things, the order is reversed. After the pleasure come the pains and the punishments, so that in this way the pleasure disappears. Just as the man who is expecting a crown of victory in the games has no perception of the present burdens, so he who is expecting punishments after the pleasure cannot reap the fruit of a pure joy, because his fear of what will come upsets everything and puts him in a state of confusion. Rather, if one should examine the matter carefully, even before the punishment that follows these actions, he would find that at the very moment he ventures to do the wicked deed, he experiences much pain.

VIII

And if you wish, let us examine this in the case of those who plunder the possessions of other men, or of those who, in one way or another, have become wealthy and have put aside all the fears, the dangers, the trembling, the anguish, the concern, and all like worries. Suppose a man has become wealthy easily and without pain and is confident of keeping his fortune. Of course, he cannot be sure of this, but still let us suppose that he is sure for the sake of argument. What kind of pleasure will he get from his wealth? Will pleasure come because he is surrounded with many possessions? This is the very thing that prevents him from enjoying gladness of heart. For as long as he desires other things in addition to what he has, he must endure torture. When his desire stops, then he can find pleasure and enjoyment.

When we are thirsty, we refresh ourselves by drinking as much as we wish. But as long as we are still thirsty, the torture of our thirst grows greater, even if we drain every spring to its dregs. The pangs of our punishment are more severe even if we drain ten thousand rivers. If you acquire everything in the world but still want more, you are making your punishment more severe because you have tasted of more numerous possessions.

Therefore, do not think that any pleasure comes to you from amassing great wealth. Consider, rather, that pleasure comes from not wishing to be rich. But if you lust after money, you never put a stop to the scourging it inflicts upon you. For this kind of desire has no end to it, and the farther you advance along the road to it, the farther off from the end of that road will you be. Is this not a paradox? Is it not madness and the ultimate insanity?

Therefore, let us keep away from this first root of evil. Let us not even touch this lustful desire. If we have put our hand to it, let us leap back from this first touch. This is what the author of Proverbs warns us to do when he is speaking of an adulterous woman and says, *Leap back, do not delay, do not draw near the doors of her house*. And I say this to you about the love of money. For if you step little by little into the sea of that madness and fall, you will not easily be able to stand up and get out of it.

Suppose you fell into a whirlpool. Even if you struggle times beyond counting, you will not easily escape the vortex. So will it be after you have fallen into this far worse abyss of covetousness. You will destroy yourself and all your possessions.[486] Therefore, I urge you, let us be on our guard against the first step and flee from little evils. For the great evils are sired by these. The man who comes to say of every sin that "nothing will come from this," little by little will he destroy himself entirely. Surely, this saying, "Nothing will come from this," has brought in vice; it has opened the doors for the robber; it has torn down the walls of cities.

It is the same in the case of our bodies. The most serious diseases grow worse when we think lightly of the less serious ones.

---

486 Cf. Acts 8:20.

If Esau had not given up his birthright, he would not have become unworthy of the blessings.[487] If he had not made himself unworthy of the blessings, he would not have desired to go on to slay his brother.[488] If Cain had not fallen in love with the chief rank and the first place but had left that up to God, he would not have had the second place. Again, when he had the second place, if he had heeded the Lord's warning, he would not have undergone the agonies of committing murder. Again, after he murdered his brother, if he had come to repent when God called him, and if he had not answered God in such shameless fashion, he would not have endured those dreadful punishments that followed.[489]

If those who lived before the law was given fell into the very depth of wickedness little by little because of their indifference, consider what we will suffer. Surely we are called to greater trials if we do not pay strict attention to ourselves or anticipate the sparks of evil deeds, and if we do not quench them before the pile is kindled into flame. Let me give you an example. Are you a man who constantly swears false oaths? You must not only stop swearing falsely, but you must stop swearing any oath. Then you will have no further trouble. It is far more difficult for a man who swears oaths to avoid perjury than for a man who swears no oaths at all.[490]

Are you a man who insults and abuses others? Do you strike them with your fists? Lay down a law for yourself not to lose your temper or ever to raise your voice. Then you will be rid of this evil fruit, roots and all. Are you lustful and dissolute? Again, set a rule for yourself not to look at a woman, not to go to the theater, not to be overly curious by leering at the beautiful aspects of other people in the marketplace. For it is far easier from the first to not look at a fair-figured woman than, after you have ogled her and stirred up your lust, to get rid of the tumult of passion she has roused in you. For such struggles are easier in their first stages. Rather, we shall

---

487 Cf. Gen 25:19–34.
488 Cf. McKenzie, *DB*, 244–245.
489 Cf. Gen 4:1–16.
490 Cf. Matt 5:33–37. See notes *ad loc.* in NAB and RNT. Also see NPNF[1] 11:425n2. Chrysostom speaks strongly against oaths and swearing especially in his *Baptismal Discourses* (trans. Harkins, ACW 31); see that work's index of words under "oaths" (p. 365) and "swearing" (p. 372).

have no need to struggle if we do not open the gates to the enemy or take in the seeds of evil.

This is why Christ chastised the man who looks at a woman and lusts after her.[491] He did this so that He might free us from greater trouble. He is ordering us to drive our adversary [the devil] out of the house before he gets stronger and while he can still be easily ejected. For what need is there to have an excess of troubles and to be locked in combat with our enemies when it is possible to set up a trophy of victory without the combat and to take the prize before the conflict? For the effort of not looking at women in the prime of their beauty is not as great a struggle as it is to restrain yourself while you ogle them. Not to ogle would be no trouble. But after you have ogled them, much toil and sweat is required to restrain your passion.

IX

Therefore, when the trouble is less or when there is no sweat or toil at all, while the gain is greater, why are we so eager to plunge into the sea of countless evils? Not only does a man who does not look with lust at a woman overcome his passion more easily; he also overcomes such lust with a greater purity. But the man who leers with lust must put forth greater effort to be freed from his passion. And he does not do this without some stain of sin — if he ever frees himself at all. The man who does not look at the sight of a beautiful body is also unstained by the lustful desire that comes from ogling at the sight. But the man who lusts to see it, after he has first destroyed his power of reason and polluted it in countless ways, then drives out the stain that his lust brought on — if he ever does drive it out.

To keep us from suffering these experiences, Christ forbids not only murder, but anger as well; He forbids not only adultery, but even a lustful look; He forbids not only swearing falsely, but all swearing whatsoever. Nor does He make the measure of virtue stop here. After He set down these laws, He went on to something that is still greater. For after He prohibited us from committing

---

[491] Cf. Matt 5:28.

murders and ordered us to keep free from anger, He bade us to be ready to suffer evil. For He told us not only to be prepared to suffer as much evil as the plotting of our enemy might wish, but to go further and to overcome his excessive madness by the abundance of our Christian virtue and way of life.

For Christ did not say, "When a person strikes you on the right cheek, be noble and endure it, and keep your peace." He went further and told us to offer the other cheek too. For He said, *Turn to him the other cheek as well.* This is a brilliant victory, namely, to offer him more than he wishes and to go beyond the bounds of his evil desire by the abundance of our own patience and long-suffering. For in this way you will put an end to his madness and receive from the second act the reward for the first. And you will bring an end to your anger against him. *Cf. Matt 5:39*

Do you see that we always have it in our power to not suffer evil? Do you see that those who would do us harm do not have this power? Rather, we ourselves have the power of not suffering evil but even of experiencing good. Indeed, what is especially marvelous is that we not only are left unhurt if we live a sober and watchful life, but we are even blessed by the very things that others do to hurt us.

Consider this. Did someone commit an outrage against you? You have the power to make this outrage turn to your own praise. If on the one hand you, in your turn, commit an outrage against him, you increase the disgrace. If on the other hand you bless and praise him who harmed you, you will see that everyone present gives you the crown of victory and proclaims your praise. Do you see how, if we wish it that way, we receive good from the things that were done to hurt us?

We can see this happening in the case of possessions, blows, and all the other wrongs done to us. But if we repay those who hurt us with the opposite treatment, we are weaving for ourselves two crowns — one for the harm we have suffered, and one for the good we have done. Therefore, when someone comes to you and says that so-and-so has done you an outrage and keeps saying bad things about you to everybody, praise the man who is calumniating you to everyone who speaks to you about him. For in this way, even if you wish to avenge yourself, you will be able to exact punishment.

For even if they are very foolish, those who hear you will be filled with your praises and will hate him for being fiercer than any brute beast, because he has caused you pain, although you had done no harm to him. Even though you suffered evil at his hands, you repaid him with the opposite treatment. And so you will have it in your power to show that everything he has said is futile and false. For when someone has felt the sting of slander and is vexed by it, his vexation offers proof that he is aware of the truth of what has been said about him. But he who smiles at the criticism leveled against him by this very action frees himself of all suspicion in the eyes of those who are present.

Therefore, consider how many good things you get from this. First, you free yourself from tumult and trouble. Second — rather, put this in first place — if you have sinned, you will strip those sins away, just as the publican did by listening humbly to the Pharisee's accusations.[492] In addition to these, you will make your soul heroic by this practice, and you will enjoy praises from all. But if you wish to take vengeance on that man, this too will follow in full measure, both when God punishes him for the things he said and, before that punishment, because your Christian way of life has become a timely blow to him.[493]

As a rule, nothing stings those who do us harm as much as when we who are hurt laugh at their insults. Therefore, just as so many good things will come from our living a Christian way of life, so too everything opposed to that lifestyle will happen to us if we act out of a meanness of spirit. For we bring disgrace on ourselves and, in the eyes of all present, we seem to be guilty of what has been said about us. We fill our souls with tumult and bring joy to our enemy. We provoke God and add to our previous sins.

Therefore, after considering all these things, let us avoid the abyss of meanness of spirit and hurry to the harbor of patient endurance. Let us do this so that we may *find rest for our souls*, as Christ has also declared. And may we come to gain the blessings of the

Cf. Matt 11:29

---

492 Cf. Luke 18:10–14.
493 Cf. Rom 12:20.

life to come through the grace and loving-kindness of our Lord Jesus Christ, with whom be to the Father, together with the Holy Spirit, glory, power, and honor, now and forever, world without end. Amen.

HOMILY 13

I

Cf. Rom 7:14

For we know that the law is spiritual, but I am made of flesh because I have been sold into the power of sin.

Paul had said that evils had become great and that sin had grown more powerful after it found its occasion and opportunity in what the law commanded.[494] So the law itself produced a result quite the opposite of the effect it was earnestly pursuing and was hurling the man who heard it into great doubt and perplexity. Next, after he has first freed the law from this wicked suspicion, he goes on to give the reason why this happened.

Someone might hear that it was through the commandment that sin got its start and that, after the coming of the law, sin came to the full vigor of life and that, through the commandment, sin practiced its deceit and brought on death.[495] To prevent anyone from thinking that the law was the cause of these evils, Paul first sets down a defense of the law that not only frees it of these accusations, but even weaves for it a crown of the highest praise. Nor

---

[494] Ernst Käsemann (*Commentary on Romans*, trans. Geoffrey W. Bromily [Grand Rapids, MI: Eerdmans, 1980], 192) points out that the verses of Romans 7:14–25 constitute a digression; they give an apology for the law. True, Paul did show (Rom 7:10–14) that sin became more powerful through the commandment (the Decalogue) of the Mosaic law, an effect opposite to the end it pursued. Now Paul must show that the law is good and spiritual, as is the soul of man, and that neither does the flesh of man cause sin; rather, it is the will of man that is responsible for the evils he commits. The death of Christ in the flesh conquered and destroyed death's power over man's flesh. See Homily 12.53 and §§ 52–53 of this homily.

[495] Cf. Rom 7:11, and see Homily 12.53.

does he do so as if he were personally granting a favor to the law. Rather, he does so as one who is setting forth a judgment common to all men.

So it is that Paul says, *For we know that the law is spiritual.*[496] This is just as if he had said that it is clear and agreed that the law is spiritual.[497] It is so far from being the cause of sin or accountable for the evils that have occurred. And see how he has set it free from this accusation but has also given it excessive praise. For after he said that the law is spiritual, he showed that it is the teacher of virtue and the foe of vice. For this is what it means to be spiritual, namely, to lead away from all sins. And this the law did do by frightening, admonishing, punishing, correcting, and counseling everything that has to do with virtue.

From what source, then, did sin come if the law is such a marvelous teacher? It comes from the 'carelessness and listlessness'[498] of its disciples. Therefore, Paul went on to add, *But I am made of flesh.* In this way he gives a sketch of the man living under the law and before the law [was given]. *Sold into the power of sin.*[499] What Paul means is that along with the necessity of dying, the throng of passions entered into man. For when his body became mortal [after Adam sinned], man then also received concupiscence[500] and anger and pain and all the other passions. All these needed great

Cf. Rom 7:14.

Cf. Rom 7:14

---

496 As Fitzmyer says (JBC, 53:77), the law is spiritual in its origin because it is given by God, as well as in its destiny because it is a means of leading man to God, and so it does not belong to the world of earthbound, natural man. It is, therefore (as Chrysostom says), a teacher of virtue, a foe of vice, and leads man away from sin.
497 Cf. §§ 41–42 of this homily.
498 The Greek word is ῥᾳθυμία ("indifference," "laziness or sloth," "lack of diligence," "negligence," or "carelessness").
499 Throughout most of Rom 7:7–25, Paul speaks in the first person, and there has been much debate as to whether or not this "I monologue" is autobiographical. In his *In Hope of Man's Glory*, C. H. Giblin considers that Paul speaks in the person of Adam and thinks that the passage is typological. Surely it is not a picture of a man in grace, but of one without Christ, voicing a desperate cry, imprisoned by sin and death, serving with his flesh the law of sin. Despite all his weakness, sinful man is not without hope. He can be rescued in his conflict with sin by the power of God's grace working through Christ Jesus. Käsemann also discusses these verses at length in his *Commentary on Romans*, 192–212. See also notes *ad loc.* in NAB and RNT, and Stevens' note in NPNF[1] 11:427.
500 The Greek word is ἐπιθυμία ("desire/sexual desire/lust").

wisdom to prevent the flood tides in us from plunging reason into the depths of sin.[501]

The passions themselves were not sin.[502] But when the countless number of them was unbridled, they had sin as the result. Let me take one passion and discuss it as an example. For instance, concupiscence is not a sin.[503] But when it goes to excess and refuses to remain within the law of marriage, when it leaps after women who are married to other men, then the matter becomes adultery — not because of concupiscence, but because of the man's unbounded lust.

Consider how wise Paul is. After he praised the law, he immediately hurried back to the earlier time. After he had shown the state of our human race in those days and its condition after it received the law, he made it clear how necessary the presence of grace was. And this was something he was eager to emphasize at every opportunity. For when he says *sold into the power of sin*, he was speaking not only of those under the law, but also of those who lived before the law, as well as of men born from the very beginning. Then he mentioned the way in which they were sold and how they surrendered.

Cf. Rom 7:15   Paul says, *For I do not understand what I do*. What does he mean when he says, *I do not understand*? He means "I am ignorant." And when did this come about? For no one ever sinned when he was ignorant. Do you see that, unless we choose our words with proper discretion and keep looking toward the Apostle's purpose and object, countless absurdities will follow? For if they sinned through ignorance, they did not deserve to be punished. It is just as Paul
Cf. Rom 7:8   said above: *For without the law, sin is dead*.[504] In that text Paul was not showing that sinners failed to know they were sinning. They did

---

501 The concepts in this paragraph are at the foundation of Chrysostom's understanding of the human condition brought about by Adam's Fall. The source of sin and evil is found in man's ῥαθυμία and his πονηρά προαίρεσις in exercising his αὐτεξούσιον. See discussion on this in Papageorgiou, "A Theological Analysis," chap. 2, pp. 50–53.
502 See NPNF¹ 11:427n1.
503 "ἡ ἐπιθυμία ἁμαρτία μὲν οὐκ ἔστιν."
504 See Confraternity note *ad loc.* and Homily 12.49.

know, but their knowledge was indistinct. Therefore, they were punished, but their punishment was not so severe.

And again Paul said, *I had not known lust*.[505] But he was not talking of a total ignorance of lust; he was talking about knowing it with the clearest knowledge. And he said, *[Sin] worked all manner of lust in me*. But he did not mean that the commandment caused the lust, but that sin — because of the commandment — brought on a heightened degree of lust. So also here it is not total ignorance that he means when he says, *I do not understand what I do*. If this were so, how would he find pleasure in the law in the depths of his heart? Cf. Rom 7:7–8

Cf. Rom 7:8

What then does he mean when he says, *I do not understand*? He means "I grow blind and dizzy; I am carried away; I have violence done to me; and, without knowing how, I am tripped up and thrown down." It is just as we usually say, "Somehow, someone came and grabbed me," when we are not using ignorance as an excuse, but when we are making it appear that we were caught by some kind of trick, circumstance, or plot.

For it is not what I wish that I do, but what I hate that I do. How then do you fail to know what you are doing? If you wish to do what is good and hate to do what is wicked, this is a mark of perfect knowledge. From this it is clear that Paul did not say *not what I wish* because he was denying free will[506], nor because he was bringing in some overpowering necessity. For if we sin against our will because we are forced to do so, there would be no reason for the punishments that were inflicted in former times. Cf. Rom 7:15

But just as when he said, *I do not understand*, it was not ignorance that he was showing us, but rather what we explained, so here, when he puts before us the words *not what I wish*, he did not mean necessity, but his disapproval of what was done. I say this because if this was not what he meant when he said, *I do not do what I wish*, how is it that he did not add, "But I do that which necessity forces me to do"? For this is what is opposed to the power of free will.

But now Paul did not say this, but instead he wrote down, *what I hate*. And he did this so that you may learn that when he said *not*

---

505 See Homily 12.47.
506 "οὐχὶ τὸ αὐτεξούσιον ἀναιρῶν, οὐδὲ ἀνάγκην τινὰ εἰσάγων βεβιασμένην." For a historical overview on "Freedom and Responsibility" and Chrysostom's understanding of it, see Papageorgiou, "A Theological Analysis," chap. 2, pp. 77ff.

what I wish, he did not take away the power of the will. What then does he mean by *not what I wish*? He means "what I disapprove of, what I do not agree with, what I do not like." To oppose this he also added what follows when he said, *But I do that which I hate. But if I do what I do not wish, I am agreeing that the law is good.*

Cf. Rom 7:15-16

II

Meanwhile, you see that the power of understanding has not been corrupted. It preserves its own noble character while it is acting. For if it goes after evil but goes after it because it hates it, this would be the greatest commendation both for the natural law and for the written law. As Paul says, it is plain that the law is good from the things of which I accuse myself when I have failed to listen to it and when I hate the wrongs I have done.

And yet, if the law was the cause of sin, how is it that Paul took delight in it but hated what it commands to be done? For he says, *I agree that the law is good. But now, no longer is it I who do that [which I do not wish to do]; it is the sin that dwells within me. For I know that in me, that is, in my flesh, no good dwells.*[507] Because of these verses we are attacked by those who slander the flesh and make it no part of God's creation.[508] What then should we say? Exactly what we said earlier when we were discussing the law. Just as Paul said there that sin was the cause of it all, so also here. For he did not say that the flesh accomplishes this, but quite the opposite: *No longer is it I who do this, but it is the sin that dwells within me.*

Cf. Rom 7:16-18

But even if Paul says that good does not dwell in it, this is still no charge against the flesh. For his statement that no good dwells in his flesh is not a proof that the flesh is evil. We agree that the flesh is not as great as the soul and that it is inferior to it. But it is not contrary or opposed to it, nor is it evil. As a lyre is subject to the musician and a ship to the helmsman, so the flesh is subject to the soul. But the harp and the ship are not opposed to those who guide and use them, but go along with them even if they, as instruments, do not have the same honor as the artists. So if a man

---

507 Chrysostom's text omits the words within brackets.
508 The Manichaeans.

says that the skill does not belong to the harp or the ship, but to the helmsman or the artist, he is not slandering the instruments. He is pointing out the great difference between the instruments and the artists.[509]

In the same way, when Paul said, "Good does not dwell in my flesh," he did not slander the body, but he did show the superiority of the soul. For it is the soul that takes in hand the whole duty of the harpist and the helmsman. And this is what Paul points out here when he puts the authority in the hands of the soul. When he has divided man into two parts, soul and body, he is saying that the flesh is more lacking in reason, devoid of understanding, and that it belongs to the things that are led, but not to the things that lead.

So the soul possesses greater wisdom and can distinguish between what should be done and what should not be done. However, it lacks the strength to control the horse, namely, the body, as it wishes. And this would constitute a charge not only against the flesh, but also against the soul. The soul knows the things it must do but does not carry out in action what seems best for it to do. As Paul says, *To wish is within my power, but I do not find the strength to accomplish that which is good.* Cf. Rom 7:18

Here again, when Paul says, *I do not find the strength*, he is not speaking of ignorance or doubt, but of a kind of spiteful action and plot on the part of sin. Therefore, to show this more clearly, he went on to say, *For I do not do the good that I wish to do, but I do the evil that I do not wish to do. But if I do what I do not wish to do, it is no longer I who do this, but the sin that dwells in me.* Cf. Rom 7:19–20

Do you see how Paul acquits both the essence of the soul and the essence of the flesh and transfers the blame entirely to the evil action? For if he did not wish to do it, the soul is freed from blame. If he himself did not accomplish it, the body is also acquitted. And the entire blame belongs to the 'deliberate choice of evil'.[510] For the

---

509 For an extensive discussion on Chrysostom's understanding of the dynamics between soul and body, and human responsibility for sin and evil, see Papageorgiou, "A Theological Analysis," chap. 2, pp. 62–71.

510 "καὶ μόνης τῆς πονηρᾶς προαιρέσεώς ἐστι τὸ πᾶν." For Chrysostom, sin is not a mere mistake, but man's "deliberate choice." Here Chrysostom differs from Gregory of Nyssa, who taught that sinning, the misuse of the freedom of choice, was an issue of "mistaken judgment" (an intellectual error) on the part of man. For more on this,

essence of the soul and the essence of the body are not the same as the essence of the 'deliberate choice'.[511] The first two essences are works of God; the third essence is a motion that comes from ourselves and is directed toward whatever object to which we may wish to lead it.[512]

Willing is a natural thing and comes from God. But such a use of the will belongs to us and comes from our own intention and purpose. *Therefore, when I wish to do good, I discover this law, namely, that evil is close at hand for me.* What Paul says is not too clear. What, then, does he mean? What he is saying is that I praise the law in my conscience, and I find that it supports me when I wish to do what is good and that it strengthens my intention. Just as I find pleasure in it, so does it praise my purpose.

Cf. Rom 7:21

Do you see how Paul shows that the knowledge of things that are good and of those that are not has been laid as a foundation in us from the beginning, and that the law of Moses praises this law and is praised by it? Paul did not say earlier, "I am taught by the law," but *I agree that the law is good.*[513] Nor will he say, "I am instructed by it," but *I delight in the law.*[514]

Cf. Rom 7:16
Cf. Rom 7:22

What does he mean by *I delight in*? He means "I agree with it as being good, just as it agrees with me when I wish to do what is good." And so, willing what is good and not willing what is evil was laid as a foundation from the beginning.[515] And when the law came, it accused many men for their evil actions and praised many men for their good deeds.

Do you see that everywhere Paul testifies to the law inasmuch as it lends a hand to help and to give an increase of intensity, but nothing more? For even when the law praises [me] and I take

---

see Papageorgiou, "A Theological Analysis," chap. 2, p. 51, n. 125.
511 προαιρέσεως.
512 Cf. Papageorgiou, "A Theological Analysis," chap. 2, pp. 62–71.
513 See § 12 of this homily.
514 See § 20 of this homily.
515 Here Chrysostom claims that the God-given natural inclination of man is to desire the good and be opposed to evil; this is the "law of nature." Cf. Homily 12.57: "As soon as God formed Adam, the Lord put in him the law of nature and established it firmly to dwell in the whole human race." See also discussion in Papageorgiou, "A Theological Analysis," chap. 2, pp. 80–87: Chrysostom considers freedom and reason as necessary attributes of the image of God in man.

delight in it and wish for what is good, nonetheless "evil is close at hand for me" and its activity is not removed. So it is that the law only becomes an ally to the man who has the intention of doing something good, inasmuch as the law wishes for the same thing as the man does.

Next, because Paul had made this last statement in a rather indistinct manner, as he goes on he explains it and makes his point more clearly. He does this by showing how evil is close at hand, and how the law helps the man who wishes to do good. For he says, *I delight in the law of God according to the inner man.* What he means is this: I knew what was good even before this. But I praise it now that I have found it set down in writing. *But I see another law in my members waging war against the law of my mind.*[516]   Cf. Rom 7:22

Cf. Rom 7:23.

III

Here again, he gives the name of *sin* to the law that was waging this war. He calls sin a law not because it deserved it, but because of the strict obedience of those who heeded it. And so, just as Mammon, or wealth, is called a master,[517] and the belly is named a god,[518] not because they deserved it, but because of the extreme slavery of those who are their subjects, so also here Paul calls sin a law because of those who are so enslaved by it. For sinners are just as afraid to put sin aside as those who have received the law are afraid to let go of this law.

What Paul means then is that sin is opposed to the law of nature, for this is the *law of the mind.* And then he brings in the armies drawn up for battle and the battle itself, and he attributes the whole contest to the law of nature. For the law of Moses was subsequently added over and above the natural law. Yet neither the one law nor the other — the one by teaching and the other by praising what had to be done — achieved any great success in this battle because the tyranny of sin was so strong in overcoming and in getting the upper hand.

---

516 See note *ad loc.* in RNT.
517 Cf. Matt 6:24; Luke 16:9, 11, 13 (and RNT note *ad loc.*). See also McKenzie, DB, 557.
518 Cf. Phil 3:19.5

Cf. Rom 7:23.   Paul showed this and made clear how strong this defeat was when he said, *But I see another law waging war against the law of my mind and making me a prisoner to the law of sin*. He did not say "to the assaults of my flesh," nor "to the nature of my flesh," but *to the law of sin*, that is, to the tyranny of sin, to the power of sin. How is it then that he says, [*to the law of sin*] *that is in my members*? And why does he say that?

Surely he does not say that because his members are the cause of sin. He is saying that because he is separating his bodily members as far as possible from the sin. For that which is in a thing is quite different from the thing in which it is. Therefore, just as the commandment is not evil because sin found its occasion from it, so the nature of the flesh is not evil even if through it sin prevailed over us. If this were true, the soul too will be evil and even more so, because the soul possesses power over our actions. But this cannot be. No, it cannot be.

If a tyrant and a robber were to seize a marvelous home and a royal palace, their action would not be a slanderous charge laid at the door of the buildings, but the accusation would go against those who plotted such deeds. But the enemies of the truth in their impiety fall into a most unreasonable state of mind and fail to perceive it. Not only do they accuse the flesh, but they also slander the law. Yet if the flesh were evil, the law would be good. For the flesh wages war against the law and opposes it. But if the law is not good, then the flesh is good,[519] because, according to these enemies of the truth, the flesh wages war and fights against the law. How is it then that they say that both the flesh and the law come from the devil, because they bring in arguments that contradict each other?

Do you see how unreasonable as well as how impious they are? But the doctrines of the Church are not like that. For they not only condemn sin, but they also maintain that God gave both laws — that of nature and that of Moses — and that both laws are opposed

---

519 As Stevens says in his note (NPNF1 11:430), it is an interesting point to see how vigorously Chrysostom opposes the idea that the flesh is essentially evil, as if it were a current notion of his time. This view, derived perhaps from Manichaean sources, had a powerful influence in the Church from early times and became the basis for rigorous ascetic practices.

to sin and not to the flesh. They do not hold that the flesh is sin, but a work of God that is very useful for the life of virtue if we are watchful and sober.[520]

Unhappy man that I am! Who will deliver me from the body of this death? Cf. Rom 7:24 Do you see how great the tyranny of evil is? It overcomes even the mind of a man who takes delight in the law. What Paul means is that no one can say that sin overcomes me because I hate the law and turn my back on it. For I take delight in it, I agree with it, and flee to it for refuge. Yet it lacks the strength to save me even when I turn to it. But Christ saved me even as I fled from Him.

Do you see how great the superiority of grace is? But the Apostle Paul did not put it this way. With a groan and a loud lament, as if there were no one to help him, he points out, through his lack of an ally [in the law], the power of Christ when he says, "Unhappy man that I am! Who will rescue me from the body of this death?" The law lacked the strength; conscience did not come to my aid. Yet I praised deeds that were good. Not only did I praise them, but I fought against what was opposed to them. When he said *waging war against,* he showed that he was in the battle line against sin.

From what source, then, will there be hope for salvation? Paul says, *I give thanks to God through Jesus Christ our Lord.* Do you see how Cf. Rom 7:25; 1 Cor 15:57 he showed that the coming of grace was necessary, and that our success is a work common to the Father and the Son? For if it is to the Father to whom Paul gives thanks, it is also the Son who is the cause of his thanksgiving.

But when you hear Paul saying, *Who will rescue me from the body of this death?* do not think that he is accusing the flesh. For he did not Cf. Rom 7:24 say "the body of sin," but *the body of death,* that is, the mortal body, the body that has been overcome by death. He does not mean the body that has generated death. So this is no proof of the evil of the body, but of the loss that the body has undergone.

It is just as if a man who had been captured by the barbarians would be said to be a barbarian not because he is one, but because he is being held captive by them. So too the body is said to belong

---

[520] ἐὰν νήφωμεν. This is the opposite state to slothfulness and indifference, which Chrysostom encourages his hearers to embrace. For a discussion on Chrysostom's understanding and use of "watchfulness," see Papageorgiou, "A Theological Analysis," chap. 4, pp. 256–264.

to death because it is held captive by death and not because it has produced death. Therefore, Paul does not wish to be rescued from the body, but from the mortal[521] body. As I have often said, he is suggesting that, from the fact that the body is subject to suffering, it has become an easy object of attack by sin.

IV

You may say, then, if the tyranny of sin was so strong before the coming of grace, why were those who sinned punished? Because they had received such commandments as could be kept and observed even when they were under the dominion of sin. Although this law did not draw them to a lofty state of life, it did allow them to enjoy wealth and possessions; it did not hinder them from having several wives, or from satisfying anger in a just cause, or from making use of luxury within proper bounds.[522]

And this condescension was so great that the law made fewer demands than those made by the law of nature. For the law of nature commanded one man to consort continually with one woman. Christ made this clear when he said, *The Creator, from the beginning, made them male and female*. But the law of Moses did not prevent a man from putting one wife aside and taking another in her stead, nor did it prohibit having two wives at the same time.[523]

Cf. Matt 19:4; Gen 1:27.

And in addition to this example, you might see that those who lived before the Mosaic law kept straight a greater number of other actions than in the law because they were instructed by the law of nature. Therefore, those who lived under the dispensation of the Old Testament suffered no harm or loss, because such moderate legislation was imposed upon them. But if, even in such a situation, they were not strong enough to prevail [over sin], the charge must be laid on their own sluggish indifference.

This is why Paul gives thanks that Christ, who did not carefully weigh any of these things, not only did not ask for an accounting of our actions, but even made us ready for a greater race. And so

---

521 This might also mean "liable to passions." Cf. NPNF[1] 11:431n1.
522 Cf. NPNF[1] 11:431n2.
523 See McKenzie, *DB*, 201, on divorce in the OT, and 548–550 on multiple wives and concubines.

Homily 13

Paul said, *I give thanks to God through Jesus Christ.* He passes over the salvation on which all were agreed and goes on from what has already been established to a further point when he says that not only were we set free from our former sins, but also that we have become invincible for the future. Cf. Rom 7:25

For Paul says, *For now there is no condemnation for those who are in Jesus Christ, [who do not walk according to the flesh].*[524] But he did not say that until he had first recalled to our minds our former condition. For after he had just said, *Therefore, with my mind I myself serve the law of God, but with my flesh the law of sin,* he now goes on to add, *For now there is no condemnation for those who are in Christ Jesus.* Cf. Rom 8:1

Cf. Rom 7:25

However, because the many people who sinned after baptism contradicted this, Paul hurried on this account to give an answer. And he did not simply say, *For those who are in Christ Jesus,* but added *For those who do not walk according to the flesh.* In this way he shows that every [sinful] action that lies in the future comes from our sluggish indifference. For now it is possible to not walk according to the flesh, but at that time it was a difficult thing to do.[525]

Next, Paul proves this in another way when he speaks the following words: *For the law of the Spirit of the life that is in Christ Jesus has set me free.*[526] Here he is calling the Spirit *the law of the Spirit.* Just as he called sin *the law of sin,*[527] so he speaks of the Spirit as *the law of the Spirit.* And yet he called the law of Moses by this name too when he said, *For we know that the law is spiritual.* Cf. Rom 8:2

Cf. Rom 8:2

Cf. Rom 7:14

What then is the difference? It is a great difference, one that knows no limits. The law of Moses was spiritual, but this is the law of the Spirit. And what is the distinction between this law and that? They are distinct because the law of Moses was only given by

---

524 The bracketed relative clause is not found in the Greek text of Aland et al., Merk, or Migne, nor in the English translations of the Confraternity ed., NAB, RNT, or JB. It does, however, appear in the Greek text of the Westcott and Hort, Tregelles, the Greek text behind the NIV, and the KJV. It must have been in the Greek text used by Chrysostom because he cites it several times in his subsequent argument, hence I have retained it in my translation. It is also found in the Latin translations of Merk and Migne.

525 No doubt, despite the wholehearted fervor of the first Christians, the new Way was strange and opposed to the lifestyle of almost all of their fellow men.

526 NAB and RNT read "you" for "me," as does Merk.

527 See § 27 of this homily. See also Rom 7:23.

the Spirit. But the law of the Spirit furnishes the Spirit abundantly to those who receive it. For this reason Paul called it *the law of life*, to distinguish it from *the law of sin*, not from "the law of Moses."

Cf. Rom 8:2   For, when Paul says, *It freed me from the law of sin and of death*, in this place he is not speaking of the law of Moses. Nowhere does he speak of that law as the law of sin. How could he call it a law of sin when, time and time again, he calls Moses' law just and holy and says that it destroyed sin? But he did call the law of sin the law that waged war against the law of the mind.[528] For the grace of the Spirit put a stop to this grievous war by slaying sin and making the contest easy for us. The Spirit first gave us a crown[529] and then drew us to the struggle with an abundance of allies to aid us in the fight.[530]

Paul constantly does this. He turns from the Son to the Spirit and from the Spirit to the Son and the Father because he reckons that all we are and have belongs to the Trinity. And he does that
Cf. Rom 7:24 here. For when he said, *Who will rescue me from the body of this death?* he showed the Father doing this through the Son.[531] And then again he shows the Holy Spirit working with the Son. Indeed, Paul said,
Cf. Rom 8:2 *For the law of the Spirit of the life in Christ Jesus has set me free.* Next, he again shows the Father and the Son working together. For he says,
Cf. Rom 8:3 *What was impossible for the law, inasmuch as it was weak because of the flesh, God has made good by sending His own Son in the likeness of sinful flesh and, as regards sin, He condemned sin in the flesh.*

Again Paul seems to be slandering the law. But if anyone pays close attention, Paul is also giving the law great praise when he shows that it is in harmony with Christ and chooses the same things. He does not speak of the wickedness of the law, but of *what it was impossible for it to do*. And again he speaks of it *inasmuch as it was weak*, but not inasmuch as it did evil or plotted against us. Nor does he consider that the weakness belongs to the law, but rather to the flesh, because he says, *Inasmuch as it was weak because of the flesh*.

---

528 Cf. Rom 7:23.
529 Against temptation. The "crown" consists of the graces given to us.
530 Against the devil's temptations.
531 Cf. Rom 7:25.

Here, however, again he is not speaking of the flesh in its essence and substance. Rather, he is giving the name of "flesh" to the more carnal sort of mind. In this way he frees both the body and the law from being objects of accusation. Yet he does this not only in this way, but also in another, as we shall see from what follows.

V

If the law was not in harmony with Christ, how is it that Christ came to its aid and fulfilled its just claim? How is it that Christ stretched out His hand to help the law by condemning sin in the flesh?[532] For this was left out when, long before, the law had condemned sin in the soul. But what of this? Did the law accomplish something greater, whereas the Only Begotten accomplished something that was less? By no means! For it was God who was the principal agent in doing what the law did, because it was God who both gave the law of nature and then added the written law to it. Besides, there would have been no need or use for the greater if the lesser had not been set down beside it.

For what good is it to know the things that must be done if no one follows through and does them? There is no benefit in this, but there is even a greater condemnation. So it is Christ who has saved the soul and who has also made the flesh obedient to its rein. To teach is an easy task, but to show a way in which these things were easily done is the real marvel. It was for this that the Only Begotten came; nor did He depart until He set us free from that difficulty.

But what is still greater is the way in which He won this victory. For He did not take a different kind of flesh, but the same flesh, which is worn out with toil and suffering. This was just as if someone saw a cheap and vulgar woman being beaten in the marketplace and should say that he was her son, whereas he was in fact the king's son. In this way he set her free from those who were treating her abusively and beating her. This is what Christ did when He confessed that He was the Son of Man,[533] stood beside her, and condemned the sin.

---

532 Cf. Rom 8:3, and see § 44 of this homily.
533 In all likelihood a messianic title, "Son of Man" occurs seventy times in the Synoptic Gospels and twelve times in John, and is used only by Jesus. It does not oc-

However, Christ did not then continue beating the woman's flesh. Rather, He continued the beating of the flesh with His own death. And in this very act, it was not the beaten flesh that was condemned and died, but the sin that had done the beating. And this was the marvel that surpassed all marvels. Unless the victory came in the flesh, it would not be such a wonderful thing, because the law accomplished a victory over death. This, however, was the marvel, namely, that it was with the flesh that Christ raised up His trophy of victory and that what had been overthrown time and time again by sin won for itself a glorious victory over sin.

See how many unexpected things happened. First, sin did not conquer the flesh. Second, sin was overcome and conquered by the flesh. And not losing a battle is not the same thing as winning a war over an enemy who had constantly beaten us in battle. The third thing is that not only did the flesh conquer sin, it beat it badly and punished it. For Christ did not commit sin, and so He conquered sin. By dying He conquered and condemned it. Although before this sin had held the flesh in scorn, Christ proved that the flesh was something to cause sin to shudder.

And so in this way Christ destroyed the power of sin and took away the death that sin had brought on. For as long as sin seized sinners, it brought them to the end of death in all justice. However, when sin handed over to death a body that it had found to be without sin, it was condemned because it had acted unjustly. Do you see how many proofs of Christ's victory in the flesh there are? First, there was the fact that the flesh was not overcome by sin; second, the fact that the flesh conquered and condemned sin; third, that the flesh did not simply conquer sin, but also condemned it because it had sinned.

For after Christ had first proved that sin had acted unjustly, he now condemned it not only by his power and might but even by the reckoning of justice. And Paul made this clear when he spoke

---

cur in the Epistles. It surely stresses the human condition of Jesus, but also often stresses His superhuman powers, especially that of forgiving sins. This latter power is highlighted in stories of sinful women whose offenses are forgiven, which dismays their accusers. Chrysostom's intent here seems to be to emphasize the two natures in Christ and to stress the human, by which His flesh was victorious over the death wrought by sin. See McKenzie, *DB*, 831–833.

Homily 13

about sin and said, *He condemned sin in the flesh*. This is just as if Paul had said that Christ had convicted it of great sin and then had condemned it. Do you see that everywhere sin has been condemned, and not the flesh? For the flesh is everywhere crowned with victory and passes sentence against sin. Cf. Rom 8:3

But if Paul should say that the Father sent the Son "in the likeness of the flesh," you would not think on this account that His flesh was of a different kind. But because Paul had said *in the likeness of sinful flesh*,[534] the word "sinful" was his reason for saying "in the likeness." For Christ did not have sinful flesh, but flesh like our sinful flesh, except that Christ's flesh was sinless. But in nature Christ's flesh was the same as ours. And so from this it is clear that the nature of the flesh is not evil. Cf. Rom 8:3

For it was not by taking a kind of flesh different from the former flesh, nor by changing this same flesh in its substance, that Christ in this way caused the flesh to win the battle. He allowed the flesh to remain in its own nature and in that way gain the crown of victory against sin; He then raised it up and made it immortal.

Someone may say, "What then does this have to do with me if these things happened in the case of that flesh [of Christ]?" It has a great deal to do with you. This is why Paul went on to say, *In order that the demands of the law might be fulfilled in us who do not walk according to the flesh.*[535] What does Paul mean by the word "demands"? He means the end, the scope, the making good of a wrong. What does he wish to say and what is he enjoining on us? That we would be free from sin. However, this is now being taken care of for us through Christ. Making a stand against sin and getting the better of it comes from Him, but enjoying the victory is ours. Cf. Rom 8:4

Shall we then sin no more? Surely, we shall not sin unless we have become extremely faint and have lost heart. This is why Paul added *in us who do not walk according to the flesh*.[536] After you had heard that Christ had freed you from the war with sin and that the demands of the law had been fulfilled in you because sin had been Cf. Rom 8:4 and 8:1

---

534 See also NPNF¹ 11:432n1.
535 See also NPNF¹ 11:433n1.
536 But see note 35 above.

condemned in the flesh, Paul added these words because he was afraid you might destroy your every defense.

This is why, after he said in that same passage, "Therefore, there is no condemnation," he went on to say, "for those who do not walk according to the flesh." And here too, after he said, "In order that the demands of the law might be fulfilled in us," he went on to say exactly the same thing — rather, not exactly the same thing, but something much stronger.

For after he said, *In order that the demands of the law might be fulfilled in us who walk not according to the flesh*, he added *but according to the Spirit*, because he was showing that we must not only keep ourselves free from evil deeds, but also that we must adorn ourselves with deeds that are good. To give you the crown belongs to Christ. But it is up to you to hold on to what has been given to you. For what the law demanded, namely, that you not become liable to its curse, this Christ has accomplished for you.

Cf. Rom 8:4

VI

Therefore, do not betray a gift so great as this; keep a close guard over this beautiful treasure. Paul is showing you in this passage that the bath of baptism is not enough for us to be saved if after baptism we do not display a way of life worthy of the gift. So again Paul is advocating the law when he says this. Even after we have given our obedience to Christ, we must do and accomplish everything in such a way that the demands of the law that Christ fulfilled remain in us and are not corrupted.

Cf. Rom 8:4

Paul says, *For they who live according to the flesh are intent on the things of the flesh; those who live according to the spirit are intent on the things of the spirit. For the tendency of the flesh is toward death, but the tendency of the spirit is toward life and peace. For the flesh in its mind is hostile to God; it is not subject to the law of God, nor can it be.*

But not even in this does Paul slander the flesh, because as long as the flesh stays in its proper place it does nothing that is unnatural. But whenever we turn everything over to the flesh and it goes beyond its proper bounds, it rises up against the soul. Then it destroys and corrupts everything, not by its own nature, but by the excess and lack of discipline that come from it.

Those who live according to the spirit are intent on the things of the spirit. For the tendency of the flesh is toward death. Paul did not say "the nature of the flesh," or "the essence of the body," but *the tendency.* And this tendency could be corrected or destroyed. He does not say this because he is granting to the flesh its own power of reasoning. Far from it! He is pointing out a grosser motion of the mind and giving it a name from the body, the part of man that is worse, just as he is often in the habit of calling the whole man *the flesh,* even though the whole man also has a soul.

The tendency of the spirit. Here again, he is speaking of the spiritual mind, just as further on he says, *He [Christ] who searches hearts knows what the tendency of the spirit is.* And he points out many blessings that arise from it, both in the present life and in the world to come.[537] For the tendency of the spirit furnishes far more blessings than the evils that the tendency of the flesh brings to us. And Paul made this clear when he said *life and peace.* For these are opposed to the tendency of the flesh. For Paul tells us, *The tendency of the flesh is toward death,* which is opposed to *life and peace.* Cf. Rom 8:27

For after Paul had said *peace,* he went on to say, *For the flesh in its mind is hostile to God,* which is worse than death. Then, after he showed that the tendency of the flesh was both death and enmity toward God, he said, *For it is not subject to the law of God, nor can it be.* Do not be upset when you hear *nor can it be,* for this difficulty has an easy solution. What Paul means here by *the tendency of the flesh* is that reasoning which is earthly, gross, and distracted toward the things of this life and its wicked actions. And Paul is saying that this cannot be subject to God.

And what kind of hope for the future is there if it is impossible for an evil man to become good? This is not what Paul says. If it were, how would Paul have become good?[538] How would the thief on the

---

537 Cf. Rom 8:28–30.
538 After persecuting the Church. See Acts 9:15–19.

cross?[539] How would Manasseh?[540] How would the Ninevites?[541] How would David have recovered himself after he had fallen?[542] How would Peter have raised himself after he had denied Christ?[543] How could a man who had lived in fornication have been enlisted into the fold of Christ? How could the Galatians,[544] who had fallen from grace, have returned to their former dignity?

Therefore, Paul did not mean that it was impossible for a wicked man to become good, but that it was impossible for a man who remained wicked to become subject to God. However, it is easy for a man to change his ways and to become good and subject to God. For Paul did not say that the man cannot be subject to God, but that the evil action cannot become good. It is just as if he said, "Fornication cannot become chastity, nor can wickedness be virtue."

Matt 7:18 Matthew also says this in his Gospel: *A bad tree cannot bear good fruit.* He was not blocking the change from wickedness to virtue, but he was saying that continuance in evil cannot bear good fruit. For he did not say it was impossible for a bad tree to become good, but that it was impossible for a tree to remain bad and to bear good fruit. But Matthew showed that the bad tree can be changed both from this passage and from another parable, in which he brings in the weeds that became wheat.[545] And on this account he hinders

Matt 13:29 the weeds from being rooted out. For he says, *No, for fear that in*

---

539 Cf. Luke 23:40–43.
540 For Manasseh see 2 Chr 33; he became King of Judah and reigned in Jerusalem for fifty-five years. He rebuilt the worship places of the Baals. The Lord spoke to Manasseh and his people, but they would not listen, so He surrendered them to the Assyrians and they were taken as captives to Babylon. Manasseh saw his error and humbled himself greatly before God. The Lord forgave him and brought him back and restored him into his kingdom. See also the Prayer of Manasseh, Ode 12 (LXX).
541 The Ninevites fasted and repented of their sins at the preaching of Jonah, and their city was spared. Cf. McKenzie, *DB*, s.vv. "Jonah" (pp. 450–452) and "Nineveh" (p. 618). Matt 12:41–42 tells us that at the last judgment the Ninevites will arise and condemn the faithless generation that rejected Jesus.
542 David repented of having murdered Uriah and of his adulterous marriage to Bathsheba. See 2 Sam (2 Kgdms) 11–12.
543 Matt 26:33–35, 69–75.
544 Cf. Gal 1:6–10, 5:1–6, 10.
545 Matt 13:24–30.

gathering the weeds you root up the wheat along with them, that is, the wheat that will spring up from the weeds.

However, when Paul says *the tendencies of the flesh,* he is talking about wickedness. By *the tendencies of the spirit* he means the grace that has been given and how it works, as can be judged in the good use of our free will. In no place in this passage is he discussing an entity or an essence, but he is talking about virtue and evil. As for what you lacked the strength to do under the law, you will now be able to do it, that is, to walk aright and without falling, if you receive the help of the Spirit. It is not enough to not walk according to the flesh. We must also walk according to the spirit.[546] Turning away from evil is not enough for us to gain salvation; we must also do what is good.

But this will be possible if we give over our souls to the Spirit and persuade our flesh to recognize its proper place. For in this way we shall make our bodies spiritual too, just as we shall make our souls carnal if we act sluggishly and with indifference.

VII

Because it was not a necessity of nature that put the gift[547] in us, but our freedom of choice that gave us the gift, it is up to you to make your bodies spiritual or your souls carnal. For Christ has completed everything that depends on Him. Sin does not wage war against the law of our mind, nor does it make us captives, as it did before baptism. All those things have been stopped and destroyed, and our passions are in fear and trembling at the grace of the Spirit.

But if you quench the light, if you cast aside the one who holds the reins, and if you drive out the helmsman, then you must lay on yourself the blame for the storms that sweep over you. Because virtue has now become an easier thing for you to lay hold of and on this account has given you great strength and motivation for living a Christian life, you must consider in what state the affairs

---

546 Cf. Rom 8:5.
547 I.e., baptism.

of men were when the law was in force and in what state they are now after grace has sent forth its light.

Things that until now no man thought possible — such as, for example, virginity, contempt for death, and other sufferings in much greater numbers — are now prospering everywhere throughout the world. And this is true not only among us, but also among the Scythians, Thracians, Indians, Persians, and several other barbarian peoples. There companies of virgins, whole nations of martyrs and congregations of monks, now outnumber those who are married. This is also true of the strictness of fasting and the superiority of poverty.

Now these are things that, with one or two exceptions, men who lived their lives according to the law could not conceive of even in a dream. Because, then, you see the true state of affairs sounding forth more clearly than a trumpet blast, do not let yourself grow soft and betray so great a grace. For it is impossible, even after receiving the grace of faith, to be saved if you are sluggish and indifferent. The wrestling matches are made easy so that you may win the contest, not so that you may fall asleep or abuse the greatness of this grace by taking the opportunity to be sluggish and indifferent, to wallow again in the mire in which you wallowed before.

Cf. Rom 8:8 This is why Paul goes on to say, *They who are carnal cannot please God*. Why is this? Are we to cut our bodies to pieces to please God and so make our escape from the flesh? Are you ordering us, Paul, to kill ourselves while you lead us on the way to virtue? Do you not see how many inconsistencies come to birth if we take what Paul says in its most literal sense? For by *carnal* in this verse Paul does not mean the body or the essence of the body; he means the carnal and worldly way of life.

He means the life that is filled with the softness of luxury and dissolute living, the life that makes the whole man flesh. Just as the wings given by the Spirit make the body spiritual, so also those who leap back from the Spirit and are slaves to the belly and to pleasure make the soul carnal as well. They do not change the essence of the soul, but they do destroy the soul's nobility.

This manner of speaking is found in many places in the Old Testament, where *the flesh* means the gross and clay-like life that has been smitten with unseemly pleasures. For the Lord said to Noah, *My spirit will not remain in these men, because they are flesh.* But Noah himself was encompassed with flesh. However, this is not the charge, namely, to be encompassed with flesh, for this is natural. Rather, the charge is that these men had chosen a carnal life. Gen 6:3 (LXX)

This is why Paul says, *They who are carnal cannot please God.* And he goes on to add, *You are not carnal, but spiritual.* Again he is not saying *carnal*, or *in the flesh*, without qualification. He is speaking of such flesh as has been dragged along and tyrannized by the passions. Someone will ask, "Why did Paul not say that, and why did he not make the difference clear?" His reason was that he wished to rouse up his audience and to show that the man who lives his life aright will not even be in the body. Cf. Rom 8:9

Because it was surely clear to everyone that the spiritual man was not in the state of sin, Paul speaks of the greater fact that man is spiritual not only in the matter of sin, but, from now on, not even in the matter of flesh. Why? Because from that very moment he became an angel, was borne up to heaven, and was merely carrying his body around with him.

But if you are slandering the flesh because Paul calls the carnal life by the name of *flesh*, so too are you slandering the world for the reason that evil is called *the world*. Christ said to His disciples, *You are not of this world*, and again He said to His brothers, *The world cannot hate you, but it hates Me.* And Paul will say that the soul is estranged from God because he called those who live in error *souls*.[548] Cf. John 15:19

But this cannot be, no, it cannot. We must everywhere attend not simply to the words, but to the thought of a speaker, and know the exact meaning of what is said. Some words are good, some are bad, and some are neither good nor bad in themselves. For example, "soul" and "flesh" are neither good nor bad, because they can become one or the other. "Spirit" is always numbered among the good words and can never become anything else. Again, the meaning of "flesh," that is, a bad action, is always bad. Why? Because it is never subject to the law of God.

Therefore, if you give your soul and body to what is better, you belong to the better part. If you give them to what is worse, then

---

548 Ψυχικούς: cf. 1 Cor 2:14.

you have stood out as a sharer in their ruin. This is not because of the nature of the soul and of the flesh, but because of the judgment,[549] which is responsible for choosing the one or the other. This is certainly so, and what has been said does not slander the flesh. Again, taking up what Paul said, let us examine it more carefully. He said, "You are not carnal, but spiritual."

VIII

What then does he mean? Were they not in the flesh, or did they go around without bodies? How can this possibly be? Do you see that he is hinting at the carnal life? And why did he not say, "But you are not in sin"? His reason was so that you might learn that not only did Christ quench the tyranny of sin, but He also made the flesh lighter and more spiritual. He did not do this by changing its nature, but rather by equipping it with wings.

Just as when fire comes together with iron, the iron becomes fire while staying in its own nature, so too, with those who believe and possess the Spirit, the flesh afterward goes over into that action and operation. It becomes entirely spiritual because it has become spiritual in all its parts, and, together with the soul, it is now equipped with wings and is like the body of Paul, who spoke these words.

Therefore, Paul laughs to scorn all soft living and sensual pleasure. He found delight in hunger, scourgings, and prisons; he did not feel pain because he was suffering these torments.[550] And it was to prove this that he said, *For our present affliction, which is light and for the moment.* That is how well he had instructed the flesh to run side by side with the spirit.

Cf. 2 Cor 4:17.

Cf. Rom 8:9 *If indeed the Spirit of God dwells within you.* Paul often uses the expression *if indeed*,[551] not to express doubt, but even when he is strongly persuaded, and he uses it in place of "because," or "for," as
Cf. 2 Thess 1:6 when he says, *If indeed it is just on the part of God to repay with affliction*
Cf. Gal 3:4 *those who afflict you.* And again: *Have you suffered so much in vain, if*

---

549 γνώμην. This term is always used by Chrysostom to denote the freedom of the will.
550 Cf. 2 Cor 11:25–27.
551 I.e., εἴπερ.

indeed it was in vain? Now if anyone does not have the Spirit of Christ. Cf. Rom 8:9 Paul did not say, "If you do not have," but he brings forward this distressing situation in the case of others. And he goes on to add, *He does not belong to Christ.* Cf. Rom 8:9

But if Christ is in you. Again, Paul says that Christ is in them. He Cf. Rom 8:10 has put the distressing situation briefly and parenthetically. He puts what is desirable both before and after the distressing part, and he states it in many words so as to overshadow what causes distress. But he is not saying that the Spirit is Christ. Far from it! What he is showing is that the man who has the Spirit not only is called Christ's, but even possesses Christ Himself. For it is impossible that Christ not be present where the Spirit is present. For when one person of the Trinity is present, the whole Trinity is present. For the Trinity is undivided in Itself and most closely united to Itself.

Someone will say, "And what will happen if Christ is in you?" *If* Cf. Rom 8:10 *Christ is in you, the body, it is true, is dead because of sin, but the Spirit is life by reason of justification.* Do you see how many evils come from not having the Holy Spirit? Death, enmity toward God, being unable to keep His laws, not belonging to Christ as you should, not having Him dwelling within you. But also consider how many blessings come from having the Spirit. You belong to Christ; you have Christ Himself; you are competing with the angels.

For this is to mortify the flesh, namely, to live an immortal life, to have from that time forward the pledges of the resurrection, to run with ease the race of virtue. For Paul did not say that for the rest of one's life the body is free from the activity of sin, but that it is even dead to sin. And this increases the ease of the contests. For such a person gains the crown because he is free from troubles and toils. Therefore, Paul added the words *because of sin* so that you might learn that it was wickedness and not the nature of the body that Christ altogether abolished.

For if it were true that Christ destroyed the nature of the body, he would also have taken away many of the things that can be helpful to the soul. However, this is not what Paul says. He means that while the body still remains alive, it is dead. For this is the sign that we have the Son and the Spirit is within us: when our bodies differ in no way from corpses with respect to committing sins.

But do not feel frightened when you hear of death. You truly have in you a life that no death will take away. Such is the life of the Spirit. No more does this life yield to death, but it exhausts and destroys death. What it receives it keeps immortal. This is why, after Paul said, *The body is dead*, he did not go on to say, "The Spirit is living," but *The Spirit is life*. He said this to show that the Spirit has the power of giving life to others.

Then, again, to hold fast the attention of his audience, Paul tells them the cause of life and gives proof for what he says. The cause is justification. For where there is no sin, death is not to be seen. Where death is not to be seen, life is indissoluble. *But if the Spirit of Him who raised Jesus from the dead dwells in you, then He who raised up the Lord will also bring to life your mortal bodies because of His Spirit, who dwells in you.* (Rom 8:11)

Again, Paul moves the discussion to the resurrection, because this hope especially encouraged the audience and made them feel secure because of what happened in the case of Christ. Be not afraid, Paul is saying, because you are encompassed with a dead body. Hold fast to the Spirit and your body, even though it is dead, will surely rise again. What about this, then? Do the bodies that do not have the Spirit fail to rise again? How must *all stand before the judgment seat of Christ*? (Cf. Rom 14:10) How will we put our faith in what is said about Gehenna? For if those who do not have the Spirit do not rise again, then there is no Gehenna.

What then is the meaning of what you just said? The meaning is that all will rise, but all will not rise to life.[552] Some will rise to punishment, and others will rise to life. This is why Paul did not say, "He will raise up," but *He will bring to life*. (Cf. Rom 8:11) And this is a greater thing than rising up, because it is given only to the just. After Paul set down the cause for this honor, which is so great, he continued his explanation by saying, "Because of His Spirit, who dwells within you." And so, if while you are still here on earth you drive away the grace of the Spirit and do not depart while this grace is still safe, you will surely perish even if you rise again.

---

552 Cf. John 5:29; 2 Cor 5:10 and RNT note.

Just as the Father will not endure to give you over to punishment while He sees His Spirit shining in you, so too if He sees the light of the Spirit quenched, He will not allow you to be brought in to the Bridegroom, in the same way as He refused to admit those [foolish] virgins.[553] Therefore, do not allow your body to live now so that it may live in the life to come. Make it die so that it may not die. For if it remains alive, it will not live; but if it dies, then will it live.

This is what happens generally in the case of the resurrection. It is first necessary for the body to die and be buried; then it becomes immortal. This also happened in the bath of baptism. The old body was crucified and buried, and then it arose. This also happened in the case of the Lord's body. For it was crucified and buried, and then it arose.

IX

Therefore, let us do this too. Let us continually mortify our body in its works and deeds. I do not mean its substance — heaven forbid! — but mortify its drives toward evil deeds. For this is life too; rather, it is the only life. I mean that we must not permit anything arising from human weakness to become a slave to any pleasures. For the man who makes himself the slave of these pleasures cannot live once he has become their servant. Why is this? Because of the despondency, the fears, and the dangers, as well as the throngs of sufferings, that such pleasures bring with them. For if that man must expect to die, he has already died before he actually does die because of his dread of death.

If he should live in fear of disease or poverty or something he did not anticipate, he is ruined and has perished. And what could be more miserable than a life like that? But not so is the man who lives for the Spirit. He stands above fears and grief and dangers and change of every sort, not by refusing to endure any of them, but, what is far greater, by scorning them when they come upon him.

---

553 Cf. Matt 25:1–13.

How is this possible? It is possible if the Spirit dwells within us continually. This is why Paul did not say, "The Spirit who dwelled within," but *The Spirit who dwells in you*, because he is pointing to a continual indwelling. Therefore, that man is most truly alive who is dead to this life. This is why Paul said, *The Spirit is life by reason of justification*. And so that what Paul said may become clearer, let us bring in the examples of two men.

_{Cf. Rom 8:11}

_{Cf. Rom 8:10}

The one man is given up to the prodigality, the pleasures, and the deceitfulness of this life. The other man has died to these. Now let us see which is the one who is especially alive. Let the one of these two be exceedingly rich and very distinguished, a man who keeps about him parasites and flatterers and who spends the whole day in reveling and drinking. But the other man spends his life with poverty, fasting, and in all other kinds of hard training and strict living. In the evening, let him partake only of the food he must have, or, if you wish, let him go two or three days without eating.[554]

Which of these two men, in our eyes, will be the one who is especially alive? I know that the general run of men will think it is the one who exults in pleasures and scatters his wealth. But we think it is the man who enjoys moderation. However, because there is still a quarrel and controversy, let us go into the houses of each of the two, and go at the time when you think the rich man is most alive, that is, at the time of his self-indulgence. And after we have gone in, let us see in what condition each of these men is. For it is from their actions that one appears to be living and the other dead.

Shall we not find then the one man among his books, or in prayer and fasting, or in some other necessary task, awake and sober, conversing with God? But we shall see the other man in a drunken stupor and in a condition no better than a corpse. If we wait until evening, we shall see this death coming upon him more and more and, after that, sleep again overwhelming him. But even in the dead of night, we shall see the first man sober and awake.

Which man should we say is more alive? Is it the one who is lying there senseless and exposed as a laughingstock to all? Or is it the one who is awake and conversing with God? If you go up to the

---

554 Cf. NPNF[1] 11:437n3. Such fasting was not uncommon in warmer climates (See Eusebius, *Ecclesiastical History* 2.17) and is still practiced in certain places.

one who is unconscious and tell him something that is necessary for him to know, he will not hear a word you speak, just as a corpse would not hear you. Whether you wish to communicate with the other man by night or day, you will see an angel rather than a man, and you will hear him speaking wisely of the things of heaven.

Do you see that this man is more alive than those who are living, while the other lies in an even more pitiable state than those who have died? And if the drunkard seems to be stirring himself to action, he sees something different from what is before his eyes. He is like those who have gone mad, or, rather, he is in a more miserable condition, even more miserable than those who have gone insane. For if anyone should do harm to those who have lost their minds, we would all feel pity for the madmen who were harmed, and we would rebuke the one who hurt them.

But if we see someone trampling on the drunkard not only do we feel no pity, but we even pass judgment against him as we see him there lying on the ground. Tell me then, is this life? Is it not a harsher fate than ten thousand deaths? Do you not see that the dissolute man is not only dead, but that he is worse off even than a corpse and more miserable than a man possessed by a demon?

While the mentally ill man is pitied, the drunkard is hated. The possessed man finds forgiveness; the other pays the penalty for his disease of madness. But if he is such a laughingstock externally, because he is drooling putrid saliva and his breath stinks from wine, think of his miserable soul buried inside such a body, as if in a tomb, and consider in what condition it is likely to be.

We could look upon this man just as we would upon a chaste, free-born maiden of high lineage and great beauty and, at the same time, see some savage, disgraceful, and unclean slave woman getting ready, with all her strength, to do violence to and trample upon the maiden. For such is drunkenness.

X

What man in his right mind would not choose to die ten thousand deaths rather than to live in such a state for a single day? For even if, as day is breaking, the drunkard rises up and seems to be sober after all his reveling, not even then does he enjoy the cleanness of sobriety. Why? Because that cloud which comes from the storm of his drunkenness still stands before his eyes. Even if he were granted the clearness of being sober, what good would it do? For the state of being sober would be of no use to him except for letting him see those who are accusing him.

For when he is behaving in an unseemly manner, he gains only this much: he does not see those who are laughing him to scorn. But when day breaks, he loses even this comfort. He hears his servants muttering, his wife's words of shame, his friends slandering him, and his enemies' scornful laughter. What could be more miserable than this life? Everybody laughs at him all day, and when evening comes he does the same shameless things again.

And what about this? Do you wish me to bring forward the greedy? For this is another and worse form of drunkenness. If greed is a drunkenness, then it is also a death, and of a much worse kind than intoxication. For being drunk with wine is not so terrible as being drunk with a lust for possessions. When one is drunk with wine, the punishment stops when the suffering comes to an end in insensibility and the ruin of the drunkard himself. But with greed, the wound passes on into ten thousand souls and kindles wars of many kinds from every side.

Come now and let us put the one beside the other. Let us see what aspects greed has in common with intoxication. Let us make a comparison now of the [two] drunkards and see in what ways greed claims a larger share of blame. Let them not be compared with that happy man who lives by the Spirit, but let them be tested one against the other.

Again, let us bring before you the table[555] that is running red with the blood of countless corpses. In what ways, then, are they similar to each other? They are alike in the very nature of the disease. But the species of drunkenness are different because one comes from wine, whereas the other comes from possessions. The disease is similar because both alike are gripped by unnatural desire. In the case of the one who is drunk with wine, the more he drinks, the more he desires. In the case of the man who is in love with money,

---

555 The money changer's table, in all likelihood.

the more he gets in his grasp, the more he kindles the flame of desire and causes for himself a more difficult thirst.

In this way, then, they are alike. But in another way, the lover of money has an advantage.[556] In what way is this? The drunkard suffers from something that is natural. Wine is warm, and increases one's natural dryness. And in this way wine makes the drunkard thirsty.[557] But what is it that makes the greedy man always want more wealth? What is it? Whenever he becomes wealthier, then especially is he in the state of poverty. This disease is hard to understand and is more like a riddle.

But, if you wish, let us take a look at them after their drunkenness has passed. But it is impossible to see the greedy man after his drunkenness has passed, because his state of intoxication never stops. Therefore, let us look at both while they are in the state of intoxication. Let us consider which one is more ridiculous by drawing an accurate picture of both of them.

Then we shall see that the man who loses his wits, as evening comes on, because of the wine he drinks, is blind to everything, even though his eyes are wide open. He moves around heedlessly and bumps into those he chances to meet. He vomits, tears his clothes, and strips them off in an unseemly manner no matter whether his wife is present, or his daughter, or a servant girl, or anybody else, and these will laugh loudly at him.[558]

Now, let us bring the avaricious man before you. What happens here is not only a matter for ridicule, but also for cursing, great anger, and ten thousand thunderbolts. However, let us now just look at the ridiculous part. For the greedy man, like the other, fails to recognize anyone, whether he is friend or foe. Like the drunkard, he is blind, even if his eyes are open. Just as the drunkard sees everything as if it were wine, so the man of greed looks upon everything as if it were money.

And when he vomits, it is much worse. For he does not throw up food, but he spews out words of abuse, of insolence, of wars,

---

556 In a bad sense.
557 This is probably the fourth-century scientific understanding of alcoholism that was available to Chrysostom.
558 ἐγγελάσεται δαψιλές. The ΕΠΕ text has Ἐγελάσατε, but from the context it seems to me that the PG text is the original.

of deaths — words that draw down on his head countless thunderbolts from above. And just as the body of the drunkard is livid and wasting away, so too is the soul of the man of greed. Nor is his very body free from this disease, but is more severely caught in its grip. Why? Worry is eating it away in a manner harsher than being drunk with wine would. And just as worry does this, so do anger and sleepless nights. So, little by little, the whole body is consumed.

The man who is in the grip of his love for drinking can sober up after the night is over. But the greedy man is constantly drunk, night and day, awake or sleeping, because he is paying a greater penalty than any man in prison, than those who work in the mines, than any other man who may be paying even more severe penalties.

XI

Tell me then, is this life? Is it not death? Is it not more pitiable than any death? Death gives rest to the body; it is free from ridicule, unseemly behavior, and sins. But these fits of drunkenness cast the body into all of these by damming up the ears, by blinding the eyes, and by keeping the mind in deep darkness. For greed does not endure to hear or speak of anything but interest, simple and compound; shameful profits; hateful deals; and servile transactions befitting a slave. The greedy man is like a dog that barks at everybody, because he hates everyone, is opposed to everyone, and attacks everyone with no reason to do so.

Greed rises up against the poor; it begrudges the rich man his wealth; it treats no one pleasantly. If the greedy man has a wife, if he has children, if he has friends, unless he can gain profit from all of them, they are more his enemies than those who are his natural foes. What could be worse than this madness? What could be more miserable? By his own efforts the greedy man is making ready for himself on every side crags, hidden rocks, precipices, chasms, and countless depths. Yet he has but one body, and he is a slave to but one belly.

If you are that man of greed and if someone should thrust you into political office, you will run away, because you are afraid of what expenses it may involve. Yet you are taking upon yourself things that will cause you more distress than any public office, because you are giving your services to Mammon. And these are services that will not only cost you more, but will also be more fraught with danger.

You are contributing your tax money to this evil tyrant — not only your money, but also your bodily toil along with its anguish and pain. You are contributing your very body too, so that you may realize some increase in your wealth from this barbaric servitude. You are a pitiable and miserable man. Do you not see each day those who are carried to their tombs? Do you not see how they are brought to those graves stripped and devoid of all possessions? They cannot take anything from their homes with them. They bring to the worms only what they are wearing.

Consider these dead men each day that passes and perhaps your sickness will become less severe. That is, unless you will become still more insane when you see how much it costs to be buried. Surely your illness is a serious one, and yours is a dread disease. This is why at every assembly in church our discourse touches on this topic [of greed]. This is why we constantly fill your ears to overflowing. We hope that some benefit can come from your growing accustomed to hearing it.

But do not grow obstinate. For it is not only on judgment day, but even before that day comes, that this ailment in its varied forms brings punishments. If I tell you of those who are constantly chained in prison, if I tell you of a man who is nailed to a lingering disease, if I tell you of someone who is struggling with famine or anything else whatsoever, I will not be able to point out anyone who suffers such punishments as those who love money.

What could be more difficult to endure than being hated by all men, than hating everybody, than being civil and pleasant to no one? What could be as intolerable as never having enough to satisfy oneself, as being always thirsty for more, as struggling with unending famine? What could be more unbearable than the distress of a hunger more difficult to endure than any of which man can conceive? What could be harsher than suffering daily pains, than never being sober, than constantly being in a state of confusion and distress?

For the avaricious submit themselves to all these torments and many more than these. While they are making profits, even if they gain for themselves the possessions of all men, they experience no pleasure. Why? Because they are aiming after still more money. And when they undergo the loss of even a dollar, they think that they have suffered a more grievous hurt than any loss. They feel that they have been deprived of life itself.

What words can put these evils before your minds? And if the evils are so great here on earth, think of the evils that will come hereafter: being cast out of the kingdom, the pain of Gehenna, the chains that constantly restrain them, the outer darkness, the venomous worm, the gnashing of teeth, the distress and affliction, the rivers of fire, the furnaces that are never quenched. Gather all these together and compare them to any pleasure that can come from money and possessions.

When you have done this, tear out this disease by its roots, so that you may receive the true wealth and free yourselves from this grievous poverty. And in this way, may you find the blessings both of the present world and of the world to come. May you obtain these blessings by the grace and the loving-kindness of our Lord Jesus Christ, with whom be glory to the Father, together with the Holy Spirit, now and forever, world without end. Amen.

HOMILY 14

I

Therefore, my brothers, we are debtors, not to the flesh,   Rom 8:12–13
that we should live according to the flesh. For if you live
according to the flesh, you are going to die; but if by the
Spirit you put to death the deeds of the flesh, you will live.

After Paul had shown how great is the reward of the spiritual life because it makes Christ dwell within us, because He makes our mortal bodies alive by lifting them up, as it were, on wings to heaven and by making the path of virtue easier, Paul then felt the need for giving an admonition. He brings in his warning when he says, "Therefore, we should not live according to the flesh."[559]

But Paul did not state it that way. Why? Because his words are much more striking and powerful when he says that we are debtors to the Spirit. He makes this clear when he says, *We are not debtors to*   Cf. Rom 8:12

---

[559] The preceding homily (13) is very important because it shows that Paul does not identify sin with the law. Sin exists not in the law, but in the will of man, whose inclination to evil was too often strengthened by what it saw proclaimed in the law. Thus a person who has not received the justifying grace from belief in Christ, or the Christian who reverts to making the law the measure of his relationship to God, will soon find that his reason, and his desire to do the good that he finds in the law, in mortal conflict with his way of life; this will leave him to the slavery of sin and the death that sin brings. He can only be saved from this slavery by the grace of God, which works through Christ Jesus. In Rom 8:1–13 we find that the law of the Spirit can come to dwell in the flesh of the sinner and regain righteousness for him. Then the old man dies and the new man, no longer a debtor to the flesh, will live in peace because of the indwelling of the Spirit.

the flesh. And he proves that this is true in every case when he says that whatever comes to us from God is not a matter of debt, but of sheer grace. But what we do after we are given this grace is no longer a matter of any generosity of ours; it is a debt. For when Paul says, *You have been bought with a price; do not become the slaves of men*, that is the very thing that he means.

1 Cor 7:23

And when he writes, *You are not your own*, Paul is pointing out the same truth. Elsewhere he again reminds us of this fact when he says, *If One died for all,*[560] *therefore all have died; and He died for all in order that those who are alive may no longer live for themselves.* By way of proving this, he says in the present text, "We are debtors." Next, after he had said, *We are not debtors to the flesh*, so that you might not again understand these words as spoken against the essence of the flesh, he did not remain silent, but went on to add, *That we should live according to the flesh*.

1 Cor 6:19

Cf. 2 Cor 5:14–15

Cf. Rom. 8:12

For we owe many things to the flesh, such as to feed it, to keep it warm, to give it rest, to care for it when it is sick, to clothe it, and to attend to it in countless other ways. So that you may not think that he is taking away this care and service, after he said, *We are not debtors to the flesh*, he explains this when he goes on to add, *That we should live according to the flesh*. What Paul means is this: "I am taking away that care of the flesh that leads to sin. In the same way, I do wish that those things that keep the flesh well to continue." And he makes this clear as his discourse goes on.

Cf. Rom 8:12

For after he said, *As for the flesh, take no thought*, he did not fall silent, but went on to add *for its lusts*. Here too he is teaching us. What he means is: "Let us take care of the flesh, for we owe it this attention. However, let us not live according to the flesh, that is, let us not make the flesh the mistress of our life." For the flesh must follow, not lead. Nor must it control our life, but it must accept the laws of the Spirit.

Rom 13:14

So Paul has defined this matter and has proved that we are debtors to the Spirit. Next he shows for what blessings we are debtors. Here he does not speak of past benefits, but of the blessings to come. And in this his prudence especially demands our admiration. Indeed, the blessings of the past were sufficient to make us

---

560 Most manuscripts omit "if" (εἰ), which is included in Chrysostom's text.

marvel. But still he does not set these blessings down at this time, nor does he speak of those ineffable benefits; he speaks only of those still to come. For a blessing once given is not as likely to lead the ordinary man on as is one expected in the future.

After Paul had added this, he first brought fear to the hearts of his hearers because of the pains and evils that come from living according to the flesh. And so he says, *If you live according to the flesh, you are going to die*, hinting that death will be eternal death for us, the death that will exact punishment and torture in Gehenna. But if anyone carefully examines the meaning of what Paul says, such a person is already dead in this life, as we made clear to you in the preceding discourse.

But if by the Spirit you put to death the deeds of the flesh, you will live. Rom 8:13 Do you see that Paul's words are not about the essence of the body, but about carnal deeds? Paul did not say, "If by the Spirit you put to death the essence of the body, you will live," but *the deeds of the flesh*. And not all the deeds, but the wicked ones. And this is clear from what follows. For Paul says, *If you do this, you will live.*

How could this be if his words were to be understood about all acts? For surely, seeing, hearing, speaking, and walking are acts of the body. If we are going to put these acts to death, we will be so far from being alive that we will pay the penalty for manslaughter. What deeds does Paul mean for us to put to death? He means those deeds that move us to wickedness, those that advance toward evil, and those that it is impossible to put to death except by the Spirit. For to put to death the other acts of the body is to slay yourself, and that you have no right to do. To put the sinful acts to death can be done only through the Spirit.

But if the Spirit is present, all the waves are checked, all the passions cower before Him, and nothing can rise up against us. Do you see how Paul bases his exhortation to us on the blessings to come and, as I said before, how he shows us that we are debtors because of these same future blessings and not only from the blessings we have already received?

For Paul means that our right action is a success that belongs to the Spirit. Not only have we been freed from our past sins, but the Spirit has made us unconquerable against future ones, because that Spirit deems us deserving of immortal life. And to state another reward, Paul goes on to say, *As many as are led by the Spirit of God, they are the sons of God.*

II

For this crown is a much greater honor than the previous one. This is why Paul did not merely say, "As many as live by the Spirit of God,"⁵⁶¹ but *As many as are led by the Spirit of God,* because he is showing that God wishes the Spirit to be Master over our life, just as a helmsman is master of the ship and a charioteer is master over a team of horses. And Paul subjects to such controlling reins not only the body, but the soul itself.

For Paul does not wish the soul to hold the power; he puts its command over the body under the power of the Spirit. He does this for fear that those who have relied on the gift of the baptismal font may grow careless afterward in following the way of life proper to a Christian. What Paul means is that even if you should receive baptism, but after receiving it you are not going to be led by the Spirit, you are destroying the dignity given in baptism as well as the privilege of being an adopted son.

This is why Paul did not say, "As many as have received the Spirit," but *As many as are led by the Spirit of God,* that is, as many as follow the Christian way as long as they live, *they are the sons of God.*⁵⁶² Paul says this because this dignity was also given to the Jews. For the psalmist says, *I have said, 'You are gods; and all of you are children of the Most High.'* And again he says, *I have begotten sons and raised them on high.* And in Exodus we read, *Israel is my firstborn.* And Paul himself says, *Who have the adoption as sons.*⁵⁶³ But Paul then goes on to prove how great is the difference between the honor of adoption in the Old Testament and in the New.

What Paul is saying is that even if the names of adoption are the same, the realities of adoption in the Old and the New Testaments

---

561 In Gal 5:25 Paul uses the word "live" (meaning "have life") as opposed to "are led by," which shows that they are "children of God." In Gal 5:18 Paul says, "If you are guided by the Spirit, you are not under the law."
562 See also John 1:12.
563 Said of the Jews.

are not the same. And he furnishes clear proof of the matter by bringing in a comparison drawn from those who were adopted, from the adoption they received, and from the things that were to come.

First, he shows what had been given to the Jews. What was given to them? A spirit of bondage. For this reason Paul went on to say, *For you did not receive the spirit of bondage so as to again be in fear.* Cf. Rom 8:15 Then Paul passes over any mention of what is opposed to bondage, namely, the spirit of freedom, but he sets down what is far greater, namely, the spirit of adoption. And through this, at the same time he brought in the notion of freedom. He did this when he said, *But you have received a spirit of adoption as sons.* Cf. Rom 8:15

This is clear. But it is not clear what the spirit of bondage is, so we must make this less hazy. What Paul has said is not only obscure, but it is difficult to grasp. For the Jewish people did not receive the Spirit. What then is Paul saying here? He is calling the letters [which spell the word] spiritual, for they were spiritual. In the same way he called the law spiritual, and the water from the rock, and the manna.

For Paul said, *All ate the same spiritual food, and all drank the same spiritual drink.* So too he called the rock spiritual when he said, *For they drank from the spiritual rock that followed them.*[564] Because all this was beyond nature, therefore he called it spiritual. But he did not call these events spiritual because at the time they occurred those who shared in them had not received the Spirit. Cf. 1 Cor 10:3–4; Cf. 1 Cor 10:4

In what sense were those letters of bondage? Put before your eyes their whole way of life and you will see this clearly. Surely punishments and retribution were never far away from them, and proportionate recompense immediately followed, just as what we might call the daily ration given to slaves. Many a terror from every side reached its climax before their eyes. Cleansing and expiation only concerned their bodies, and self-control extended only to their actions.

This is not the case with us. Both our thoughts and consciences are cleansed. Christ did not only say, *Thou shalt not kill,* but *Thou shalt not be angry*; he did not only say, *Thou shalt not commit adultery,* Cf. Matt 5:27–28

---

564 See notes *ad loc.* in Confraternity and RNT. See Exod 16:15, 35; 17:6; Num 20:11.

but *Thou shalt not look with wanton eyes.* Christ said this so that it might not be from fear of punishment in the present life, but from our desire for Him, that our virtuous habits and all our good actions would come.

Nor did Christ promise a land flowing with milk and honey,[565] but He does make us joint heirs with the Only Begotten.[566] In this way He makes us stand apart from the things of the present life, and He promises to give us such things that are especially fitting for those who are the sons of God to receive. These include nothing that appeals only to the senses or only to the body; all of them are spiritual.

Even if the Jews were called sons, they were called sons only as slaves. But because we have become free, we have received sonship by adoption and are waiting for heaven. With the Jews He spoke through the mouths of others; with us He speaks in His own person. They do everything they do because they are motivated by the fear of punishment; we, who are spiritual, act out of yearning and desire. Theyments. They act like hirelings and obstinate men, and never do they stop their murmuring. But we do everything to please our Father. When benefits were given to them, they blasphemed. When dangers come our way, we are grateful.

If both of us must be punished because we have sinned, even here there is a great difference. We are not stoned and branded and maimed by the priests, as they are, so that we may be converted. It is enough that we be kept from our Father's table and away from church for a certain number of days.[567] Among the Jews, adoption was an honor in name only. But here with us, the realities followed, namely, the cleansing of baptism, the gift of the Spirit, the granting of other blessings.

And it is possible to mention more of these gifts that show our nobility of station and the meanness of their condition. Paul hints at all of these by speaking of the Spirit, the fear, and the adoptive

---

565 Cf. Exod 3:8. This promise was made to Moses, not to the Christians.
566 Cf. Rom 8:17.
567 No doubt a reference to the penances imposed on public sinners — excluding them from the Divine Liturgy and participation in the Eucharist.

sonship. And he gives another proof of our having the adoption of the Spirit. What then is this? *By virtue of which we cry, 'Abba! Father!'*[568]

III

The initiated know how great a thing this is, because with good reason they were bidden to speak this word first in the prayer of initiation.[569] But what about this? Did the Jews not call God "Father"? Are you not listening to Moses? For he said, *You have forsaken God, who begot you.* Do you not hear Malachi? He reproached the Jews and said, *One God created us, and there is one Father of all of us.* Yes, but even if these words and more than these were spoken, nowhere do we find them calling God by this name[570] or praying in such words. Cf. Deut 32:18
Cf. Mal 2:10

However, all of us — priests, private citizens, rulers, and subjects — have been ordered to pray with these words. And this is the first sound we utter after those marvelous birth pangs and this strange and unusual law of childbirth.[571] But if in any other instance the Jews ever called God by the name of "Father," they did so of their own mind. However, those who are in the state of grace call God their Father because they are moved to do so by the action of the Spirit.[572]

Just as there is a spirit of wisdom that makes those without wisdom wise — and this is revealed in their teaching — there is also a spirit of power by which the feeble have raised the dead and have driven out demons. And there is a spirit of the gift of healing, and a spirit of prophecy, and a spirit of tongues.[573] So too there is a spirit

---

568 In Mark 14:36, during His agony in the garden, Jesus calls on His Father (with this Aramaic term of endearment, Abba) to let this chalice pass from Him, but acknowledges that the Father's divine will must be done rather than what His human will might prefer. Hence "Father" is a term of obedience as well as endearment. As used liturgically by Christians, it entails the obedience of the adopted sons to their heavenly Father. See note on Mark 14:36 in RNT; and Fitzmyer, JBC, 49:26 and 53:84.
569 See Cyril of Jerusalem, *Catechesis* 23.11.
570 I.e., "Abba."
571 In baptism.
572 Chrysostom shows in this paragraph that it is the Spirit who empowers those endowed with charismatic gifts. For more on these gifts see §§ 78-83 of this homily.
573 Cf. 1 Cor 12:7-11.

of adoption. As we know, the spirit of prophecy is a gift by which the one who possesses it foretells the future. However, he does not do so because he speaks of his own knowledge, but because he is moved by grace. So surely the spirit of adoption is that gift by which the one who has received it calls God his Father because he has been moved by the Spirit.

Because Paul wishes to show that this is a genuine birth, he uses the Hebrew language. For he not only said "Father," but *Abba, Father*, because this word is a special sign of trueborn children when they speak to their father. And so, after he had spoken about the difference between the adoption of the Jews of old and the adoption that comes from the Christian way of life, the grace given in baptism, and the freedom, Paul brings in another proof of the superiority, which goes with this adoption.

Cf. Rom 8:16 What is this difference? Paul says, *The Spirit himself gives testimony to our spirit that we are sons of God.* For it is not only from the language that I am strengthened, Paul is saying, but from the cause from which the language had its birth. For we say these words when the Spirit says them. And Paul revealed this more clearly when he said Cf. Gal 4:6 in another place, *God sent the Spirit of His Son into our hearts, crying out, 'Abba, Father.'*

When Paul says, *The Spirit gives testimony to our spirit*, what does he mean? He means the Paraclete together with the gift given to us. For the voice comes not only from the gift, but also from the Paraclete who gives the gift. For the Paraclete Himself, by means of this gift, taught us to speak these words. And when the Spirit gives testimony, what doubt can be left? If a man, or an angel, or an archangel, or some other such power, makes this promise, then there might be reason for some doubt.

But when it is the loftiest Essence that gives this gift and bears witness in the same words with which He commanded us to pray, who could thereafter doubt our dignity? When the emperor chooses someone and proclaims to all men the honor done to his chosen one, none of his subjects would dare to contradict him.

Cf. Rom 8:17 Paul then says, *But if we are sons, we are also heirs.* Do you see how little by little he makes the gift greater? Because it is possible to be sons and not to become heirs — for not all sons are heirs — Paul added this, namely, that we are heirs. For the Jews, along with not having the same sort of sonship as we do, are also cut off from the inheritance. *For he will utterly destroy those evil men and will give over the vineyard to other vinedressers.* Cf. Matt 21:41

And before that, Christ had said, *Many will come from the east and the west and will feast with Abraham. But the sons of the kingdom will be cast outside.* Nor did Paul stop with this, but he set forth something still greater. What was this? That we are heirs of God. Therefore, he added *heirs of God*. And what is still more, he says that we are not merely heirs, but also *joint heirs with Christ*. Cf. Matt 8:11–12 Cf. Rom 8:17 Cf. Rom 8:17

Do you see how Paul strives to bring us close to the Master? Although not all sons are heirs, he shows that we are both sons and heirs. Because not all heirs are heirs to large fortunes, he shows that we also have this advantage because we are heirs of God. Again, because it is possible to be heirs of God but in no way a joint heir with the Only Begotten, he shows that we have this privilege too.

See how wise Paul is. He condensed the bitter things when he was telling what those who were living according to the flesh will suffer — for example, that they are going to die.[574] But when he fixed on the more favorable things, he brings his discourse into a wide-open space, and he expands his discussion on the recompense of the rewards by showing how varied and great are the gifts we receive. For if being God's son was an ineffable grace, consider how great a gift it is to also be an heir. And if this is a great gift, being a joint heir is much greater.

After he showed that the gift[575] was a gift of grace, he went on to make what he said worthy of belief when he said, *If only we suffer with Him, so that we may also be glorified with Him.* What Paul means is that if we have shared with Christ in suffering, much more will we share with Him in the things that are good. For if He granted such blessings to those who had done no good deed, when He sees them undergoing such sufferings, how will He fail to requite them all the more? Cf. Rom 8:17

---

574 Cf. Rom 8:13, and see § 7 of this homily.
575 The gift of baptism.

IV

Then, after Paul showed that it was a matter of giving in return, so that what he said might be credible and so that no one would doubt it, he again shows that all he has been talking about has the virtue of a gift of grace. First, he shows this so that what he says may be believed even by those who doubted, and so that those who accepted it might not feel ashamed because they were receiving salvation forever as a free gift. Second, he shows this so that you may learn that God goes far beyond your toils by what He gives in return. Surely, Paul made this first point clear when he said, *If only we suffer with Him so that we may be glorified with Him*. He proves the second when he went on and stated, *The sufferings of the present time are not worthy to be compared with the glory to come that will be revealed in us*.

Cf. Rom 8:18

In an earlier text Paul had demanded that the spiritual man correct his habits when he said, *You are not debtors to live according to the flesh*, so that such a man might prevail over lust, anger, money, vainglory, and envy. But here, after he reminded him of the whole gift, both what has already been given and what is to come, and after he raised him up with hopes and placed him near to Christ, after he showed him to be a joint heir with the Only Begotten, he then boldly leads him forth to the risks and dangers. For us to prevail over the passions within us is not the same thing as to endure those trials — the scourgings, the famine, the pillaging, the prison chains, the executions. For these require a spirit that is much more noble and vigorously strong.

Cf. Rom 8:12

And see how at the same time he checks the arrogance and uplifts the spirits of the combatants. For after Paul had shown them that the rewards are greater than the labors, he exhorts them to great efforts. But he does not let them grow proud, because they are still outdone by the crowns of victory given in return. And in another passage Paul also says, *For the present burden of our affliction is light enough and earns for us an eternal weight of glory beyond all comparison*.

Cf. 2 Cor 4:17

His discourse was being delivered to men possessed of a deeper kind of wisdom, so here he is not dismissing their sufferings as light. But he is offering consolation to them for the pains they are suffering in the light of the return that will be theirs in the blessings to come. And so he says, *For I reckon that the sufferings of the present time are not worthy to be compared.* He did not say "with the rest and relaxation that will come," but what was much greater, namely, *with the glory to come.* For where there is rest, by no means need there be glory.   Cf. Rom 8:18

But where there is glory, by all means must there also be rest. Then, after he said the glory was to come, he shows that it is already here. For he did not say, "Compared to the glory that is going to be," but compared to the future glory *that will be revealed in us.* He puts it this way because the glory is present now, but it is hidden from sight. He said this elsewhere and in clearer language when he stated, *Our life is hidden with Christ in God.*   Cf. Rom 8:18

Cf. Col 3:3

Therefore, put your confidence in this glory. It has already been prepared for you and is waiting for your labors to end. But if the fact that it is still going to come and is not yet here causes you to grieve, then let this very thing cause you to rejoice, namely, that it is something great and ineffable, that it far surpasses your present condition, and that it is being stored up for you in heaven.

For Paul did not merely write, *the sufferings of the present time,* but he speaks in this way to show you that this other life is superior not only in quality, but in quantity too. For those sufferings, whatever they may be, are embraced in the present life. But the blessings of the future life are stretched out over endless ages. Because Paul could not tell us of these blessings one by one, nor could he explain them in words, he gave them the name of *glory,* after the thing that above all others seems to be most desirable to us. For this glory seems to be the sum and summit of all blessings.

To urge his audience on in another way, Paul elevates his discourse to a higher plane by speaking of the creation. He establishes two points by the words he is about to use, namely, disdain for the present life and desire for the future life. And the third after these, or rather the first, is when he shows how the human race was so much sought after by God and in what high honor He holds our nature. And after these, all the teachings that the philosophers set forth about this world are swept aside like a spider's web or a child's toy by this one doctrine.[576]

Cf. Rom 8:19–20

Let us listen to the very words of the Apostle so that these matters may become clearer. Paul says, *The created world eagerly awaits the revelation of the sons of God. Creation was made subject to vanity and futility not of its own accord, but by the will of him who subjected it in hope.* What Paul is saying is this. Creation itself feels severe labor pains as it waits for and expects these blessings about which we just now spoke. For eager waiting is intense expectation. As his discourse becomes more emphatic, he turns this whole created world into living persons by personifying it.

The prophets do this too when they bring in the rivers as clapping their hands,[577] the hills as leaping up, and mountains as becoming skittish.[578] The prophets do not wish us to think that these inanimate things are possessed of living souls, nor would they have us endow them with any power of reason. The inspired writers only wish us to learn how great the blessings are. For these gifts are so great that they reach even to things that lack perception.[579]

V

The prophets also do this same thing in the case of sad events. They speak of the vine and also the wine as weeping,[580] and the mountains and the ceilings of the temple as howling,[581] so that again from these we may know how extreme the evils are. Because the Apostle remembered what the prophets had said, he personifies creation and says it groans and feels the pangs of birth. It was not because he heard groans coming from earth and sky. He is only showing how extremely good the future blessings are and the desire of creation to be freed from the evils that were holding it in their grasp.

---

576 Cf. Homer, *Iliad* 15.367.
577 Cf. Ps 97/98:8.
578 Cf. Ps 113/114:4.
579 Cf. Stevens' note in NPNF[1] 11:449.
580 Cf. Isa 24:7 (LXX).
581 Cf. Amos 8:3.

Creation was made subject to vanity and futility, not of its own accord, but by the will of him who subjected it. What does Paul mean when he says, *Creation was made subject to vanity and futility?* He means that it became subject to corruption. Why and on what account? On account of you, the human being. When you received a body subject to death and suffering, the earth too received a curse and brought forth thorns and thistles.

But after the heavens have grown old along with the earth, they will later change to a better lot. Listen to the prophet when he says, *In the beginning, O Lord, You laid the foundation for the earth, and the heavens are the work of Your hands. They shall perish, but You remain. Like a garment, they will grow old, and as a cloak will You fold them, and they will be changed.*

Isaiah too revealed this when he said, *Lift up your eyes to the heavens above and look on the earth below. For the sky is darkened like smoke, and the earth shall grow old like a garment, and the inhabitants will die in like manner.* Do you see how creation became the slave of vanity and how it is escaping corruption? The psalmist said, *Like a cloak you will fold them and they will be changed.* And Isaiah said, *And the inhabitants will die in like manner.* However, he was not speaking of total destruction.

For the inhabitants, that is, men, will not undergo total destruction, but a temporary one, and through it they will be changed into an incorruptible state.[582] And it will be just the same with creation. Isaiah showed this by saying *in like manner.*[583] And Paul will go on to say this too. However, at the present time he is speaking of the bondage itself, and he is showing why it became the bondage it was. And he names us as the cause.

What about this, then? Was creation treated maliciously because it suffered what it did because of another's sins?[584] By no means! Surely it came into being on my account. Therefore, because it came into being for my sake, how would it be treated unjustly when it suffers what it does for my correction? Besides, there

---

582 Cf. 1 Cor 15:53–56.
583 See also 2 Pet 3:13: after the last judgment, the universe will be transformed by the reign of God's justice "into a new heaven and a new earth." Cf. Isa 65:17–18; 66:22. See also Acts 3:21; Rom 8:19–25; Rev 21:1; Matt 19:28.
584 The sins of Adam and his descendants.

is no need to raise the question of right and wrong in the case of things that lack souls and powers of perception.

But because Paul has personified creation and made it into a living thing, he does not use any of those reasons that I mentioned. Indeed, he uses another kind of language because he is eager to bring the greatest comfort to his audience. What is this other kind of language? "What have you to say?" he means. "Creation was treated badly and suffered. It became corruptible because of you. But in no way was it treated unjustly. Certainly, it will again become incorruptible for your sake." This is what Paul means when he says *in hope*. [Cf. Rom 8:20]

But when Paul says, *Not of its own accord was it made subject*, he did not say this to show that creation was possessed of the power of will, but so that you may learn that everything came into being because of the care and concern of Christ. And this was not an achievement of creation itself. Now tell me what he means by *in hope*. He means that *creation itself also will be delivered*. [Cf. Rom 8:21]

And what does Paul mean by *itself also*? He means that not only you, but also what is inferior to you and has no share with you in either intellect or sense perception. This too will have a share with you in the blessings. For he says, *It will be delivered from its slavery to corruption*. That is, no longer will it be corruptible, but it will follow and go along with the beauty of your body. Just as when your body became corruptible, creation itself became corruptible, so too when you become incorruptible, creation itself will follow and go along with you again.[585] [Cf. Rom 8:21]

And to show this, Paul then went on to add, *Into the freedom of the glory of the sons of God*, that is, because of their freedom. Just as the nurse who reared the son of a king enjoys with him the blessings of power when that prince comes into his father's rule, so also does [Cf. Rom 8:21]

---

[585] Giblin (*In Hope of God's Glory*, 394–395) points out that Paul sees all creation corrupted by the sin of Adam and his descendants (cf. Rom 8:20). Paul also seems to suppose that all creation will undergo a future transformation proportionate to that which Paul expects for the risen sons of God. It would seem, however, that the creation made subject to Adam and his descendants is not to be taken as the norm for imagining the glory to be revealed in the brothers of the new Adam. Rather, we should see the norm for imagining the glory of the new creation in the risen Jesus and those who will be raised, body and soul, to join Christ, their brother in heaven.

creation. That is what Paul means. Do you see that in all respects man takes the lead, and that it is for his sake that all things are made?

Do you see how Paul brings comfort to those who are struggling in the contest and how he shows the ineffable loving-kindness of God? Why, he says, are you grieving over your temptations? It is because of yourself that you are suffering; creation is suffering because of you. Not only does Paul comfort and console. He also shows that his words deserve our belief.

For if creation has hope because it came into being in every way for your sake, much more should you have hope, you through whom creation is going to enjoy all those good things. And likewise, when a son is going to appear at an occasion of dignity, men will clothe even the slaves with brighter garments for the glory of the son. So too does God clothe creation with incorruptibility for the freedom of the glory of his sons. *We know that all creation groans and is in agony until now.* Cf. Rom 8:22

VI

See how Paul shames his audience when he all but says, "Do not be worse than creation, and do not be fond of dwelling in the things of the present life." For not only should we not cling to them, but we should groan for the delay of our departure from this world. For if creation does this, much more is it right for you to show this same response, because you have been honored with the power of reason.

But this was not yet strong enough to shame them. Therefore, he went on to say, *But not only creation, but we ourselves, who have the first-fruits of the Spirit, groan within ourselves,*[586] that is, we who have already tasted the things to come. For even if a man is made of the hardest stone, the gifts already given to him are enough to raise him up and lead him away from the things of the present life and lift him up to the future blessings in two ways; namely, because the Cf. Rom 8:23

---

[586] The first-fruits given in baptism are still incomplete. While we live in our earthly bodies, we can only hope for the future blessing that will bring us to the fullness of adoption, which will come with the inheritance of a risen body like that of Christ Himself.

gifts are so great, and because the first fruits are so numerous as well as so great.

For if the first fruits are so great that through them we are freed from our sins and find justification and holiness, if by them those men of former days drove out demons and raised the dead by the shadow of their garments,[587] consider how great the whole crop must be. If creation, which lacks mind and reason, knew nothing of these first-fruits but still groaned, how much the more must we give the same response?

Then, so that Paul might not give the heretics a handle for argument and might not appear to be rejecting the present world, he says, *We ourselves groan*, not because we are finding fault with or accusing the present system, but because we are aiming at greater things. Paul made this clear when he added, *While we are eagerly waiting for the adoption as sons*.

Cf. Rom 8:23
Cf. Rom 8:23

Tell me, Paul, what are you saying? You constantly turned this way and that, and kept crying aloud that we had already become sons. And now you put this blessing among things to be hoped for when you write that we must wait for it? Paul sets this straight in what follows when he says *the redemption of our body*, that is, perfect glory. For now the fate that will be ours stands in shadows until our last breath. For many who were sons have become dogs and slaves.

Cf. Rom 8:23

If we die with good hope, then the gift of sonship cannot be removed. It is clearer and greater, and it need not fear any change from death or sin. This grace will then be secure when our body will be separated by death from its countless passions. For this is complete redemption and not simply redemption, but such a redemption as will never turn back to its former slavery.

So that you may not be at a loss when you are constantly hearing about glory but never having a clear knowledge of it, Paul partially reveals the future when he sets before you the change of your body and, along with it, the change in the whole of creation. And he made this clearer in another place when he said, *Who will refashion the body of our lowliness, conforming it to the body of His glory*. And in still another place he also said, *But when this mortal body puts on*

Phil 3:21

Cf. 1 Cor 15:54;
Isa 25:8; Hos 13:14

---

587 Cf. Acts 5:15.

immortality, then will come to pass the word that was written: 'Death is swallowed up in victory.' What Paul was showing us was that with the corruption of the body, the constitution of the things of this life will also come to an end. And again he wrote in another passage: *For this world as we see it is passing away.* 1 Cor 7:31

And Paul goes on to say, *For in hope were we saved.* The fact that he spent time on the promise of things to come seemed to cause pain to the weaker ones in his audience, because those blessings are only a matter of hope. This was the case, even if he had proved previously that hope is far surer than the things we see in the present life. He proved this when he discussed at length the gifts that have already been given and when he showed that we had already received the first-fruits of these blessings. Cf. Rom 8:24

To prevent us from seeking for everything in the present life and from betraying the nobility of birth that comes from faith, Paul says, *For in hope we were saved.* What he means is something like this. We must not seek for everything in the present life; we must also have hope. For this is the only gift we contribute to God, namely, to trust and believe in Him who has promised the blessings of the life to come. And it was in this way alone that we were saved. And if we destroy this hope, we have destroyed our entire contribution. Cf. Rom 8:24

For I ask you, Paul is saying, were you not liable for countless evil acts? Were you not in despair? Were you not under the sentence of judgment? Were not all men powerless to save you? What, then, did save you? It was your hope in God;[588] it was your belief in him regarding the things he promised and gave. You had nothing more to contribute. If, then, this hope saved you, hold on to it now too. For it is clear that the hope that furnished you with such great blessings will not deceive you about the blessings to come.

When you were dead and lost, when you were a slave and an enemy, hope took you and made you a friend, a son, a just man, and a joint heir. It gave such great blessings as no one ever expected. After such liberality, such kindliness in taking you to Himself, how

---

588 See NPNF¹ 11:446n1: "This blending of faith and hope illustrates the connection of faith and love, the Object of our love being now known by faith, and appropriated by hope. The personification which follows is a powerful way of representing that in us which apprehends God as itself His gift."

will He fail to satisfy you in the future? And so, do not say to me, "Hopes again, expectations again, faith again!" For this was the way you were saved from the start; this was the only dowry you contributed to the Bridegroom.

Therefore, hold fast to it and guard it. For if you demand everything in this life, you have lost those good deeds of yours by which you became brilliant and illustrious. And this is why Paul went on to say, *But hope that is seen is not hope. For how can a man hope for what he sees? But if we hope for what we do not see, we wait for it with patience.* That is, if we are going to look for everything in this life, what need is there for hope?

Cf. Rom 8:24–25

What then is hope? It is confidence in the future. For what great demand does God make of you, because He Himself has given you blessings, complete in every respect, from His own possessions? One thing only He asks of you, namely, hope, so that you too may have something to contribute to your own salvation. And so Paul was hinting at that when he added the words "But if we hope for what we do not see, we wait for it with patience."

Just as God rewards with a crown the man who toils and endures hardship and undergoes countless labors, so also does He reward with a crown the man who hopes. For the word *patience* belongs to hard work and much endurance. Nevertheless, God has granted the crown also to the man who hopes, so that He might bring solace to his work-wearied soul.

VII

Next, Paul shows that we enjoy much help to make the task of hoping light when he goes on to say, *But in like manner, the Spirit also helps our weakness.* For the one part of the task is yours, that is, the part of patience; the other part is furnished by the Spirit, who prepares and encourages you to hope. And through this hope, He again makes your task a lighter one.

Cf. Rom 8:26

Then, so that you may learn that this grace stands beside you not only in your toils and dangers, but that it works with you in things that seem to be very easy, and that on every occasion it contributes its share to the alliance, Paul goes on to add, *For we do not know what*

Cf. Rom 8:26

we should pray for as we ought. He says this to show the great concern of the Spirit for us, and also to teach us not to think that the things that seem to human reason to be beneficial and desirable are entirely so.

For because it was likely that when they were being scourged, driven into exile, and suffering countless dreadful things, they should seek a respite and think that it might be advantageous to pray and ask this favor of God, Paul is saying this to them. "Do not think that the things in your eyes seem that advantageous are entirely beneficial." Certainly we need God's help for this. Man is so weak, and of himself he is nothing. This is why Paul says, "For we do not know what we should pray for as we ought."

So that the disciple might no longer be ashamed of his ignorance, Paul showed that their teachers were also ignorant in these very matters. For he did not say "You do not know," but *We do not know.* Nor was he only being modest in what he said, as he made clear in other passages. For in his prayers Paul never stopped begging that he might see Rome, but his petition was not granted at the times he made this request.[589] And many times he called for help for the thorn that was given to him in his flesh, that is, by reason of his dangers.[590] Yet he completely failed to find relief.

In the Old Testament neither was Moses' prayer answered when he begged to see Palestine.[591] Nor was Jeremiah heard when he made supplication for the Jews,[592] nor Abraham when he made intercession for the people of Sodom.[593] *But the spirit himself pleads for us with unutterable groanings.* What Paul is saying is not clear, because many of the wonders that happened in those early days no longer occur at the present time. Therefore it is necessary to instruct you on the situation at that time. In this way what I have to say will be clearer in the future.

What was the situation at that time? To all the baptized in those days, God gave different charismatic gifts, which indeed were called spirits. *For the spirits of the prophets are under the control*

Cf. Rom 8:26

1 Cor 14:32

---

589 Cf. Rom 1:10–13.
590 2 Cor 12:7–9.
591 Cf. Deut 3:26.
592 Cf. Jer 15:1.
593 Cf. Gen 18–19.

of the prophets, Paul has said. So one man had the gift of prophecy and foretold the future. Another had the gift of wisdom, and he taught the rank and file. Another had the gift of healing, and he cured the sick. Another had the gift of miracles, and he raised the dead. Another had the gift of tongues, and he spoke in different languages.

Along with all these, there was also the gift of prayer, and this too was called a spirit. The one who possessed this gift prayed on behalf of all the people. Because we do not know all the things that are beneficial for us, we demand in prayer things that will not help us. This is why the charismatic gift of prayer came into one of those who were then alive. And he was appointed to pray for what was for the common advantage of the whole Church and for the benefit of all. And he taught the others [the things for which they should pray].

And so it is that in this place Paul calls this kind of charismatic gift a spirit. And the soul that receives this gift, Paul says, groans and intercedes with God. For the one who has been deemed worthy of this gift first stands, filled with compunction and groaning in his mind, and then falls down before God to beg for the things that are beneficial for all. In present times the deacon is a symbol of this man when he offers up the prayers on behalf of the people. And Paul is making clear what this very spirit was when he says, *The spirit himself pleads for us with unutterable groanings. And he who searches the hearts.* [Cf. Rom 8:26–27]

Do you see that here it is not a question of the Paraclete, but of the spiritual heart? Because if this were not the case, Paul would have had to say, "But he who searches the Spirit." So that you may learn that Paul is speaking of the spiritual man and the one who has the charismatic gift of prayer, he went on to say, "But he who searches the hearts knows what the spirit," that is, the spiritual man who has this gift, *desires because he pleads for the saints according to God.* [Cf. Rom 8:27]

Paul does not mean that the spiritual man is teaching God what God does not know, but he put it this way so that we may learn to pray for those things that are necessary and to ask God for the things that are pleasing to Him. For this is what the words *according to God* mean. And this was also for the purpose of consoling those who came to him and for the purpose of their best instruction.

For it was the Spirit, the Comforter, who provided the gifts and gave the countless blessings. As Paul says, *All these things are the work of one and the same Spirit.* And it is for our instruction that this takes place, as well as to show His love; [it is for this reason] that the Spirit condescends to such a degree. And it is from this love that the one who prays comes to be heard, because his prayer is made *according to God*. Do you see in how many ways Paul instructs them in the love that was shown on their behalf and in the honor that comes to them? 1 Cor 12:11

VIII

What is there that God has not done for us? On our account He made the world corruptible. For our sake He allowed the prophets to be ill-treated. He sent them into slavery for our sake, and for our sake He let them fall into the furnace and to endure evils beyond number. He made them prophets for our sake, and He made the apostles for us. He gave His Only Begotten for our sake, and for our sake He punishes the devil. He seated us at His right hand, and for us He was reproached. As the psalmist says, *And the reproaches of them that reproached You are fallen upon me.* Cf. Ps 68/69:9

Yet, even though we stood apart from God after such great blessings, He does not desert us. Again He entreats us and makes others ready to entreat on our behalf, so that He may grant us His grace. This happened in the case of Moses. Surely God said to him, *Let Me alone and I will utterly destroy them.*[594] And God did this to bring Moses to make entreaty for them. And God does this same thing now. It was on this account that God gave the charismatic gift of prayer. He does not do this because He stands in need of entreaty, but so that after we had been saved with little or no effort on our part, we might not become more careless. Cf. Exod 32:10

Often, on David's account or for this or that other man, God says that He is reconciled with them because He is again proving this

---

[594] Referring to the incident of the golden calf that the Israelites worshipped in the desert.

very point, namely, that a set form may be added to the reconciliation. God did this even though He Himself would appear to possess a greater loving-kindness if He were not to say to them that it was because of some prophet or other, but that it was through Himself that He was putting aside His anger.

But God was not eager to do this, so that the basis for their reconciliation might not be the starting point of sluggishness and laziness for those who were being saved. This is why God said to Jeremiah, *Do not deem it right to pray for this people, because I will not listen to your prayer.*[595] God did not say this because He wished that prophet to stop praying when He deemed it right — for God is very desirous that we be saved — but God said what He did to frighten those people. Because the prophet knew this, he did not stop praying.

So that you may learn that it was not because God wished Jeremiah to stand aside, but to make the people ashamed that He said this, listen to God's words to Ezekiel: *Do you not see what they are doing?*[596] And when He says to the city, *Though you should wash yourselves with niter and multiply soap, still you are stained before Me,*[597] God does not say this to throw them into despair, but to rouse them to repentance and conversion.

Just as in the case of the Ninevites, when God spoke of an indefinite sentence but did hold out hopes for an easier one, He frightened them the more and led them to repentance,[598] so He does the same thing here, both to rouse up the Jews and to make the prophet more venerable so that in this way the people might listen to him. Then, because they remained stricken with their incurable disease and were not chastened when the others were carried off to captivity,[599] he first exhorted them to remain there.

---

595 Spoken to Jeremiah when he was praying for the Israelites, who had again fallen into idolatry.
596 Words spoken to Ezekiel by the angel (representing the voice of God) who points out to the prophet a pagan statue of Jealousy at the north gate of Jerusalem.
597 Words spoken by the Lord God through his prophet, chiding the Jews for their idolatrous practices. The niter is the lye used in making soap.
598 Cf. Jonah 3.
599 In Egypt.

Because they were impatient but were daring enough to desert to Egypt, God permitted this, but He asked them not to desert to impiety as well as to Egypt.[600] Because they did not obey His request, God sent the prophet along with them so that they might not after all suffer complete shipwreck.[601] Because they did not follow when God called, He then followed them to correct them and to hinder them from going further in their iniquity. God acted just like a loving father acts toward a son who is unlucky in everything he does. The father takes his son everywhere he goes and follows the son wherever he goes.

This is why God not only sent Jeremiah into Egypt, but also sent Ezekiel to Babylon. And they did not refuse to go. For when they saw that their Master had such a deep love for His people, they continued to do the same. It was just as if a right-minded servant were to take pity on a worthless son because he saw his father grieving and striking his breast over him. And what did the prophets not suffer on account of those people? They were cut to pieces; they were driven out; they were reviled; they were stoned; and they suffered countless tortures. However, after all these torments, they kept running back to their people.

Surely Samuel did not stop grieving for Saul[602] even though he had been sorely insulted by him and had suffered damage beyond remedy at his hands. Yet he remembered none of these things. Jeremiah had composed written dirges for the Jewish people.[603] Yet when the general of the Persians gave him permission to dwell without fear and in full freedom wherever he might wish, he preferred the affliction and misery of his people in an alien land to living at home.[604]

So too Moses left the royal palace in which he was living and hurried to share the calamities of those Hebrews.[605] And Daniel remained without food for twenty-six days,[606] afflicting himself

---

600 Cf. Jer 44:5.
601 Jer 44:28.
602 Cf. 1 Sam (1 Kgdms) 16:1.
603 The Book of Lamentations.
604 Cf. Jer 40:1–6.
605 Cf. Exod 2:10–15.
606 Cf. Dan 10:2–4. For Daniel's fast, see Harkins, St. John Chrysostom: Discourses,

with a most oppressive fast, so that he might reconcile God to his people. And while the three boys were in the furnace in the midst of such a fierce fire, they sent up a supplication for the people.[607] They felt no grief on their own account, because they were saved; but because they thought that at that time especially they had the freedom to speak, for that reason they prayed for the people.

Cf. Dan 3:15^{LXX} — This is why they said, *With a contrite soul and a spirit of humility, let us be accepted.* For those people, Joshua also tore his garments.[608] On their account, Ezekiel grieved and lamented when he saw them slain.[609] And Jeremiah said, *Let me alone; I will weep bitterly.*[610] And before that, when he did not dare to pray openly for total remittance of their dreadful deeds, he sought for a fixed day when he said, *How long, O Lord?* For the race of the holy ones is filled with love. This is why Paul said, *Put on, therefore, as God's chosen holy ones, the children of mercy, kindness, and humility.*[611]

IX

Do you see how accurate his words are? Do you see how Paul wishes us to be constantly merciful? For he did not simply say "be merciful," but *put it on*, in order that mercy may always be with us as our garments are always with us. Nor did he simply say "mercy," but *the bowels of mercy*, so that we may imitate natural love. But we do quite the opposite. Even if someone comes up to us and asks for one small coin, we insult him, abuse him, and call him an impostor.

Do you not shudder and blush when you call a man who is begging for bread an impostor? Even if such a person is guilty of imposture, this is why he deserves to be pitied, because he is so pressed with hunger that he takes such a character on himself. And this makes us deserve the charge of cruelty. Because we do not allow ourselves to give readily what they ask, they are forced to

---

85–86 and notes.
607 Cf. Dan 3:1–90. See Harkins, *St. John Chrysostom: Discourses*, 86 and notes.
608 Cf. Josh 7:6.
609 Cf. Ezek 9:8.
610 Text should read "Isaiah" for "Jeremiah."
611 σπλάχνα οἰκτιρμῶν ("children of mercy/compassion"). See G. W. H. Lampe, ed., *A Patristic Greek Lexicon* (Oxford: Clarendon Press, 1961), 1249–1250, for the various uses of σπλάχνα.

contrive countless devices so that they may deceive our inhumanity and soften our hardness of heart.

Besides, if he were to ask for silver or gold, there would be a reason for you to suspect him. But if he approaches you because he is in need of food, why do you display your "wisdom" at the wrong time? Why are you so precise and exact in accusing him of laziness and sloth? For if we must say such things, we must not say them about others, but about ourselves. Certainly, when we approach God and ask pardon for our sins, recall these words and you will know that you yourself will hear them with more justice from God than the poor man heard them from you.

Still, God never said such words to you as "Get out of here! You are an impostor, because you constantly go to church and listen to My laws. But in the marketplace you set gold, pleasures, friendship, and simply everything above My commandments. Now you are humble, but after your prayer you are bold and cruel and inhuman. Therefore get out of here and never come back to Me."

For we have deserved to hear these words and many more than these. Yet God has never reviled us in such a way. He is long-suffering; He fulfills everything on his part; and he gives us more than the things for which we ask. Therefore let us keep this in mind, and let us free from poverty those who ask us for help. And if they are impostors, let us not be precise and exact. For in the same way we are in need of salvation, along with forgiveness and loving-kindness and abundant mercy.

For it is not possible, no, it cannot be, that those whose life is examined by our methods would ever be saved. All would have to be punished and come to utter ruin. Therefore let us not be bitter judges of others for fear that we will have an exact accounting demanded of us. For we have sins that are beyond all pardon. So let us show greater mercy to those who have committed sins too great to be forgiven, so that we may store up in advance such mercy for ourselves. Yet, however many are the things on which we pride ourselves, we will never be able to contribute such love for mankind as we need from the loving-kindness of God.

How could it be anything but absurd, when we are in need of so many things for ourselves, to make such an accurate examination of our fellow servants and to do nothing of the sort against ourselves? For you are not showing in this way that he is undeserving of your kindness as much as you are demonstrating that you yourself are unworthy of the loving-kindness of God. For the man who makes an exact examination of his fellow servant will much more find God doing this same thing to him.

Let us not, therefore, speak against ourselves, but let us furnish our fellow servants with what they need, even if they come to us because they are lazy and sluggish. Surely we commit many sins because we are lazy and sluggish. Rather, we commit all of them because of such carelessness. Yet God does not call upon us immediately to pay the penalty. He gives us a fixed time for repentance,[612] while each day He nurtures us, instructs us, and supplies us with all other things so that we may emulate His mercy.

Therefore, let us get rid of this inhumanity, let us cast out this savagery inasmuch as we are benefitting ourselves more than we are helping others. For we are giving to others our silver, our bread, and our clothing. But for ourselves, we are storing up beforehand the greatest glory, a glory that no words can express. For after we have received immortal bodies, we will be glorified and reign with Christ.[613]

How great this is we will know from this — rather, we will never know it clearly in this life. However, so that, after you have been led up from the blessings that are among us here on earth, you may grasp at least some knowledge of this, I will try to set before you what I have said as best I can. Tell me this. After you have grown old and spent your life in poverty, if someone promised to make you a young man on the spot, to bring you to the peak of youth, to make you very strong and handsome beyond all others, and then to give you the kingdom of the whole earth — and that for a thousand years — a kingdom possessing the deepest peace, what would you choose to do and undergo for the fulfillment of such a promise?

See, now. Christ is not promising you these, but gifts much greater than these. For the distance between old age and youth is

---

612 Chrysostom sees our time in this life as a time of exercise in the spiritual struggle, as athletes exercise in the stadium.
613 A clear reference to the resurrection of the body.

not so great as the difference between mortality and immortality. Nor is the difference between a kingdom and poverty to be compared to the difference between the glory to come and the glory of the present life. The difference is as great as that between dreams and reality.

X

Still, I have said nothing yet. For no words can make clear how great the difference is between the blessings to come and those of the present life. As far as time is concerned, our minds cannot even grasp the difference. How could anyone compare a life that has no end with the present state of our lives? As for the peace of the future life, it is as far removed from the peace of the present world as is the difference between peace and war. And as for incorruptibility, it is as much better than corruption as a pure pearl surpasses a clod of clay. Indeed, if someone were to try to tell how great the difference is, he would not be able to make it clear to you.

If I compare the beauty of our bodies after they have been glorified to the light of sunbeams, if I compare this beauty to the brightest lightning, I still will be saying nothing worthy of the splendor of our bodies. How much money, how many bodies — rather, how many souls — would it be worth our while to give up in exchange for these gifts? If here and now someone brought you into the palace so you could converse with the king before the eyes of all, if you could share the king's table and join him at the banquet, you would say that you were happier than any man in the world.

But you are going to mount up to heaven and stand beside Him who is the King of the whole universe; you will vie with the angels in brightness; and you will enjoy that ineffable glory. If you have to give up your money, as you must, if you must lay aside this present life, are you hesitating to leap up and rejoice and to soar up on wings of joy?

To get a public office that would give you the opportunity to defraud people — and I would not call such fraud profitable — you throw in all your possessions and you borrow from others. Nor do you shrink from putting up your wife and children as security for the loan. But when the kingdom of heaven is set before you, an office from which no one is trying to oust you, when God bids you to take not a part of a corner of the earth, but the whole of heaven, do you shrink back and hesitate? If the portions of the heavens that we see now are so beautiful and bring us such delight, do you gape after money and fail to consider how beautiful and delightful must be the upper heaven and the heaven of heavens?

Because it is not yet possible to see these things with our bodily eyes, rise up in your thoughts and, as you stand above the heaven we see, look up to the heaven above this one to the limitless height, to the light filled with awe, to the throngs of angels, to the endless ranks of archangels, to the other incorporeal powers. After you come down from on high, take hold of the image[614] of the things we have about us. Sketch out the things you see belonging to an earthly king.

For example, sketch out the king's men in their armor of gold; the teams of white mules ornamented with gold trappings; the chariots crested with jewels, spangled with fluttering gold leaf and cushioned with snow-white pillows. Picture the soldiers with silken dragons on their garments, carrying shields with golden bosses and jewel-encrusted straps reaching to their rims, riding on horses with gilded trappings and golden bits.

But we see none of these things when our eyes behold the king. He alone turns our eyes to him with his garments of purple, his crown, his throne, his brooch, his shoes, and the great splendor of his appearance. After you have brought all these together in an exact picture, then take your thoughts away from them and turn your minds to the things above and to that dread day when Christ will come. For on that day you will see no teams of mules, nor golden chariots, nor dragons and shields, but things that are filled with great awe and that cause such deep consternation as to astonish the incorporeal powers themselves. For Jesus has said, *The powers of heaven will be shaken.* (Cf. Matt 24:29)

For on that day the entire heavens will be opened, the gate of those vaults will swing wide, and the only begotten Son of God will come down. He will not be surrounded by twenty or a hundred

---

614 Cf. Plato, *Republic* 7.516.

armed men, but by thousands and tens of thousands of angels and archangels, cherubim and seraphim, and all the other powers. Everything will be filled with fear and trembling, while the earth bursts apart with all men who have ever lived since the day of Adam's birth up to that day. All will rise from the earth, and all will be caught up,[615] when Christ reveals Himself with a glory so great that the sun and the moon and every light will lie hidden when the rays of His glory shine upon them.

What words will set before us that blessedness, that splendor, that glory? Alas, my soul! For tears and deep groans come upon me when I think from what blessings we have fallen, and from what happiness we are estranged. For estranged we are — I am still talking about myself — unless we shall do something great and wonderful. Let no one here speak of Gehenna. Surely, to fall from such great glory is a far more bitter fate than any Gehenna. Estrangement from that joyful lot is worse than ten thousand punishments.

Nonetheless, we continue to gape after this world and to take no thought of the wickedness of the devil, who by little things takes away from us the things that are great. He gives us clay so that he may snatch gold from us. Rather, he gives us these little things so that he may snatch heaven away from us. He shows us a shadow so that he may rid us of the reality. He shows us phantoms in our dreams — for that is what the wealth of this world is — so that when day breaks he may show us that we are poorer than any man.

XI

After we ponder these thoughts, late though it is, let us flee from his treacherous guile and go over to the things to come. For we cannot say that we were ignorant of how perishable the present life is. Each day the things of earth shout out louder than a trumpet how worthless, how ridiculous, how shameful, how dangerous are the pitfalls of the present life. What excuse will we have for pursuing with such great zeal these things that are so filled with dangers and disgrace, while we flee from those that are free from

---

615 Cf. 1 Thess 4:17.

risk and make us shine with glory, so that we may surrender our whole selves to the tyranny of money?

Our slavery to possessions is harsher than any tyranny, as all know who have been deemed deserving to be freed from it. Therefore, so that you may learn the beauty of this freedom, burst your chains and leap away from this trap. Do not let gold lie hidden in your home. Instead of gold, store up what is more valuable than hoards of wealth, namely, mercy and love for your fellow men.

These give us the freedom to approach God; wealth submerges us in deep shame and makes the devil pant to pursue us. Why then do you put weapons in the hands of your enemy and make him all the stronger? Arm your own right hand against him and bring all the beauty of your house into your soul. Stow all your wealth in your mind. Instead of a strongbox and a building, let heaven keep guard over your fortune. Let us throw all our possessions around ourselves to defend them, for we are much better than walls and more dignified than the paved floor of a house.

Why, then, do we spend all our efforts on those possessions while we neglect ourselves? We cannot take them with us when we depart this life. Often we cannot hold on to them while we are still here on earth. But it is possible to possess our wealth in such a way that we are seen to be wealthy here on earth and also in heaven hereafter. For the man who carries his fields, his home, and his gold in his soul, wherever he is seen, he is seen together with his wealth.

You will ask how this can be done. It can be done and with the greatest of ease. If you have transferred that wealth into heaven through the hands of the poor, you will have transferred it all into your own soul. Even if death overtakes you, no one will take your wealth away from you, and you will go to heaven a rich man. Such was the treasure that Tabitha had.[616] It was not her house that extolled her, nor its walls, its stone, or its columns. It was the bodies of the widows she clothed, the tears she shed. It was death that was the runaway, and life that came back to her again.

Let us make ready such storerooms for ourselves, let us build such houses for ourselves. God Himself brought the poor into

---

616 Cf. Acts 9:36–40.

being out of nothing. You did not allow those whom God had created and to whom He had given life to perish from hunger or future misery; you cured, set straight, and in every way supported the temples of God. What words could match those for usefulness and glory?

If you have not learned clearly with what honor God has adorned you when He ordered you to give relief to those in poverty, ponder over this with yourself. If God were to have given you such great power that you could hold the sky upright when it was falling, would you not have considered that accomplishment an honor far beyond your powers? See that He has now deemed you worthy of a greater honor. He has entrusted to you to straighten out those whom He holds in higher regard than the heavens.

For of all things visible, nothing is equal to man in God's esteem. Surely it was for man's sake that God created the heavens, the earth, and the sea. But He takes greater pleasure in dwelling with men than in the sky. But still, even though we know this, we bestow no care or forethought on men who are the temples of God. We leave them neglected while we build large and splendid houses for ourselves.

This is why we are stripped of all blessings. This is why we are more the beggars than those in extreme poverty. Why? Because we are beautifying these houses of ours, but we cannot take them with us when we leave this earth. Yet we have rejected and sent away those temples of God, although we could have transferred them to heaven to await us when we ourselves leave this life. For even though the bodies of the poor have dissolved into dust, they will surely rise again.

After gathering them all together, God, who laid this charge on us, will praise those who have taken care of His poor. He will look with admiration on them because they lifted up the poor when they were about to fall down, now from hunger, now from nakedness and cold. Still, despite all the praises promised to us, we still put it off and draw back from undertaking that noble charge.

Christ does not have a place where He might rest,[617] but He goes about as a stranger, without a cloak or food. You are making ready

---

617 Cf. Matt 8:20; Luke 9:58.

for yourself suburban estates, baths, covered walks, and countless rooms in your thoughtless vanity. You have not shared with Christ even a small corner of a roof. Yet you beautify and adorn an attic for ravens and vultures. What could be worse than this insanity? What could be more grievous than this madness? For these are signs of the ultimate derangement. And whatever you may call it, you will fall short of calling it what it deserves to be called.

However, even if this disease is difficult to deal with, it can be driven out. It is not only possible, but it is easy to do so. It is not only easy, but it is far easier to be freed from this destruction than from diseases of the body. How is this true? It is true because the Physician is greater. Therefore, let us bring Him to ourselves and ask Him to help us. Let us contribute our fair share — I mean our good will and our desire. He will need nothing else. If only He gets this much from us, He will contribute His entire share. Let us, then, make our contribution, so that we may enjoy true health and may attain to the blessings of the world to come by the grace and loving-kindness of our Lord Jesus Christ, with whom be glory to the Father, together with the Holy Spirit, now and forever, world without end. Amen.

HOMILY 15

I

However, we know that for those who love God,   Rom 8:28
all things work together unto good.[618]

It seems that Paul set this whole section into motion with an eye toward those who are in danger; and not only this section, but also in the verses just before the words [of today's text]. Surely when he said, *The sufferings of the present time are not worthy to be com-*   Cf. Rom 8:18 *pared with the glory to come*, and when he said, *All creation groans*, and   Cf. Rom 8:22 also when he said, *In hope were we saved*, and again: *We wait for it with*   Cf. Rom 8:25 *patience*, and still again: *We do not know what we should pray for as we*   Cf. Rom 8:26 *ought*, all these verses were spoken to those at risk.

For Paul was instructing them not to choose just those things that they themselves would consider to be beneficial, but the things that the Spirit might suggest. Certainly, many things that seemed profitable to them sometimes brought considerable harm. For example, rest and freedom from danger and living without fear seemed to them to be beneficial. And what is strange if they

---

618 An important verse that, with the following two (8:29–30), outlines the Christian vocation as designed by God, namely, to be conformed to the image of His Son, so that Christ might be the firstborn among many brothers (8:29). Those whom God chooses are those whom God foreknew (8:29). Those who are called (8:30) are predestined to be conformed. Paul wishes to emphasize the care that God has taken for the Christian's salvation; see RNT notes on these verses. See also the note on vv. 28ff. in NAB; and Fitzmyer, *JBC*, 53:91. But Chrysostom points out that in the verses preceding Rom 8:28–30, Paul has fixed his attention on those in danger and at risk.

thought these were beneficial when they seemed to be such even to the blessed Paul?

However, Paul later learned that the things that are contrary to those are the beneficial things, and when he learned this, he accepted them. Three times he had begged the Lord to be freed from dangers. But after he heard Christ say, *My grace is sufficient for you, for My strength is made perfect in weakness,* Paul then rejoiced when he suffered persecution, when he was cruelly treated, and when he suffered incurable ills. For he said, *I am satisfied with persecutions, with insults, with distress.* This is why he also said, *We do not know what we should pray for as we ought.* And he urged everyone to make room for the Spirit. For the Holy Spirit has great concern for us, and this is pleasing to God.

Cf. 2 Cor 12:9

Cf. Rom 8:26

And so, after Paul prepared them for the contests with these texts, he added today's verse to give them a reason strong enough to regain them for himself. For he says, *We know that for those who love God, all things work together unto good.* And when he says *all things*, he means even the things that seem painful. Even if tribulation, poverty, imprisonment, death, or any other thing whatsoever should come upon us, God can change all these to their opposites. For this is a mark of His ineffable power, namely, to make the things that seem to cause distress to be light and no burden for us, and to turn them into what is helpful for us.

This is why Paul did not say that nothing dreadful comes upon those who love God, but that "they work together unto good." What he means is that God has used the grievous things themselves to bring credit to those who have been plotted against. This is a much greater thing than stopping the grievous things from coming upon us or destroying them after they have come.

This is what God did in the case of the furnace in Babylon.[619] He did not prevent the three boys from falling into it, nor did he quench the flames after those holy ones had been cast into the fire. He permitted the fire to burn on, and by these very flames he made them greater objects of wonder.[620] Likewise, in the case of the

---

619 Cf. Dan 3:16–24.
620 Cf. Dan 3:32.

apostles,[621] God wrought other such great miracles. For if human beings who have learned to live the Christian way of life can use the nature of things for an opposite purpose, even while living in poverty they can appear to be better provided with resources than the rich. They can shine forth even when they are held in contempt.

God will do much more — things like these and even greater things — for those who love him. We need one thing only, namely, to love Him with a genuine love, and all the other things follow from that. Just as what seemed to be harmful to Paul's audience really helped them, so too the helpful things do harm to those who do not love God. Even the display of miracles by Christ and the correctness of His doctrines harmed the Jews, as did the wisdom of His teaching. Because of His miracles and doctrines, they called Him possessed of the devil;[622] because of His wisdom, they said He made himself equal to God;[623] because of His miracles, they tried to kill Him.[624]

However, even though the robber [on Calvary] was nailed to the cross and crucified, even though he was reviled and was suffering countless torments, he not only was in no way harmed, but earned the greatest blessing from his pain.[625] Do you see how, for those who love God, all things work together unto good? Therefore, after Paul mentioned the great blessings that far surpass human nature, because it seemed beyond belief in the eyes of many, he proves it from past blessings when he says, "For those who are called according to His purpose."[626]

---

621 Cf. Mark 16:17–18.
622 Cf. John 8:48.
623 Cf. John 5:18.
624 Cf. John 11:53.
625 Cf. Luke 23:40–43.
626 Cf. Rom 8:28. See Stevens' note (NPNF1 11:454): "Chrys. apprehends well the practical purpose for which the apostle introduced verses 28–30. Notwithstanding all the imperfections of the Christian's spiritual life (26, 27) and the trials which have been so fully described (1–24) we have the assurance that all these things are working in accordance with God's gracious plan for his ultimate good. In passing over from the idea of believers as those who love God to its counterpart that they are those called according to His purpose…The apostle develops from this idea of *purpose* a series of conceptions designed to emphasize the believer's security. 'You who love God can be sure of the outcome of all suffering in good for you are included in God's purpose which he purposed in Christ Jesus our Lord.' (Eph. iii. II.) You have all the

Consider what is meant by the calling. Why did not Christ call everybody from the start? Why did he not call Paul himself along with the others, because the delay seemed to be harmful? Yet the facts show that this delay was for the best. And Paul speaks here of the purpose so that he might not give the whole importance to the calling. If he did not speak in this way, the Gentiles and the Jews would be sure to contradict him. For if the calling alone were enough, why were not all saved?

This is why Paul said that not the calling alone, but also the purpose of those who are called, is what produced salvation. For the call carried neither necessity nor force. Surely all were called, but all did not listen or obey. *For those whom He has foreknown He has also predestined to become conformed to the image of His Son.* Do you see the weight and importance of this honor? For what the Only Begotten was by nature, this they too became by grace. Still, Paul was not satisfied with saying "conformed," but he also added something else, namely, *That He should be the firstborn.* Nor did Paul stop there. He brought in still another thing when he said *among many brethren*, because by all these things he wished to make the relationship clear. You must consider that all these were said with regard to the Incarnation. For according to the Godhead (θεότητα), Christ is the Only Begotten.

Cf. Rom 8:29
Cf. Rom 8:29

II

Do you see what great gifts He has given us? Therefore, do not doubt about the future. For Paul also shows His care for us from another source when he says that this was prefigured in this way from the beginning. Men take their ideas about things from the things themselves. But for God, from long ago, these things have been decided upon, and from old He has been well disposed toward us. Therefore, Paul says, *And those whom He has called, them He has also justified.*[627] He justified them through the bath of regenera-

Cf. Rom 8:30

---

strength and solidity of God's eternal plan on your side. When the divine purpose of redemption was before the mind of God in eternity, you were the propsective participants in it, as truly as you are now the real participants." Cf. § 10 of this homily.
627 The bath of regeneration is, of course, baptism.

tion. "Those whom He has justified, them He has also glorified."⁶²⁸ He glorified them through grace, through sonship by adoption.

What then shall we say to these things? This is just as if Paul should say, "Say no more to me about dangers and the plots from every side." For if some there are who do not believe in the blessings to come, still they could say nothing against the blessings that have already come, I mean such blessings as God's friendship toward you from the beginning, your justification, and your glory. Surely God gave you these graces and gifts by means of things that seemed to be painful. And what you considered to be shameful, such as the cross, the scourging, the shackles, these are the things by which He set the whole world straight. *Cf. Rom 8:31*

Just as by the things that He Himself suffered, even though they bring sadness to men's eyes, just as He used these to effect the freedom and salvation of all human nature, so also is He accustomed to do with the sufferings that you endure. For He uses your trials and torments to bring about your glory and renown. *If God is for us, who will be against us?* *Cf. Rom 8:31*

Someone may say, "Who is not against us?" Surely the world is against us, both rulers and people, both kinsmen and citizens. Still, those who are against us are so far from acting maliciously against us that they become the causes for us to win crowns of victory, even if they have no intention to do so. They help us to gain countless blessings because God, in His wisdom, turns their plots so that they win for us salvation and glory. Do you see how no one is against us?

Certainly this made Job's glory brighter,⁶²⁹ namely, that the devil was armed against him. For surely the devil stirred up his friends against him; moved his wife against him; made his sores, his servants, and countless other tricks and devices do him harm. Still nothing was against him. Yet this was nothing great for Job, even

---

628 Cf. Rom 8:30.
629 Satan was behind all Job's losses, woes, and misfortunes, because the devil wished to prove to God that Job's virtue was in reality Job's self-interest. But Job will not blame God for his troubles. The result is that God doubles his blessings, thus proving that if God is for us, no one can be against us. We may not realize it at the time we are suffering them, but all our bad fortunes and travails are blessings because God is with us.

though it was very great. But what was far greater was the fact that everything turned out to be for his benefit. Because God was for him, the things that seemed to be against him all turned out to be for him.

This also happened in the case of the apostles. Surely the Jews, and those of the Gentiles, and the false brethren, and rulers, and people, and famine, and poverty, and ten thousand other things were against them. Yet nothing was against them. For these all made them glorious and manifest from every side. They made them objects of praise and commendation in the sight of both God and men. Consider how great was the word Paul spoke about the faithful who really believed and were truly crucified.

Paul's word was such as not even the emperor wearing his crown could accomplish. For against him are many barbarians fully armed for hostile invasion, many plotting bodyguards, and many of his subjects, who often enough are in a constant state of rebellion. And there are countless other dangers. But against the man of faith who truly pays heed to the laws of God, neither man nor demon nor anything else will be able to make a stand.

For if you take away his money, you have supplied him with recompense. If you have cursed him, because of your curse you have made him more glorious in the sight of God. If you bring him to starvation, his glory and reward will be greater. If you hand him over to be slain — which seems to be the harshest of all punishments — you are weaving a crown of martyrdom for him. What then could be equal to this way of life, when nothing can be against it? Even those who appear to be plotting against it help it no less than the very ones who confer benefits upon it. This is why Paul said, "If God is for us, who will be against us?"

Next, because Paul was not satisfied with what he had already said, he sets this down here as well. And it is the greatest sign of Christ's love for us, the sign to which Paul constantly returns. I mean the slaying of the Son. What Paul is saying is that God not only justified and glorified us and made us conformed to that image, but for your sake He did not spare His Son. For this reason Paul went on to say, *He who has not spared His own Son, but has delivered Him up for us all, how can He fail to grant us also all things with Him?*

Cf. Rom 8:32

Paul has written these words with abundant warmth and excessive love, so that he may demonstrate God's love. How then will God forsake us on whose behalf He has not spared His own Son, but has delivered Him up for us all? Ponder on how great a goodness it takes not to spare His own Son, but to deliver Him up on behalf of all, including the worthless, the arrogant, and those who blasphemed Him. *How can He fail to grant us also all things with Him?*

What Paul is saying is something such as this. If God granted us His Son, if God not only made us a gift of His Son, but even delivered Him up to be slain, why, after you have received the Master, are you uncertain about the other blessings? Why do you feel doubtful about your possessions when you have the Lord? God has given the greatest gift to His enemies. How will He fail to give the lesser gifts to His friends? *Who shall make accusation against the chosen ones of God?* Cf. Rom 8:33

III

Here Paul is speaking against those who say that faith is not profitable and who refuse to believe in the sudden change.[630] See how quickly he stops up their mouths by the worthiness of Him who did the choosing. Paul did not say, "Who will bring accusation against the servants of God," or "of God's faithful ones," but *against the chosen ones of God*. For election is a sign of virtue. For after a trainer of horses has chosen colts as fit for the race track, if no one can find fault with them, [all is well]; but he will become a laughingstock if anyone can find fault with his choice.

But when God has chosen souls, those who find fault with His choice are the ones who are laughed to scorn. *It is God who justifies! Who shall condemn?* Paul did not say, "God who forgives sins," but what was a much greater thing: "God who justifies." For when the decision of the judge, and such a Judge as God, has declared a man just, what would the accuser deserve?

Therefore, it is not right to fear temptations. For God is with us, and He has proved this by the things He has done. He did not do this for the nonsensical foolishness of the Jews. For He has

---

630 Effected in baptism.

certainly chosen and justified us. And that is indeed wonderful, because He justified us by the death of His Son. Who then will condemn us, because God has given us the crown of victory, because Christ was slain on our account? Not only was He slain, but after that He intercedes on our behalf. For Paul says, *For it is Christ who died — yes, and rose again from the dead — who is at the right hand of God, and who intercedes on our behalf!* [Cf. Rom 8:34]

Although He has appeared in His own dignity, He has not put an end to His care for us. He even intercedes on our behalf and still keeps watching and guarding us with the same love. Christ was not satisfied with dying only. He not only did the things that were His to do; He also called on Another [the Father] to help him. And this especially is a sign of the greatest love. This is the only thing Paul wishes to show by the word *intercede*, and he is using a way of speaking that is more condescending and better suited to humans. He does this so that he might show how great Christ's love for us is.

Paul also does this because if we do not understand the words *God has not spared* in this same way, many inconsistencies will result. And so that you may learn that this is what he wishes to point out, after he said earlier, *Who is at the right hand*, he then went on to add, *He makes intercession for us*. Because Paul had shown the parity of honor and equality of rank of the Father and the Son, the intercession of the Son would not then be seen as a mark of inferiority, but only as a sign of love. [Cf. Rom 8:32; Cf. Rom 8:34; Cf. Rom 8:34]

Because the Son is the life and the source of all blessings, because He possesses the same power as the Father both to raise up the dead and bring them back to life and to do all other things, how would He have need to intercede with the Father to help us?[631] He freed those in despair and who had been condemned from that condemnation by His own power and made them just and sons. He led them to the highest honors and brought into act things that had never been hoped for.

After Christ had accomplished all this, and after He had revealed our human nature on the kingly throne, how did He stand in need of intercession for the easier things? Do you see how it is clear in

---

631 Cf. John 5:19, 31, 36.

Homily 15

every way that Paul has spoken of this intercession for no other reason than to show the warmth and abundance of Christ's love for us? Even the Father is seen to be urging men to be reconciled to Him. *On behalf of Christ, therefore, we are acting as ambassadors, because the Father is appealing through us.* Cf. 2 Cor 5:20

Nonetheless, even though God is appealing through us, even though men are acting as ambassadors to other men on behalf of Christ, we do not consider on that account that anything is done that is unworthy of that divine dignity. From all that has been said, we gather one thing only, namely, the intensity of Christ's love. However, if the Spirit pleads with unutterable groanings,[632] if Christ died and intercedes for us,[633] and the Father has not spared His own Son for you,[634] if God has chosen you and justified you,[635] why then are you afraid? Why do you tremble when you are enjoying such great love and concern?

Indeed, it is because of this love and concern, after Paul has shown God's great providence for us from the very beginning, that he feels free and boldly proceeds to say what follows. He does not say that you ought to love God as God loves you, but, as if he had been inspired by this ineffable providence, he says, *Who shall separate us from the love of Christ?* He did not say "of God," because it makes no difference to him whether he calls Christ by the name of Christ or of God. *Shall tribulation, or distress, or persecution, or hunger,* Cf. Rom 8:35 *or nakedness, or danger, or the sword [separate us]?*

Notice the prudence of the blessed Paul. He did not speak of the things by which we are made captives every day, for example, the love of money, the desire for glory, the tyranny of anger. Rather, he lists things that are far more tyrannical than these, things that are strong enough to overwhelm human nature itself. He names things strong enough to force open the firmness of our wills, even though we are often unwilling to submit to them, things like tribulation and distress.

Even though the trials of which he has spoken are easy to count, each one of those enumerated involves countless other chains of

---

632 Cf. Rom 8:26.
633 Cf. Rom 8:34.
634 Cf. Rom 8:32.
635 Cf. Rom 8:30.

temptations. For when Paul speaks of tribulation, he includes imprisonment and bonds, calumnies and banishments, and all the other hardships. He is enumerating a vast sea of dangers in a single word. He is simply revealing to us by one term all the dread things that occur among men. Yet he still has the boldness to face them all. This is why he brings them forward in the form of a question. He does this just as if no one could deny that nothing will be able to move a person who has been loved so much and who has enjoyed so great a providence.

IV

Then, so that it might not look as if these things were signs that he had been forsaken, Paul brings in the prophet who had foretold this a long time ago when he said, *For Your sake we are killed all the day long; we are counted as sheep for the slaughter.* That is, we are exposed to all things to suffer evil because of them. But still, against so many and such great dangers and against these new horrors, the reason and purpose for these conflicts is a sufficient encouragement — not only sufficient, but much more than that.

<small>Cf. Rom 8:36, quoting Ps 43/44:22</small>

What Paul means is this. It is not for men, nor for any other living creature, that we suffer these things, but for the King of all things. Christ adorns them not only with this crown, but He has encircled their heads with another crown, one that is varied and diverse. Because they were men, they could not endure innumerable deaths. So he shows them that the prizes are not made less on this account. Even if it was our lot to die only once, God has granted us to suffer death each day by our own choice, if we are willing to do so.

From this it is clear that we will leave this world with as many crowns as the days we have lived — rather, with many more. For on a single day it is possible to die once, or twice, or many times. And he who has prepared himself for this always receives his complete reward. This is what the psalmist hinted at when he said *all the day long.* This is why the Apostle also brought him before his audience, to rouse them up all the more.

<small>Cf. Ps 43/44:22</small>

What Paul means is this. Those who lived in Old Testament times, those who had the land as the reward for their toils, those who had the other prizes that perish along with the present life — those men looked down in scorn on the present life with its temptations and dangers. What pardon then would we have if we show weakness and cowardice after the promise of heaven, the kingdom above, and the ineffable blessings, by failing to come up to the same measure as those men of old?

But Paul did not say that. Rather, he left this up to the consciences of his audience. He is satisfied with the quotation alone. And he shows that their bodies became their sacrifice, and that there is no need to be upset and troubled, because it was God who managed things in this way. And he encourages them in other ways as well. To prevent anyone from saying that he is simply philosophizing before he has experienced the reality, he went on to say, *We are counted as sheep for slaughter,* meaning the daily deaths that he, the Apostle, endured.

Do you see Paul's courage and fairness? What he means is that just as those sheep did not resist when they were slaughtered, so neither must we. But because the weakness of the human will had grown afraid even after such great blessings, see how again he rouses his audience and puts them on a lofty and exalted plane. For he said, *But in all these things we overcome because of Him who has loved us.* Cf. Rom 8:37

The wonderful thing is that not only do we now overcome, but we overcome by the very things that were plotted against us. Not only do we overcome, but we are more than conquerors, that is, we conquer with every ease and without sweat and toil. For without enduring the real torments, but by merely setting our mind and will straight, we erect on every side our trophies of victory against our enemies.

And with good reason. For it is God who fights the battle at our side. However, do not fail to believe this. If we were being beaten back, we would overcome those who were beating us. If we were being put to flight, we would conquer those who were pursuing us. If we were dying, we would put to flight our living foes. For when you add God's power and love, there is nothing that will stop these wondrous and unexpected things from happening. There is nothing that will prevent the light of victory from shining upon us.

For these victors did not merely conquer; they conquered in such a wondrous way so that you may learn that, for the adversaries who plotted against them, the war was not being waged against men, but against the unconquerable might and power of God. Consider the Jews, who had those apostles in their midst and who were at such a loss when they said, *What shall we do with these men?* For this is the marvelous thing: that, even though the Jews had the apostles in their grasp and had them subject to their legal judgment, even though they had them imprisoned and scourged, those Jews were at a loss and helpless. Why? Because they were overcome by the very things by which they expected to win a victory.

Cf. Acts 4:16

Neither a tyrant, nor the people, nor ranks of demons, nor the devil himself had the strength to overcome those apostles. All these foes suffered major defeats when they saw that everything that they devised against their captives turned out to be in the apostles' favor. This is why Paul said that we become more than conquerors. For this was a new way to win a victory, namely, to win by the things devised against them and never to be overcome, but to go into those battles as if they were masters of how the conflict would end. "For I am sure that neither death, nor life, nor angels, nor principalities, nor powers nor things present, nor things to come, nor height, nor depth, nor any other creature will be able to separate us from the love of God that is in Christ Jesus our Lord."[636]

V

These are great things that Paul has said. But we do not understand them because we do not have his great love. Still, even though the words are great, Paul wished to show that they were nothing as compared to the love with which he was loved by God. Then he sets down his own love after God's love, so that he may not seem to be boasting about himself. What he is saying is something such as this.

---

636 Cf. Rom 8:38–39.

Why speak, he means, of things present and evils inherited in this life? Even if someone should speak to me of things to come, of powers like life and death, of powers like angels and archangels and every creature above, even these are insignificant in my eyes compared to the love of Christ. For not even if someone were to threaten me with death — that future death that never dies — in order to separate me from Christ, nor if he were to promise me unending life, I would not accept it.

Why speak, he means, of the kings and consuls here on earth, or of this man or that? Even if you were to speak to me of angels and of all the powers above, of all the things that are and of all that will be, both those on earth and those in the heavens, both those under the earth and those above the heavens, all these are insignificant in my sight when compared to the love of Christ. Then, as if these were not enough to prove the passionate love[637] that he had, in order to suggest many other things that were just as great, he said, "Nor any other creature." What Paul means is something such as this. Even if another creature were as great as the visible and the invisible creation, nothing would separate me from that love.

However, Paul did not say this because angels or the other powers would try to do this — heaven forbid! — but because he wished in the strongest possible way to show the love he had for Christ. For he did not love Christ because of the things that are Christ's; he loved those things that are Christ's for the sake of Christ, because he looked only to Christ Himself. He only feared one thing, namely, that he might fall from that love he had for Christ. For this loss of love is more terrifying than Gehenna itself, just as abiding in His love is more desirable than the kingdom itself without the love for Christ.

For what reason, then, can we be worthy at all, when Paul feels no amazement even for the blessings of heaven when compared to his love for Christ, while we hold things of mire and clay in greater honor than the honor in which we hold Christ. And while Paul is willing to fall into Gehenna and to be banished from the kingdom for his love for Christ, if the choice were put before him [rather than to be separated from that love], we do not even hold the

---

637 τὸν πόθον.

present life in scorn. Do we then deserve even to touch Paul's sandals, since we have fallen so short of his nobility of mind and soul?

For the sake of Christ, Paul considers that even the kingdom is nothing; but we take slight thought of Christ, and make great account of the things that are His. Indeed, I wish we would make great account of the things that are Christ's! But as things are now, not even this is so. Although a kingdom lies before us, we let it go and pursue shadows and dreams all the days of our lives. Yet, because God loves mankind and is so gentle, He does the same thing a loving father would do if his son grew discontented with living at home day after day. If this should happen, the father would wisely keep him at home by other means.

Because we do not have the love and desire for God that we should have, God keeps putting many other things before us so as to hold us close to Him. But not even in this way do we continue to stay at home. Rather, we run off to our childish games. But Paul did not act in this way. Like a free and well-born son who loved his father, he sought only to be with the Father and did not take so much account of the other things. Indeed, he set much more store by the other things than the boy did. But Paul did not honor the Father and the Father's things in the same way. When he looked to the Father, he considered the Father's things of no value. He would choose to be with the Father, even if he should be punished and scourged, rather than to be separated from the Father and living a life of luxury.

VI

Therefore, let us shudder — those of us who do not hold possessions in scorn for the sake of God. Rather, I should say those of us who do not hold possessions in scorn for our own sakes. For it was Paul alone who suffered all things for the sake of Christ, not for the sake of the kingdom or for his own honor, but because of his love and goodwill toward Christ. But neither Christ nor the things of Christ draw us away from the things of this world. Like serpents or vipers or pigs, or even all these together, we drag ourselves about in the slime.

How are we any better than these snakes and pigs, we who have so many and such great examples but who still keep looking down and cannot look up to heaven for even a brief moment? God gave us His Son, but you do not even share a piece of bread with the Son who was given for your sake, for the Son who was slain on your account. And it was for your sake that the Father did not spare Him, and this even though He is the true Son of the Father. But you do not so much as look at Him, even though He is wasting away with hunger. You do this even though the money you are going to spend for this food comes from the things that are His, even though what you spend is really for your own sake.

What could be worse than this transgression? He was given for your sake; He was slain for your sake. It is for your sake that He goes about hungry; it is from what is His that you should give, so that you yourself may reap the benefit. Yet, even so, you refuse to give. Could stones be more senseless? Even though so many things are urging you to act, you persist in this state of savagery. And this is the work of the devil.

Christ was not satisfied with death and the cross alone. He even accepted to become poor and a stranger, a beggar and naked, to be thrown into prison and to undergo sickness, so that in this way He might call you to Himself. He says, "If you do not answer My call because I suffered on your behalf, take pity on Me because of My poverty. If you are unwilling to take pity because of My poverty, be moved because of My sickness; turn to Me because I am in prison. If these things do not make you feel love for your fellow man, show your willingness to comply with My request because what I ask is easy for you to do.

"For I ask for nothing that will cost you much. All I ask for is a piece of bread, a roof for My head, the consolation of a few words of comfort. If, after these, you still remain savage and unsubdued, become a better man, even if it is for the sake of the kingdom and the rewards that I have promised. Do you consider these of no account? At least for the sake of humanity, be moved when you see Me naked and when you recall the nakedness I endured on the cross for your sake.

"If you are unwilling to recall that nakedness, then recall that nakedness for which I suffer now in the persons of the poor. I was bound for your sake during My passion, and for your sake even now I am still in chains. You should be moved by the bonds I suffered during My passion or by those I still suffer. And you should be willing to show some pity for Me. I fasted for your sake, and for your sake I am hungry again. I was thirsty when I was hanging on the cross, and I still thirst in the persons of the poor, so that by both these thirsts I may draw you to Myself and make you love your fellow men for your own salvation.

"Therefore, even though you owe Me a return for countless good deeds, I do not ask you for this because you are in My debt, but because I am offering you a crown for showing favor to Me. I am giving you the kingdom as a gift in return for these small favors. I am not saying, 'Free Me from poverty,' nor 'Give Me your wealth,' even though I became poor for your sake. But still I am asking for a piece of bread, and a garment, and a small comfort for My hunger.

"And if I am thrown into prison, I am not forcing you to loose My chains and release Me, but I ask one thing only — that you come to visit Me because I have been put in chains on your account. Then I have received favor enough, and, in return for this favor only, I am offering you heaven as a free gift. Even though I have set you free from more dangerous chains, I am satisfied with only this much, namely, that you be willing to visit Me when I am in prison."

"Of course, I can give you a crown even if you do not grant Me these favors, but I wish to be in your debt so that your crown may bring you some feeling of confidence. And this is why, even if I am well able to feed and nourish Myself, I go about begging and holding out My hand as I stand at your door. For I deeply desire that you will feed Me, because I love you very much. This is why I long to share your table, as is the custom for those who love each other. And I find pleasure in this. When the whole world is watching, then will I proclaim and extol you. When everyone is listening, I will point out the one who has fed Me."[638]

---

638 Again Christ is identified with the poor, the hungry, the naked, and the imprisoned. Although we could ease His suffering with our alms, we neglect to do so even though the wealth we have is a gift from Him. Even though we owe it all to Him, we refuse to pay it back to Him in the persons of the poor and needy. If we refuse them

Yet when someone feeds us, we are ashamed and we hide our faces. But because Christ loves us very much, even if we remain silent, He then speaks up and, with much praise for us, He tells what we have done. He is not ashamed to say that we have clothed Him when He was naked and fed Him when He was hungry. Therefore, let us store all these things in our heart; let us not stand there until it is time to shout our approval, but let us fulfill in act the things of which I have spoken.

What good is there in your shouting and applauding?[639] I seek one thing only from you: proof in deeds, obedience in acts. That is applause enough for me. This is what brings profit to you. And that is brighter and more shining than a crown for me. After you have left the church, prepare this crown for yourselves and for me through the hands of the poor, so that we may live together in good hope during the present life and, as we depart to the life to come, we may find countless blessings. May it come to pass that all of us attain these blessings through the grace and loving-kindness of our Lord Jesus Christ, with whom be glory, power, and honor to the Father, together with the Holy Spirit, now and forever, world without end. Amen.

---

our help, we are refusing to give Him what is His and what is only put in our care to be used for those who need it.

639 Chrysostom's audiences frequently shouted and applauded the rhetorical splendor of his words. This seems to have been one such occasion.

BIBLIOGRAPHY

Altaner, B. *Patrologie*. 6th ed. Freiburg, 1963. 5th ed. translated by H. C. Graef (Edinburg and London, 1960).

Ameringer, Thomas E. "The Stylistic Influence of the Second Sophistic on the Panegyrical Sermons of St. John Chrysostom: A Study in Greek Rhetoric." PhD dissertation, The Catholic University of America, 1921.

Arndt, W., and F. W. Gingrich. *A Greek-English Lexicon of the New Testament*. Chicago, 1957.

Barth, Karl. *Epistle to the Romans*. Translated by E. C. Hoskins. Oxford, 1968.

Baur, Chrysostomus. *John Chrysostom and His Time*. Translated by M. Gonzaga. Westminster, MD: Newman Press, 1959.

Brown, Raymond E., Joseph A. Fitzmyer, and Roland E. Murphy. *Jerome Biblical Commentary*. Englewood Cliffs, NJ: Prentice-Hall, 1968.

Burns, Mary Albania. "Saint John Chrysostom's Homilies on the Statutes: A Study of Their Rhetorical Qualities and Form." PhD dissertation, The Catholic University of America, 1930.

Carter, R. E. "The Future of Chrysostom Studies." *Studia Patristica* 10. Edited by F. L. Cross. Berlin: Akademie-Verlag, 1970.

Chadwick, H. "Rufinus and the Tura Papyrus of Origen's Commentary on Romans." *Journal of Theological Studies*, n. s., 10 (1959): 10–42.

Copleston, Frederick. *A History of Philosophy*, vol. 1. Westminster, MD: Newman Press, 1946.

Ἰωάννου Χρυσοστόμου Ἔργα. Ἕλληνες Πατέρες τῆς Ἐκκλησίας, τόμ. 16B–17. Θεσσαλονίκη: Πατερικαὶ Ἐκδόσεις Γρηγόριος ὁ Παλαμάς, 1985.

Ferguson, Everett, ed. *Encyclopedia of Early Christianity*. New York and London: Carland Publishing, 1990.

Field, F. *Joannis Chrysostomi Interpretatio omnium epistolarum Paulinarum*. Bibliotheca Patrum. Oxford, 1845.

Giblin, Charles Homer. *In Hope of God's Glory: Pauline Theological Perspectives*. New York: Herder and Herder, 1970.

Gorday, Peter. *Principles of Patristic Exegesis: Romans 9–11 in Origen, John Chrysostom and Augustine*. Studies in the Bible and Early Christianity 4. New York and Toronto: Edwin Mellen Press, 1983.

Guinan, Michael. *Job*. Collegeville, MN: Liturgical Press, 1986.

Harkins, Paul W., trans. *St. John Chrysostom: Baptismal Instructions*. Ancient Christian Writers 31. Mahwah, NJ: Paulist Press, 1963.

———. *St. John Chrysostom: Discourses against Judaizing Christians*. The Father of the Church 68. Washington, DC: Catholic University of America Press, 1979.

Hoffman-Aleith, Eva. "Das Paulusverständnis des Johannes Chrysostomus." *Zeitschrift für die Neutestamentliche Wissenschaft* 38 (1939).

Käsemann, Ernst. *Commentary on Romans*. Translated by Geoffrey W. Bromily. Grand Rapids, MI: Eerdmans, 1980.

Kelly, J. N. D. *Golden Mouth: The Story of John Chrysostom; Ascetic, Preacher, Bishop*. London: Duckworth, 1995.

Lagrange, M. J. *St. Paul: Épitre aux Romains*. 7th ed. Paris: J. Gabalda, 1950.

Lampe, G. W. H., ed. *A Patristic Greek Lexicon*. Oxford: Clarendon Press, 1961.

Maxwell, Jaclyn L. *Christianization and Communication in Late Antiquity: John Chrysostom and His Congregation in Antioch*. Cambridge: Cambridge University Press, 2006.

Mayer, Wendy, and Pauline Allen. *John Chrysostom*. London and New York: Routledge, 2000.

McKenzie, John L. *Dictionary of the Bible*. Milwaukee: Bruce Publishing, 1965.

Merzagora, A. "Giovanni Chrisostomo, Commentatore di S. Paulo." *Didaskaleion* n.s. 10 (1931).

Migne, Jacques-Paul, ed. Patrologia Graeca. 161 vols. Paris, 1857–1866.

Murphy, F. X. "The Moral Doctrine of St. John Chrysostom." *Studia Patristica* 11 (1972).

New Catholic Encyclopedia. New York: McGraw-Hill, 1967.

The Nicene and Post-Nicene Fathers, Series 1, ed. Philip Schaff. Vol. 11, *Saint Chrysostom: Homilies on the Acts of the Apostles and the Epistle to the Romans*. Translated by J. B. Morris and W. H. Simcox; revised with notes by George B. Stevens. Reprint, Grand Rapids, Michigan: Eerdmans, 1980.

Papageorgiou, Panayiotis. "A Theological Analysis of Selected Themes in the Homilies of St. John Chrysostom on the Epistle of St. Paul to the Romans." PhD dissertation, The Catholic University of America, 1995.

Papageorgiou, Panayiotis. "Chrysostom and Augustine on the Sin of Adam and Its Consequences." *St. Vladimir's Theological Quarterly* 39, no. 4 (1995): 361–378.

Quasten, Johannes. *Patrology*. Vol. 3, *The Golden Age of Greek Patristic Literature from the Council of Nicea to the Council of Chalcedon*.

Westminster, MD: Newman Press, 1960.

Rahlfs, Alfred, ed. *Septuaginta*. 2 vols. Stuttgart, 1935.

Sanday, William, and Arthur C. Headlam. *A Critical and Exegetical Commentary on the Epistle to the Romans*. Edinburgh: T&T Clark, 1902.

Schelkle, K. H. *Paulus Lehrer der Väter: Die altkirchliche Auslegung von Römer 1–11*. Dusseldorf, 1956.

Staab, Karl, ed. *Die Pauluskommentare aus der griechischen Kirche*. Neutestamentliche Abhandlungen 15. Munich: Aschendorff, 1933.

Trakatellis, Demetrios. "Being Transformed: Chrysostom's Exegesis of the Epistle to the Romans." *Greek Orthodox Theological Review* 36, nos. 3–4 (Fall/Winter 1991): 211–229.

Turner, H. E. W. *The Pattern of Christian Truth*. London, 1954.

Uleyn, Arnold. "La doctine morale de S. Jean Chrysostome dans le commentaire sur S. Matthieu et ses affinités avec la diatribe." *Revue de l'Université d'Ottawa* 27 (1957).

Wilamowitz-Moellendorff, Ulrich von. *Die Kultur der Gegenwart*. Berlin, 1905.

Wiles, Maurice F. *The Divine Apostle: The Interpretation of St. Paul's Epistles in the Early Church*. Cambridge: Cambridge University Press, 1967.

Index

A

Abel 68, 174
  from the treachery of Cain 54
  received justification 180
  slain 158
Abraham 39–41, 94, 113, 145, 174, 188, 291
  as a patriarch 94, 113
  believe in God 136
  death of the body 203
  faith credited as justice 139
  faith of 161
  father of the uncircumcised 140
  God is not the God of the dead, but of the living 203
  God's command 181
  God's justice and limitless power 150
  led Isaac up the mountain 14
  as a prophet 113
  received circumcision 140
  received justification 135, 139, 143
  son of David 113
  sons 109
  statement of 166
  strengthened in faith 147
Absurdity, idolatry and 106
Abuses 157
  proselytes 92
  spirit of those who 226
Adam 190, 225
  birth 301
  disobedience 175, 179–180
  fell into sin 174
  God formed 229
  sin 177, 200
  sinned and his body became subject to suffering 222
  a type of Jesus Christ 175
Adoption
  as sons of God 19, 188, 276, 288, 308
  an honor 278
  of the Jews 280
  justification and 178
  in Old/New Testament 276
  spirit of 279
Adoptive sonship 20
Adversus Julianum 1.27 xiii
Affliction 75
  burden of 282
  distress and 272
  external matters of this world 163
  God to repay 262
  misery of people and 295
  present 262
  tribulation and 75–76
Allegory xi
Amalek/Amalekites 14, 145
Amendment and reconciliation 76
Angels 10
  archangels and 317
  dwelling 153
  Gospel of 84
  heaven forbid 317
  life of 203
  messenger to summon and console 85
  throngs of 300
Anger and passion 53
Aphrodite, lust 106
Apollo 50

Apostles [2], 103, 171,188, 307, 310
  blessed 19, 22
  Jews 316
  purpose and object 242
  thought 175
Archippus 5
Aristotle 49
Arrogance 93
  of Jews 91, 111
  madness for glory 90
  pride and 29
  senseless obstinacy and 227
  uplifts spirits of combatants 282
Asclepius 50
Athenians 34, 60
St. Augustine (Adversus Julianum 1.27) xiii

B

Babylon
  Ezekiel to 295
  foreign land 105
  furnace in 306
Banishments 314
Baptism 38, [139], 194–195, 200, 222, 251, 259
  bath of 265
  cleansing of 278
  dignity given in 276
  faith and 204
  first-fruits given in 287
  gift of 204
  grace given in 280
  into death 184
  in Jesus, Christ 192
  law and 218
  second bath of 196
  sins after 192
  spirits 291
Barbarians 249, 260
  house slaves 65
  land of exile 202
  natural law 229
  Scythian and 46
  sin is more tyrannical than 105
Baur, Chrysostomus
  John Chrysostom and His Time xiv
  positive view of Chrysostom xiv
Biblical Exegesis, Homilies on Romans as xiii–xvi
Blasphemy 94, 104
  against God 94
  curses and 171
  God 149
  passionate rage and 171
Blessedness 138, 301
Blessed, transgressions are forgiven 203
Blessings
  eternal 133
  God 293
  justification and 201
  pains and 168
  unworthy of 235
Body
  beautiful 236
  Christ's 53, 122, [125], 156, 193, 207, 220
  corruptible 75, 129, 286
  corruption 289
  dead 263, 270, 285
  diseases 304
  good as dead 147
  immortal 180

Index

mortal 197, 199, 201, 241, 249–250, 288
mortify 265
murderer separates the soul from 61
of old man 195
paralyzed 115
perishable 129
putrefaction 169
redemption 288
resurrection of xvii
reverence 53
of sin 194, 198, 200, 249
slander 245
soul and 63, 169, 204, 221, 245, 261
soul in Gehenna 37
spiritual 260
stands midway between evil and virtue 198
strength of 20
Brown, R. xviii

C

Cain 54, 157
Calling
  alone 308
  body of ours 194
  drawing and 85
  to holiness 19
  the letters spiritual 277
  Spirit the law of the Spirit 251
Calumnies 314
Calvin, J. xviii
Carelessness, listlessness of disciples 241
Celibacy
  pattern for 123
  poverty 222

Charity 121
Chastisement 44
Christ 4, 6, 8, 13, 17, 20–21
  Adam a type of 175
  address to His disciples 261
  anointed 11
  authentic worshippers 12
  in baptism 192
  beating of the flesh with His own death 254
  birth breaking the law of nature 15
  body 53
  chastised man who looks at woman and lusts after her 236
  condemnation 251
  condemnation by 181
  correctness of His doctrines 307
  death of 160–161, 166, 174, 185, 195–196, 240
  desires 152
  destroyed the power of sin 254
  did not lie 2
  doctrines of 24
  eternal life through 182
  faith in xvii
  fear of punishment 278
  forbidding murder, anger, adultery and lust 236
  forgiveness, justification, and life 43
  glorified and reign with 298
  glory 152
  God judging hidden secrets of men through 82
  gospel and 83
  grace and loving-kindness 55

human nature 312
hunger along with horses, mules, couches, and footstools 209
identified with the poor 27, 320
intensity of love 313
Last Supper 26
laws of 89
love of 88
loving-kindness 42
new commandment 126
not commit sin 254
not recognizing any distinction of persons 130
not satisfied with death 319
offending 85
Peter burned with love for 87
power of 152, 230
reconciliation 167
resurrection of xvii
revealing Himself with a glory 301
reverence for 155
Romans hiding themselves from 36
for the sake of Christ 317
salvation 133
shaped His teaching 15
sinful flesh 255
suffer disgrace 172
in suffering 281
threatened people with Gehenna 222
tyranny of sin 262
who lived before the coming of 76
witnesses 174
working to bring immortal life 133

Christianity xvii
Christians 90, 209, 220
  antiquity xviii
  catechesis xix
  Church 98
  doctrine xvii
  interpretation of Scripture xix
  life 172, 259
  living and good conduct 203
  spiritual life 307
  tradition xvii
  vocation as designed by God 305
  way of life 238, 307
Chrysostom, St. John
  ability to understand and interpret Epistles of St. Paul xiii
  Anomoean (neo-Arian) heretics 41
  application of rhetoric to his sermons xvi–xvii
  audiences 321
  authorship xiii
  Biblical texts translation xvii
  "body of sin" 194
  citations from Old Testament xvii
  commentaries on the New Testament xiv
  commentary on Romans xii
  commentary on St. Paul xii
  concupiscence 194
  different from Gregory of Nyssa 245
  doctrine of "original sin" xiii
  dynamics between soul and body 245
  emphasizing St. Paul's desire to visit the Romans 30

INDEX

exegesis of Romans xi
exegetical methodology xi
"experience" as only way to explain God's love 173
exposition of the Epistle xiv
God-given natural inclination of man 246
last judgment 45
love of God 89
opposes the idea that the flesh is essentially evil 248
Paul's treatment of significance of faith of Abraham 134
Pelagian connection xiii
ranking xviii
scientific understanding of alcoholism 269
strongly against oaths and swearing 235
"thorn in the flesh" of 2 Cor 12:7 21
ultimate punishment 54
understanding dynamics between soul and body 221
understanding of the human condition 242
usage of colorful terms and images to express his understanding of love 172
views of Quasten, Johannes on works of xiv
Ὁρισθέντος 16

Church
  advantage 292
  assembly in 271
  Christian 98
  distributions of ministries 12
  doctrines of 248
  fighting against 122
  interpreters xiv
  members of 25
  sacred enclosure of 154
  theology and life of the early 5
  worship 26

Circumcision 77
  Abraham received 140
  becoming uncircumcision 95
  of the flesh 142
  forgiveness 139
  important according to Jews 94
  Jews 97
  justifying by faith and uncircumcision through faith 135
  not an elitist moral sign 90
  Paul, St. rejecting 95
  superfluous 96

Cleansing
  of baptism 278
  expiation and 277

Commandments
  advent of sins after 240
  God 136

Commendation and praise 310

Conceit
  of arrogance 29
  man not achieve anything 39
  minds 170
  pagans 49
  proud and 23, 29, 110

Concupiscence 241–242

Condemnation 176
  by Christ 181
  death and 177, 180
  punishment and 161

Condescension 250

Conflagration 62

Conscience 65, 82
  bad 164
  clean 21
  examining self 27
  good 21
  reason and 83
  wicked deeds 21
Contentiousness 75
Continence and self-control 232
Converts
  Dionysius the Elder 34
  Dionysius the Younger 34
  from Judaism 6
  Jewish 6, 93
  pagan 6, 29
Cornelius 77, 119
Council of Constantinople, condemnation of Theodore work by x
Covetousness 51
  evils 205
  worse abyss of 234
Creation
  achievement of 286
  beauty of 226
  corrupted by the sin of Adam 286
  desire of 284
  God's 244
  hope 287
  servants by 10
  severe labor pains 284
  sinner's knowledge 71
  subject to vanity and futility 285
  visible and invisible 317
  of the world 46
Cross
  baptism 184
  burial and 185
  of Christ 36, 165
  death and 195, 319
  God's ineffable kindness 160
  pagans with arguments based on 49
  preach the 37
  robber (on Calvary) nailed to 307
  work of his ineffable loving-kindness 37
Crucified One
  Romans were bidden to worship 23
  worship of 36
Curiosity questions 41
Curses
  blasphemies and 171
  God 124

D

Dangers and temptations 314
Daniel 5
  fullness of grace 53
  in the lion's den 53
  remained without food for twenty-six days 295
David 14
  Abraham and 113, 136
  forgiven sinner blessed 139
  freed from punishment 85
  having murdered Uriah 258
  justified "blessed" 138
  to level the charges 109
  person who is called blessed 138
  preaching Him who has His generation 15
  Saul did kill 123
  two forms of death 203
Deacon 292

Dead
  baptism 195
  corpses of 206
  to the law 219, 229
  life to 146, 153, 197, 199
  to live 115
  lost and 289
  Moses 10
  resurrection from 15
  rise from the 161, 220
  to sin 104, 184–185, 192, 195–196, 263
  womb of Sarah 147
Death
  Adam's sin brought 200
  of Christ 160, 161, 166
  condemnation and 177, 180
  descendants 175
  life and 317
  not an unmixed evil 181
  painful 306
  physical 178, 180
  resurrection and 185
  sin and 174
  spiritual 178
Deeds
  doctrines and 71
  evil 231–232, 235
  good 109
  honor and the disgrace coming from 80
  punishment and reward dependance on 78
  virtuous 94
Demons
  dwelling with 124
  mouths of 37
  neither man nor 310
  nor ranks of 316
  possession by 124
  raised the dead and 279, 288
Descendants
  death 175
  sinners 180
Desire
  leading the sexes together 59
  love of 88
  patient 225
  sinners 205
  unnatural 268
  wicked 68
Devil
  confers justification 183
  taking desire 59
  wickedness of the 301
Dignity 57
  of God 41
  greatness and 189
  honor and 60
  positions of 75
  of the teacher 224
Diodore of Tarsus
  commentary on Romans xi
  divine οἰκονομία xi
  exegesis of Romans influenced by Chrysostom and Theodore xi
  influence on Chrysostom's approach xvii
  teacher of Chrysostom and Theodore xi
Dionysus 50
  drunkenness 106
Discourse 67
  of Paul, St. 43
  up to God 145

Disobedience
  Adam 175, 179–180
  man 178
  sinners 179
Doctrines
  of Christ 24
  Christian xvi
  deeds and 71
  evil 69
  good name and good 46
  heretical 2
  impiety 59
  lying and false 34
  miracles and 307
  of the Church 248
  of "original sin" xiii
  of the truth 44
Dreams
  bad conscience 232
  men who lived their lives 260
  phantoms 301
  pursue shadows and 318
  reality and 299
Dress, adornment of 21
Drunkenness 268–269
Dry anointing 60

E

Ease
  exceeding power and 120
  facility in observing the law 92
  His suffering with our alms 320
  of the contests 263
  race of virtue 263
  repayment 132
  in struggle 201
Egypt 185
  Jeremiah into 295
Egyptians 50
  punished by God 37
Election
  as a sign of virtue 311
  was from God 12
Elisha 54
Endurance
  anoint with the oil of 164
  harbor of patient 238
  master of noble 53
  patience belonging to hard work 290
  shame not seem to be beyond 215
  tribulation makes for 164
Envy
  evils 126
  flame of 123
  grudging and 24
  malice and 121, 128
  murder coming from 68
  sickness of 126
  soul of 22
  vice of 123
Ephesians, Paul, St. aroused the 190
Ephesus 93
Epistles 3
  to the Colossians 4
  to the Corinthians 3–4
  to the Galatians 5, 181
  to the Hebrews 4, 9, 189
  to the Philippians 2
  to the Thessalonians 3–4
Esau 235
Eunuchs 62, 65
Eve 225
Evils

INDEX

abundance of 69
becoming great and sin growing more powerful 240
countless 128
covetousness 205
deeds 231–232, 235
enormity of 62
ignorance of scriptures 2–9
intention 225
justice and 214
men 225
pains and 275
root of 205
set free from former 203
of sin 177
wickedness and 77
Exodus 276
Ezekiel
  to Babylon 295
  God's words to 294
Ezekiel (Hebrew prophet) 5

F

Faith 40
  of Abraham 94, 161
  baptism and 204
  Gehenna 264
  in God 136
  justification of 139
  people imprisoned by the law 182
  promise as outcome of 144
  salvation 144, 151
  testimony to 142
  weakening in 147
Famine 310
  poverty and 207
Fasting 123

life with 266
not uncommon in warmer climates 266
prayer and 266
superiority of poverty 260
Fate
  bitter than any Gehenna 301
  harsher than ten thousand deaths 267
fear
  of devil 151
Fear
  blessings to come 181
  destroy both body and soul in Gehenna 37
  of disease or poverty 265
  freedom from 57
  of Gehenna 85
  of God 8, 27–28, 62–64, 73, 84, 99, 115
  of Jews 228
  of punishment 278
  temptations 311
  trembling and 31, 72, 301
Fidelity 69
  of God 100
Filadelfia, described 3
Fitzmyer, J. xviii, 241
Forgiveness
  circumcision 139
  of God 122
  Jesus 43
  loving-kindness and 298
  Paul, St. 138
  of sin 114
Fornication 61–62, 258
Freedom
  to approach God 302

of choice 96
salvation and 309
of speech 105
tranquility and 232
Friendship
  God's 309
  human 89
  love and 88, 188, 190
  "Sharing salt" 156

G

Gehenna 60–62, 129, 205, 222
  Christ threatened people with 222
  face of God 85
  faith 264
  fire of 206
  freedom from 172
  God threatening with 86
  pain of 272
  Paul, St. speaking of 59
  Paul, St. willing to fall into 317
  punishment and 89, 168, 201, 207, 275, 301
  sufferings 89
Gent
  enjoying advantage over the Jews 108
Gentiles 67, 91, 93–94, 119, 124, 144, 160, 308–309
  accountable to God 111
  enjoying advantage over the Jews 108
  foes 103
  Greek 76
  to have the rights of kinship 135
  Jews advantage over the 77, 111
  objects of admiration 81

Paul, St., accused the 108
praised by Paul 82
reasoning power 92
receiving honor 78
uncircumcision and 95
Giblin, C. H. 241, 286
Gluttony 128
God
  abandoned 69
  accountable to 111
  adoption as sons of 19
  assuring Cain of his right of primogeniture [125]
  as weapons for justice 198
  blasphemy 94, 150
  blessed 52
  blessings 43, 57, 85, 130
  bodiless 48
  both lover and beloved 172
  Christian vocation as designed by 305
  commandments 64, 136
  commands 40, 104
  condemnation of 84
  condemning self and 72
  creation 244
  curse 124
  delivering lusts in heart to unclean practices 51
  destined Jeremiah to be His servant 12
  dignity of 41
  discourse up to 145
  dishonor by transgressing the law 93
  essence 41
  esteem 303
  eternal plan 308

Index

failure to discover 48
faithfulness of 229
faith in 136
fear of 27, 63–64, 84
fidelity of 100
forbidding 31
forgiveness 122
formed Adam 229
freedom to approach 302
freeing from punishment 137
friendship 309
fulfillment of promise 165
Gentiles are accountable to 111
gifts 39, 145
giving importance to actions rather than quality of persons 79
glory of 49, 113, 122, 149, 172
goodness 73
gospel of 12
grace of 25, 30, 99, 162, 176, 202
granting justification in abundance 38
has not done for us 293
heirs of 281
honor and loving-kindness 101
honor from 158
hymns to 105
image of 207
immortal 48
ineffable kindness 160
ineffable liberality 182
intelligence 57
Jews knowledge of 90
Jews offending 94
Jews outrage 93
judging hidden secrets of men 82, 84
judgment of 44, 70–71, 74, 83
justice and limitless power 150
justice of 102, 110, 115, 199
justification of 112–113
justifying circumcision by faith and uncircumcision through faith 135
kindness 22, 86
kingdom 172
knowledge of 46–49, 162
leave the dead to bury their dead 203
long-suffering 72
love 85, 158, 165, 172
love assures salvation 174
love Him with a genuine love 307
loving-kindness of 74, 287
lusts after monstrous deeds 58
making man independent for choosing good and avoiding evil 82
making people fear by talking about punishment 74
manifestation of his justice 115
man loving relationship with 173
nature 79
offending 85
opposite response 28
oracle of 100
ordinance of 69, 105
partiality 79
plans of salvation 10, 15, 39
power 37, 43, 115, 118, 146
power leading to salvation 37
power of sin and 196
promise 147–148
providence 35, 82, 119
provident 49

providing mind and powers to
　　men 51
provoke 238
punishment by 73, 238
as respecter of persons 79
rewards with crown the man 290
righteous judgment 103
salvation 134
securing peace and holiness of
　　20
sent Ezekiel to Babylon 295
sent Jeremiah into Egypt 295
strength of sin and greater grace
　　of 177
threatened punishment 170
threatening with Gehenna 86
true philosophers resembling 52
trustworthy testimony of 25
truth and glory 103
unjust in punishing 102
victory 102
virtuous 99
will 59, 79
willing 246
wished Jeremiah to stand aside
　　294
words to Ezekiel 294
words unsupported by evidence
　　147
world became guilty before 134
wrath of 44–45
Gorday, Peter xv
Gospels
　of the angels 84
　Christ and 83
　promise of blessings 43
Grace
　apostleship and 16
　eternity by 42
　fullness of 53
　gift of 28, 216, 281
　given in baptism 280
　of God 30, 99, 162, 176, 201
　Jews receiving greater 38
　justification and 179
　loving-kindness and 21, 55, 66, 89
　of the Spirit 264
　overflowing 178
　peace and 18–20
　preeminence of 230
　sins 176
　of the Son 176
　superiority of 249
Gratification, natural means of 57
Greeks
　abandoning error 104
　equality of honor 80
　idolatry 105
　Jews possessing no advantage
　　over Greek because of cir-
　　cumcision 90
　Jews requiring greater need of
　　grace than 80
　judged without the burden of the
　　law 80
　left without excuse or defense 78
　myths 119
　natural law 229
　Paul, St. accusing the 78
　Paul, St., no difficulty in assailing
　　104
　punishment 79
　salvation 90, 99
　sunk in idolatry 99
　superior to the Jew 82
　without the law 80

Gregory of Nyssa 245
  Origen's legacy of duality of man transmitted to Chrysostom through xi

H

Habakkuk 39
Hagarenes 145
Haggai 5
Harkins, Paul W., views of xvii–xix
Harlots, intercourse with 60
Heathen 63
Hebrews
  calamities of 295
  language 280
Hell 62, 204
Hemorrhage, woman with the 152
Heresies
  begotten 124
  chief 2
  Gnostic 5
Heretics
  Anomoean (neo-Arian) 41
  hear the voice of the Spirit 39
  an opportunity for argument 220
Hermes (messenger of God) 3
Hoffman-Aleith, E., critics on Chrysostom's ability to understand Paul xiv
Holy Spirit 8, 16, 21, 42, 55, 66, 165, 173, 306
Homosexual acts 60
Homosexual men 56
Honor
  dignity and 60
  immortality and 74
  loving-kindness and 101
Hope
  Abraham belief 146
  blessings lie in 164
  does not disappoint 165
  in the future blessings 167
  of the glory of God 162–163
  in God 289
  good 21, 87, 231, 288, 321
  ill-founded 165
  for salvation 249
Humility
  God's grace and 25
  of mind 19
  spirit of 296
Hurt
  double 215
  God 52
  grievous 272
  inflammation of the brain 59
  laugh 238
  mortal 157
  suffer 157

I

Idolatry
  absurdity and 106
  Greeks sunk in 99
Idols
  abominate 93
  Egyptians 50
  knowledge and glory on 46
  worshipped 47, 77, 105
Ignorance
  sin through 78
Immortality 181
  honor and 74
  incorruptibility and 75
  mortality and 299

Impiety and godlessness 70
Imprisonment 314
  painful 306
Incarnation 308
Inhabitants, souls of the 63
In Hope of Man's Glory (Giblin) 241, 286
Inhumanity
  get rid of 298
  to man 207
Iniquity 68
  assent to 75
  for lawlessness 213
  sin as weapons of 198
Injustice
  against the king 46
  eunuchs 62
  God's victory 102
  in matters of money 45
  toward women 45
  unrighteousness 198
Insult
  abuses and 235
  avoid 53
  to circumcision 96
  from strangers 61
  glory of God 119
  God's gifts 44
  Jews heaped 102
  man suffers no harm 52
Intercourse
  between woman and mam 59
  with harlots 60
  with imprisoned virgin forcefully 61
Intoxication 268–269
Irenaeus, theology of xi
Irrationality 37

Isaac 14, 23, 40, 113, 188
Isaiah 13, 93–94, 109, 168, 285
Ishmael, descendants of 147
Ishmaelites 145
Italy 34

J

Jacob 23, 40, 113, 188
Jephthah 191
Jeremiah 47, 54, 86, 291, 294
  destined by God to be His servant 12
  into Egypt 295
  reporting what God had said about his ministry 12
Jerome Biblical Commentary (Brown, Fitzmyer and Murphy) xviii
Jerusalem 3
Jerusalem Bible (JB), consultation from xvii
Jews 12, 279, 308
  advantage over the Gentiles 77, 111
  advantages from God 93
  apostles 316
  arrogance of the 91
  becoming unclean and unjust 229
  betrayed themselves 117
  called sons 278
  calm down haughtiness of the 141
  circumcision important according to 94
  dishonor God 93
  enjoying larger share of teaching and instruction 76
  equality of honor 80

Index

Gentile Greek and 76
Gentiles accountable to God 111
Gentiles enjoying advantage over 108
genuine relationship with Abraham 135
glories of the 90
Greeks superior to the 82
haughty in their thoughts 92
knowledge of God 90
madness of 225
murderous 54
offending God 94
outrage God 93
patriarch and friend of God 135
possessing no advantage over Greek because of circumcision 90
praised by Paul, St. 92
prophet calling the Jews uncircumcised 94
prophets 294
punishment 79
realization of their own sins 110
religious culture of 76–78
repress their arrogance 111
requiring greater need of grace than the Greeks 80
sluggish indifference 111
to live a life of moderation 118
violence of the 109
vulgar 182
Job 77
  blows and wounds 54
  devil induced 190
  glory brighter 309
  Satan behind losses, woes, and misfortunes 309
  trials of 190
  won a crown of victory 22
John, gospels of 9
Jonah 5
Joseph 68
Josephus 93
Joshua 296
Judaism 81, 99
Judas 225
Judea 23
Judgment
  condemnation 177
  deliberation and 223
  future 77
  of God 44, 70–71, 74, 83, 102, 136
  good 47
  imperfect 169
  legal 316
  of Christ's 45
  Paul, St. 120
  prudent 9, 94
  Quasten xiv
  sagacious 97
  wisest of peoples 60
Justice
  evil and 214
  freedom from 214
  of God 102
  servants of 215
Justification
  Abel received 180
  Abraham 138–139, 141–143, 161
  Adam's sin in paradise 177
  adoption and 178
  blessedness 138–139
  blessings and 201
  Christ 43

court's decrees 102
deaths 192, 201
devil confers 183
faith and 38, 108, 115, 135, 139, 144
God grants 38, 112–115, 134, 183
grace and 177, 179
holiness and 288
involving two deaths 192
Jews 38
man faith 137
patriarch receiving 140
salvation and xvii
saving souls through 43
sign of 141
sinners 39
superiority of 138

K

Käsemann, Ernst 240
Kindness 29
  of God 85
  imperial 38
King of Judah 258

L

Lagrange, M. J., Chrysostom's interpretation of Paul in Homilies on Romans xiv
Last Supper 26
Law
  accusation against the 227
  baptism and 200
  convicts one of transgression 200
  is spiritual 241
  natural 228
  not in harmony with Christ 253
  slandering the 223
  wickedness 252
Lawful copulation, lack of 59
Lawless/lawlessness 58
  behavior 61
  due to shameless deeds of men 58
  iniquity for 213
  intercourse with harlots 60
  power of 214
  slavery and 214
Law of Moses
  dies without any mercy 204
  law of sin and of death 252
  natural law 247
  Paul's objective to abrogate 228
  praises this law 246
  preventing man from putting one wife aside 250
  spiritual 251
Life
  of austerity 24
  Christian 195
  conduct 10
  death and 316
  eternal 74, 182
  immortal 133, 203
  of moderation 118
  soft and dissolute 170
  of virtue 65, 231
  virtuous 92
Lord of Elijah 131
Loving-kindness
  forbearance and 116
  forgiveness and 297
  of God 74, 286
  grace and 55, 66, 89
  honor and 101

Index

Luke 14, 17
  gospels of 9
Lusts
  after monstrous deeds 58
  Aphrodite 106
  in heart to unclean practices 51
  for money 205, 234
Luther, M. xviii

M

Man
  disobedience 179
  evils 224
  gift of prophecy 292
  God judging hidden secrets of 84
  good action 176
  greedy 269
  in his right mind 267
  inhumanity to 207
  loving relationship with God 173
  mentally ill 267
  must not commit adultery 93
  offense 176
  punishment 180
  ridiculous nature 64
  sinner 180
  souls 177
  spiritual 292
Manasseh 258
Manichaeans 197, 224
Mark 14
  as apostle 12
  gospels of 9
Marriage
  adulteress of the widow 220
  adultery 242
  after death of first husband 219
  injustice toward women 45
  undermining 53
Martyrs
  congregations of monks and 260
  countless hosts of 223
  crowns of 180
  memorials of the 1
Matthew 14, [88], 97
  as apostle 12
  bad tree cannot bear good fruit 258
  book of the origin of Jesus Christ 113
  evangelist 12
  gospels of 9, 13
Melanchthon, P. xviii
Melchisedek (priest) 77
Mercy 69, 296
Micah 86
Milesians 16
Mind
  callous and unfeeling frame of 86
  intention 96
Miracles 13
  God 17, 306–307
  Jesus 15, 307
  raised the dead 292
Moderation, Jew to live a life of 118
Money
  borrow 129
  evil tyrant 271
  gathering 2
  for the glory of the king 46
  greed for 225
  injustice in matters of 45
  lend 127
  loss of 232
  lust for 205, 234

possessions and 106, 205, 272
receive 132
someone owed 130, 179
in treasuries 25
Mosaic law 228–229, 240, 250
Moses 9–10, 14, 54, 99, 174
   law of 228, 247, 250
   leaving the royal palace 295
   praise of law 246
   prayer 291
   void the law 204
Murphy, R. xviii

N

Natural affection 69
Natural law 228
   barbarians 229
   family feeling 69
   Greeks 229
   salvation 108
Natural pleasures 170
Natural uncircumcision 97
Neologism [87]
New American Bible (NAB), consultation from xvii
New Testament 226, 276
Ninevites 77, 258, 294
Noah 54, 174, 261
Nobility 157, 160

O

Obedience, to the faith 17
Obstinacy 93
Old Testament 9, 13, 39, 109, 250, 260, 276, 291, 315
   sacrifices in the 114
Onesimus 4–5

Only Begotten 40, 168, 178, 188, 253, 278, 281–282, 293, 300, 308
Oppression and trials 54
Origen (Alexandrian scholar) x
Original sin, doctrine of xiii
Over-confident 72

P

Pagans 47, 48
   confidence in 155
   Gentile grief 67
   madness 50
   sacrifices [114]
Pains
   blessings and 168
   evils and 275
   ultimate 89
Palestine 291
Paraclete 292
Pardon and excuse 75
Passions
   anger and 53
   blasphemy and 171
   as disgraceful 56
   restrain 236
   sinful 221, 223
   sins 242
Patience 74
   hard work and endurance 290
Patriarchs 160
   Abraham 94
   friend of God 135
   honored 146
   messenger to summon and console 85
   receiving justification 140
Paul, St.

Index

Abraham faith and justification 149, 160
Abraham received circumcision 140
Abraham received justification 143
accusations against men 68
accused the Gentiles 108
accusing not only Jews but whole human race 83
accusing the Greeks 78
Adam died and people became mortal 180
Adam sinned and his body became subject to suffering 222
advantages of the Jews 93
agreed to circumcision 96
anxiety 33
apostleship 11, 16, 18
Apostle to the Gentiles 16
apostolic prudence 82
aroused the Ephesians 190
bath of baptism 256
bearing witness to the Thessalonians 24
beheaded by order of the tyrant 35
blessed 85
blessedness to justification 139
body of death 249
But I am made of flesh 241
called as an apostle 11–12
called law of nature a commandment 229
calling God as his witness 25
calling Greeks, Gentiles who adored God 77
calling himself a servant of Christ 10
calls death the wages of sin 217
call sin unrighteousness 198
calm down haughtiness of the Jews 141
candor and prudence 11, 16
carelessness and lack of concern 76
cause of all evils 205
cause of life 264
chastisement 44
Christ's death 161
Chrysostom's ability to understand and interpret Epistles of xiii
Chrysostom's exegesis xiv
circumcision becoming uncircumcision 96
circumcision profitable if keep the law 94–95
circumcision profit with a good life 98
clarification on "according to the Spirit of holiness" 15
clarification on "who was declared (Ὁρισθέντος)" 16
comfort and console 287
commentary by Chrysostom on xii
commit sin 201
consciences of his audience 315
console and encourage 30
courage and fairness 315
creation 284
creation corrupted by the sin of Adam and his descendants 286
dead to the law 219
death of Christ 174

death of one or the other partner 218
deeds of 14
defending circumcision 98
demanded great strictness of life 213
demean other races 91
denouncing rulers of Rome 70
descendants of Ishmael 147
desire of men and women coming from greediness 58
destroy the dignity of the law 218
determination 195
dignity and worthiness of person 114
discussing grace 226
dishonor God by transgressing the law 93
distinction of Jews before the Greek 38
does not dishonor the law 97
earnestness 76
Epistle 110
Epistles, time and order of 2–9
equality of honor of the Jew and the Greek 80
evils becoming great and sin growing more powerful 240
exalted language usage 44
exceeding power 120
faith a law 117
faith credited to Abraham 95
Father sent the Son 255
favor of the Jews 223
fear of God 27–28
fear to the hearts of his hearers 275
fidelity of God 100

forgiveness 139
For I do not understand what I do 242–243
fornication 61
For without the law, sin is dead 242
frightening his audience 78
"from the Father and from the Son" 20
gaining luster from those who insulted him and plotted against him 54
Gehenna and punishment 201
Gentiles objects of admiration 81
genuine birth 280
gives thanks to Christ 250
glory of the sons of God 286
God as respecter of persons 79
God granting justification in abundance 38
God is not the God of one portion, but is the Father of all 145
God justifying circumcision by faith and uncircumcision through faith 135
God's gifts 202
God's grace 25
God's great providence for us 313
God's ineffable liberality 182
God's love assures salvation [174]
God's victory 102
"God who forgives sins" 311
"Good does not dwell in my flesh" 245
good name and good doctrines 46
gospel and Christ 84
grace 28

great power 135
He condemned sin in the flesh 255
heretics 220, 288
his desire 33
his discourse 43
for in hope were we saved 289
hunger and nakedness 21
identify source of the trouble 174
idolatries 49
if Christ is in you 263
I give thanks to God through Jesus Christ our Lord 249
ignorance of teachers 291
I had not known lust 243
impiety 59
impiety and godlessness 70
importance of faith 142
inclusion of the Psalms 109
instilling fear into man 70
inventors of evils 68
Jews requiring greater need of grace than the Greeks 80
judging another, you condemn yourself 95
judging others, not themselves 71
judgment 120
judgment of God 74
justification and faith 39
justification more august and sublime 138
justification of God 112
kindness of heart 32
lacking skill 7
law is holy 229
law of life 252
law of Moses 228
law of the mind 247

letter kills, but the spirit gives life 224
liable for countless evil acts 289
life incapable of dissolution 196
living without the law at one time 227
love and concern 26
love for God 22
manifestation of God 134
man who is dead is justified from sin 218
married woman bound to her husband by the law as long as he lives 218
men abandoning natural intercourse with women 56
men dishonoring the natural means of gratification 56
mentioned weapons and a king 216
missionary preaching and teaching 5
modesty 34
natural sexual intercourse forbidden to women 56
no difficulty in assailing the Greeks 104
not prefixing his name to Epistle to the Hebrews 9
not satisfied with arguments 220
offence and grace 103
Old Testament 109
only speaking of licentiousness and impurity 51
on truth of God and lies of man 102
on use of circumcision 100
pain of 35
pardon and excuse 75

paths of impiety 45
patriarch 174
pattern of knowledge and of truth 92
people who are in danger 305
perception 57
physical death 178
power of God 118
praise for the Gentiles 82
praises of the Jews 92
preaching 18, 25–26, 35
preeminence of grace 230
prefix his name in his Epistles 9
previously rejecting circumcision 95
proclaim the gospel of God 12
promise as outcome of faith 144
proof that God endowed men 46
prophet 314
prudence 313
prudent and blessed soul 57
prudent judgment 9, 94
punishment 59
recognizes two uncircumcisions 97
relationship of faith 145
rescue from body of death 252
resurrection 264
revelation of God 74
revelation of the sons of God 284
ridiculous nature of Jews 92
sagacious judgment 97
salvation 135
salvation missing for the Greek 90
sending his petitions to God on behalf of whole world 25
sin as law 247
sin came from transgression of the law 175
sinner of any excuse 52
sins of excuse 56
slander the flesh 256
Sold into the power of sin 241
solving one absurd objection with another 102
Son of God arrival with countless angels 45
soul of 7, 18, 27, 35
sovereignty sin 198
speaking against those who say that faith is not profitable 311
speaking of sin in paradise 175
speak of Gehenna 59
Spirit of God 276
spiritual death 178
spirit who dwelled within 266
stand against an urgent necessity 225
stressing on equality 19
suffered persecution 306
tendencies of the spirit 259
tendency of the flesh is toward death 257, 259
tentmaker 34
testifying characteristics of Romans 23
"the power of God leading to salvation" 37–38
They who are carnal cannot please God 260–261
tyranny of avarice 93
tyranny of evil 249
tyranny of sin 250
uncircumcision and circumcision 119

Index

uncircumcisions 95
uses the word "called" 18
varies his message 43
verse from the Psalm 138
victory by the necessary proofs 219
view of Christianity xvii
views of shameless deeds of men 58
views on creation of the world 47
views on who was declared Son of God in power 15
view that gospel is source of salvation and eternal life 43
We are not debtors to the flesh 274
weeping and grieving over his sins 85
wickedness 198
wife called an adulteress if husband alive 219
willing to fall into Gehenna 317
wisdom 49, 219
wise nature of 281
wishes to be constantly merciful 296
word "live" (meaning "have life") 276
words for private citizens and subjects 71
world became guilty before God 134
writings used as authoritative Christian writings ix
written testimony 138
You are not your own 274
Perception, souls and powers of 286
Persecution 306, 313

Persians 31, 260, 295
Persuasion 148
Perversity 59
  of men 45
Pharisees
  accusations 238
  scribes and 200, 222
Philosophers, resembling God 52
Philosophy 52
  Christian way of life 52
  man suffers no harm at hands of those who insult him 52
  thick beard and short tunic 34
Piety
  desert to Egypt 295
  devil persuaded Jephthah to slay his daughter 191
  reverence and 28
  sacred rituals 77
Plato 34, 50
  Aristotle opposing 49
  collection of poets 50
  Euthyphro 6 51
Pleasures
  adulterers 232
  enjoyment and 234
  evil deeds 231
  life of virtue and 65
  natural 57, 170
  in punishment 59
  sight of your possessions 128
Poverty 310
  celibacy and 222
  consolation in 132
  easing 121
  famine and 207
  fear of 265
  painful 306

superiority of 260
Preaching
  apostolic 23
  austere life 24
  continuous gift of 18
  gospel of His Son 24–26
  of Jonah 258
  Paul's missionary 5
Pride 93
  arrogance and 29
Prodigality 266
Prophecy, spirit of 279
Prophets 88, 314
  accusations made by 93
  as accuser 93
  calling the Jews uncircumcised 94
  Jews 294
  justification of God 113
  law and 110
  messenger to summon and console 85
  sad events 284
  slew of 86
  sufferings 295
Providence of God 35, 82, 119
Prudence 77
Punishments 59, 85, 91, 104, 137
  adulterer 71
  condemnation and 161
  dependance of rewards on deeds 78
  to devil imposed by God 150
  dreadful 232, 235
  escape 106, 112
  freed from 60, 178, 215
  Gehenna and 89, 168, 201, 207, 301
  gift of grace 182
  God 73, 170, 238
  God unjust in 102
  Greek condemned without 80
  Greek escaping 78
  inexorable and intolerable 45
  of Jew and the Greek 79
  man 180
  ordinary men 88
  Peter denied Christ and not grieved because of 87
  pleasure in 59
  retribution and 277
  salvation 108
  sin and 214
  stoppage when the suffering comes to an end 268
  threatening with 89
  threat of 43, 60
  torture and 275
  for transgressions of the law 76
  trodden underfoot the Son of God 204
  ultimate 41, 44, 110

Q

Quasten, Johannes xii

R

Rahab 39
Reasoning powers 65, 83, 92
Reconciliation 294
  amendment and 76
  Christ 167
Redemption 114
Regeneration, bath of 308
Remission 116

INDEX

from sins 182
Resurrection 148, 160, 193
   death and 185
   incorruptibility and immortality 75
   life after 62
Retribution and punishments 277
Righteousness 102
   sanctification 213–214
   sin 198, 202
Romans
   central argument of 112
   considering rulers equal to God 36
   hiding themselves from Jesus 36
   management of affairs of 32

S

Sabbaths 98, 142
Sacrifices 98, 142
   in the Old Testament 114
   pagan 114
Sacrilege 93
Salvation 38, 117, 251, 282, 308, 320
   faith and 136, 144, 151
   freedom and 309
   gift for self 90
   God 134
   God's love assures 174
   Greeks 98
   hope for 249
   human race 111
   missing for the Greek 90
   natural law 108
   neglecting 89
   punishment 108
   sinners 167

Sarah, dead womb of 147
Satan 89, 125, 190
   behind all Job's losses, woes, and misfortunes 309
Saul (king) 41
Scriptures
   'Abraham believed God 136
   anointed 11
   Christian interpretation xix
   Chrysostom, J. xviii
   Ishmaelites 145
   seriousness of the evils 2–9
   two become one flesh 59
Scythians 18, 31, 37, 46, 260
Self-control and continence 232
Self-destruction 128
Self-indulgence 266
Servants
   accusation against God 311
   by creation 10
   gentler 64
   Jews 10
   of justice 215–216
   maidservants 211
   righteousness 213
   tasks 32
   thoughtless house 64
   unprofitable 126
Sicily 34
Sinners 67, 69
   descendants 180
   desire 205
   disobedience 179
   enemies and 166
   forgiven 139
   knowledge 71
   man 180

meaning 180
not satisfied with evils 68
repentance 73
salvation 167
sin seized 254
Sins
  accusations against 230
  Adam 174, 177
  after baptism 192
  came from transgression of the law 175
  commandment 240
  committed 64, 68, 183, 201, 298
  criminal acts and 67
  death and 174
  destroy the soul 204
  destruction of 199
  evils becoming great and sin growing more powerful 240
  forgiveness of 114
  freed from 202
  grace and 176
  greatness of 183
  grievous 72
  passions 242
  punishment and 214
  recognition of 111, 115
  remission from 182
  secret 83
  seized sinners 254
  servitude to 214
  slavery to God 215
  slaves to 201, 214
  sovereignty 198
  strength of 177
  taking occasion and opportunity through the commandment 228
  through ignorance 78
  unnatural 67
  unrighteousness 198
  as weapons of iniquity 198
  wickedness and 87
  with faithful 67
Slavery
  disgraceful 232
  lawlessness and 214
  to possessions 302
Slaves 65
  to sin 201, 214
  of vanity 285
Socrates (Phaedo 118) 50
Sodom 62, 226, 291
Sodomites 63
Solon 60
Souls
  characteristic of 149
  of the inhabitants 63
  men 177
  powers of perception 286
  sins destroy the 204
  wisdom 245
Spirits
  anointed 11
  antiquated law 223
  baptism 291
  furnishes the Spirit 252
  grace of the 264
  of humility 296
  of wisdom 279
  of prophecy 279
Sufferings
  dangers and 54
  Gehenna 89
  prophets 295

Swearing
  any oath 235
  falsely 235, 236
Syllogisms 49
Syrians 23

T

Teachings
  Christ 14
  Christian xv
  Diodore xi
  doctrinal 183
  of the faith 23
  God instruction and 47
  ignorance and lack of skill do not hinder 8
  Jew getting larger share of 76
  Paul's missionary preaching 5
  spiritual man 292
  wisdom of 307
Temper, lose self 235
Temptations 54
  dangers and 314
  fear 311
  trials and 74
Theodore of Mopsuestia
  commentary on Romans xi
  influence on Chrysostom's approach xvii
Thracians 18, 260
Timothy, Paul's letter 4
Transgression 223, 319
Trials
  oppression and 54
  temptations and 74
Tribulation 313
  affliction and 75–76
  blessings 164
  enduring/endurance 29, 164
  exult in 163–164
  imprisonment and bonds 314
  painful 306
  struggles 163–164
  suffer due to laxity 171
Triumph, uncircumcision 97

U

Uncircumcisions 77
  circumcision becoming 96
  Gentile and 95
  natural 97
  Paul, St. recognizing two 97
  triumph 97

V

Vanity
  futility and 284
  Gentiles 77
  pagans' conceit and 48
  pretense and 39
  slave of 285
  thoughtless 304
Vengeance, deserve 104
Victory of God 102
Violence of the Jews 109
Virgin
  forceful intercourse with imprisoned 61
  plight of 61
Virginity, practicing 223

W

Watchfulness 249
Wealth

blessings 20, 179
bodily beauty and 64
of Christian tradition xvii
confidence in 131
exults in pleasures and scatters 266
in the temples of the idols 93
leave to children 131
as lord 106
luxury and 23
in mind 302
possessions and 233
poverty and 65
of reasons 81
riches and 151, 270
Romans 36
safe with God 132
Wickedness 68, 131
  Christ's death 166
  of the devil 301
  evils and 77
  justice of God 102
  of the law 252
  natural evil 231
  sins and 87
  to virtue 258
Widows
  bodies of 302
  no longer a wife 217
  protecting the 26
  second marriage 220
Wisdom 49
  of Paul, St. 49
  soul 245
  spirit of 279
Woman
  prostitutes 65
  with the hemorrhage 152
Worship
  of beasts 49
  Christ 230
  of the Church 26
  God 24–25
  idols 77, 105
  Jewish 26
  Romans bidden to worship the Crucified One 23
Wrath
  of God 44–45, 102
  of the Jew 80
  storing 73, 77

Z

Zeal 4
  after baptism 192
  of Archippus 5
  to Christ 110
  earnestness and 192
  Jews 91
  Paul's 17
Zechariah 5
Zephaniah 5

www.ingramcontent.com/pod-product-compliance
Lightning Source LLC
Chambersburg PA
CBHW052055300426
44117CB00013B/2142